NORTH AMERICA

A GEOGRAPHY OF CANADA
AND THE UNITED STATES

NORTH AMERICA
A GEOGRAPHY OF CANADA
AND THE UNITED STATES

BY

J. H. PATERSON

LECTURER IN GEOGRAPHY IN THE
UNIVERSITY OF ST. ANDREWS

THIRD EDITION

OXFORD UNIVERSITY PRESS

Oxford University Press, Ely House, London W.1

GLASGOW NEW YORK TORONTO MELBOURNE WELLINGTON
CAPE TOWN SALISBURY IBADAN NAIROBI LUSAKA ADDIS ABABA
BOMBAY CALCUTTA MADRAS KARACHI LAHORE DACCA
KUALA LUMPUR HONG KONG

FIRST EDITION 1960
SECOND EDITION 1962
THIRD EDITION 1965
FILMSET BY BAS PRINTERS LIMITED
OVER WALLOP, HAMPSHIRE
AND PRINTED IN GREAT BRITAIN BY
BILLING AND SONS LIMITED
GUILDFORD, SURREY
REPRINTED WITH CORRECTIONS
1966

CONTENTS

CONTENTS

CONTENTS

LIST OF MAPS AND DIAGRAMS

LIST OF MAPS AND DIAGRAMS

LIST OF PLATES

LIST OF PLATES

AUTHOR'S NOTE

THE regional geographer is essentially a gatherer of Other Men's Flowers. It is not, usually, the transmission of new facts that justifies his authorship, so much as the rearrangement, into more significant patterns, of facts which are already known. This book represents a search for such rearrangements, as it traces new patterns emerging from the familiar facts of the geography of North America at mid-century.

In the course of such a search as this, the geographer inevitably finds that he has to revalue, or even to discard, some of the symbols of his shorthand which have served over past decades—such labels, for example, as the 'Manufacturing Belt' or the 'Cotton Belt'. I believe that, in some cases, their use has actually masked a more logical analysis of the geographical facts than they themselves provided, and I have tried to show how and why they have served their time. So much has changed in North America since they were first invented.

Chapters VIII to XIX of the book deal with the regions of North America, and all of these regions are familiar to geographers. I have not, however, devoted much attention to their exact definition on the ground, nor attempted to map them. Rather, I have allowed them to define themselves, in terms of the regional problems which confront them. Among a forward-looking people like the North Americans, the bonds of regional sympathy are tied less by topography or climate than by a shared concern for the future of the community.

In dealing as a geographer with these problems, however, I have tried to keep in sight the fact that they are human problems. Thus, for example, in the sections on manufacturing I have usually cited the statistics for employment rather than output. Although the employment figures admittedly tell only a part of the story, and tend to mask the effects of automation and increased efficiency, nevertheless they serve as a better expression of the human side of the ever-changing relationship between man and environment.

With regard to some of these regional problems, I have merely raised questions which I hope may provoke thought and discussion. With others, I have hinted at a judgement which is, obviously, personal and therefore liable to challenge. To an extent unknown in the longer-settled lands of Europe, however, the problems of resource use and geography are, in newer lands, subjects of public interest and debate, and millions of Americans have made their own personal judgements on these technical problems. In making mine, I have drawn upon as wide a range of literature and opinion as possible, besides incorporating, in two or three places, findings based on my own research.

In writing about this fast-developing continent, an author quickly realizes that he can never be entirely up to date. I have therefore thought it best to draw the line, statistically, at the point reached by the 1957 editions of the *Canada Yearbook* and the *Statistical Abstract of the United States*, and all tables of figures not attributed to another source are taken from these publications. Since they were issued, of course, development has continued apace—in Canada, for example, the output of natural gas has virtually doubled, and in California the population has increased by, probably, another million and a half—but at least they form a base line for future reference.

Many people have helped me with the writing of this book, and I gratefully acknowledge all the assistance I have received; initially from the Commonwealth Fund, whose generosity enabled me to spend two years in North America; then from the American geographers who showed me sections of their country; and more recently from the staff of the American Library in London, the Librarian at Canada House, and, on specific matters, from the Canadian Wheat Board, the Quebec Hydro-Electric Commission, and the Tennessee Valley Authority.

St. Andrews,
January 1960

AUTHOR'S NOTE TO THE
THIRD EDITION

MUCH of the text of the original edition of this book was written during the mid-1950's, a period which, we can now appreciate, marked the end of the 'post-war' years, and the start of a period in which the effects of the war that ended in 1945 were overlain by other, more immediate influences on the life of North America's peoples. When that text was written, there was still a 'dollar gap' to worry European governments, and the era of jet air travel had scarcely begun. No wonder, then, that an author who committed himself to print in an age that now seems practically medieval should feel embarrassed to re-read his earlier work, and should be anxious to revise his conclusions.

The present edition of this book therefore differs a good deal from its predecessors—about a quarter of it has been re-written —not only in that the statistical information and reading lists have been brought up to date, but also in that emphases and conclusions have been adjusted in the light of more recent experience, of fuller reflection and, as always, of helpful comment by numerous colleagues and readers on both sides of the Atlantic. To all those who have suggested ways in which the book could be improved, I wish to express my sincere thanks. Among them, I should like to single out Professors J. Lewis Robinson, Clarence W. Olmstead and Richard Hartshorne.

Discussion with American geographers has underlined one of these comments which I should like to mention specifically here. Anyone who compares this book—and, incidentally, other British regional texts—with its American counterparts will notice at once that, while the American regional geographies begin their treatment of the first areal sub-division almost immediately, my own book contains no less than seven chapters of generalities before the strictly regional treatment begins. This difference is not fortuitous: it represents a basic divergence of policy for which each author accepts individual responsibility. My own method has been based on the assumption that, in dealing with an area of whatever size, the geographer's clearest method of presentation is to say first all that can be said about the area as a whole, and only to begin his breakdown for regional and sub-regional treatment when increasing differences between one part and another oblige him to do so. *September 1964*

I

THE PHYSICAL BACKGROUND

1. *Introduction*

THE continent of North America has an area of some 8·3 million square miles. Of this total, about 900,000 square miles are accounted for by Mexico and the countries that border the Caribbean, while the Arctic Archipelago of Canada, the almost uninhabited islands which lie within the Canadian sector of the Arctic regions, account for a further 700,000 square miles. The area with which this book is chiefly concerned is represented by the remaining 6·7 million square miles, which are divided, politically, into:

Canada (less Arctic Archipelago)	3·1 million square miles
Continental U.S.A.	3·6 million square miles[1]

Translated into distances, these dimensions mean that the part of the continent which we are considering stretches across almost 50° of latitude, from the Florida Keys to the northern tip of mainland Canada, and across 115° of longitude, from the east coast of Newfoundland to the Bering Strait. The railway distance from Halifax in the east to Prince Rupert in the west of Canada is more than 3,750 miles; from New York to San Francisco is some 3,000 miles, and from Brownsville, on the United States–Mexican border, to the 49th parallel that marks the boundary between Canada and the U.S.A., is 1,600 miles. Thus Prince Rupert is as far from Halifax as the mouth of the Congo is from London, and New York is as far from San Francisco as it is from Ireland.

2. *The Physiographic Divisions*

For ease of reference the North American continent may be divided, north of the United States–Mexican border, into seven main physiographic provinces, as shown in Fig. 1.

THE ATLANTIC AND GULF COAST PLAINS

From western Texas to New York the North American con-

---

[1] Including Alaska (0·6 million square miles).

THE APPALACHIAN SYSTEM

In eastern North America mountain-building processes went on, at intervals, throughout Ordovician, Devonian, and Permian times. The area affected by these processes forms a wide belt, with a marked north-east to south-west trend, from Newfoundland to central Alabama. This area, diverse in present character but unified by its physical history, may be called the Appalachian System. It falls into three sections: a southern section, stretching from Alabama to the valley of the Hudson and including the Appalachian Mountains proper; a New England section, from the Hudson to central Maine; and a north-eastern section, covering northern Maine and the Maritime Provinces of Canada.

(a) *The Southern Section.* In the south the system is formed by two parallel belts. On the east is that of the 'old' Appalachians, made up of Pre-Cambrian igneous and metamorphic rocks. On the west is a 'new' belt, formed by the upthrust edge of the great Palaeozoic floor that covers the central lowlands of North America. Each of these belts has an eastern edge different in form from the western, so that this further subdivision gives the system four provinces.

On the eastern, or seaward, edge the old rocks have been severely eroded to form a gently-sloping, dissected plateau surface known as the Piedmont. From its junction with the coastal plains at the Fall Line (see p. 183) it rises gradually to 1,200 or 1,500 feet, where it merges with the wooded mountains. These mountains represent the western half of the 'old' Appalachians, an area less heavily eroded than the Piedmont, and so rising in places to a present level of 6,000 feet or more. In the Great Smokies and the Blue Ridge of the southern states this mountain barrier is virtually uninterrupted, but it subsides northward, and in northern Virginia and Pennsylvania it becomes low and discontinuous.

When the 'new' belt of the Appalachians in the west was upthrust, the Palaeozoic strata, which formerly lay almost horizontal, were severely contorted along the line of junction with the older formations to the east. This junction zone now shows a remarkable series of folds, running parallel with the trend of the system, and known as the Ridge and Valley Province. This 'corrugated' area is from 25 to 80 miles wide, and through it run the north-flowing Shenandoah and the south-flowing Tennessee, with their tributaries, while east-flowing rivers like the Potomac are forced to cut through the ridges in a series of gaps.

West of the fold zone, and above a high scarp face (known in Pennsylvania as the Allegheny Front), lies the fourth, or inland, province of the system. It is a plateau section, where the Palaeozoic formations retain almost the same undisturbed bedding as they had before the upthrust. The Cumberland Plateau in Tennessee and Kentucky lies at about 2,000 feet, and levels rise to twice that height in West Virginia. Northward the plateau stretches almost to the southern shores of the Great Lakes; westward it drops away to the lowlands. Among its sandstones and limestones lie the vast coal measures of the great Appalachian coalfield.

(b) *The New England Section.* North of the Hudson the Pre-Cambrian and Palaeozoic belts of the Appalachian System continue into New England. The first of these is represented by the heavily eroded uplands of New England that correspond to the Piedmont. The Ridge and Valley Province of the Palaeozoic belt, on the other hand, can be traced running north through the Hudson Valley, and so by way of the Champlain Lowland to where it merges into the down-faulted St. Lawrence Valley. On the west the Plateau Province terminates in the Catskill Mountains.

The uplands of New England form a plateau surface which drops gently eastward to the sea. They are surmounted by groups of peaks that represent harder masses of rock, which have resisted the attacks of three, or perhaps four, cycles of erosion. Such peaks have received the name of monadnocks, after Mount Monadnock in New Hampshire. The uplands have two axes, separated by the lowlands that extend from New Jersey north through the Connecticut Valley. The western axis is marked by the line of the Green Mountains, and is carried north by that of the Notre Dame and the Shickshock Mountains, which stretch into the Gaspé Peninsula of Quebec. None of these is as much as 4,500 feet high. The eastern axis runs through the White Mountains (where Mount Washington reaches 6,288 feet) and into Canada's Maritime Provinces. The whole surface of New England has been heavily glaciated, and much of the detail of the landscape is due to the action of the ice.

(*c*) *The Maritimes–Newfoundland Extension*. While the Appalachian mountain-building processes extended their influence to northern Maine and the Maritime Provinces, and traces of the system persist as far east as Newfoundland, the present structure of the area bears little relation to that farther south. Huge igneous intrusions have occurred, to form batholiths that constitute the Central Highlands of New Brunswick and the hills of the 'arm' of Nova Scotia and Cape Breton Island. Between these old formations in Nova Scotia and the equally old rocks of the Canadian Shield, a wide basin has been formed in which younger beds—Permian and Carboniferous—are to be found. These underlie the lowlands round the Bay of Fundy and Prince Edward Island. On the southern shore of the Bay of Fundy the same feature that forms the Connecticut Valley —a band of young sandstones and shales of Triassic age— occurs again to form the Annapolis Valley of Nova Scotia.

THE LAURENTIAN OR CANADIAN SHIELD

Much of eastern Canada is covered by more than a million square miles of metamorphosed Pre-Cambrian rocks, which form a vast block known as the Laurentian Shield. Beneath the Palaeozoic strata that border it on the south, on the west, and round Hudson Bay, there can be traced the continuation of the Shield, underlying much of central Canada and the Great Lakes region as well.

Wide areas of this ancient rock mass have been severely compressed and contorted, and in the zones of disturbance a large variety of minerals is to be found. The present surface of the Shield, however, bears little relation to the previous disturbance. Through a long history of erosion, culminating in severe glaciation, it has been converted into an even peneplain surface that dips gently away from a level of 1,700 or 2,000 feet along its south-east (or St. Lawrence) edge, until it disappears below younger formations just south of Hudson Bay.

The Shield is nearly all Canadian, but it has two southward extensions into the U.S.A. which share its main characteristics. One is in the Adirondack Mountains of northern New York State, and the other forms the Superior Upland in northern

Wisconsin and Michigan. On the west the Shield sinks beneath later materials along a line that runs through Lake of the Woods, Great Slave Lake, and Great Bear Lake to the Arctic seas. On the east it includes Labrador, with its monadnock ranges, and it can also be traced to Newfoundland.

The tremendous forces of glaciation scoured the smooth peneplain in almost unobstructed action. Today the result of this action remains in an absence of soil cover and in a chaotic drainage system. Glacial detritus has dammed and diverted streams, creating a rocky landscape strewn with lakes and swamps. Sometimes, however, these lakes have disappeared, leaving behind them their clay-filled beds, and thus offering some prospect of fertility in this otherwise infertile world of the Shield.

THE CENTRAL LOWLAND

Between the Appalachian System in eastern North America and the Rocky Mountains in the west is a vast lowland area. As far as relief is concerned, the Gulf Coast Plains and much of the Laurentian Shield, which have already been described, belong to this lowland also. It is only on geological grounds that they are separated from it, for one is younger, and the other older, than the region we are now considering.

Even with the coastal plains and the Shield excluded, the remainder of the lowland area is of enormous extent. From the edge of the Appalachian Plateau in Ohio to Denver, at the foot of the Rockies, is 1,200 miles. From north to south the dimensions of the region are even more impressive—40° of latitude, or over 2,500 miles, from the edge of the coastal plain in Texas to the delta of the Mackenzie at 70° North.

Spread across the Central Lowland are Palaeozoic beds of great thickness, evenly deposited on the floor of a former sea. In the north-east these overlap the Shield, while on the south they are themselves submerged below the later deposits of the coastal plain. In the east, as we have seen, they end in violent contortions against the wall of the 'old' Appalachians. In the west they terminate against the Front Range of the Rockies, and on the north they reach the Arctic Ocean.

The Central Lowland comprises several sections. These may be described as the Eastern Transition Belt, the Mississippi–

Great Lakes Section, the Ozark–Ouachita Province, and the Great Plains.

FIG. 2. The Central Lowland: Location Map of Physical Features.

(a) *The Eastern Transition Belt.* Between the Appalachian Plateau, where the Palaeozoic formations have been upthrust, and the Mississippi Valley, where they lie even and almost undisturbed, there is a transitional area, sometimes known as the Interior Low Plateaux. As the effects of the Appalachian mountain-building processes spread farther afield they became less violent, and in the Transition Belt merely created some slight folds, and a gentle westward dip away from the mountains. This area has, for the most part, a sandstone cover underlain by Carboniferous limestone. The latter gives rise to areas of karst topography and to such limestone features as the Mammoth Cave of Kentucky. Of more importance to the economic life of the region is the effect of this folding in creating two domes, whose sandstone cover has been removed by erosion, leaving limestone basins—the Blue Grass Basin of Kentucky and the Nashville Basin of Tennessee. Both of these have long been famous for the excellence of the pastures on their lime-rich soils.

(b) *The Mississippi–Great Lakes Section.* This section constitutes the eastern half of the Palaeozoic lowlands. It is a true, structual plain, whose flatness is emphasized by the fact that, as far south as the Ohio and Missouri Rivers, the solid surface is masked by a mantle of glacial drift. Here, as on the Shield, glacial action has effected the drainage system, and the area abounds with lakes. Before the coming of the cultivator, who has drained the land, swamps were also widespread. The slight folding that has disturbed the area accounts for its only significant physical features. These are synclines in Ohio and Illinois which contain coal measures, and a basin centred in southern Michigan, whose rim is marked by cuestas that form an almost perfect semicircle round it. The best-known of these is the Niagara Cuesta, a 'rim' of magnesian limestone which underlies the Falls, and from there runs northwards across a string of islands in Lake Huron, and west and then southwards through Upper Michigan into Wisconsin.

West of the Mississippi the strata dip very gently westward, while, equally gently, the land surface rises. The result is a series of east-facing scarps of beds which become progressively younger as they are encountered going west. The most prominent of these scarps, the Missouri Coteau, is usually taken to delimit the section on the west.

(c) *The Ozark–Ouachita Section.* West of the Mississippi, and near where it merges into the Gulf Coast Plain, the Central Lowland is interrupted by a group of low mountains which are sometimes known as the Interior Highlands. These highlands are formed by two separate features. In the north is a dome which is flanked by rocks of Carboniferous age, and at whose crest Pre-Cambrian granites are exposed. This area forms the Ozark Plateau. To the south, beyond the Arkansas River, lie the Ouachitas, fold mountains which closely resemble in structure the Ridge and Valley of the Appalachians; indeed, they were created by the same mountain-building movements. The highest points in the Ouachitas are at 2,800 feet and in the

Ozarks at about 1,700 feet.

(*d*) *The Great Plains*. The eastern edge of the Great Plains, in the neighbourhood of the Missouri Coteau, lies at about 2,000 feet above sea-level. The western edge, where the Front Ranges of the Rockies abruptly rise, is at an elevation of 4,000 to 5,000 feet, giving an average slope of 8 to 10 feet per mile across the area. These plains are, nevertheless, a true part, structurally, of the Central Lowlands. They extend from Mexico northward until, narrowing between the Shield and the Rockies, they reach northern Alaska.

As in the western part of the Mississippi–Great Lakes Section, the strata underlying the Great Plains continue to dip westward towards a trough at the foot of the Rockies. The eastward slope of the land surface, however, is due to the fact that the present surface is formed by a mantle of recent, and often quite unconsolidated, materials from the Rockies, transported and spread by the east-flowing rivers. This smooth surface mantle is disturbed only by the effects of erosive agents upon it. Wind and water have cut deeply into the soft, loose materials washed down from the mountains. In Nebraska a belt of sand hills have been formed by the force of a virtually unobstructed wind, while in the Dakotas—and, to some extent, in all the river valleys that cross the plains—water erosion has created the fantastic Badland topography for which the plains are famous.

Only one major break interrupts the evenness of the plains —the Black Hills of South Dakota, which rise to over 7,000 feet. Here the old, crystalline continental bedrock breaks through to the surface in a domelike swelling, and forms a welcome change from the monotony of the plains.

THE ROCKY MOUNTAIN PROVINCE

Late in Cretaceous times tremendous mountain-building processes disturbed the western half of the North American continent, where a long series of sedimentary beds lay evenly spread over the ancient continental floor. This disturbance, which was accompanied by volcanic activity, is known as the Laramide Revolution. It resulted in a great uplift, accompanied by folding and faulting, of the areas which are now known as the Rocky Mountain Province and the High Plateaux.

The uplift led to a much intensified attack by erosive agents in the Tertiary period that followed. From the highest parts of the west, thousands of feet of sedimentary cover were removed, and the Archean floor was exposed. Elsewhere, however, the cover has been preserved, usually by down-faulting, and it is the various strata of this sedimentary covering, with their characteristic horizontal bedding, that give to the landscape of the west many of its particular splendours.

We must now define more closely the nature of the Rocky Mountains. On the east (Great Plains) fringe of the area affected, the Laramide Revolution threw up two parallel anticlines, running generally from north to south. These anticlines, now eroded down to their crystalline cores, form the mountain chains that constitute the Rocky Mountains proper and that extend, with some interruptions, from the Brooks Range in Alaska, south across Canada and the U.S.A., to about 35° North, with traces of extension beyond this into Mexico. The peaks of these Front Ranges rise abruptly above the Great Plains to heights of from 10,000 to 14,000 feet.

The Front Ranges are backed by an area of scattered mountains, interspersed with plateaux. The whole province has an east–west width of between 100 and 300 miles. Most of the mountain ranges follow the general north–south trend of the Rockies, a trend which is accentuated by faulting. Across the boundary between the U.S.A. and Canada, for example, runs the remarkable Rocky Mountain Trench, a fault valley 900 miles long, and occupied in turn by the Columbia, Fraser, Parsnip and Finlay Rivers. Elsewhere, however, volcanic activity has created great structureless batholiths, like the mountains of central Idaho, where 20,000 square miles of granite form a wilderness area that rises above 12,000 feet, and remains almost impenetrable to the present day.

All through the Rocky Mountains, indeed, the effects of vulcanicity have been great. Lava flows cover much of northern New Mexico, and in Wyoming visitors flock to Yellowstone National Park to watch over 3,000 geysers and hot springs that are still active on this 7,000-foot plateau in the heart of the mountains.

In the Cordilleran barrier there are two principal breaches. One of these is in the far north, at the southern end of the

Mackenzie Mountains, where the Liard River flows through the break, and is followed by the Alaska Highway. The other is a breach of the utmost importance for transcontinental communications, and occurs in Wyoming. The old Oregon Trail (see p. 161) made use of this route, on which wagons could be hauled over the continental divide without difficulty —without, indeed, more than a distant glimpse of the mountains. Today, on the main line of the Union Pacific Railroad from Chicago to California, the railway traveller glides over the 7,000-foot pass without any impression of climbing, and only careful observation will mark the whereabouts of the watershed.

THE HIGH PLATEAUX

West of the Rocky Mountains proper lies an area whose astonishing physical features are the product, in about equal proportions, of crustal faulting, volcanic activity, and intense recent erosion by down-cutting rivers. The basic form of the area is that of a series of plateau-steps, some of them almost as high as the Rockies themselves, and almost all above 3,000 feet. In the south-western United States, however, the 'steps' descend fairly regularly from the Rockies for 500 miles westwards, to the remarkable hollow of Death Valley, at 280 feet below sea-level. Farther north the plateau province is narrower, so that its width in British Columbia is no more than 100 miles.

The development of these plateaux, like that of the Rockies, resulted from the Laramide Revolution, and they form a series from Mexico to the Bering Strait. On the whole their different levels are the result of faulting. For the rest they possess two common characteristics. The first is that the original relief, whether it was based on the old continental floor or on the later Palaeozoics, has been smoothed by recent deposits. Over wide areas, notably in the Great Basin of Utah and Nevada, these are ordinary alluvia, but elsewhere lava flows of great extent are found, lying ten or twenty deep in regular horizontal layers. The second common characteristic is that throughout the province there seem to have been great amounts of recent uplift, and the resultant spectacular patterns of erosion are epitomized by the Grand Canyon of the Colorado.

Several parts of the province can be distinguished. In the south-east lie the Colorado Plateaux, developed on horizontal Palaeozoics and dropping by cliff-steps from 11,000 to 5,000 feet above sea-level. Through the sandstones and limestones of this sedimentary cover the Colorado and its tributaries have cut gorges up to 5,000 feet deep. In the Grand Canyon the river has cut down through the whole series of Palaeozoics to the Archean floor, thus exposing a giant cross-section of the continent's physical history.

The western edge of the Colorado Plateaux is marked by a great fault at the foot of the Wasatch Mountains, and west of this lies the Great Basin, stretching for 500 miles from north to south and from east to west. Most of this is an area of inland drainage. The Basin is divided, however, into numerous sections by faulted mountain blocks, a few score miles in length, and running, for the most part, regularly north and south. In between the ranges, recent alluvia and lake-bed deposits fill the Basin. The Great Salt Lake, which today occupies some 2,000 square miles at the eastern edge of the Basin, is only a remnant of the former Lake Bonneville, ten times as large, whose shoreline can be traced on slopes that are a thousand feet above the level of the present lake.

North of this 'basin and range' country lie the plateaux of the Columbia River and of British Columbia. These are most easily described as lava seas. The surrounding walls of the Rockies and the Cascade and Coast Mountains formed 'shores' within which the flows were dammed, so that in places they have been built up to a thickness of as much as 2,000 feet. Northward through British Columbia the plateaux become more dissected and interrupted than farther south, but the High Plateaux Province continues, with some breaks, all the way across the Yukon to central Alaska.

THE PACIFIC COASTLANDS

The most westerly physiographic province of North America is filled with a remarkable variety of natural wonders, and it is, indeed, only a common history that links its varied landscapes with each other. In this province are found the highest and lowest points of the continent, its deepest valley and its only remaining (recently) active volcanoes.

On the American shores of the Pacific, the trend of the land features is almost everywhere parallel to the shoreline. These features form three belts, and this triple-banded effect can be traced from Mexico to Alaska, with only a short break in the region round Los Angeles.

On the inland edge of the province, adjoining the High Plateaux, is a mountain chain comparable in size and splendour with the Rockies. From southern California this chain, the Sierra Nevada, stretches north to become the Cascade Range in Oregon and the Coast Mountains when it reaches British Columbia. It culminates, in the Alaska Range, in North America's highest peak, Mt. McKinley (20,320 feet). Throughout its great length it is cut by only three low-level crossings: the valleys of the Columbia, Fraser, and Skeena Rivers. Formed mostly of old crystalline materials occurring in the shape of batholiths, its crestline is crowned by scores of volcanic cones. These cones, whose lavas lie thick over the ranges, form outstanding peaks like Mt. Whitney and Mt. Rainier (both over 14,400 feet). In Alaska recent uplift has created block mountains like the St. Elias Range, which rises in places above 18,000 feet.

Much of the eastern side of the mountains is faulted and very steep. From Mt. Whitney to Death Valley is only 70 miles in distance, but nearly 15,000 feet difference in elevation. The west side of the mountains, particularly the Sierras, is notable for its ice-carved valleys—Yosemite, with its waterfalls and its 3,000-foot cliffs, and King's Canyon, with its unrivalled depth of 8,000 feet.

West of the mountains is a line of depressions—the Central Valley of California, the Willamette Valley, Puget Sound, and the coastal channels of British Columbia. Created in conjunction with the uplift of the mountains, these depressions have been filled, at various times, with ice, mud flows, and alluvia. Today they are submerged in the north but dry in the south, where up to 2,000 feet of materials have been deposited to form fertile farmlands, the agricultural heart of the Far West.

Bordering the coast itself is yet another mountain chain. In California it is composed of rolling hills, 2,000 to 3,000 feet high. These enclose the Central Valley on the west, except where the sea breaks through them, at the Golden Gate at San

Francisco. This coastal chain continues into Oregon, but north of the Columbia it becomes higher and more rugged, until it reaches Puget Sound and the 9,000-foot Olympic Mountains. North of the Strait of Juan de Fuca the ranges are discontinuous, and are represented by Vancouver Island and by the long chain of islands that flanks the coast beyond, as far as the Aleutians.

This triple belt of the Pacific coastlands is recognizable everywhere except in the extreme south-west of the United States. Here it is interrupted by faulting in an east–west direction, which has created a lowland corridor that links the coast with the southern tip of the Great Basin. The coastal hills and the Sierra Nevada meet and enclose the southern end of the Central Valley of California, and to the south of their junction in the Tehachapi Mountains lies the lowland route to the interior (Fig. 1, 7[1]) dominated today by the great urban area of Los Angeles.

3. The Glaciation of North America

Of decisive importance in shaping the physical and cultural patterns of present-day North America was the epoch in the continent's history when some three-quarters of its surface was covered by ice. Glacial erosion smoothed its rugged relief and re-formed its drainage patterns; glacial deposition covered a million square miles with drift, which filled former valleys and provided materials for some of the continent's most fertile soils. On the farmlands of the Middle West it is to the Ice Age as much as to any other single factor that the modern farmer owes his prosperity.

Although the ice was once continuous from coast to coast, it is necessary to distinguish between two separate parts of this great cover. Over the north-east of the continent there spread the vast Laurentide Ice Sheet. In the north-west and west, on the other hand, a separate system of glaciers—usually known as the Cordilleran System—formed in the mountains, from which it spread to cover the intermontane zone. While remnants of this western system are still to be found in the northern Rockies and the mountains of the northern Pacific coast, the Laurentide Sheet, although much greater in extent, has disappeared entirely from the North American mainland, and today remains only on the mountains of Baffin and Ellesmere Islands.

THE LAURENTIDE ICE SHEET

The ice probably originated in the Hudson Bay or Labrador region. From there it spread across eastern North America, almost to the foothills of the Rockies, and at its maximum extent covered some 4·8 million square miles. It is suggested that it originated in a series of valley glaciers which grew slowly until they became sufficiently widespread to affect the climate; thereafter they would grow with increasing rapidity, expanding in the direction from which most precipitation was being received—in this case, the west. Over so large an area ice would probably accumulate at varying rates, and so domes or 'centres' of ice would be built up in the areas of most rapid growth. There seem to have been two such centres—the Labrador and the Keewatin—one to the east, and the other to the west, of Hudson Bay; but these centres may have shifted their position with the passage of time. From them the ice flowed outwards in all directions.

Southwards the ice spread over New England and the Adirondacks, as far as northern Pennsylvania. But on this all-important southern edge of the sheet, where the force of the ice movement was becoming weaker, the direction of movement tended to be influenced by the pre-existing relief features, such as the Superior Upland and the Niagara Cuesta. Diverted by these the southern edge of the ice formed a series of southward-moving lobes. Under the influence of climatic fluctuations these advanced and retreated several times during the glacial epoch, so that the southern limit of the sheet varied in position from time to time. On the whole, however, its maximum southward extent is marked today by the line of the Missouri and Ohio Rivers, which first developed as streams flowing along the ice front.

Beneath most of the vast area of the Laurentide Sheet the principal action of the ice was erosive. Over most of the area north of the present Great Lakes there was little glacial deposition, but a widespread scouring. Relief was smoothed, soil cover was removed, and a new and often inconsequent drainage pattern was imposed on the area. Today, as we have already

PLATE I

The Canadian Rockies: Mount Assiniboine (11,870 feet) from the north. This mountain, part of the main chain of the Rockies, stands at the southern end of the line of national parks in the vicinity of Jasper and Banff, Alberta

PLATE II

The Colorado Plateau: Looking down the canyon of the Little Colorado River from above Grand Falls, north-east of Flagstaff, Arizona. The horizontal bedding of the rocks and deep incision of the river are both characteristic of the plateau, whose surface is here lying at about 5,000 feet

seen, the features of this region are an infertile surface and a maze of swamps and lakes.

Along the southern margin of the sheet, however, erosion gave place to deposition, and scouring to infilling. Here the action of the ice produced a series of highly significant land-

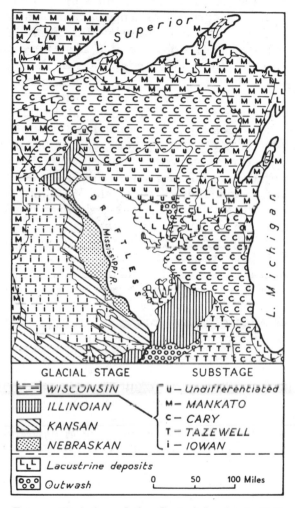

Fig. 3. Glaciation of the Central Lowland: Drift Covers in the Mississippi–Great Lakes Section. (After the *Glacial Map of North America*, published by the Geol. Soc. of America, 1st ed., N.Y., 1945.)

scape features. Foremost among them is the mantle of glacial drift that covers virtually the whole area. Varying in thickness from a foot or two to 150 feet, the drift has completely reformed the topography of central North America.

It is this drift cover—the ground moraine, or till, left by the Ice Sheet—which serves as the best guide to the advances and retreats of the ice under the influence of climatic fluctuations. Each new advance produced a fresh layer of drift. From the evidence these provide, it is deduced that there were four main periods of southward advance, or 'glacial stages', separated by interglacial periods. The earliest glacial stage, the Nebraskan, was followed (in each case the name is borrowed from one of the states most affected) by the Kansan and the Illinoian, and finally by the Wisconsin, during which the ice reached its maximum southward extent. As the most recently deposited drift, the Wisconsin overlays the older mantles, which, as the map on p. 17 illustrates, protrude at its edges. Providing, as it does, the most abundant materials for study, the Wisconsin Stage has been further divided into four sub-stages, which seem to correspond to minor fluctuations within the major advance.

The interglacial periods, also, are not without their importance. They were evidently long enough to permit both the development of a vegetation cover and the formation of wide belts of loess. This accumulated on the bare, ice-free surfaces after each retreat and locally, as in the 'loess state' of Iowa, it is of the utmost importance to agriculture.

Thus the glacial and interglacial deposits are often interleaved, and together form a thick cover which bears no resemblance, either in relief or in soil type, to the earlier surface that can be identified beneath it. While the material of which the till is composed varies in character from boulders to fine clays, on the whole it produces excellent soils.

The second main feature of this zone of deposition is the great number of moraines and hills of glacial origin. The edges of most of the drift belts are marked by end moraines. On the map these often appear—especially on the till plains south of the Great Lakes—as semi-circular ridges that reveal how, at the limit of its advance, the ice front consisted of a series of lobes. Farther east, in New England, these same end moraines are today represented by the line of islands which fringes the region's southern coast—Nantucket, Martha's Vineyard, and Long Island. Elsewhere, as in Wisconsin, the moraines form long, straight ridges running from north to south. Drumlins abound, especially in the Great Lakes shorelands of Wisconsin, Michigan, and western New York; they generally appear in clusters containing dozens together, orientated roughly north–south by the direction of ice flow.

Lying as it does in the heart of the present Great Lakes, the peninsula of southern Ontario possesses these morainic features in very large numbers. The centre of the peninsula is covered by glacial drift with drumlins, and is almost surrounded by a horseshoe of morainic hills, formed by lobes of ice pressing south into the lake basins on either side of it. Outside this horseshoe lie clay and sand plains; these are relics of the bed of the far larger lakes which formerly occupied the basins of Ontario, Erie, and Huron, and surrounded an Ontario 'island' much smaller than the present peninsula.

The third feature of note is the effect of glaciation on the drainage pattern. Before the glacial epoch the drainage of the whole Midwestern area was probably eastwards and then northwards towards Hudson Bay. When the ice began to retreat northwards the residue of the sheet blocked this route to the sea and melt-water accumulated along the ice front in a series of huge lakes. These reached as far west as Lakes Agassiz and Regina on the Canadian prairies, and together covered an area several times larger than that now occupied by the five Great Lakes. The development of the Missouri–Ohio drainage system, while it provided an outlet southward for some of the melt-water, further dislocated the earlier drainage pattern, and wide-spread damming and river diversion occurred.

As the location of the ice front changed, so the form of these lakes varied. First one outlet and then another was uncovered by the ice, giving a fresh escape route for the melt-water. As each outlet was cleared and deepened by erosion, the lowering of the water level resulted in the abandonment of an earlier, higher route. At one period or another this great expanse of water seems to have drained away either south-west and southwards to the Mississippi, or south-eastwards into what are now the Susquehanna and the Hudson, or north-eastwards into the St. Lawrence, when eventually that route was cleared. Today

C

the Great Lakes represent a remainder of this great body of water, whose past presence is attested by the old lake beds which provide the farmers of Illinois, Minnesota, and Manitoba with some of the world's flattest and most fertile farmlands.

In all this drift-covered expanse one small part stands out as an exception—the Driftless Area of Wisconsin. By some trick of relief—probably the sheltering effect of the Superior Upland— this area was by-passed by the ice. Walled in on two sides by the Wisconsin terminal moraine, its features are water- and not ice-formed. Its relief is more broken than that of the surrounding areas; its soils are the poorer for being drift-free; economically, it shows a marked inferiority to the areas outside the moraine wall.

THE CORDILLERAN GLACIATION

The Cordilleran System ultimately covered almost the whole of what are now western Canada and Alaska, and isolated ice caps spread over the higher areas as far south as the mountains of northern New Mexico. With its heavy precipitation, the Mountain West, and particularly British Columbia, was a centre of accumulation. From the heights of the two main mountain chains the ice tended to flow both east and west, so that eventually the westward-moving ice from the Rockies and the eastward flow from the Sierras and Cascades coalesced to form a complete cover over the intermontane zone.

With the ending of the glacial epoch, the intermontane basins became filled with melt-water. As in the east, drainage was dislocated: outflow to east and west was barred by the mountains; northward the remains of the ice blocked all outlets. Only in the extreme south was there an open route to the sea. The Great Basin of Utah and Nevada became the bed of glacial Lake Bonneville. It is of this great body of water, ponded between the southern Utah divide and the retreating ice front, that the present Salt Lake is a relic, its shoreline lying 1,000 feet below that of its predecessor. Ultimately, Lake Bonneville drained off northwards into the swollen Columbia, to whose post-glacial volume the Dry Falls in the Grand Coulee (see p. 446), with their 3½-mile brink, bear eloquent testimony.

Of this Cordilleran System, the icefields of Alaska remain to the present day as substantial reminders. Farther to the south, small glaciers still flank the peaks of British Columbia and the state of Washington, as far south as Mount Rainier.

4. The Climate of North America

The Florida Keys, the southernmost point of the U.S.A., lie just north of the Tropic of Cancer; the northern tip of the Canadian mainland lies at 72° North. With a latitudinal spread of nearly 50°, therefore, the area we are considering has a wide variety of climates. At one extreme are the frostless islands of the Gulf of Mexico; at the other the Arctic conditions of the Canadian Northlands. On the Pacific coast there are stations which record over 200 inches of precipitation per annum, while a few score miles inland there are areas with less than 10 inches. The east–west dimensions of North America are equally significant. There are points in the central plains which are more than 1,000 miles from the sea, so that they experience to the full the climatic extremes of a continental interior. On the other hand, within this great land area there is room for a chain of inland seas—the Great Lakes—over 700 miles from east to west, and for the 750-mile penetration of Hudson Bay south-ward from the Arctic Ocean, both of which have specific effects upon the climatic régime of eastern North America.

AIR MASSES

For all its variety, however, the climate of North America is the product of relatively simple controls. Over the greater part of the continent east of the Rockies it is the behaviour and inter-action of two air masses that is responsible for weather changes. These are the polar continental air mass centred on the Canadian Northlands, and the tropical maritime air mass of the Atlantic–Gulf of Mexico area. West of the Rockies and on the Atlantic seaboard three other air masses play a part of vary-ing importance in weather controls—the polar maritime air of the northern Pacific and of the northern Atlantic, and the tropical maritime air mass over the Pacific which affects the southwestern U.S.A. and Mexico.

Polar continental air from the first of these air masses spills out from its source area in northern Canada and is associated in summer with cool, clear weather, and in winter with cold waves that bring spells of bitter weather to the northern interior and frost danger to the usually milder regions farther south. Tropical maritime air from the Gulf, on the other hand, flows northward from its source region over a warm ocean. In summer it is associated with high temperatures and oppressively high humidity over much of eastern North America, while in winter Gulf air brings mild spells and rain or fog to the cold interior.

As the general position of these air masses shifts with the sun, so they tend to dominate different parts of the continent in summer and winter, and there is at all seasons a zone over which they are in conflict; a zone in which the effects sometimes of one, and sometimes of the other, are dominant. In summer this zone of conflict runs south of the Great Lakes, so that the Midwest experiences an alternation of warm, humid weather of the type produced by Gulf air and cooler, less humid weather introduced from the north. In winter, on the other hand, when the whole system shifts south, the zone of conflict lies over the Gulf coast, and most of the interior is dominated by the cold air flow from the northern high-pressure area, with occasional breaks from the south, which may have the welcome effect of alleviating winter cold, but may also cause fog and brief, dangerous thaws.

This zone of conflict between North America's two most important air masses is an area where atmospheric disturbances are frequent, and consequently it is crossed by an unusually large number of storm tracks, even for a middle-latitude region. Cyclonic storms are generated all along the contact zone between the two air masses, and move from west or south-west to east, across the U.S.A. and southern Canada. The water expanse of the Great Lakes seems to be a factor in making them converge on the line of the St. Lawrence Valley and the New England–Maritimes area.

It is, then, the interaction of these two air masses that produces the weather experienced by southern and central North America, and so by a high proportion of the continent's population. West of the Rockies, however, the situation is quite different. Penetrations of Gulf air are rare, and the main interaction of air masses is between polar continental from the Northlands and polar maritime air from the Pacific. In winter, the Pacific air brings wet and (for these latitudes) mild weather to the coastlands: the amount of precipitation falls off southwards. Occasionally the Pacific air penetrates, though cooler now and drier, to the east of the Rockies. In summer, the northern Pacific is dominated by a high-pressure system, and the influence of polar maritime air on west coast weather becomes stronger. At this season, however, it is associated with dry, rather cool weather.

The extreme south-west of the U.S.A. lies within the sphere of influence of tropical maritime air. Although dominant along the coast of Baja California, this tropical air (which is associated with the warm dry conditions along that desert coast) is kept from extending its influence far to the north by the strength of the flow of polar air throughout most of the year.

On the Atlantic coast, in a similar way, the weather is produced by the interaction of three types of air—the polar continental and the Gulf air, as is the case over most of eastern North America, together with polar maritime air from a source area near Greenland. The southward penetration of this polar maritime air affects the coastlands of the north-east, bringing cold and drizzle in winter, and lower temperatures with moderate precipitation in summer. Its sphere of influence, however, does not extend southwards much beyond Chesapeake Bay.

TEMPERATURE

The wide range of climatic conditions in North America is clearly marked in the temperature statistics. There are only narrow coastal areas in the continent which do not experience extremes of either winter cold, or summer heat, or both. The Gulf coast and Florida have a seasonal régime of warm winters and hot summers; the mean January temperature is more than 50° F. and the mean July figure is above 80° F. At the other extreme, north-eastern Canada experiences the cold winters and cool summers (with a mean of less than 50° F. for all 12 months of the year) of a polar climate. Over most of the land mass, therefore, the chief feature of the temperature régime is its continentality, with a characteristically large annual range of temperature (up to 80° F. in north-western Canada), a wide diurnal range in winter, and an alternation of cold winters and hot summers separated by only brief transitional seasons.

The majority of North Americans live, therefore, in areas where the mean January temperature is below 32° F. The January isotherm of 32° F. runs from the Atlantic coast just south of New York, past Philadelphia, and then almost due west, through southern Indiana and Illinois, to south-eastern Colorado, while almost all of the Mountain West experiences a January mean well below 32°F. The January mean in Chicago

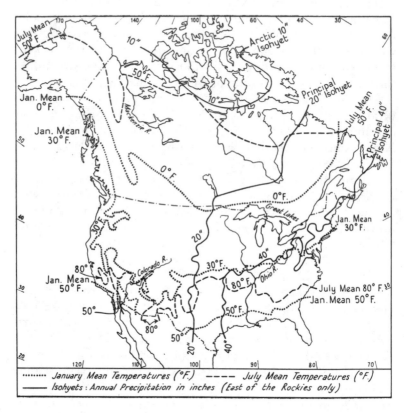

FIG. 4. The Climate of North America: Selected Isotherms and Isohyets.

is 25° F.; in Montreal it is 14° F., and at Winnipeg, which is the coldest of North America's large cities in winter, the mean temperature for the month is —3° F. The average figures, however, conceal the characteristics of this winter cold which are, firstly, that during the daytime the temperature will frequently rise above freezing point, only to fall to 10° or 0° F. at night, and secondly, that the means are depressed by extremely low temperatures occurring in periodic 'cold waves', rather than by consistently cold weather throughout the winter.

By contrast with the continental interior, the southern and western coastlands—from Virginia to Oregon—everywhere enjoy a January mean of more than 40° F. A regular winter migration of Americans takes place from the interior to these areas, where the influence of the ocean gives the smaller annual temperature range which is characteristic of maritime climates. The smallest temperature ranges in North America occur on the coast of central California (where, in exceptional locations, the annual range is less than 10° F.), at Key West, Fla. (a range of 13° F.), and on the coast of Oregon and Washington (14° to 16° F.).

If most Americans spend at least one month of winter at a mean temperature of 32° F. or below, it is also true that, in almost every major city, they languish through one or more summer months with a mean of 70° F. or above. The 70° F. July isotherm follows fairly closely the boundary of dense settlement across the central Great Lakes; Chicago experiences a July mean of 74° F., and Montreal one of 70° F. Farther south July means of 80° F. or above are general in Oklahoma, Arkansas, and the states lying to the south and south-east of them. Where these high summer temperatures are associated—as is the case almost everywhere east of the Mississippi— with high humidity, the resultant summer weather is extremely oppressive, both by day and by night, and it is necessary to travel either northwards or else to the Mountain West to find the relief of lower humidity and wider daily temperature ranges.

In the Mountain West summer conditions vary with altitude, but days are generally warm and nights pleasantly cool. On the Pacific coast there is a steady decrease of summer temperature from south to north; the July mean at San Diego is 67° F., and at Victoria, B.C., is 60° F. The moderating influence of the Pacific extends, however, only a short distance inland; the Central Valley of California experiences July means in excess of 80° F., while less than 200 miles inland lies Death Valley, with its forbidding July average in excess of 100° F.

PRECIPITATION

The parts of North America which receive most precipitation are firstly, the mountains of the northern Pacific coast and, secondly, the southern Appalachians and the south-eastern states. If the remainder of the continent is regarded as a rough triangle with its apex in the far north-west, then the south-eastern one-third is mainly humid, and the south-western and northern two-thirds are semi-arid or arid. Expressed in other terms, the pattern is that virtually all of the land mass lying east of 98° W. longitude and south of the 60th parallel has 20 inches or more of rainfall per annum, while north and west of these lines is a dry belt that stretches to the Arctic and westward almost to the Pacific coast.

Rain-bearing winds reach the continent from the North Pacific, and from the Atlantic and Gulf of Mexico where these seas border the continent on the south-east. The winds of the North Pacific immediately encounter the abrupt rise of the great mountain ranges of the Pacific coast; they shed their moisture in abundance, leaving the greater part of the area between the coastal mountains and the Rockies in the rain shadow. The behaviour of the rain-bearing winds of the south-east is governed almost equally by factors of relief, but in this case by the *absence* of any significant mountain barrier to their advance, so that their effect is felt over the whole continent east of the Rockies and south of the Laurentian Shield.

Movement of the pressure systems, on which these rain-bearing winds depend, creates seasonal variations in rainfall. West of the Rockies, in the sphere of influence of North Pacific air, there is everywhere a marked winter maximum. Even in the areas of the British Columbia coast where the annual rainfall is more than 100 inches, July and August have little rain, while farther south, in California, where the total amount of precipitation is much smaller (it is 20 inches at San Francisco and 10 inches at San Diego), there may be as many as four summer months that are completely rainless, after the familiar pattern of Mediterranean-type climates. Farther inland, in the desert basins, while the amounts of rainfall received are even smaller than on the California coast, much the same régime holds good; in the west, summer rains, apart from thunderstorms, are experienced only in the higher parts of the mountains.

East of the Rockies the situation is reversed; here only a small area shows a winter maximum. Elsewhere, as Fig. 5 shows, where there is any significant maximum, it occurs in the warmer months. It may occur, however, in spring, as in the central Corn Belt, or in early summer, as in the Great Plains, or in late summer, as in north-eastern Canada, and this distinc-

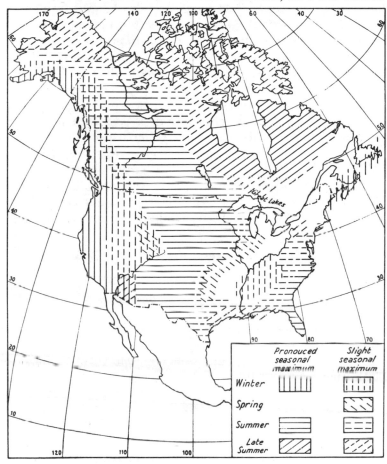

FIG. 5. The Climate of North America: Seasons of Maximum Precipitation. The map, which is based on data for some 250 stations, shows the season or seasons having precipitation maxima. Where two maxima occur in the year, this is indicated by cross-hatching.

tion is of great importance to the farmer. In the Agricultural Interior and on the Great Plains, growing-season rains favour the growth of crops. In areas of late summer rain, on the other hand, the maximum occurs too late to be of much agricultural value.

The only area of winter maximum east of the Rockies lies on the eastern coast of Labrador, Newfoundland, and the Maritime Provinces. Over the whole triangle of land lying between the Great Lakes, the St. Lawrence, and the Atlantic, rainfall is plentiful throughout the year, because the presence of these water bodies tends to attract to the area depressions travelling on almost all the continent's east-bound storm tracks. Thus New York has 3 to 4 inches of rainfall monthly, and Toronto 2 to 3 inches. But where, in addition, the presence of polar maritime (Atlantic) air makes itself felt (see p. 25), along the north-east coast, the winter's rainfall is supplemented from this source and exceeds that of the other seasons.

CLIMATIC REGIONS

Using these details, we can now attempt a classification of the climatic regions of North America. The simplest way to consider these is to group them as follows:

(a) The northern fringe of the continent,
(b) The Pacific coastlands,
(c) The mountainous west,
(d) The south-east,
(e) The continental interior.

(a) The northern fringe of the continent is an area of polar climate which finds its counterpart in northern Siberia. The boundary of this region runs somewhat north of the Arctic Circle through northern Alaska and as far east as the 110th meridian, and then turns south-east across the middle of Hudson Bay and northern Labrador to the Strait of Belle Isle; thus the climatic heart of the North American Arctic is situated over the northern end of Hudson Bay.

(b) The Pacific coastlands fall into three climatic regions.
1. Between approximately the 40th and 60th parallels there is a coastal belt with a cool temperate marine climate which resembles that of north-western Europe or New Zealand, except that the summers are drier, so that British exiles may feel that in coastal British Columbia they have discovered an

almost idealized version of the climate of their homeland.

2. Between 30° and 40° North—that is, roughly, throughout the state of California—is a belt of warm temperate climate of the western margin type usually known as Mediterranean, whose characteristics are a dry summer and moderate winter rain. In other words, the lack of summer rainfall, already

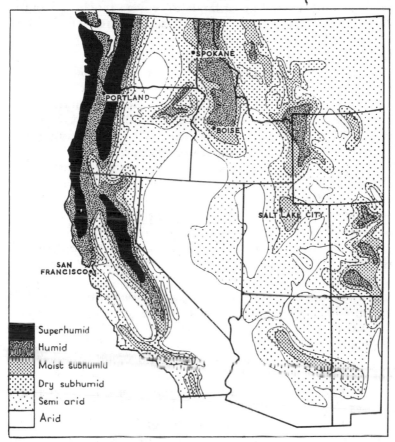

FIG. 6. The Western U.S.A.: The Climate of the U.S.A. west of the Rockies, according to the classification of C. W. Thornthwaite, and showing the wide variety of climatic circumstances induced by the varied relief. (Based on a map appearing in *Geog. Review*, vol. xxxviii (1948), p. 94, and reproduced by permission.)

noticeable in the cool temperate belt, becomes more marked as the summers become warmer going southward. But it is an over-generalization, as we shall see in Chapter XVII, to describe the climate of California simply as Mediterranean. This it is only in the broad pattern of seasonal variations; in detail, the local conditions produced by relief are both complicated and varied.

3. On the coast south of 30°—that is, in Lower California and Mexico—but extending inland to cover much of southwestern U.S.A., is a region of true desert climate, which corresponds with the desert regions in similar latitudes in northern Africa, in Australia, or north of the Persian Gulf.

(c) Inland from the Pacific coast relief is too varied to permit of the accurate identification of climatic regions, but in general there is a transition from true desert climate at the lowest elevations, in the Lower Colorado Basin and the Great Basin of Utah–Nevada, to semi-arid, or steppe, conditions at middle elevations, and to a montane régime at greater heights, where precipitation increases, and average temperatures decrease, with increasing elevation. Thus most of the continent east of the Pacific coastlands and west of the 100th meridian (that is, including much of the Great Plains) has a middle latitude steppe régime, modified by altitude, like that of the middle elevations between the Central Asian Mountains and the Russo-Siberian Plains.

(d) The south-eastern United States, as far inland as about the 38th parallel, has a climatic régime which can be described as humid sub-tropical, or as warm temperate, eastern margin. It finds its counterpart in southern Brazil and the Plate River region, or, with variations produced by the action of the monsoon, in south-eastern China. Winters are mild, summers are hot, and rainfall is distributed fairly evenly among the seasons of the year, with a tendency to a summer maximum that decreases towards the north-west.

(e) The climate of the remainder of North America falls, under any classification, into the category of continental régimes; there are the wide annual range of temperatures, the rapid diurnal variations in winter, and the modest rainfall which are characteristic of a continental interior. Whether this general heading of 'continental' is to be subdivided on a basis of temperature or of precipitation is a matter of personal choice. If the criterion of temperature is used, then the governing factor is the heat of summer, and the interior can be divided on this basis into three east–west belts, with a region of cold continental climate adjoining the polar region in the north, and belts of cool continental and warm continental climate lying between it and the 38th parallel. If the criterion of precipitation is used, then the interior would be classified, in north–south belts, as mostly humid continental, with a sub-humid transition belt separating the eastern interior from the steppe (or, as it might be called, the semi-arid continental) belt of the west. In either case the climatic analogy is with western Russia where there occurs, in the same way, a north–south sequence based on the northward decrease of summer heat, and an east–west sequence based on precipitation.

5. *The Soils of North America*

The general pattern of North America's soil regions is dictated by the climatic factors which we have just considered. All the world's great soil groups are represented somewhere in the continent, with the exception of the true lateritic soils of tropical forests and grasslands, which occur only as far north as Cuba and Yucatan. Within this general pattern, however, North America possesses a wide variety of soils which depend for their character not on climate but on age or on local factors of relief or bedrock, and some of these special soils are of peculiar importance to the farmer or the conservationist. Before dealing with the broad soil groups based on climatic differences, therefore, it is as well to be aware of the wide soil areas which do not fit into such a classification.

INTRAZONAL AND AZONAL SOILS

The soils for which a classification based on climate is either inadequate or misleading are of two kinds.

(*a*) *The Intrazonal Soils.* By this term is understood mature soils to whose structure some local influence of bedrock or relief has given a particular character. To this category belong, among the soils of the settled part of the continent, those known as 'half-bog', which are found along the flat seaward edge of the Atlantic and Gulf Coast Plain from North Carolina to central Texas. A second example of intrazonal soils is provided by the

Rendzinas of central Texas and central Oklahoma, and the High Lime soils of eastern Manitoba. These are groups of soils developed on a soft limestone or chalk base which have, in consequence, a high lime content in spite of the effects of leaching; they thus appear, from their chemical composition, to have been formed in a drier climate than is actually the case. A third example is provided by the so-called planosols of the Agricultural Interior. These are soils developed on the loess and drift plains of Illinois, Iowa, and Missouri where, in the post-glacial period, deposition has created an exceptionally flat surface and affected drainage; poor soil drainage and absence of surface erosion have created a soil in which the upper layers are leached and the subsoil includes a layer of clay hardpan.

(b) *Azonal Soils.* These are soils which are immature; that is, they are composed of materials so recently accumulated, or so lightly bound, that no true soil profile has developed. Such materials cover a significant fraction of the whole area of North America, and include both lands of agricultural value and areas of waste. For fertility, few areas can rival the alluvial plains of the Mississippi Valley and the Central Valley of California, both of which belong to this category. On the other hand, the loose cover of the Sand Hills section of Nebraska is a trap for the unwary cultivator, for the sand, produced by the breakdown of Tertiary sandstones, is entirely unconsolidated beneath a thin layer of grass roots. In the Mountain West azonal materials include the thin, stony cover of the mountains, the alluvia collected in the desert basins, and the most recent of the lava flows on the lava plateaux of the Pacific North-West.

GENERAL CLASSIFICATION

In the general classification that follows, therefore, these important exceptions must be borne in mind. The exceptions apart, the soils of North America fall into the three main categories of (a) soils of the humid east and the cool north, (b) transitional soils, and (c) soils of the dry west.

It is no coincidence that it was an American—C. F. Marbut—who first proposed the classification of soils as 'pedocals' and 'pedalfers'. Pedocals (the syllable '-cal' is an abbreviation for 'calcis' or 'calcium') are soils in which carbonate of lime accumulates. Pedalfers (the '-al' indicates aluminium and the '-fer' iron) are soils in which not lime but compounds of aluminium and iron accumulate. The factors that decide which of these two processes takes place are mainly climatic. Lime accumulation is a feature of the soil profile of semi-arid and arid regions;

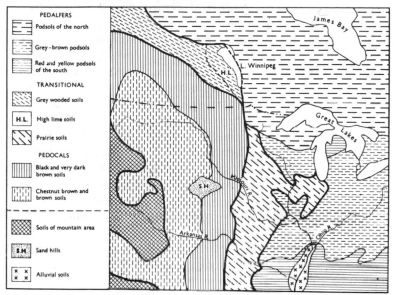

FIG. 7. Soil Regions of the North American Interior.

the depth at which the accumulation takes place varies with the rainfall, so that in the driest areas accumulation takes place near, or even on, the surface, while with increasing rainfall it occurs at greater depths. In humid regions, however, the process of leaching tends to remove the calcium carbonate from the soil and to lead instead to the formation of a layer of compounds of aluminium and iron. Thus the terms 'pedalfer' and 'pedocal' may generally be used to describe the soils of humid, or of semi-arid and arid regions respectively, and while most of the soils of eastern and northern North America belong to the former group, those of the west belong to the latter.

(a) *Soils of the East and North.* The regions of the far north that experience a polar climate are characterized by tundra soils. Here the important soil-controlling factors are the lack of heat, which discourages organic processes of soil formation, and the permafrost (or permanently frozen) layer that lies a short distance below the surface. As a result of these influences the shallow soil layer is wet and badly drained. The soil profile usually consists of one or more layers of peat, covering a grey subsoil which extends down to the permafrost layer, lying at a depth that may vary from 5 or 6 feet to a few inches below the surface.

South of the tundra soils is a wide belt of podsols; it stretches from central Alaska to Newfoundland, while on the south its boundary is roughly that of the Laurentian Shield and the New England Upland. It is the characteristic soil of the belt of cold continental and cold maritime climates, and of the coniferous forest zone to which they give rise. Under this natural forest cover, the soil profile exhibits a surface layer of only partly decayed vegetation, covering a light grey, heavily leached horizon that in turn overlays a brown subsoil. Associated as they are with slow decomposition and plentiful soil moisture, the podsols are generally acid in reaction, and of limited agricultural value unless they are limed; even so, they may be too stony or sandy for use other than as pastures.

The podsol belt is in turn succeeded, to the southward, by a belt of transitional soils, podsolic in character, but of greater usefulness to the farmer. Among these are the grey-wooded soils of the north-western Prairie Provinces, and the brown and grey-brown podsols that cover a large, and agriculturally important, area of eastern North America. South of the Laurentian Shield and the New England Upland these podsolic soils cover the peninsula of southern Ontario, much of the Agricultural Interior, and the Atlantic coast states as far south as about 38° N. latitude; that is, they are the soils of the mixed and deciduous forests that cover this area. These podsolic soils differ from the true podsols in that they are found in regions which either are drier than the podsol zone (as is the case with the grey-wooded soils) or have warmer summers and a higher evaporation rate, so that humus formation is more rapid and leaching less severe than on the true podsols. Consequently, once cleared, they respond more readily to fertilization and cultivation than do the podsols.

South of the 38th parallel, and as far west as eastern Texas, is the zone of red and yellow podsols, the soils of the warm temperate south-east. With the heavy rainfall and the mixed forest cover of this region, the podsols, under a thin layer of vegetable litter, are strongly leached and acid in reaction. Their colour indicates that, with the higher temperatures of the south-east, the podsols are becoming lateritic; weathering and leaching have gone deep, and aluminium and iron oxides are being produced which, in the more extreme climatic conditions of the tropics, form a crust of laterite.[1] Such soils are easily cultivated but easily destroyed; their content of organic matter is generally low, and both care and fertilization are necessary to keep them in constant cultivation.

(b) *Transitional Soils*. In the Agricultural Interior of the continent the transition from the soils of the humid east to those of the semi-arid west is marked by a series known as the prairie soils. These display features characteristic of both east and west in that, while they are non-lime-accumulating like the podsols, they are grassland soils like the chernozems which adjoin them on the west. They are found, as we shall see in the next section, where the eastern forests give way to the western grasses, and they cover much of Iowa, Illinois, southern Minnesota, and eastern Kansas. A somewhat similar transitional role is played, in the Canadian Prairies, by the grey-wooded soils already mentioned, for although they are classed as podsolic, and support a forest cover, they also have a deep layer of lime accumulation.

(c) *Soils of the West*. Adjoining the transitional prairie and grey-wooded soils on the west and south respectively are the pedocals of the semi-arid west. The outer belt of these, in the region where rainfall is 20 to 30 inches per annum, is represented by the chernozems, or black earths. These soils, which formerly supported a tall grass vegetation with scattered groves of trees, are found in a narrow north–south belt through the eastern Dakotas, and parts of central Nebraska and Kansas; from North Dakota the belt swings west to form a rough semi-circle around the dry heart of the Prairies of Canada, where

---

[1] In *Physical Elements of Geography* (4th ed., McGraw Hill, 1957), V. C. Vinch, G. T. Trewartha, and Associates point out (p. 448) that, whereas the terms *laterite* and *lateritic* have often been used generally, in descriptions of the soil processes of humid tropical and sub-tropical regions, it is more correct to confine their use to special cases in which the mineral laterite is present, and in describing the general processes to use the terms *latosol* and *latosolic*. Both sets of terms are given here to avoid confusing the reader who may be familiar with only one of them.

the chernozems underlie what is known as the Park Belt. The black upper horizon of these soils is rich in organic matter and highly productive; the lower horizons vary in character, but include a layer of lime accumulation between 2 and 3 feet below the surface.

On the inner, or drier, edge of the chernozems the black earths become progressively lighter in colour and more alkaline in reaction, and grade into the chestnut-brown soils of the central Great Plains. These in turn give place in the north to the brown soils, and in the south to the reddish-browns, of the driest lands east of the Rockies—the 12- to 15-inch rainfall belt between southern Alberta in the north and western Texas in the south. In this last belt the soil profile consists of a brown or red topsoil which, under irrigation, is highly productive, and a subsoil which becomes grey or white, and highly calcareous, a foot or two below the surface.

Although, geographically, the sequence of soils is interrupted at this point by the Rocky Mountains, it is continued in the deserts west of the mountains. Many of these areas are covered, as already noted, by recent alluvia, but elsewhere there is a widespread cover of red, brown, and grey desertic soils. The characteristic profile of these reveals a lightly coloured surface layer, whose colour depends on the nature of the parent rock; it is often covered with a gravel or pebble desert floor. Lower horizons are grey or white in colour. Both soil and subsoil are highly calcareous, and the accumulation of salts may form layers of hardpan either at, or just below, the surface.

The soil regions of the Pacific coastlands, west of the mountains, are a reproduction, over a smaller area, of those of the continental interior. While, as we have already seen, a large part of the Central Valley of California is floored with recent alluvia, in the northern section of the valley and on the low hills of the California coast are found soils similar to the prairie type of the Midwest. Northward, up the coastal lowlands and on the lower hills, the prairie type gives way to the grey-brown podsols associated with the cool temperate marine climate of Washington and British Columbia. Inland, the one important area of soil diversity in the west occurs, as might be expected, in the relatively low-lying Columbia Basin, with its varied agricultural development. Here, where rainfall increases from west to east across the Basin, and from the centre towards the northern and southern rims, there is a core area of chernozems in the Palouse country of eastern Washington, flanked on the drier side by brown soils and on the moister side by soils of the prairie type, as in the Agricultural Interior.

6. *The Vegetation of North America*

To the early European settlers, North America was a land of forests. As the French on the St. Lawrence and the English on the Atlantic coast moved inland, they found little break in the monotony of the trees, and their economy became a forest-based economy, like that of the Indians they encountered. Only after settlement from the east coast had penetrated 500 or 600 miles inland did the pioneers emerge from the forest into the 'oak openings' and small prairies of the area south of the Great Lakes. Since by this time they had come largely to depend on the forest and its denizens for their livelihood, they regarded the treeless horizons with considerable suspicion, while the true grasslands farther west found them, as we shall later see, almost wholly unprepared.

Only in the south-west of what was later to become the U.S.A. did the Spaniards, pushing north from Mexico, encounter open country. In southern Texas they entered, at its south-western corner, a great triangle of natural grassland, whose apex was in the oak openings of the Midwest, and whose base lay along the foothills of the Rocky Mountains northward roughly as far as the 52nd parallel.

Although, within the settled area of eastern North America, the original forest cover has largely been removed (to be replaced either by farmland or by second-growth forest), nevertheless the general pattern of vegetation regions, dictated as it is by climatic factors, remains recognizable.

THE FORESTS

(*a*) *Extent and character.* Before the coming of the white man it seems that forests covered slightly less than a half of the area of what is now mainland Canada and the U.S.A.; that is, some 3 million square miles out of 6·1 millions. In addition, rather more than one-third (that is, some 200,000 square miles) of

Alaska was forest-covered. Today this area has been reduced, by exploitation and destruction, to about 2·5 million square miles.

This original forest cover was diverse in character, but almost continuous in extent, over the eastern parts and much of the north of the continent. Indeed, it is simplest to state that it extended north and west from the middle Atlantic seaboard until it encountered one or another of three limiting circumstances: cold, dryness, or high altitude.

On the north the forest thins out and gives place to the heaths and mosses of tundra vegetation, roughly along the boundary line of the region of polar climate (that is, where all twelve months have a mean temperature of less than 50° F.). Here the governing factors are the onset of Arctic cold, the lack of summer heat, the dryness of the western Arctic, and the presence of the permafrost layer which prevents the roots of trees from penetrating to a depth sufficient to support growth. This northern forest boundary runs from the Mackenzie Delta to, and across, the middle of Hudson Bay, and thence into northern Labrador.

South of this line a belt of forest spreads across the whole breadth of the continent, except in the west, where the cover is broken by the rise of North America's loftiest mountains— those of Alaska and the northern Pacific coast. In Alaska and northern British Columbia, in consequence, the forests are largely confined to the interior valleys and the coastlands. This continent-wide forest cover extends south, with no other serious interruption, until it reaches the tree frontier imposed by increasing aridity in the south-western section of the continent.

This dry and largely treeless area lies south and west of a line running from southern British Columbia along the 52nd parallel to the Prairies, and then south-eastwards to the apex of the treeless triangle already described, which is located south of the Great Lakes. Along this boundary cause and effect are interwoven in the vegetation pattern; on the one hand, increasing aridity, and especially seasonal drought, discourages tree growth; on the other, where grassland has become established, young tree shoots compete unsuccessfully with quicker-growing grasses.

From the apex of the triangle in the east, the southern side runs west and south in a broken line to central Texas. Along this line, as on the northern side, the luxuriant tree growth of the eastern Gulf coast and the south-eastern states is thinned by diminishing precipitation, increasing evaporation rates, and by markedly seasonal rainfall, which favours the growth of grasses against that of trees.

The remaining forest areas of North America can best be described as three southward penetrations, across the treeless area, of the forests on its northern side. They correspond to the areas of higher rainfall that lie along the Rockies, the mountains of the Pacific, and the coast north of the 40th parallel, and together they form an important part of the commercial forest resources of the continent.

The Rockies are, in general, tree-covered on their middle slopes. The lower limit of the forest—represented by scattered and bushlike pinyon and juniper—is encountered between 4,000 and 6,000 feet; and the treeline is, according to slope and exposure, between 9,000 and 11,000 feet, with alpine meadow and bare rock above it. On the higher sections of the inter-montane plateaux, also, wherever rainfall permits, various forms of open forest are found.

On the great ranges of the Far West are found the continent's largest and most valuable stands of timber. In the Pacific North-West the forests are continuous from sea-level up to the timber-line at 6,000 to 8,000 feet. In California, where precipitation is less heavy, an intermediate vegetation belt, known as chaparral and composed of bushes and small trees, intervenes before the true forest begins, about 2,000 feet above sea-level.

The coastal hills themselves are tree-clad roughly as far south as the Golden Gate, and intermittently beyond there. In the Pacific North-West the coastal forests, like those of the Cascades inland, are composed largely of Douglas fir. But the distinctive feature of the California coast is the redwood belt, the habitat of the continent's largest tree species. These giant trees, the sequoias, owe their presence not so much to the rainfall (a moderate 30 to 50 inches) as to the humid atmosphere created by the coastal fogs of central California (see p. 405).

The northern forests are almost entirely coniferous in character, while those of the Great Lakes region and southern New

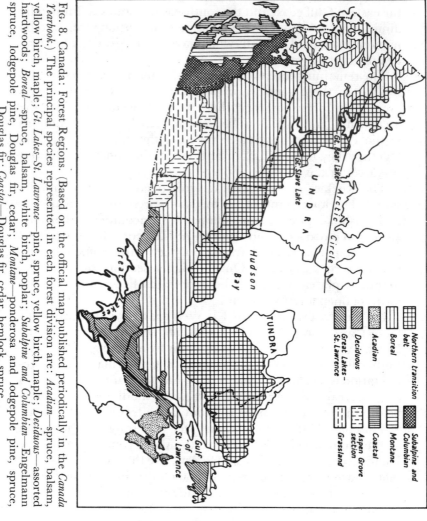

Fig. 8. Canada: Forest Regions. (Based on the official map published periodically in the *Canada Yearbook*.) The principal species represented in each forest division are: *Acadian*—spruce, balsam, yellow birch, maple; *Gt. Lakes–St. Lawrence*—pine, spruce, yellow birch, maple; *Deciduous*—assorted hardwoods; *Boreal*—spruce, balsam, white birch, poplar; *Subalpine and Columbian*—Engelmann spruce, lodgepole pine, Douglas fir, cedar; *Montane*—ponderosa and lodgepole pine, spruce, Douglas fir; *Coastal*—Douglas fir, cedar, hemlock, spruce.

England are mixed; like those of the Appalachians, they mark the transition to the deciduous forests of oak, beech, and hickory which are found in the southern interior of the continent. In the Mountain West the distribution of species—most of them coniferous, such as spruce, fir, pine, and larch—is governed largely by altitude, but no inventory, however brief, can overlook the magnificent stands of Douglas fir that spread densely over the whole coastal belt of the Pacific North-West, and that represent the most valuable single forest resource of North America.

(b) *The Forests as Resources.* Of the million square miles of forests remaining in the U.S.A., some two-thirds are classed as 'commercial', while in Canada, about 60 per cent. of the 1·6 million square miles of forest are said to be 'productive'. These forest resources have been tapped to supply the needs of a continent which consumes more than half the pulp and paper production, and over 40 per cent. of the lumber production, of the world. Both nations began by possessing roughly equal areas of forest, but since both population and demand are ten times greater in the U.S.A. than in Canada, it is not surprising to find, firstly, that after three centuries of exploitation the U.S.A. has only 70 per cent. of its cover and 10 per cent. of its virgin saw-timber left, and secondly, that it has come to rely heavily on the production of Canadian forests to meet its own gigantic demand for wood products. In fact, the annual drain on the total timber resources of the U.S.A. in the 1950's has been 50 per cent. greater than the annual growth, while in the most valuable part of the nation's forests— the great softwood stands of Oregon and Washington—the drain has been more than twice the annual growth.

In Canada, by contrast, some two-thirds of the productive forests remain unexploited. The factor which governs their future use is not demand—that may be taken for granted—but accessibility. Exploitation naturally began in the areas of easiest access, along the shorelines and the southern edge of the great boreal forest, while tomorrow's reserves lie, to a large extent, either in the western mountains or north of the St. Lawrence–Hudson Bay watershed, whence the rivers on which the logs would be floated run north into the wilderness.

The exploitation of the continent's forests has created

industries of great size. While the actual logging operations employ a good deal of labour, much of this employment is seasonal, and is carried on by part-time farmers or fishermen. It is the processing of the forest products which has become so important. In Canada, wood products—lumber, wood pulp, and paper—form the basis of the country's largest group of industries, a group employing 15 per cent. of Canada's industrial workers, and contributing more than one-quarter of the value of the country's exports. In the U.S.A., the forest products industries accounted in 1958 for 7 per cent. of the nation's industrial employees. Locally, of course, these industries play a far more important role than even these figures would suggest. In Oregon, for example, the 1958 Census of Manufactures showed that these industries gave employment to nearly 60 per cent. of the state's industrial workers.

THE UNFORESTED WEST

In the semi-arid and arid west of the continent the natural vegetation is grass and shrubs. Only on the slopes of the mountains, where precipitation is higher, or along river courses where moister conditions are found, is tree growth encouraged. For the rest, it is the quantity of precipitation, and its seasonal distribution, that govern the character of the vegetation. This means, as we shall see again in Chapter XVI, that there is a sequence of vegetation types that holds good, either between the desert heart of the area and its more humid fringes, or between the lowest levels of the western basins and the lower tree limit on the mountains. Within these sequences, it is possible to distinguish four main types of natural vegetation: tall grass; short grass; sagebrush with grass; and desert shrub.

The tall grass prairies, most of which have now been brought under the plough, occupied the eastern apex of the treeless triangle, where annual rainfall is between 20 and 35 inches per annum. The vegetation of this region consisted of both tall and short grasses growing together, with such varieties as the bluestems (*Andropogon*) reaching 6 feet or more in height. The dense root network developed by these abundant grasses has produced the deep humus layer that makes the chernozem soils of the tall grass prairies famous.

As the tall grass is the vegetation of the black earths, so the chestnut-brown and brown soils farther west are related to the short grass prairies. Short grass is probably the most extensive, and certainly the most valuable, vegetation type of the unforested west. It is made up of a wide variety of species, among which some of the commonest are the wheatgrasses (*Agropyron*), gramas (*Bouteloua*), and buffalograss (*Buchloë dactyloides*). Within this region, which stretches from central Texas and New Mexico to the southern Prairie Provinces, the native grasses grow from 1 to 3 feet high; their height is restricted by the shallower percolation of water in the 12- to 20-inch rainfall zone and the consequent limitation on root development.

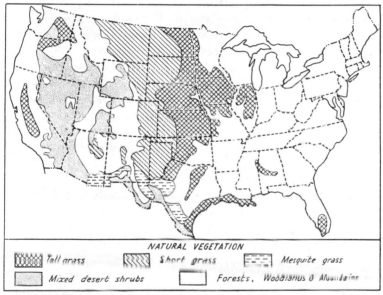

FIG. 9. Grasslands of the U.S.A.

While the main area of short grass vegetation is on the Great Plains, this type of vegetation is, or was, to be found in modified form in two other areas of significant extent in the west. One of these is in the south-western United States, between western Texas and Arizona, where the vegetation is classified as semi-desert grass. It differs from the true short grass prairie in its composition—dominant species are gramas, dropseeds (*Sporobolus*), and curly-mesquite (*Hilaria belangeri*), growing, as on the

Great Plains, from 1 to 3 feet tall—and in the fact that there is generally a scattering of shrubs, or even small trees, accompanying the grasses, particularly mesquite and creosote. The existence here of some 50 million acres of semi-desert grass is due to the fact that, unlike the areas of true desert that adjoin them, these lands receive sufficient summer rainfall (from the Gulf of Mexico) to support grasses; their combination of grass and shrubs thus marks a transition between the true grasslands and the scrub of the deserts.

Short grass prairies are also found in the Pacific coastlands, especially on the foothills surrounding the Central Valley of California (where they lie below the chaparral in the altitudinal sequence) and in the Palouse region of Washington and Oregon. This is the area of Pacific bunchgrass, where grasses similar to those found on the Great Plains originally covered some 60 million acres. Most of these grasslands, however, have by now either been ploughed up, or have been overgrazed by stock and invaded, in consequence, by sagebrush and shrubs.

The combination of sagebrush and grass is as much a feature of the unforested parts of the High Plateaux as short grass is of the Great Plains. It is a combination which is estimated to cover 250 million acres of the west. The intermontane region, as we saw in an earlier section, generally has a winter–spring rainfall and where, in addition, annual rainfall is below 20 inches, conditions favour the growth of woody shrubs rather than grasses. The typical cover is therefore a combination of sage and grass, in which the proportions of the two vary according to the rainfall, the grasses disappearing altogether on the desert margins.

Where the grasses maintain so precarious a hold, however, their disappearance may equally well be the result of overgrazing by livestock. The sagebrush, of which there are a great variety of types, with wide climatic tolerance, offers little forage to stock (although game animals feed on it), so that it will flourish while the grasses decline. Western ranchers resort to spraying and brush-beating to try to keep the scrub down, but only careful management (discussed more fully in a later chapter) will enable the grass cover to flourish[1].

[1] It is interesting to note that, while the ranchers generally regard sagebrush as something useless to be eliminated, at the same time western experimental stations are attempting to breed new varieties which will be palatable to stock.

In the lowest and driest parts of the west, finally, if and where a vegetation cover exists, it is composed of scattered desert shrubs, mostly woody in character. Over most of the dry area, creosotebush is characteristic, while on the highly alkaline surfaces of salt deserts and old lake beds, varieties of sage and other alkali-tolerant shrubs are found . In the deserts of southern California and southern Arizona are to be found, in addition, a variety of large cacti whose bizarre shapes make them one of the tourist attractions of the south-west.

FURTHER READING

(a) Physiography and Glacial Geography

This subject is more than adequately covered, for the general reader, by W. W. Atwood's *Physiographic Provinces of North America*, which in turn owes much to the earlier work of N. M. Fenneman, *Physiography of the Eastern United States* and *Physiography of the Western United States*, and his shorter 'Physiographic Divisions of the United States', *A.A.A.G.*, vol. xviii, pp. 261–353. The information in the section on glaciation is largely based on the work of R. F. Flint, especially on his *Glacial Geology and the Pleistocene Epoch*, chapters 11–14, and 'The Stagnation and Dissipation of the Last Ice Sheet', *Geog. Review*, vol. xix, pp. 256–89.

On the glaciation of Canada, there is an interesting series of articles in *Cahiers de Géographie de Québec*, Nos. 8 and 10.

(b) Climate

For the U.S.A., the Dept. of Agriculture *Yearbook*, 1941, 'Climate and Man' gives comprehensive coverage of the subject, while among a host of looser references may perhaps be mentioned the series of articles by R. DeC. Ward, on specific aspects of North American climate, which have appeared in the *Geog. Review*. For Canada the general reference is *Climatological Atlas of Canada*, prepared by M. K. Thomas, while the *Canada Yearbook*, 1959, carried a good short article, 'The Climate of Canada'.

(c) Soils and Vegetation

The U.S. Dept. of Agriculture's *Yearbook* on soils (1938 and 1957), grass (1948), and trees (1949) leaves little unsaid on these topics. Shorter references, however, are largely confined to introductory chapters in larger volumes, as in the case of D. F. Putnam's *Canadian Regions*, or to regional articles. But for both the U.S.A. and Canada see *A World Geography of Forest Resources*, ed. S. Haden Guest, J. K. Wright, and E. M. Tcclaff, chapters 6–8; 'Forest Regions of Canada', by W. E. D. Halliday, *Can. Geog. Journal*, vol. xix, pp. 229–42, and H. L. Keenleyside's 'The Forests of Canada', ibid., vol. xli, pp. 2–15.

II

THE POPULATION

1. *The Indians*

THE earliest European immigrants to the New World found a native population already in possession. It is not clear how large this 'Indian' population was, but it soon became apparent that, as far as North America was concerned, the great majority of the Indians were concentrated on the plateaux of Mexico. In the rest of the continent there were probably about 1 million Indians, of whom some 200,000 lived in what is now Canada.

Among these original Americans, however, there were wide differences of culture and language. Living close to nature, the Indians had adapted their economies to their environment. In the remote north the Eskimos lived by hunting and fishing, while in the east most of the tribes combined hunting with a primitive agriculture that produced corn and squashes. In the south-west were the pueblos where, by 1500, a remarkable urban culture had reached and passed its climax, while elsewhere roamed tent-dwelling pastoralists or food-gatherers, like those of the Great Basin of Utah, whom pioneers of the 1830's reported to have the world's lowest standard of living.

These cultural variations, moreover, were not permanent. The pressures of war, famine, or disease would force a tribe to move its hunting grounds, abandon its fields, or adopt new forms of economy. One of the most striking of these changes must have occurred about the year 1300, when a number of the largest pueblos in Utah and Colorado were apparently abandoned, swiftly and mysteriously. But the greatest changes of all, both in location and in livelihood, were brought about by the introduction of the horse.

The Great Plains had formerly been the home of a few pastoralist tribes. Across them roamed herds of bison, which were largely immune to the attacks of hunters moving on foot. But about the year 1600 horses, which had been introduced into the New World by the Spaniards, became available to the Indians, and their coming made possible a new way of life. Travelling on horseback and hunting the bison in groups, the plains Indians became the 'new-rich' of seventeenth-century America. So strong was the attraction of this new way of life that other tribes moved into the area. From the eastern woodlands the Blackfoot and Cheyenne tribes trekked west, followed later by the Sioux and others; from the Rocky Mountain foothills came the Comanche; from the south-east came tribes that abandoned agriculture for the new life of the plains. And hard on the heels of the last arrivals came the white man, to inaugurate the era of 'Cowboys and Indians' in the west.

From the eastern seaboard the tide of white settlement flowed west. The fate of the Indian tribes whose lands lay in its path was varied. In Canada contact was on the whole peaceful, and a proclamation of 1763 laid down that no Indian could be dispossessed of his lands without his own and the Crown's consent. There were few 'Indian wars', and the Indian Act of 1876 insured the status of the Indian people. In the United States, however, less happy conditions prevailed. The westward thrust of the white settlers forced tribe after tribe off its hunting grounds, and while the policy of the government was at most times reasonable, its good intentions were constantly overtaken by the swiftness of the white advance; another war followed and another tribe withdrew, broken, to the west. Lands reserved for the Indians were subsequently found to be wanted for white settlers. Ultimately, the tribes were assigned reservations in the least desirable—which generally meant arid—sections, and the hunter-nomads were encouraged to become farmers, but lacked either the temperament or the ability to make the change. Inevitably the wasteful, extensive system of Indian land use had to give way before the demands of the nineteenth century. But the manner of the change leaves abundant cause for regret.

The Indian population reached a low point at the end of the nineteenth century, but since that time, under more enlightened policies, it has increased again. Today there are rather more than 600,000 Indians in Canada and the U.S.A., although intermarriage has made definition difficult. Their reservations cover 55 million acres in the United States, and about 6 millions in Canada. On the reservations they retain many of the traditional forms of tribal life and government, but large numbers have left the reservations to seek work elsewhere. While the standard of living on some of the reservations is lamentably low, other groups, such as the Indian wheat farmers in Oregon, share the prosperity of their white neighbours. Elsewhere, justice seems to have been belatedly served by the discovery that the lands which were turned over to the Indians, in the nineteenth century, because the white man did not want them have proved, in the twentieth, to be rich in oil or uranium.

2. *The Immigrants*

In the year 1800 there were about 5,500,000 people in the territories now covered by the U.S.A., and some half a million in Canada. Immigration from Europe had been proceeding slowly for two hundred years, to the French areas along the St. Lawrence, to the Spanish lands on the Gulf of Mexico, or to the Atlantic seaboard where English culture and institutions dominated a cosmopolitan society that included groups of Germans, Dutch, and Scandinavians.

For the first few years of the nineteenth century the tempo of immigration remained slow. But, for the United States, the hundred year period between the end of the Napoleonic Wars and 1914 was the century of the immigrants—over 30 million of them arrived. In Canada the main phases of immigration came later. The first decade of the twentieth century saw 1,800,000 arrivals, and between 1914 and 1951 the total was 2,500,000, most of whom came either in the 1920's or after 1945.

What were the causes of this greatest of modern population movements? They are to be sought largely in the conditions prevailing in the countries of the Old World, both political and social. War, disease, industrialization, agricultural enclosure, religious persecution; all these are mirrored in the rises and falls of the immigration rate. Perhaps the most basic reason of all was the great increase in population which began in Europe about 1800 and which dislocated the agricultural and social systems of the continent. Basic, too, was the rapid progress of industrialization which threw the artisan out of work and created instead the demand for factory labour. Then, as the balance between the continent's economy and its growing population became more delicate, so the effects of crop failure or disease became more catastrophic. Every political rearrangement—the Vienna settlements, the Prussian annexation of

PLATE III

The Expanding Cities of the West: (1) Denver, Colorado. Between 1950 and 1960, the population of Denver's metropolitan area increased by 51%, to a total of 929,383. Centre foreground, the state capitol of Colorado, with the business district behind it. Beyond, the railway belt, the wooded suburbs, and the irrigated Piedmont stretching to the foot of the Rockies

PLATE IV

The Expanding Cities of the West: (2) Vancouver, B.C. In 1941, the population of Greater Vancouver was 351,500; by 1961, it had reached 778,000. View from the south-east, showing, upper centre, Stanley Park and the Lion's Gate Bridge; right centre, the passenger shipping terminal; lower left, lumber rafts awaiting processing in False Creek

Schleswig, or, above all, the Treaty of Versailles—created a new class of refugees. Singly or in groups, driven out or encouraged to leave so that others might remain and survive, the surplus population of Europe found its way to the ports and took ship for the New World.

M. L. Hansen, chronicler of the 'Atlantic Migration', has pointed out that there were three main periods in the 'immigrants' century'. From 1830 to 1860 the movement was largely one from the Celtic fringes of the British Isles and from the middle Rhine, especially Hesse. Scottish crofters dispossessed by the advent of sheep farming joined with Irish peasants dispossessed by their landlords. This movement reached its peak after the terrible famine years of the 1840's. Then, from 1860 to 1890, Englishmen mingled with Germans and Scandinavians in a second great wave. Finally, between 1900 and 1914 (and in Canada between 1900 and 1955), the majority of the immigrants came from the Slav countries of eastern Europe, with a strong flow also from the Mediterranean lands to the U.S.A. The peak was reached in 1907, when the United States admitted 1,285,000 immigrants.

The war of 1914–18 created upheavals in Europe on a gigantic scale. Had emigration been unrestrained, there is no doubt that millions would have left the continent for America. In view of this prospect, the U.S.A. felt it necessary to limit by quota the number of immigrants that might be received. The quota, as fixed in 1927, permitted the entry of only 150,000 immigrants each year. Since the quota for each nation was based on the number of persons of that nationality or origin in the U.S.A. in 1920, the system favoured Great Britain and virtually excluded the nationals of the south and east European countries, whose need for relief and degree of unrest were greatest. Even although the 1927 law was modified, under that of 1952 the quota for the Republic of Ireland, with less than 3 million nationals, was three times as great as that for Italy, with 50 millions.

Between the two World Wars, therefore, it is not surprising to find that the stream of emigration to the U.S.A. not only dried up but, on balance, was reversed. Only for persons born in Canada, Mexico, and the Latin American countries was entrance to the U.S.A. unrestricted by quota. After 1945 the arrangement continued in force (with certain concessions to help European displaced by the war) until 1965, when it was finally abolished.

In Canada a government policy designed to foster the growth of the population has brought in two main waves of immigrants. The first of these was between 1900 and 1914, when the Prairie wheatlands were being opened up, and it reached a peak of 400,870 arrivals in 1913. It was largely British, but contained many Slavs, and by the time it subsided, the most common language, after English, on the prairies was Ukrainian. The second wave of arrivals has come in the years since 1945: during the two decades since then more than 2 million immigrants have entered Canada. About one-third of them were from Great Britain, but large numbers have come from Germany and Italy also, while many have been refugees displaced by political changes in Eastern Europe.

Where in the New World were these immigrants to settle? While the ports of entry were filled with a cosmopolitan population in transit, away from the coast there was a tendency for immigrants to settle in 'national' areas. West of Lake Michigan, for example, people of Scandinavian stock are in a majority over much of Wisconsin, Minnesota, and Iowa, while other areas are as markedly German or Finnish. In some cases this is due simply to the fact that the earliest arrivals encouraged their friends at home to join them. In others it is a product of organized, or group, emigration like that of the Pennsylvania Dutch or the Mennonites. In the emigration zones of Europe a system of recruiting existed which provided everything needed for door-to-door emigration. In yet other cases it reflects the *time* of arrival in North America. As settlement extended across the continent, so each decade introduced its own economic frontiers and its own labour needs. The 1860's saw the beginning of the Scandinavian immigration; they saw also the exploitation of the timber resources of Wisconsin and Minnesota, and thither went the Swedes and Norwegians as lumberjacks and frontier farmers. The Ukrainians who arrived in the 1870's were recruited to work in the rapidly expanding coal-mining areas of Pennsylvania; those who followed them in 1900 went west to the Prairies as wheat farmers.

Wherever possible, the immigrants sought work and conditions comparable with those they had left in the Old World. Italians who had raised Leghorn poultry in Italy could start afresh with Rhode Islands in New England, or establish market gardens and vineyards. Cornish miners worked the Wisconsin lead at Galena, or the copper of Upper Michigan. But the great immigrant problem was that so many of the newcomers were European peasants, possessed of a single skill, and that skill in limited demand in a society that was both industrializing and also mechanizing its agriculture.[1] All that many could offer was the strength of their arms, and so they tended to drift into poorly paid labour gangs, often separated from their families. For many, the process of settling in the paradise of the west was hard and long-drawn-out.

On the Pacific coast there was another class of immigrant— the Oriental. Chinese labour virtually built California between 1850 and 1880. Japanese market gardeners became wealthy and successful. But the very efficiency of the frugal Oriental was his undoing; the cry of unfair competition and undermined standards was raised, and in 1882 the United States passed an exclusion law. In 1952 the immigration quota for both China and Japan was set at 100.

3. The Negroes

In 1960 there were just under 19 million Negroes in the U.S.A., and they formed 10·5 per cent. of the population. They were the descendants of the slaves brought into North America by the slave-traders of Spain and England from 1600 onwards, until the trade was outlawed in the nineteenth century.

In the early days of the colonies there was a pressing need for labour. We have already seen that in North, as opposed to Central, America the native population was sparse; moreover, it was generally hostile, and could not be put to work in the way the Spaniards had conscripted the docile natives of the Caribbean. The Spaniards themselves early resorted to importing African slaves, but in the English colonies the process was more

[1] The one area of America where they might have practised their peasant farming was the South. But in that region the climate was against them, there was no easy way to acquire land, and for labourers the employment question was overshadowed by that of slavery; farm labour was provided by the Negroes. For these and other reasons, very few of the century's immigrants settled in the Southern states.

E

gradual. Originally, the labour shortage was met by the *indenture* system. An individual would contract to work for a colonist for a limited period, in exchange for his passage and subsistence, and at the end of his term would become a free settler. It was only gradually that this temporary slavery came to be distinguished from that of the Negroes, for whom there was no terminal date. The first Africans were brought to Virginia in 1619, but slavery was not made legally hereditary until 1662. For Massachusetts the comparable dates were 1636 and 1641. In 1705 a law was passed classifying slaves as a form of real estate.

It was in the plantation states of the south-east that slavery flourished, where, in the hot, humid climate, the plantation owners needed abundant and acclimatized hand labour for the

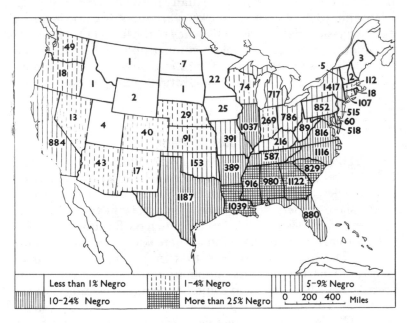

FIG. 10. U.S.A.: Distribution of Negro Population, by states, 1960. The shading indicates the percentage of the population of each state which was Negro in 1960, and the number gives the actual Negro population (in thousands).

cultivation of tobacco, rice, and cotton. Whatever questions existed in Southerners' minds about the moral legitimacy of slavery were swamped by the demand for labour, as cotton-growing spread across the south-eastern states in the early nineteenth century. Perhaps the greatest tragedy of all for the Negroes was that the South committed itself so completely to cotton cultivation that in the end, in spite of many a voice raised in protest against the system, it *could* not discard slavery and survive.

Civil war and emancipation left the Negro population solidly concentrated in the south-east, free, but tied economically to the same cotton lands as before the war. Today, nearly a century later, the old slave states still contain 57 per cent. of North America's Negroes (Texas, Georgia and North Carolina each contain about 6 per cent. of the total), but the concentration in the south-east is less marked. One of the most notable population movements of post-1914 North America has been the migration of Negroes from southern farms to northern cities. The opportunities of industrial employment created by the two World Wars have given impetus to this movement, which has brought the Negroes north in such numbers that there are now well over a million of them in New York City, a million in the Chicago area, and half a million each in Philadelphia and Detroit. Washington, the national capital, has become the first major city to record a census population which is more than 50 per cent. Negro. And between 1940 and 1960 the Negro population of Illinois increased from 387,000 to 1,037,000, to give it more coloured people than Alabama or Mississippi.

The result of this movement has been to involve the northern states (where people were, in the past, free to theorize about race relations) in the problem which has for so long dominated the South. Today, people in the north was well as the south are confronted with the question of whether Negroes can compete for jobs on equal terms with white workers: of whether Negroes should be free to live in any street where they can afford a home. And whatever the Civil Rights Act may achieve in the future, every city, northern or southern, at present has its Negro quarters, to which social pressures confine the coloured people. These are often housing areas near the city centre which have been abandoned by their former white residents, who have moved out to pleasanter suburbs. But because they are generally areas of old and cramped buildings, and because the Negro immigration has been so large and so rapid, such districts quickly deteriorate into overcrowded, derelict 'blight' areas. Unless city authorities take drastic action to provide a residential outlet for the Negroes—and many of them, including New York and Chicago, are doing what they can—it seems as if this pressure and this process may continue indefinitely.

The legal status of the American Negro has enormously improved since the early years of this century. The extent to which his social and economic status has improved, on the other hand, varies considerably from state to state and between city and countryside. But with the passing of the old agricultural pattern in the southern states (see Chapter XIII) and the gradual implementation of legal rulings about equal opportunities for Negroes, there is no question that, in years to come, the Negro's chance of improving his lot and of taking his full place as a valued member of his community, whether north or south, should be infinitely greater than that of his unprivileged forbears.

4. The Melting Pot

The well-worn phrase, 'the melting pot', describes the way in which elements of the population of four continents have been set down in the United States and have there merged into one distinctive American society. The phrase rings less true for Canada, for there the melting pot, although real enough, has been devoted to a particular kind of carefully-preserved bi-metallism—the British and French connexions. While the creators of the United States set out deliberately to achieve a society in which political, social, and religious neutrality would produce a new and distinctive way of life, the Canadians have preserved, with equal care, a link with the culture of those countries which have contributed most to their own.

In Canada, in any case, the numerical predominance of the British and French stocks is marked. In 1961 these two groups made up nearly 75 per cent. of the population. In the U.S.A., on the other hand, while in 1790 the British element in the young republic represented 80 per cent. of the population, by 1920 immigration had reduced this figure to less than 50 per cent. Germany, Ireland, and the countries of southern and eastern Europe had made their contributions to the melting pot, the contents of which, although largely European in origin, were certainly well mixed. Thanks in large part to the system of public education, with its careful nationalistic emphasis, the American objective had been achieved; the immigrants had been merged into the American nation.

There has always been a certain opposition in the U.S.A. to the admission of new immigrants. On the whole, however, this reaction has been notably slight, considering how unprepossessing was the appearance of many of the new arrivals, bewildered peasants disembarking after a nightmare Atlantic crossing. At the times of greatest influx it must indeed have appeared that American culture and institutions were in danger of being swamped by aliens. There have, in fact, been efforts to halt immigration—by old colonial elements fearing the introduction of so much Mediterranean and Slav blood into Anglo-Saxon America, and, more reasonably perhaps, by those who feared that the introduction of so much cheap labour into the economy would undermine the position of the Ameri- · can worker. That this fear has never become a reality is probably due to the fact that the growth of the U.S.A. has been so rapid that labour has always been in short supply.[1] Only in a few depression years has it become redundant, and at such times, in any case, the stream of immigration has tended to dry up of its own accord.

Most of the immigrants have readily adapted themselves to American political and social ideals and have been anxious to prove themselves good citizens—some hundreds of thousands did so with telling effect in the Union armies in 1861–5. At the same time, wherever a group of fellow-countrymen congregated, they kept alive some remnants of the culture of their homeland—a church, a newspaper in their own tongue, or a group for folk-dancing or singing. In general, the larger the alien community, the slower was the process of assimilation and the stronger the nostalgic nationalism. But for the immigrants'

[1] Maldwyn Jones puts the fears of the 'old' Americans in perspective by writing, 'Indeed, since it was the unskilled labour provided by the "new" immigrants which alone made possible America's phenomenal industrial expansion in the late nineteenth century, it was to them that native Americans and older immigrants were indebted for the increased opportunities available for skilled, white-collar, and professional workers.' *American Immigration*, Univ. of Chicago Press, 1960, p. 218.

children the situation was very different. With no language barrier to overcome they made wider social contacts than their parents. For them the cultural relics of the homeland, like their parents' accent, were largely curiosities. The influence of the school quickly overcame the alien influence of the home and produced, as it was intended to produce, a new generation of Americans.

5. *The Case of French Canada*

To every mention of the melting pot and every suggestion of assimilation to a common cultural denominator, one group has remained doggedly opposed—the French Canadians. United culturally by language and religion, and represented politically by Quebec, the second most populous province of Canada, they have succeeded as has no other national group in maintaining their distinctiveness through every vicissitude of the continent's political history.

That the French Canadians have achieved this privileged position is due, politically, to their bargaining power—their numerical strength and their concentration in one key province. This power they exerted in 1867 to ensure that the new system evolved for the government of all Canada should be federal, and that the new Province of Quebec should preserve intact its distinctive institutions. French Canada, then, is a product of a federal constitution and of the determination of a powerful minority, a minority to whom, as G. S. Graham writes, 'national survival had become the dominating passion'.

The heart of French Canada, today as in the seventeenth century, is along the Lower St. Lawrence. The area reaches west through Montreal, which is a bilingual metropolis, to a short distance west of the Ottawa River. South of the St. Lawrence, however, most of the settlement was originally British, but this area has now been largely taken over by French Canadians, who have spread, in addition, into New Brunswick and over the border into New England. 28 per cent. of all Canadians speak French as their mother tongue, and in Quebec the French speakers make up four-fifths of the population of the province.

This cultural cleavage at the heart of the Canadian federation is of the utmost significance. It grew out of the conflicts of colonial days, and was widened by a religious cleavage and, in Quebec, by a separation between two school systems. Originally, it was essentially a division between a French Catholic rural population and a British non-Catholic population that dominated much of the urban and commercial life of the region. Yet although the church and the countryside no longer exercise so strong an influence on the French population, the separatism of the French element is actually growing rather than diminishing.

There are several interesting aspects of this special position of French Canada. One of them is that among the French Catholic families the birth rate has always been high—a good deal higher than for Canada as a whole. There seemed a possibility that the French population might ultimately grow to outnumber the remainder, and the statistics of population increase have been watched with close attention, especially in the post-war years, when many of the immigrants from Europe were Roman Catholics. However, during the past decade the Quebec birth rate has been falling, and by 1961 was close to the national average.

Militating, in any case, against this numerical increase is the second factor of change in the situation. It is that the strength of French Canadian culture lay in the rural settlements with their traditional way of life. In the villages of the French *habitants* the two most powerful influences were the church and the family, and there was little to challenge their control. But the increase in population has forced sons and daughters to seek employment elsewhere, while the cities offer to them—as to the younger farm population everywhere —a wider variety of interests and prospects than is to be found at home.

So there has been a move to town which has inevitably weakened the ties with the traditional culture. For one thing, the old controls are relaxed; for another, much of the industry of the cities is owned and managed by non-French Canadians. English is the language of industrialism and English, or American, is the culture of the industrial towns.

Nevertheless, there is a third factor in the situation whose effect must be taken into account. As the political voice of separatism grows stronger—and whatever the reasons, this is the case—so it becomes important for businesses operating in French Canada to transact their affairs in French. The result is that companies operating all over North America find it advisable to set up branches in Montreal or Quebec, where business is carried on in French, and executives whose base is in the industrial cities of English-speaking Ontario spend their evenings learning French.

6. *Distribution of Population—Canada*

The census taken in 1961 revealed that the population of Canada at that date was 18,238,000, or 4 millions more than at the 1951 census. Over 3·8 million square miles of territory, however, this represents a very low average density of population. And for vast areas of the country even this average figure is misleading, for the Canadian population is gathered in a series of clusters along the southern border, leaving huge northern expanses virtually uninhabited.

From either a strategic or an economic point of view this distribution of population is highly unsatisfactory. A narrow corridor round the north-east tip of the U.S.A. links the Maritime Provinces with the rest of the country. The southward extension of the Laurentian Shield to the shore of Lake Superior virtually cuts Canada in two. Beyond the Prairie Provinces rise the Rockies and the British Columbia Coast Mountains as further obstacles to movement, while the capital of Canada's newest province, Newfoundland, lies over 1,000 miles by sea from Quebec, and more than 600 miles from Halifax.

The Prairie Provinces account for some 17 per cent. of Canada's population, and the Atlantic Provinces for 10 per cent. Over 60 per cent. of the total, however, are to be found in the two provinces of Ontario and Quebec; to be precise, in the southern fringes of these two provinces. Grouped along the St. Lawrence Valley and in the peninsula of south-western Ontario is more than half of Canada's population.

That these widely separated groups of settlers ever formed the Canadian Federation may be taken as a tribute to skilful diplomacy and as a measure of the fear inspired, north of the border, by the military strength of the U.S.A. in 1865. It has

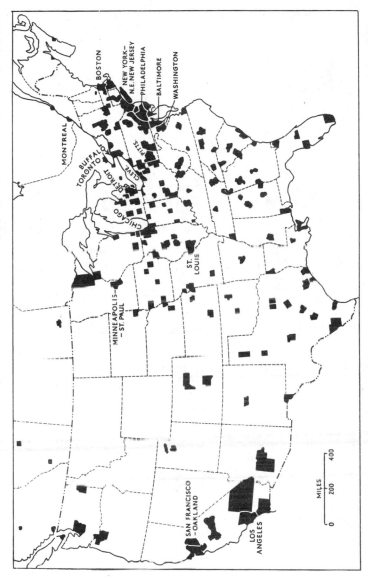

Fig. 11. North America: Metropolitan Areas. The cities identified on the map are those with populations of more than one million in 1950. Note that, owing to the method adopted of delimiting these Areas (generally by using the county boundaries), the size of the Metropolitan Area bears no necessary relationship to the population of the city and suburbs enclosed by it. This is especially true in the western U.S.A., where virtually the whole population of a county may be concentrated in one city. Thus the largest Metropolitan Area of all, in southern California, is San Bernardino S.M.A., whose population in 1960 was only 809,782.

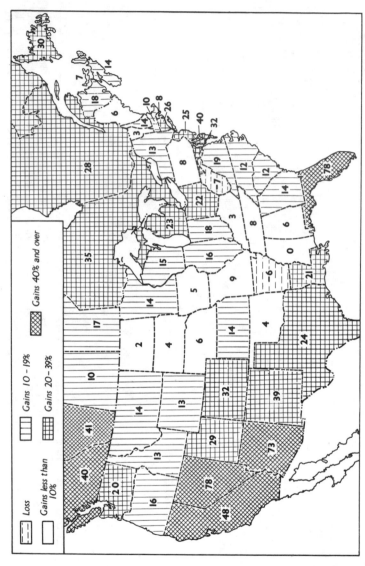

Fig. 12. The Population of North America. Percentage changes in population between the censuses of 1950 and 1960, by states and provinces.

often been remarked that it is easier for each of these Canadian population clusters to communicate southwards with the United States than with its neighbour on either side; certain it is that, up to 1960, the normal road route from east to west across Canada ran south of the border. Moreover, even when the nation has solved all the problems of intercommunication between its existing parts, there still remains the task of integrating with the remainder of the state the great empty area of the Northlands.

Canada's population increased by $6\frac{3}{4}$ millions between 1941 and 1961, but this increase was by no means equally shared among all its clusters. With a gain of 4,300,000 (60 per cent.), the main Ontario–Quebec concentration took the lion's share of the increase, and British Columbia exactly doubled its small 1941 population. By contrast, the Atlantic Provinces increased their population by 32 per cent., and Saskatchewan by only 11 per cent.

In the east, then, the population has been increasing relatively slowly. Settled early, these areas have been the scene of no striking recent development, and have attracted only a small number of immigrants. Apart from Halifax there is no large city, and today's immigrant almost always makes for the towns, with their industrial and commercial opportunities, rather than for the remote farmsteads of a region such as this.

In Quebec, a quarter of a million post-war immigrants and a high rate of natural increase among the French Canadian rural population are contributing to a threefold expansion: (1) in the rural Eastern Townships, which have, for some years now, been receiving the overspill from the crowded farm areas along the St. Lawrence; (2) in the cities of the St. Lawrence Valley; and (3) on the northern frontiers, where pioneer farmers and lumbermen are spreading north over the Shield in the Lake St. John and Abitibi areas. In Ontario similar trends are evident. Among recent immigrants one out of every two have made for this province, contributing in the first instance to the city populations of Toronto, Hamilton, and London, and spreading from there to the smaller centres. Along the northern edge of the Palaeozoic formations, where they adjoin the Shield, there is again a frontier zone, in this case a frontier with outliers in the various Clay Belts on the

Shield farther north. But a geological map remains the best key to the distribution of Ontario's population, which is almost wholly concentrated in the south-western peninsula.

In the Prairie Provinces a steady trickle of workers has been leaving the farms. This migration, as we shall see, has occurred in many other farm areas, and especially in the comparable Great Plains region of the U.S.A. While some of the migrants move to the towns, many have left the area to resettle in British Columbia. Between 1941 and 1951, the province of Saskatchewan actually lost 64,000 inhabitants through this rural exodus. But in the 1950's and 1960's this loss has been more than offset by the growth of the Prairie cities, a growth due partly to industrial development and partly to the spectacular rise in oil and gas production.

In the west, the population of British Columbia, like that of other parts of the Pacific coast, has increased very rapidly, but outside the metropolitan area of Vancouver it is a population largely scattered, over a huge area, in remote valleys and on islands. The Vancouver district has been the goal of many immigrants, but the province also includes a pioneer fringe along the Peace River, whose settlements have contributed to the provincial increase.

Finally, the Northwest Territories and Yukon, which between them comprise nearly 40 per cent. of Canada's area, possess only 0·2 per cent. of the population—some 37,000. Half of these are Indians and Eskimos, the Indians generally to be found in the forested areas of the north and the Eskimos on the tundra. The other half of this sparse population is to be found in mining communities and trading posts, and on tiny patches of cultivation dotted through a vast wilderness, upon whose surface development, up to the present, has hardly made a scratch. The white population of the Northlands, though it has increased since 1941, is far below the figure for the halcyon days of the gold rush, sixty or more years ago.

7. Distribution of Population—the U.S.A.

At the census of 1950 the United States had a population of 154·8 millions. By that of 1960, this figure had risen to 179·3 millions, so that it was increasing by almost 2½ millions annually. Less than one-tenth of this growth was due to immigration. This remarkable post-war increase had come unexpectedly, to confound earlier forecasts, and was the basis of calculations predicting a population of more than 200 millions by 1970. In this increase only three states failed to share—West Virginia, Arkansas, and Mississippi (which showed no change)—but the rate of increase varied from state to state and was generally greatest in the west and south-west and least in the Great Plains region and the lower Mississippi basin.

The average density of population was about 50 persons per square mile over the country, but the state density varied from 2·6 in Nevada to 812 in Rhode Island. The highest overall densities were to be found in the manufacturing areas of the north-eastern states; outside the industrial regions the highest densities were in the south-east. West of the Mississippi and Missouri Rivers increasing aridity and mountainous terrain reduced the density of population to 7 or 8 per square mile in the Great Plains, and to zero in the deserts of Nevada and California. Beyond these empty areas lay a series of population clusters along the Pacific coastal fringe from Puget Sound to the Mexican border.

While the American population has thus been increasing, its distribution is also continually changing. One of the features of American life that must constantly impress the European is the mobility of the population. To a degree unknown in older lands, it is geographically unattached and prepared to move long distances in search of economic gain or pleasanter living conditions. Out of this mobility have come, in recent years, three great movements of the population.

The first of these is a movement from the country to the cities, which we have already noted in Canada. Although difficulties of census division and definition mask the precise figures, it seems clear that during the decade 1950–60 the equivalent of one-third of the 1950 farm population left the farms, and that at the same time the urban population increased by one-third. The circumstances surrounding this exodus are examined in Chapter IV; mechanization was a factor, and so, too, was a general increase in the pressure of competition in some branches of agricultural production. By 1960, 69·9 per cent. of the population was classed as urban.

The second movement is from the centres of the cities to the suburbs. It reflects a rising standard of living and modern housing concepts, and since it brings outside the city boundaries a large population whose interests lie mainly within the city, it tends, statistically, to counteract the movement first described. To distinguish, therefore, between the farmers and the mere country residents, the rural population is divided into two categories: 'farm' and 'non-farm'. It is the 'farm' section which, as we have seen, has suffered such a decline over the past decade; the 'non-farm' element has considerably increased.

The best impression of the combined effects of these two movements is obtained from the population figures for the so-called Standard Metropolitan Statistical Areas (S.M.S.A.s). These cover the 212 largest cities and comprise not only the city proper but also the suburbs—sometimes several counties in extent. They give, therefore, a fairly accurate impression of the size of the whole built-up area. For each large city, consequently, two population figures can be given—that for the city alone and that for the S.M.S.A.[1] While in most cases the former has increased only slowly, the average increase for the S.M.S.A.s between 1950 and 1960 was 26 per cent. Two-thirds of the population of the U.S.A.—112 million people—lived in these 212 areas in 1960.

By far the greatest metropolitan area in the U.S.A. is that of New York–North-Eastern New Jersey with 14·7 million inhabitants, an increase of 14·3 per cent. between 1950 and 1960. It is followed by Chicago with 6·8 millions, Los Angeles with 6·7 millions, and nineteen other areas with more than a million inhabitants. Among the major cities, however, the highest *rates of increase* were to be found, not among the giants of the east (Pittsburgh and Boston were at the bottom of the list in 1960), but in the cities of Florida, Texas and California—Miami–Fort Lauderdale, Dallas and Houston, Los Angeles and San Diego. Among the smaller cities, those which expanded fastest were all to be found in the same southern and western regions, from Orlando in Florida, through Midland and Odessa in Texas, Phoenix in Arizona and Las Vegas in Nevada, to San Jose in California. The only S.M.S.A.s that lost population during the

---

[1] Throughout this book population figures given for cities are in every case those for the S.M.S.A., where such a unit exists, unless otherwise noted.

decade were in the declining coalfield areas of Pennsylvania and West Virginia.

The rapid growth of western cities is one aspect of the third and most spectacular movement of the population—westward. This movement has been in progress for so long that it has become a tradition, but never before have so many Americans followed Greeley's classic advice to go west as in the past twenty years. All the Pacific coast and most of the Mountain states felt the impact of this movement, and California, the principal objective of the migrants, increased its population by 48 per cent. or 5·1 million people between 1950 and 1960.

The reasons for this latest phase of the historic westward drift are fairly clear. It is, in the first place, a move to a more favourable climate. Businessmen impressed by low plant heating costs, pensioners seeking a pleasant retirement; ex-Servicemen who discovered, through war-time postings, that there are parts of the U.S.A. where winter clothes are unknown and fuel bills are negligible: all these have joined the movement west or (for Florida and Texas share these advantages) south. Secondly, the climate and the scenic wonders of the western states, increasingly publicized, form the basis of a vast tourist industry, whose growth in turn reflects a rising standard of living and more leisure to explore the continent. This tourist industry provides a livelihood for thousands, and does much to explain the 78 per cent. increase in Florida's population in the years 1950–60, and the 73 per cent. of Arizona.

The third reason for the drift, difficult to define and yet undeniable, is provided by the glamour of the New West. It is a movement from farms on the interminable plains, or from industrial valleys devoid of romance, to Hollywood and the land of film stars and sudden fame; to the fabulous oil-rich cities of Texas, where wealth abounds. And as the treasure hunters and businessmen arrive, so local markets and service industries are created in their turn to add momentum to the westward movement.

FURTHER READING

MOST works on the North American Indians deal with particular tribes, and from an archaeological or anthropological standpoint, but *The North American Indian Today*, ed. C. T. Loram and T. F. McIlwraith, gives a more general picture. For studies of the immigrants and the 'melting pot', see

Maldwyn Jones' *American Immigration*, M. L. Hansen's *The Atlantic Migration*, *1607–1860* and *The Immigrant in American History*, O. Handlin's *The Uprooted*, and, for a survey of individual national groups, *One America*, ed. F. J. Brown and J. S. Roucek. The history of the American Negroes is traced in *From Slavery to Freedom*, by J. Hope Franklin, or *The Strange Career of Jim Crow*, by C. Vann Woodward. See also 'The Changing Distribution of the American Negro', by J. Fraser Hart, *A.A.A.G.*, vol. l, pp. 242–66, and 'The Nonwhite Population Surge to our Cities', by P. F. Coe, *Land Economics*, vol. xxxv, pp. 195–210. On French Canada, see A. Siegfried's *Canada*, or *The French Canadians, 1760–1945*, by F. Mason Wade, and 'The Spread and Migration of French Canadians', by N. McArthur and M. E. Gerland, *Tijds. voor econ. en soc. geog.*, Jaarg. 52, pp. 141–7.

For Canada, the *Year Book* contains census data. Other useful references are 'Canadian Indians Today', by W. Dunstan, *Can. Geog. Journ.*, vol. lxvii, pp. 183–93; 'The Canadian Ecumene—Inhabited and Uninhabited Areas', by R. T. Gajda, *Geog Bull.*, No. 15, pp. 5–18, and 'Conurbation Canada', by N. Pearson, *The Canadian Geographer*, vol. v, pp. 10–17.

For the U.S.A., the literature resulting from the 1950 census was summarized in 1958 by W. Zelinsky in 'Recent Publications on the Distribution of Population in the United States', *A.A.A.G.*, vol. xlviii, pp. 472–81. Among this literature, E. L. Ullman's article on the westward movement, 'Amenities as a Factor in Regional Growth', *Geog. Review*, vol. xlvi, pp. 119–32 should be specially noted. Since 1958, population movements have been analysed by W. Zelinsky in 'Changes in the Geographical Patterns of Rural Population in the United States, 1790–1960', *Geog. Review*, vol. lii, pp. 492–524, J. P. Gibbs in 'The Evolution of Population Concentration', *Econ. Geog.*, vol. xxxix, pp. 119–29, the editors of *Fortune* in *The Exploding Metropolis*, and R. M. Northam in 'Declining Urban Centres in the United States', *A.A.A.G.*, vol. liii, pp. 50–9.

III

CONDITIONS OF
ECONOMIC DEVELOPMENT

THE patterns of a country's human geography are shaped not only by the physical factors that govern land use or routeways, but also by the social and political conditions under which settlement and development take place. In North America there are a number of such conditions whose effects on the distribution of economic activity have been of great importance, and it is the purpose of this section to call attention to these effects, as a necessary preliminary to the study of the continent's regional geography.

1. *A Federal Constitution*

Both Canada and the United States have federal constitutions. The significance of this fact for our present purposes is that, while the central government alone possesses authority in such spheres as foreign policy or defence, the local units—the provinces in Canada and the states in the U.S.A.—possess wide powers over their internal affairs, including power of taxation. Since in practice each unit pursues its own financial policies, notable differences in economic conditions may occur between adjacent states or provinces.

Some of these differences are large in scale and have important effects on landscape patterns. A state may set out to attract new industries by constructing a tax system that favours manufacturing, and hope thereby to lure producers from other states where tax rates are higher. State governments are commonly judged by their success in bringing new business to the state through such policies. In a highly competitive economy like that of the U.S.A., unfavourable local legislation may seriously handicap local producers. One of the chief reasons cited by the textile manufacturers of New England, for example, for their inability to compete with their rivals in the south (see p. 152) was the high level of taxation and compulsory welfare expenditure required by the state governments of

F

Massachusetts and Rhode Island, and this has been a contributing cause of the industry's move southward. By contrast,
the state of Nevada has built a flourishing tourist trade on an
absence of controls, legalized gambling, and the slogan that
'anything goes'.

The same differences are to be found, however, on a much
smaller scale. Petrol costs more at the Kentucky end of the Ohio
River bridges (thanks to a higher state tax) than it does at the
Indiana end, half a mile away, a fact of which local motorists
are naturally aware. Patterns of exploitation on an Alberta oil
field are different from those in Texas. In short, although in the
U.S.A. the erection of barriers to inter-state commerce is
specifically forbidden in the Constitution, differences in fiscal
and resource policies are in both countries sufficient to provide
both location incentives and inter-state rivalries.

A corollary of the division of powers between the federal and
the state or provincial governments is that, if the powers of the
states are limited, so too are those of the central government, in
the U.S.A. more narrowly than in Canada. The United States
Constitution specified the powers of the federal government,
and reserved all other powers (Tenth Amendment, 1791) to
'the States respectively, or to the people.' In order to intervene
in any internal affairs, therefore, the federal government must
first prove its constitutional right to do so. In any action that has
the appearance of a new departure, it can count on the dogged
opposition of those who are 'states-righters'.

A good example of this constitutional problem is to be seen
in recent regional developments such as those in the Tennessee
and Missouri Valleys. In these areas, which cover several states,
what is clearly needed is a concerted, supra-state plan. But all
that the federal government may implement is a project for improving the navigation of the Tennessee—or Missouri—since
the Constitution gives the federal authority the task of removing
barriers to inter-state commerce (in this case, river traffic), but
gives it no power to plan states' economies for them. This may
explain the federal government's apparently excessive pre-
occupation with rivers rather than regions. (For a further
discussion of this point, see p. 320.)

Thus, somewhat backhandedly, does the federal government
overcome its constitutional limitations. In spite, however, of the

opposition of the states-righters, the federal authorities of the U.S.A. have greatly increased their sphere of operations in recent years, at the expense of the states. The reasons for this need not here concern us, but in the long run the effect will be to eliminate some of the present local differences in the national economy. In Canada, curiously enough, the reverse process has taken place, with the provinces increasing their sphere of effective control and consequently diverging from one another on points of policy.

One further aspect of the federal relationships with states and provinces which concerns the geographer is the problem of federal ownership of land. In the United States, between 1780 and 1848, the federal government came into possession, by treaty, by purchase, or by agreement with the states, of wide areas east of the Mississippi and of virtually the whole area west of the river except Texas. This great expanse it has gradually given away or sold (the process by which this was done is outlined on pp. 79–81), but it still retains some 400 million acres for which it has full responsibility. In some of the western states the public domain represents a high proportion of the total area (in Nevada over 80 per cent.). The states thus face a situation in which the largest landlord in the state, and one over whom they have little control, is the federal government.

Needless to say, this situation leads to a good deal of agitation in the west for the handing over of the remaining 400 million acres of public land to local authorities or private owners. The problem is complicated by the fact that, as we shall see, much of the public domain is multi-purpose land—it serves for grazing, for forestry, for recreation, and for watershed control simultaneously—and so is unsuited to single-purpose use by individuals.

In Canada the situation is rather different. Although the federal lands cover almost 1,000 million acres, all but a few hundred thousand of these are accounted for by the North-West Territories (N.W.T.) and Yukon, which are administered by the Ottawa government. Title to empty lands in the then-existing provinces passed to the provincial governments after federation in 1867, and to the Prairie Provinces in 1930, so that today the holdings of the provinces exceed 1,000 million acres. Thus although 2,000 million acres of Canada are publicly owned, there is a clear geographical division between federal and provincial responsibility (the only significant exception being the federal control of the Indian Reserves within the provinces), and there is consequently not the clash of ownership which complicates the administration of the western United States where federal, state, and private lands are intermingled.

2. Sectionalism

The existence of only two nations in the 7 million square miles of Anglo-America means that there is plenty of scope for the development of loyalties more local than the national. To some extent, allegiance to the province or state meets this social need, but the particularly American phenomenon is sectionalism—a unity of outlook and interest within a region.

That this is so is due in the first place to the factors of distance and isolation. Over so large an area natural conditions are varied enough to give to regions conflicting needs and interests, and to draw together into sectional groups states or provinces with similar characteristics of environment or economy. Secondly, the sectional feeling derives importance from the fact that the boundaries of the states and provinces are for the most part arbitrarily drawn along lines of latitude or longitude, and do not correspond with any geographical reality. Thus the section is the more natural, if informal, sub-division of the nation.

In Canada the development of sectionalism follows naturally from the division of the populated areas into four parts, each isolated from the other three by circumstances of physical geography. The long debate that preceded federation in 1867 gave expression to this sectional feeling. While there were admittedly the complicating factors of French Canada and of United States' expansionism, there was also much discussion of the sectional issues—of tariffs and their effects, of hinterlands for ports, and, above all, of the transcontinental railway links upon the promise of which the adherence of British Columbia to the federation was ultimately confirmed. That the reconciliation of such conflicting sectional interests should ever have been made possible constituted, as one writer has expressed it, 'the miracle of union'.

Two other examples of sectional conflicts in North American history call for mention. One is the long continuing friction, on both sides of the border, between the settled East and the moving frontier. This somewhat over-dramatized aspect of American history may be explained in various terms. It was a conflict between those who, confronted by the apparently unlimited prospects of the empty West, wanted freedom to occupy and exploit it, and those far to the east who wanted to control the occupation. It was a conflict between those who saw the possibilities but lacked the resources to develop them and those who could finance and equip the expansion—but on their own terms. It was a conflict between those who, in their own view at least, did the work and took the risks, and those others— bankers, railwaymen, government officials—upon whom they depended for supplies, transport, and markets.

In this case, of course, the sections moved geographically as the frontier advanced; St. Louis or Winnipeg, once full of the pioneer spirit, became conservative and 'Eastern' by contrast with Denver or Edmonton. But of the whereabouts of the sections in the other great conflict there could be little doubt, for the dividing lines were crystallized in secession and battle. Sectionalism—or a 'form of regional persecution complex' as it has been called found its classic expression in the American Civil War of 1861–5.

The Civil War, as Lincoln constantly emphasized in his efforts to preserve the Union, represented a clash between sectionalism and nationalism. Southern feeling—the regional persecution complex—was fostered on the economic side by federal tariff policies unfavourable to Southern exporters, on the political side by the swelling anti-slavery campaign. And quite apart from these threats to Southern interests was another sectional issue which was resolved by the war: would the great new West become tributary to the North or to the South?

In the event, sectionalism was defeated but not eliminated. (Indeed, in the South it has achieved, with judicious treatment, an aura of romance.) The purpose of these paragraphs is to call attention to its present importance in American geography. In very general economic terms the legacy of these early sectional conflicts was domination of the South and West by the North-East.

The basic issue can be simply stated: within a large, free-trade area like Canada or the U.S.A., there is nothing to prevent one section from exploiting the resources of another and from running them down to a dangerous degree for its own profit, provided that it has the economic power to do so. In other words, it is possible to have all the economic features of colonialism, within the boundaries of a single country, and under the

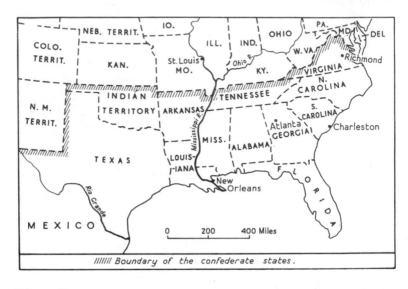

FIG. 13. The Confederate States ('The South') in the American Civil War, 1861–5.

banner of free enterprise. While this is a matter in which fact easily succumbs to feeling, and it is not necessary to accept all the charges made by the South and West against the North-East, it must be recognized that the northern Atlantic seaboard states in the U.S.A., and the Montreal–Southern Ontario region in Canada, have achieved a remarkable dominance in the economic affairs of the two countries.

This is not the result of superior natural resources. It seems to have been due primarily to the availability of capital supplies in these two areas. Capital, as we shall see in Chapter XIII, was the commodity in shortest supply in the South after the Civil War, while in the West capital was almost always in short supply, to finance the tremendously rapid spread of agriculture and communications. The high level of interest rates on loans has been a perennial complaint of Western farmers.

The other major—and related—factor making for the colonialism of the South and West was the control of the railways by Eastern interests. In the West, as we shall later see, the early railways were the arbiters of success or failure; the settlers bought, sold, and shipped goods on their terms. The railways' monopoly was complete, and, even if they did not abuse it, they exerted an all-important influence on the development of the West. Furthermore, as is explained in the next section, the railways have been able to use, as a potent instrument, their system of freight rates. Since freight charges are not calculated simply on a distance and weight basis, they could be manipulated to help or to handicap the shipper. By this means, in fact, the railways could place a whole section at a disadvantage. Complaints of such treatment came recurrently from British Columbia and the Prairie Provinces for many years. In the same way, a long-standing grievance of the South found expression in a case that came to a head in 1937, in which it was claimed that the structure of rates for goods moving from south to north encouraged the shipment of Southern raw materials (to be processed in Northern factories), but hampered the northward movement of Southern manufactures (which would compete in Northern markets).

Whatever validity attached to the somewhat crude popular concept of a ruthless East oppressing its Southern and Western dependencies, however, has been dwindling in recent years. The natural richness of these regions has enabled them to assert themselves, and to generate more than enough capital—especially from oil—to finance their own development. Feeling that, in the past, their resources have been exploited by and for other sections, they have built up their own industries, and have used their political influence in Ottawa and Washington to obtain a generous share of federal expenditure on new plants and projects. Indeed, it is this competition for a bigger share of public spending which represents the main field of sectional rivalry at the present day, a rivalry different in form from those of the past, but still an important factor in the continent's geography.

3. *The Freight Rate System*

Mention has been made of the part played by the freight rate system in consolidating the dominance of east over west in North America. We must now return to consider the subject in a wider context, as a necessary preliminary to understanding the location of economic activity in Canada or the U.S.A.

In all such activity the cost of transport, whether of raw material supplies or of finished products to market, is an important factor. The greater the distances involved in assembling or selling the goods, the more important does this element become in the final cost. But in North America there is

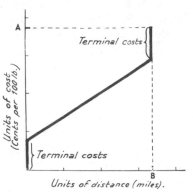

FIG. 14. Freight Rates: Basic cost diagram, to indicate a cost *A*, for moving a unit quantity of freight *B* miles. Compare with Fig. 15.

an additional consideration that greatly increases the significance of freight costs. This is the special nature of the rate structure, and it is the purpose of this section to attempt a brief explanation of what is actually a most complicated matter.

To weigh a shipment of goods and calculate the charge for carrying it a given distance does not at first sight appear complicated. The basic conditions are indeed simple. To the transport company, the cost of carrying freight is represented by the graph in Fig. 14. It costs something to load the goods aboard the train or truck; thereafter the cost increases with distance, but on a long haul the terminal costs form a smaller proportion of the total, and the cost *per mile* is less, than on a short haul.

However, neither all freight nor all haulage is uniform, and the actual slope of the graph depends on a number of factors. Some kinds of goods, such as precision instruments or fish, require more care in carriage than others, like coal or scrap iron; and for each class of goods the carrier fixes a *Class Rate*. Then again, the cost of transport is higher in mountain or desert areas than in level, well-settled regions; and the freight rate legitimately reflects this fact. Again, the cost graph may be adjusted to take account of savings made when a large amount of any one kind of goods is being carried between two particular points. Large shipments, and especially large and regular ship-ments, are for several obvious reasons cheaper to handle than small loads that need sorting in half-empty trucks; and so for larger quantities the carrier can reduce his costs and offer a lower *Commodity Rate*, applying between the points he specifies.

For the complications which follow from these simple facts two things are responsible. One is the factor of competition, and the other is the policy of the Canadian and United States governments of using freight rates to stimulate economic de-velopment. In short, the American rate structure is governed not merely by *cost* of service, but also by *value* of service to the shipper.

Each transport company, whether dealing in land, water, or air haulage, is out to offer acceptable terms to shippers of goods and to capture their business for itself. A century ago, when canals and railways were being built in North America by the score (many of them unwisely and on inadequate capital re-sources), it was often a matter of life or death to the carrier to capture the traffic of a city or area from his rivals. In these circumstances savage 'rate wars' developed, which frequently led to the ruin of all those involved; and the freight rate 'struc-ture' became simply a series of special arrangements between carriers and shippers, reflecting their relative bargaining strengths. Already in the 1850's a number of states had set up government bodies to safeguard the public interest in efficient transport service, and inevitably the federal governments were drawn in, to check what had become a scandal. In 1887 the United States established the Interstate Commerce Commis-sion (I.C.C.), and in 1903 the Canadian Government provided for a Board of Railway Commissioners (renamed the Board of Transport Commissioners (B.T.C.) in 1938, and given powers over air and water transport also).

But while these controls checked the worst abuses of the system, the freight rate structure remained basically un-changed, a mass of millions of separate agreements between carriers and shippers. The commissions have merely acted as referees, and they see to it, by enforcing certain rules of the business, that a reasonable degree of competition is maintained.

Indeed, if a local market is in the undisturbed possession of one

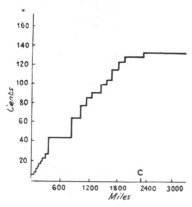

set of producers, the commissions may *create* competition, by allowing producers from elsewhere an exceptionally low rate into the market. To do this, they sometimes have to break their own golden rule— that if there are two points on the same line, the rate to the farther one must not be less than that to the nearer one. The commissions' basic aim is to ensure that the public is

FIG. 15. Freight Rates: The structure of the transcontinental commodity rate on citrus fruit, from California to New York, in 1947. *C* marks the location of Chicago on the distance scale. (From S. Daggett and J. P. Carter, *The Structure of Transcontinental Railroad Rates*, Univ. of California Press, 1947.)

provided with efficient service and is safeguarded against costly monopoly. To achieve this, they support the bargaining power of the shipper against the carrier, and of the carriers against each other.

Some of the best known special rates are the transcontinental commodity rates, approved by the I.C.C., that have been agreed between the railways and the Californian fruit growers. The rate on oranges (Fig. 15) may serve as an example. Oranges are grown both in California and in Florida. But California is twice as far from the great markets of the north-eastern states as Florida is, and there is little possibility of the Californian oranges competing in these markets unless they can be cheaply transported to the east. To the western railways, therefore, the alternatives are cheap carriage or no carriage at all, and so they have set up a low commodity rate on Californian oranges to New York, a rate so favourable, in fact, that the Californian growers can fully hold their own with their Floridan competitors.

On a much broader scale, the Maritime Provinces of Canada put forward the claim that, owing to their geographical isolation from the rest of the country, they were entitled to a lower level of rates than other sections, in order to be able to place their produce on the home market on competitive terms. The

Canadian Government accepted this argument, and by an act of 1927 reduced the whole railway rate level for the Maritimes by 20 per cent.

With the passing of time the nature of the competition among the carriers has changed. Under increasing pressure from road hauliers the railways have stopped fighting each other, and have instead banded together to preserve their interests. In certain limited spheres water routes also provide a challenge that forces a special reduction in freight rates by rail. Instead of bidding separately for traffic, therefore, the railways negotiate their rates through regional committees of their representatives, watched over by the I.C.C., the B.T.C., and the state commissions.

But the functions of the commissions are not purely preventive. It was early recognized that the freight rate structure could have an important *positive* influence on the development of a country or region. The Canadian Government has been very sensitive to this fact, particularly since it became the owner of one of Canada's two great railway systems. Its chief concern has been to assist the outward movement of Canadian raw material exports and the forward movement of settlers' necessities into the frontier zones. Thus in 1897 it concluded with the Canadian Pacific Railway the Crow's Nest Pass Agreement, whereby, in exchange for a subsidy, the railway agreed to fix low rates on a number of commodities from the western frontiers, particularly grain. This favourable rate on grain has remained to the present time, justified on the ground that, as the 1951 Royal Commission on Transport stressed, production of grain for export is for Canada 'an industry requiring special consideration as in the national interest'. In economic terms, therefore, this low rate, secured by the government, acts as a subsidy to the grain producers.

The Canadian Government has been careful to maintain a general level of rates comparable with that of the U.S.A., since over many routes, and notably the transcontinental ones, the Canadian and United States railways compete with each other and with the sea routes through Panama. A higher rate level in Canada, added to the greater physical obstacles on the Canadian side of the border, would be certain to divert business to the American carriers, at the expense of the Canadian.

The general level of freight rates in both countries has long varied from region to region. Mention has already been made of complaints on this score by the southern states of the U.S.A. (p. 73), and of the successful application by the Maritime Provinces for a regional rate cut. Undoubtedly these differences have had a significant effect in modelling the present economic geography. Both governments, however, are now committed to a policy of uniform rate levels for all regions, so that in the future no section of the country will be handicapped—or helped—in this way. But the influence of the millions of separate bargains which together constitute the American freight rate system will certainly remain.

4. Conservation of Natural Resources

There remains one further factor of the social background to be considered, without which no study of the human geography of North America could be regarded as complete. It is the growth of a popular movement towards the conservation of the continent's natural resources.

One of the major decisions facing the population of any area is the *rate* at which its resources shall be used. Many of them are irreplaceable; others are replaceable only by slow processes such as soil formation or forest regeneration. To use these assets more rapidly than they are replaced, or to use more of them than current need justifies, is wasteful exploitation; a rate of use which is adjusted to speed of replacement and to current need represents conservation. Experience on almost every new frontier of settlement supports the general statement that waste and exploitation accompany the first settlers, and that regulation of use is the only alternative to a rapid deterioration of the area's natural resources. Upon a community's willingness to accept such regulation depends the future of its supplies of minerals, timber, water, or food. Of the existence or absence of these policies of regulation the landscape will often contain visible evidence; there is a landscape of conservation and a landscape of waste.

Throughout the first three centuries of European settlement in North America the continuing impression made upon the settlers was one of inexhaustible natural riches. In a land where space was unlimited, where the forest seemed to go on for ever, where fish and game abounded, the early generations of Americans can be excused for feeling that they need never fear a permanent shortage of the materials necessary for a livelihood. If they exhausted the possibilities of one area, they could always move on. Imbued with this spirit, they did move on, until there stretched across the continent a series of frontiers, littered with the debris of exploitation and abandonment. In the north the fur men cleared the forests of fur-bearing animals. In the Great Lakes area the lumbermen passed through with all the devastating effect of a forest fire, cutting out only the species of timber they could market, and leaving behind the tangled remnants of the forest cover as useless cutover. In the south farmers grew cotton or tobacco until the soil had lost its virtue, and then abandoned their farms and moved west to repeat the process on newly cleared lands. As the tempo of development and the speed of the frontier's advance increased during the second half of the nineteenth century, the problem of exploitation came to a head. All too clearly, as the century closed, Americans came to realize that the richest resource base has its limits and that the great bonanza had better end.

From the beginning of the present century onwards a new spirit has begun to prevail. The change has come slowly, for there have been many setbacks. Every sudden increase in demand for food or timber—such as those caused by the two World Wars—leads to a new wave of exploitive cutting or ploughing, and it is asking much of a farmer who has known lean times to surrender the chance of a quick profit today to the thrifty virtue of conservation and better harvests in a distant tomorrow. The great dustbowl years of the drought-ridden 1930's came after conservation had been officially preached for forty years. Nevertheless, there is no questioning the improvement that has taken place. It is well exemplified by a single example: in Wisconsin, where in the period 1880 to 1900 the lumbermen wrought utter havoc, courses in conservation are today compulsory for all those who are in training to be teachers. So far, in two generations, has the chastened spirit of conservation spread.

In a matter of such national importance the attitude of the federal government has naturally had a decisive influence.

Indeed, the federal authorities must bear their share of the responsibility for the damage that has been done, partly because they were the original holders of most of the lands in question, and partly because it was their own attitude to these lands that set the tone for the individuals who later misused them.

In the United States the federal government, as we have seen, began to acquire title to unoccupied lands as early as 1780, when the states surrendered their claims to large and often ill-defined areas of the west. The Louisiana Purchase of 1803 enormously enlarged the federal holdings. Westward expansion was already under way, and the question faced the federal government of how to dispose of its newly acquired empire. It could either sell it or give it away; treat it either as a source of revenue or as providing homes for future Americans, and after a series of programmes designed to do the former, it eventually shifted its policy firmly to the latter. From about 1830 onwards land sales for revenue purposes declined.

It was in the 1850's, when continuous settlement had reached roughly the line of the Mississippi, that a new federal policy emerged. This policy had two foundations. The first, and earlier, of these was the impression that Congress had corporately formed of the American west, on the basis of early travellers' reports. It was highly unfavourable. The concept of a 'Great American Desert', that began just beyond the west bank of the Mississippi, was still in vogue. Moreover, the corollary of this concept was clear—if the land was worthless, it mattered little how it was treated. The official attitude all too rapidly found expression in the behaviour of the individual settler. Not for several decades was the lesson learnt: that it was precisely in these lands beyond the Mississippi that the greatest care in land use was required, if the natural hazards were to be overcome.

The second foundation of federal policy in the years after 1850 was the conviction that the national interest demanded the rapid settlement of the west. An apparently Manifest Destiny to build the republic from sea to sea had brought union with Texas, secured the Pacific North-West (the Oregon boundary), and swept California and the south-west into the nation after the barest formalities of war and treaty with Mexico. Nation building was in the air, and the 1850's saw the beginnings, on a large scale, of the 'give-away' federal policy for the west. In 1856 Congress gave the first railway land grant to the Illinois Central, and in 1862 came the Homestead Act, which offered settlers title, for a nominal fee, to a 'quarter-section' (160 acres) of public land after five years' residence and use.

We shall have cause to return later to a further consideration of both these actions (p. 120). For the present, it is sufficient to note that they opened a period during which the federal government gave away, almost without monetary return, about half of the 1,400 million acres it had earlier acquired. In doing so, it placed responsibility for the development of the empty areas firmly on the individuals and corporations to whom the grants were made.

This then, was the atmosphere in which expansion took place beyond the Mississippi and into the western Great Lakes region. The national policy of cheap land for all, with special provision for settlement by small units, may have been ideologically commendable, but it meant the surrender of a responsibility which the federal government was ill-advised to abandon if the resources of the west were to be rightly developed.

Only gradually, and largely on account of the abuses of private exploitation, did the responsibility of the government for supervising western development come to be recognized. Alongside its grants to individuals, the federal government made over huge areas to the western states, thus passing its problem on to them. Finally, in the last decade of the nineteenth century, the tide turned and the conservation movement was born. Together with a nation-wide programme of education in land use, there developed the policy of land reservation. Begun in 1891, and actively pursued by President Theodore Roosevelt in the first years of the present century, this policy meant the withdrawal from further public entry of lands whose resources —in the first instance, timber—made them of value to the nation. National parks and national forests were set up, and in these the federal government undertook to regulate land use. Later, the open grazing lands of the public domain were similarly brought under control. On the remnant of the public lands, at least, conservation came into its own. But by 1900 less

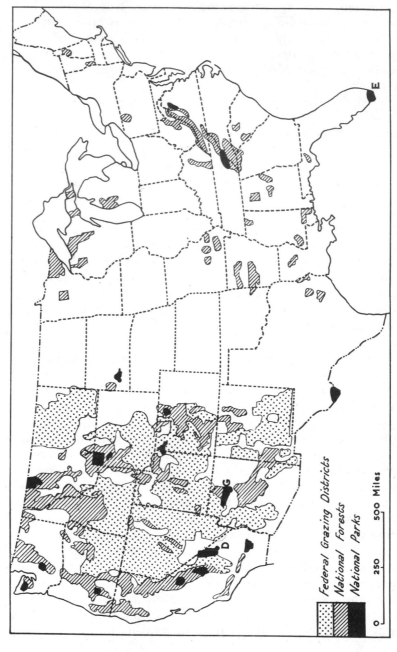

Fig. 16. U.S.A.: The Public Domain, showing the main areas of National Forests, National Parks, and grazing lands administered by the Bureau of Land Management. (Y = Yellowstone, G = Grand Canyon, D = Death Valley, E = Everglades.)

than half the original area remained under federal control. In the meantime, the situation had been deteriorating back in the eastern states. The pressure of an increasing population upon land and resources used with traditional American freedom had made deforestation, soil erosion, and diminishing crop yields common. The vicissitudes of business during and after the First World War, which culminated in the great depression of 1929–33, made it clear that a new approach to the problem of resource conservation must be made. As if to underline this, the droughts of 1934 and 1936 produced the famous dustbowls in the southern Great Plains. In 1936, therefore, the Soil Conservation Service was established, with the task of organizing farmers into district groups for the development of anti-erosion measures, and of instructing them in more scientific methods of land use.

In spite of these remedial measures, the standard of conservation practice in the U.S.A. is far from being uniformly high. But it is important for critical outsiders to understand the position. While it is common knowledge that, for example, many American farms still suffer seriously from soil erosion, it is much less well known that there exists on the statute book of nearly every state affected by erosion the legislation necessary to remedy the situation—to force farmers to be conservationists. The law can be invoked against unscientific farming.

The reason why this second fact is not so well known is simple: the law has never been enforced. To the Americans, this is a test case for their democratic principles. They believe that farmers—or lumbermen—can be made good citizens by education, and should not be coerced. Rather, then, than curtail the farmer's liberties by law, they will accept the present damage to soil or forest, and wait in hope that the quietly educational efforts of the Soil Conservation Service, and the realization that conservation pays, will ultimately bear fruit.[1] And gradually their faith seems to be finding its vindication. The dustbowl, then, is as much a social and political phenomenon as a physical one.

In Canada the situation has been generally similar to that in

[1] In the event, 33 states originally gave legal powers of regulation to Soil Conservation Districts, but in few districts have these been adopted, and in several states the powers have been withdrawn again. The matter is fully discussed by S. V. Ciriacy-Wantrup, in *Resource Conservation*, Univ. of California Press, 1952, pp. 291–2.

G

the U.S.A., and after 1862 necessarily so. The governments of both countries adopted the view that they should encourage a rapid settlement of their empty western lands, and they have in a real sense, therefore, been competing with each other for settlers. In the great westward movement of the period after 1860, the international boundary west of the Great Lakes had little significance for the settlers, whose selection of the United States or Canadian side often depended more on the availability of good land than on political allegiance.

When, therefore, the Homestead Act of 1862 made 160 acres of United States land available at virtually no cost, the Canadian Government had necessarily to take the first opportunity, after purchasing the prairie lands in 1870, to make a similar offer. The Canadian Homestead Act of 1872 served this purpose. Furthermore, the system of railway land grants which had been adopted in the U.S.A. was repeated when, in 1881, the contract for a Canadian transcontinental railway was signed. The Canadian Pacific was to receive the huge total of 25 million acres as its subsidy (reduced later to about 18 million), and moreover was free to pick and choose, as the United States railways had never been able to do. In the Prairies, as a result, the C.P.R.'s was the dominant influence, and while it early adopted an intelligent land policy, it was strictly a business enterprise, governed by financial considerations.

In Canada as a whole, however, government control of national resources has been somewhat closer than in the U.S.A. For this fact the decision to hand over control of the public lands to the provinces may have been responsible. In certain respects the contrast is marked. In the north-western forest states of Washington and Oregon, for example, the rate of timber cutting has until recently far exceeded the rate of growth. In British Columbia, however, where some 90 per cent. of the forest is owned by the province, it has been possible to keep the annual cut to a figure lower than the total annual increment. Again, when the big Alberta oilfields came in after 1947, the government took immediate steps to regulate the development and, profiting by the unhappy experience of some of the oil regions south of the border, to avoid wastage by restricting competitive drilling. On the whole, then, the time lag between the development of the United States' west and that of Canada gave the latter time to profit by the former's mistakes, and the allocation of all crown lands to the provinces gave local governments an immediate stake in the orderly development of their resources.

The rate of use of the world's natural resources has greatly increased in the first half of the twentieth century. This is a result partly of the tremendous increase in world population and partly of the technical revolution which, particularly in the western world, has so markedly enlarged the productive capacity of the individual. Crudely put, this means that man can now overwork his soil and strip his forest land more swiftly and thoroughly than ever before. The continuing problem of the North American nations is to reconcile a growing capacity to produce with a strictly limited resource base, and to do it, in accordance with their political beliefs, with as little formal regulation as possible.

FURTHER READING

ON the workings of the federal system in the U.S.A., there are a number of textbooks which give abundant detail. The Canadian system is best studied by means of one of the several excellent histories of Canada which have recently appeared. On the subject of sectionalism, the reader can consult *Regionalism in America*, ed. M. Jensen; *City, Region and Regionalism*, by R. E. Dickinson, or, for a more forceful approach, *Revolt of the South and West*, by A. G. Mezerik. The freight rate structure is discussed in *Economics of Canadian Transportation*, by A. W. Currie, and for the U.S.A. in numerous textbooks, including *Economics of Transportation*, by D. P. Locklin, or *Principles of Inland Transportation*, by S. R. Daggett. See also *The Structure of Transcontinental Railroad Rates*, by S. R. Daggett and J. P. Carter.

Among numerous works on conservation by scholars in different fields, the best geographer's contribution is probably *Conservation of Natural Resources*, ed. G. Harold-Smith. For the political and social aspects, see *Conserving Natural Resources*, by S. W. Allen, or *Resource Conservation*, by S. V. Ciriacy-Wantrup.

On all the subjects with which this chapter deals, one of the best short references available is the chapter on economic aspects of governmental affairs in the U.S.A., contributed by E. A. Ackerman to *The Changing World*, ed. W. G. East and A. E. Moodie.

For studies of specific resources in the U.S.A., the publications of The Twentieth Century Fund and Resources for the Future, Inc. should be consulted. For Canada, see the two volumes of *Resources for Tomorrow*, background papers for a conference under that title held at Montreal in October 1961.

IV

AGRICULTURE

1. *The Agricultural Regions*

F EW maps of North America are more familiar to the eye than that on page 87. Based on the county statistics of farm activity, it reveals the basic generalization that North American agriculture falls geographically into a series of belts or regions, in each of which one type of farming, and in some cases one crop, predominates. Indeed, apart from the size of the entirely blank areas (which cover some 92 per cent. of the total area of Canada), perhaps the most significant feature of the map is the relative smallness of the sections labelled 'general farming'—those regions whose agriculture is assorted enough to defy more detailed classification.[1] Everywhere else the main agricultural emphasis is clear.

It must at once be understood, however, that these agricultural regions are not permanent divisions. They represent simply the present state of development of a pattern which has been evolving for three hundred years, and which has, as a matter of fact, changed quite significantly even in the short period since the Second World War. It now seems likely that the pattern of belts—Cotton Belt, Corn Belt, and so on—with which the geographer has become so familiar, will prove to be no more than a passing phase. The cartographer of the future will almost certainly have to map smaller and more numerous agricultural regions, for while specialization in agriculture is increasing rather than diminishing, today it is specialization by the individual farmer rather than by a whole region. True general farming is dying out in face of this individual specialization but so, too, is the old region-wide concentration on a single crop.

2. *The Formative Factors*

What are the forces that have brought into being such an agricultural pattern as this, and that are now changing it

---

[1] The 1959 Census of Agriculture in the U.S.A. classified only 9 per cent. of the nation's farms as 'general'; in all others, one product or group of products accounted for 50 per cent. or more of farm sales.

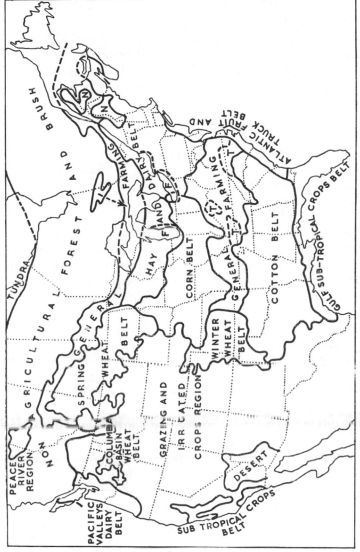

Fig. 17. North America: Agricultural Regions. (F = Fruit regions of the Great Lakes' shore, N = Non-agricultural lands within the northern General Farming Belt, T = Sections of the southern General Farming Belt specializing in tobacco.)

once again? For the sake of convenience, we may divide them into three groups, and say that they are historical, environmental and economic.

HISTORICAL DEVELOPMENT

Much of the story of American agriculture takes its character from the fact that the continent was settled by agriculturalists spreading westwards from the east coast. The earliest settlers on the Atlantic seaboard had necessarily to be as nearly self-supporting as possible. They brought with them wheat and livestock, learned the use of corn (maize) and squash from the Indians, and imported little but sugar. Hemmed in along the coast and the St. Lawrence by mountains, forests, and Indian opposition, they had to make the best of the available lands, unsuitable for cultivation though they often were, since the state of communications made it virtually impossible to transport food beyond the confines of the individual community.

As time went on, the agricultural necessity in which the transport problem involved the settlers was modified in two ways. Firstly, the gradual improvement of communications did away with the need to produce every requirement in each settlement, and made possible a regional division of labour. Areas particularly suited to the production of one crop began to specialize in it. The new situation also meant that the intensive forms of farming could be practised nearest to the settlements, where land was in greatest demand, and that the extensive forms—notably the growing of cereals and the raising of sheep —were relegated to the fringes of the settled area, where space was no problem. Provided that transport facilities were satisfactory, this represented the most economical form of land use.

The second modifying factor was the discovery, made as the frontier of settlement moved westward, that beyond the mountain barrier were wide expanses of the continent which were more fertile and easier to farm than the original agricultural lands along the east coast. To the hill farmer of New England or the western Piedmont, the level grassland of Kentucky and the forest openings of Ohio or southern Ontario seemed a paradise indeed. Once the interior was settled and linked by river, canal, or railway with the Atlantic seaboard, the high-cost, marginal farming which had been forced upon the east coast

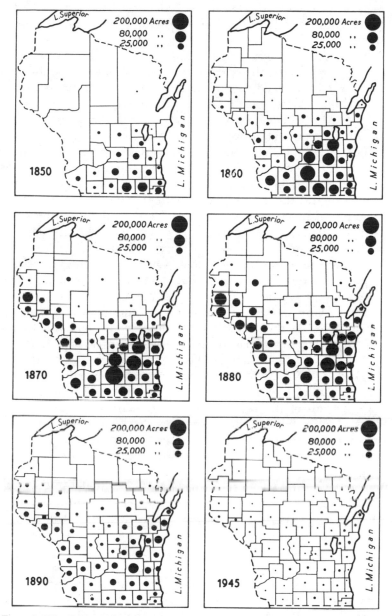

FIG. 18. The Wheat Belt Moves West: A series of maps of Wisconsin, showing how the Belt traversed the state during the period 1850–90, as it moved towards its present location in the Dakotas. (From *A Century of Wisconsin Agriculture*, Wisconsin Crop and Livestock Reporting Service, Bull. No. 290, 1948.)

states could not hope to compete with that of the favoured interior.

The effects of these two processes have been most marked.

1. *Geographically*, the effect has been that the centres of production have moved westward, their position dictated by the availability of transport facilities. The clearest example is that afforded by wheat, and is illustrated by the maps in Fig. 18. Before the year 1825 most of North America's wheat crop grew in New England, as far north and west as Vermont. In 1825, however, the Erie Canal was opened, linking the Hudson River with the eastern Great Lakes region. Such a revolution in transport costs did this event bring about that the centre of wheat production promptly moved from New England to the open lands on the Lake Erie shore of western New York. Through the period 1830–40 the wheatlands spread farther westward, this time into Ohio and south-western Ontario. The next decisive step was the development of a railway network throughout the Great Lakes region. This occurred during the 1850's—New York and Chicago were linked in 1852—and made available for wheat growing the grasslands of Illinois. Through the 1860's and 1870's the process continued, with the centres of production moving on westward across Wisconsin and Iowa. The 1880's, marked as they were by the construction of the Northern Pacific and Canadian Pacific Railways and a number of shorter lines, saw the end of the process—the establishment of the Wheat Belts which appear on the present map, in Kansas, the Dakotas, and the Prairie Provinces. Here aridity brought to a halt a movement which had covered 1,200 miles in seventy years.

2. *Economically*, the effects of these processes have been no less striking, and it is interesting to notice that there is a close parallel with the agricultural situation of Great Britain over the same period. For eastern North America, as for Britain, the opening up of new agricultural lands, fertile and extensive, meant severe competition for the farmers of the older areas. At the same time, moreover, as the railway network was spreading westward, there occurred a parallel technical advance in the manufacture of agricultural machinery, which brought further advantages to the farmers of the level, open interior lands where the machines could best be used, and further increased the handicap of the less favoured eastern regions.

What happened was that the Easterners were forced to retreat from one form of agricultural production to another. Except in a few specially favoured areas, the eastern farmers could profitably produce only what could not easily be shipped into the region from outside. Their farming had to fulfil two conditions: that production should be intensive, and that it should be concentrated on commodities for whose sale closeness to market, the Easterner's one solid advantage, was of prime importance. In these circumstances, a concentration on dairy products and fresh vegetables could safely be predicted, and this prediction is largely borne out by facts. Yet even with this limited range of output, the eastern farmer depends for his ability to sell upon first class communications. Without them, as we shall later see, he is likely to be deprived of a market altogether.

The early settlers on the Pacific coast found themselves confronted by a situation not unlike that of the seventeenth-century immigrants to the Atlantic seaboard. In the 1840's their supply route lay round Cape Horn, or at best crossed the Isthmus of Panama; their penetration inland was shallow, and the settlements had necessarily to be self-supporting. It is interesting, therefore, to notice that there occurred in the isolation of the west an agricultural development on much the same lines as that which has already been described in the older settlements of the east. Local self-sufficiency gradually changed to regional specialization. Today the west coast has its Wheat Belt in eastern Washington, and its Hay and Dairy Belt in the Willamette–Puget Sound Lowland. Recently, it has even developed its Cotton Belt in central California, although this bears little resemblance to its older eastern counterpart. Only the Midwestern Corn Belt, product of a unique combination of physical and economic circumstances, has no replica in the west.

As the mining booms of the 1840's and 1850's brought prospectors and camp followers to the west coast, the early farmers enjoyed a seller's market so profitable as to lure many an unsuccessful Forty-Niner away from his mining to the safer business of feeding his more persistent partners. So long as western agriculture fulfilled this limited function of local supply, its problems were few. But with the passage of time two changes took place. Firstly, in spite of the region's phenomenal population growth, the total agricultural output quickly grew to exceed western demand. Secondly, the Pacific coastlands developed a series of speciality crops which were, and are, produced not for the local but the national market. The combined effect of these two changes is to make today's western farmer dangerously dependent on outside markets, and so also on his means of transport to those markets. Here his isolation beyond the mountains counts against him. Before they can begin to sell in the main markets of the continent, Californian oranges must travel 1,600 miles from Los Angeles, and Washington apples a similar distance from the valleys of the Cascades. British Columbia's farmers are, if anything, worse off in this respect than those farther south. For many western products the Panama Canal offers a better route to market, even to the North American market, than do the transcontinental roads and railways.

Meantime, what is to be said of the great intermediate region that divides east from west—the Agricultural Interior? Between the Ohio, the Missouri, and the Laurentian Shield are to be found some of North America's most favoured farmers. They possess all the advantages of their fellow farmers to both east and west of them, and yet escape most of their problems. Farmers in the east have the advantage of a large urban market close at hand, but lack wide stretches of fertile farmland. Farmers farther west have space and fertility in plenty, but have the problem of getting their produce to distant markets, as well as the hovering threat of climatic variability. The Midwesterners, on the other hand, have both fertile drift plains to cultivate and excellent markets in the cities of the Manufacturing Belt; they have at their disposal, moreover, a communication network which is probably unrivalled throughout the world. The area produces no major export crop, and markets or processes a large proportion of its output within its own boundaries. With a remarkable degree of balance between crop and livestock production, as also between rural and urban population, it is not surprising that this largely self-contained region possesses the highest average of farm prosperity in the continent.

Westward and southward of this region of what might be called agricultural equilibrium, the situation of the farmers

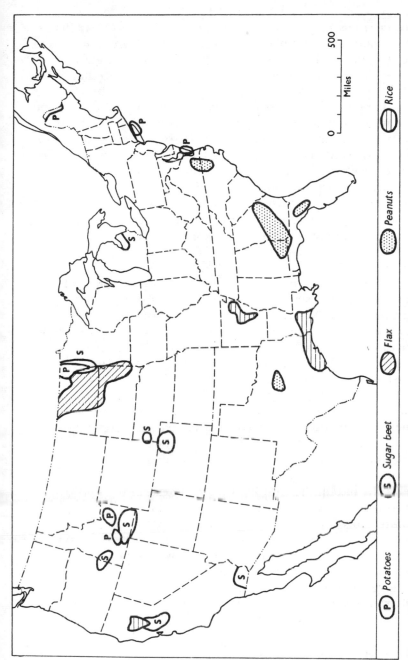

Fig. 19. The U.S.A.: Crop Specialization. Many of the less important field crops grown by American farmers show an even stronger local concentration than the major crops like corn and cotton. On this map, the areas indicated in each case contain more than 90 per cent. of the total U.S. acreage devoted to the crop in question.

P Potatoes

S Sugar beet

Flax

Peanuts

Rice

0   500
Miles

becomes less favourable. Westward, across the Great Plains, this decline can be explained in terms of increasing distances to market and of climatic hazards. Prosperity in a single year, or in a series of as many as ten years, may be equal to that of the Midwest, but there can be little security. Drought, dust, or grasshoppers will redress the balance. Southward, the decline can be accounted for by the fact that, beyond the Ohio, there are not the urban markets upon which Midwestern equilibrium depends, even if there were a southward continuation of Midwestern soil fertility. Furthermore, the pattern and, in the long run, the prosperity of southern agriculture has been distorted by its historic loyalty to King Cotton. Only since the Second World War, as Chapter XIII describes, has any semblance of a Midwestern type of equilibrium emerged.

ENVIRONMENTAL FACTORS

The preceding paragraphs have outlined some of the historical circumstances which are responsible for the present pattern of North American agriculture. They have been presented first because all too often they are lost to sight behind the physical factors of climate, relief, and soil, which are much more accessible to the geographer in search of explanations. It must now be recognized, however, that the ultimate control of this pattern is not human but natural; and, on the continental scale we are considering, the principal environmental influence is climatic. Thus the migration of the Wheat Belt from New England to the western plains, which has already been described, was the outcome of economic change, but it was confined within limits set by climatic factors—on the north by temperature and on the west by aridity. Again, in the south-west, the spread of slavery as an institution was checked not merely by political force (for it was legal in areas which it never touched) but by the climatic limits of the region in which cotton, its economic accompaniment, could be grown. Where the Cotton Belt could not reach, slave-owning lost much of its purpose.

In general, where the boundaries of the agricultural regions run from east to west, they are determined by temperature, and where they run from north to south, by rainfall.[1] The northern

---

[1] The one major exception is the southern limit of the Cotton Belt, which is governed by the heavy summer rainfall on the Gulf Coast, and not by temperature.

limit of successful cotton cultivation is governed by the diminishing length of the frost-free season. The northern limit of the
Corn Belt depends upon the amount of summer heat required
to ripen the corn, and its boundary with the Winter Wheat
Belt in the south-west upon the prevalence of dry summer
winds in that quarter, which parch the corn. The northern
limit of the Spring Wheat Belt is a product not only of poor soils
and distance to market but also of diminishing amounts of
summer sunshine and increasing frost hazards.

The rainfall control of the longitudinal boundaries is most
clearly seen on the Great Plains. The cultivation of cotton, corn,
and hay in the south, centre, and north respectively of the
Agricultural Interior, give place along the 25- or 20-inch
isohyet to wheat growing, and this in turn is abandoned in
favour of range livestock farming farther west, where the
precipitation drops to 12 or 15 inches annually.

Thus the major agricultural divisions reflect climatic influences. On a smaller scale, relief and soil account for local
differences. The ruggedness of the Mountain West, the lack of
soil over much of the Laurentian Shield, the sandy character of
the southern Pine Barrens, and the inadequate natural drainage of the low-lying Florida Everglades all serve to illustrate
the limiting effects of the natural environment on the North
American farmers. So, too, do the ravages of various crop and
animal diseases. Of these perhaps the best known is the cotton
boll weevil, of which one of the U.S. Department of Agriculture's publications comments that 'it has encouraged diversification of crops in the Cotton Belt more than has any other
single factor' since its appearance in the 1890's.

A further comment in this section must be devoted to those
parts of the map of agricultural regions which are blank. A
combination of the factors we have been considering, both
natural and economic, makes them unsuitable for farming
under present conditions. In the United States these empty
areas appear to be relatively small and scattered. The largest of
them are in the western states: the desert of southern California
and Arizona, where average rainfall is below 5 inches, and the
rugged, and in part snow-covered, terrain of the Sierra Nevada
–Cascade chain and the central Rockies. But the map of this

western region is misleading, for over much of the Range Livestock Belt farming is very extensive indeed. The difference between the apparently 'farmed' and 'unfarmed' areas may be no more than the difference between complete emptiness on the one hand and stocking at the rate of one head of cattle to every 100, or even 200, acres on the other. Furthermore, in the mountains and the desert margins such stocking is only seasonal, and the sum total of agricultural activity in any area may be represented by the presence of a few sheep which find summer grazing in the open forest, or above the tree line. Thus the map gives an exaggerated impression of the 'agricultural' west.

In the east non-agricultural lands are found in the swampy and sandy areas of the south-east, and in the forested uplands of northern New England. Here, as in the Canadian provinces across the border, remoteness from markets combines with poor soils and the cost of forest clearance to militate against the development of agriculture. Indeed, as we shall later see, the farming frontier has tended to withdraw rather than advance in this area over the past fifty to seventy years.

In Canada the non-agricultural areas cover the greater part of the country. Over much of the empty north physical conditions of climate and soil are too harsh for successful farming, but even where some form of cultivation could be carried on, distance from market limits expansion along the agricultural frontier. There are, in fact, considerable sections of these empty spaces which could be farmed, given the necessary conditions of demand for their products. But with the present Canadian population, the need to compete with farmers located far closer to markets and ports, and the cost of clearing or draining these lands, their development must wait, for the most part, an unpredictable future.

ECONOMIC FACTORS

We have considered the historical and environmental influences which have gone into the making of North America's agricultural pattern. But farming is a business, and we must now turn to the third set of factors which influence that pattern—the economic considerations.

Since 1914 the fortunes of American agriculture have undergone tremendous fluctuations. The wars created a worldwide demand for agricultural produce, which resulted in high prices and prosperity for the farmers. But this demand also encouraged a dangerous over-expansion, both of area cultivated and of output achieved, and in the post-war periods it was necessary to adjust production to the conditions of peace and of renewed world competition. After the First World War the farmer's fortunes rapidly declined, and they had already reached a low level when in 1929 began the great business depression that stifled foreign trade, reduced domestic demand, and threw hundreds of thousands out of work. Following upon these disasters, a series of bad seasons for the Agricultural Interior during the 1930's came as an added blow. To the outside world, the cumulative effect of the farmers' misfortunes was dramatically illustrated by the ravages of soil erosion. Unable to bear the expense of conservation farming at such a time, the farmers watched helplessly while the wind of the Great Plains blew out the dustbowls, and the heavy rains of the south-east washed away topsoil that had lost its virtue through the cultivation upon it of the same crops for decades at a stretch. Drastic government action was necessary in the U.S.A. and in the Canadian Prairie Provinces to re-establish even moderate prosperity for the farmers, before the outbreak of the Second World War in 1939 brought them back into their own.

Once again the war raised prices and output; once again the war's end in 1945 left the farmers' future uncertain. This time, however, there were two factors which eased the position and insured the farmers, at least temporarily, against rapid price declines. One was the tremendous post-war need for agricultural produce in the devasted areas of Europe and Asia. To the North American farmer this meant that the high war-time level of demand continued for several years, while his government shipped relief supplies to countries in need. Only gradually did the old problems of overseas trade and competition reappear. The second relieving factor for the farmers was that their political position was much stronger in 1945 than in 1919, and consequently they were able to secure by political pressure a continuation of the war-time system of price supports, to insure themselves against another rapid fall of prices like that which had occurred in the 1920's.

Through all these fluctuating fortunes, however, certain permanent features of North American agriculture are evident. (*a*) *Low intensity of land use*. Almost the first impression of rural North America that strikes the European eye is the amount of waste land that is to be found, even in areas of relatively dense settlement. Such was the speed of the westward movement of the frontier in the nineteenth century that, except in some parts of the Atlantic seaboard, settlement was never—by European standards—compact. The land policies of both governments encouraged a loose and generally careless occupance of the land. At the same time, the knowledge that there was more room farther west encouraged the pioneers to move on as soon as they considered that the older regions were becoming too crowded or too civilized. Long before all the lands east of the Mississippi were occupied, the restless pioneers were opening up the Great Plains and the Pacific coast. With land to be had virtually for the taking, there was no point in being crowded. On the other hand, the low cost of land west of the Appalachians and the Laurentian Shield meant that there was no point in costly improvement schemes either; the obvious course was to pick the best lands and avoid those which needed money spent on them. It was cheaper and easier to move to the oak openings of Illinois than to stay and clear the forest in Kentucky, and there was no useful purpose in staying to drain a few swampy acres in Ontario when miles of fertile prairie were open to occupation under the Homestead Act in Manitoba.

The cheap land policies of both governments were thus responsible for the diffusion of settlement across the continent. Even when land values began later to rise, many of the former waste-lands remained, and to this day have never been considered worth the cost of improvement.

(*b*) *Tendency to produce surpluses*. In order fully to understand this feature of American agriculture, however, another factor must be borne in mind: that the Americans can *afford* wasteful land occupance because their agricultural output has been consistently greater than their needs. Despite the tremendous population increases of the past century, it is not scarcity but recurrent surplus that has harassed the American farmer. Plenty has created more problems than want, or, in a telling phrase of Alistair Cooke's, 'American agriculture is sick from its

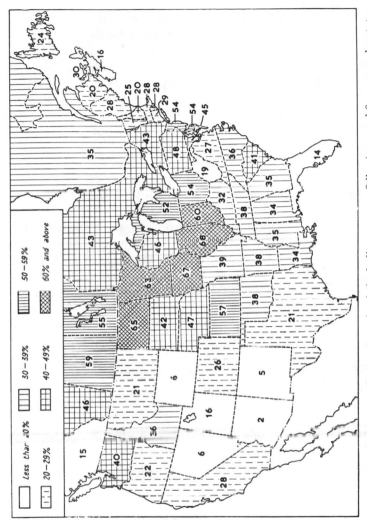

Fig. 20. North America: Ratio of cropland (including summer fallow) to total farm area, by states and provinces. (Based on census data for the 1949 harvest season in the U.S.A., and the 1951 harvest season in Canada.)

H

own success.' In these circumstances, the question of recovering land left waste in the rush of western settlement has remained largely academic.

This persistent tendency to over-produce has two causes. One is the constant development of new farm lands in the west, whether in the initial expansion, or later by irrigation. Generally speaking, the opening up of these lands was not a product of need for food but of settlement policy; the principal motive was to provide homes where agriculture could yield an income, rather than farms to meet a national need for expanded output. The encouragement of farming was thus unrelated to either present surplus or predicted shortage.

The other cause of over-production is the entirely worthy one of increasing efficiency. Not only have new lands been brought into production, but a greater output has been secured from the old. The effect of this increase in efficiency has been striking. In the U.S.A., between 1930 and 1960, the population increased by roughly a half, and the index of agricultural output by 70 per cent. Yet the acreage under crops in the country in 1960 was actually 8 per cent. *less* than in 1930. Each unit of land in 1960 was feeding three people, where thirty years before it had fed two.

In Canada, with its low population density and its imperial connexion, the production of an agricultural surplus for export is basic to the national economy. Its farmers produce regularly for export markets, chiefly in Great Britain and the U.S.A. But in the United States a number of the main farm products appear only irregularly on the international market; there is a huge home market to satisfy, and only the surplus is exported in any particular year—if a market can be found for it. The most marked of these fluctuations have occurred in the export of American wheat. During the period 1930 to 1940, the United States' exports rose as high as 123 million bushels in 1931 and 106 million in 1938, while in the years 1934–6 there was actually a net import. These marginal exports, then, represent a sort of safety valve; if the international market fails to absorb the surplus, a more drastic solution must be sought. Before the war the surplus was either burned or dumped; now the government buys it and itself shoulders the task of deciding what to do next.

(*c*) *Size of farms.* Traditionally, North America is a land of small, owner-operated farms. Such a rural society has been an American ideal: every man should own the land he farmed, and tenancy should be considered not merely undesirable, but almost evil, an infringement of the liberties of the individual. The land policies of both governments were set up to favour the small farmers, with elaborate (though not always successful) safeguards to stop the large-scale speculator. The basic unit of land grant was set at the 'family' size of 160 acres, and up to 1935 that was exactly the average size of the American farm.

To explain this rather over-emphatic attitude, which hardly fits today's facts, we should, perhaps, recall how large a proportion of all Americans are descended from European peasants and tenants, for whom a grasping landlord was their hereditary enemy, his demands the chief reason for their emigration, and whose fondest hope was one day to own their own land. By a coincidence, this dislike of tenant status is encouraged by the fact that the two areas where tenancy figures have long been highest—the Old South and the Great Plains— are also the areas where natural conditions demand most care on the part of the farmer, and most quickly show up bad farming. Be that as it may, government schemes offer tenants loans on easy terms to buy themselves out.

But in reality this ideal of the owner-farmer has little connexion with the real life of the 1960's. While the poor tenants of the South are disappearing, tenancy is on the increase in so prosperous an area as the Corn Belt (where the price of land is so high that many farmers cannot afford to buy it). And in a continent where industrial and commercial units often reach mammoth proportions, there seems no good economic reason why the farm unit should not follow suit.

(d) *The farm income.* In North America, just as in Great Britain, the farmers have had to struggle to obtain a fair share of the prosperity enjoyed by their nation. Despite their efforts, the income from agriculture has been consistently lower than that from industry or commerce, and most townspeople tend to assume that it is predestined by nature to be so, and protest at the 'feather-bedding' of the farmer.

In Britain, one of the main causes of depression in agriculture was the low tariff policy which was adopted in the 1870's, in order to help the nation's industries. By an interesting contrast,

the farmers in the U.S.A.—whose position before 1939 was just
as unfavourable as that of British farmers—also suffered from
the country's tariff policy, but in this case from the *high* tariffs
the U.S.A. imposed. Ever since the Civil War, the country had
maintained a high level of tariffs, in order to help American
industry by excluding foreign manufactures from the American
market. But foreign countries retaliated by imposing tariffs in
their turn and this closed to the American farmers the overseas
markets which, as we have already seen, they need as a
'safety-valve' for their surpluses.

Burdened with these surpluses, the American farmers have
fought hard, through their political organizations, to obtain
their share of the nation's prosperity. In particular, they have
campaigned—and successfully—for the system of price supports, which began in the 1930's, to be continued. Thanks to
these supports, and to technical progress, it has been possible
for the farmers in some favoured areas, such as California and
the Corn Belt, to close the gap between rural and urban standards of living. But in spite of continued subsidy by the government, the 1950's were a decade of only patchy prosperity on
the farms, and this is likely to make the farm income one of the
hottest political issues in the American arena for some time to
come.

The situation of the Canadian farmers has been somewhat
different from that in the U.S.A., firstly because of the different
role played by agricultural exports in the national economy,
and secondly because the financial resources of the Canadian
government have been so much smaller than those of its United
States counterpart. No Canadian government could overlook
the importance of raw material exports in the nation's economic
life; and, even if it did so, the representatives at Ottawa of the
Prairie Provinces and the Maritimes could be relied upon to
keep it reminded. Canadian policy has accepted, and been
adapted to, the nation's role as a primary producer, and even
though, since 1939, Canada has made a vast amount of progress as an industrial power, it is still as a primary producer
that she chiefly figures in international trade (see Chapter VII).
On this ground, at least, Canadian farmers have no reason to
feel that their interests have been overlooked.

But if Canadian agricultural policy has in general taken

account of the farmers' needs, it has also been realistic, in the sense that the government has expected the farmers to compete in international markets without a large measure of financial help—help which, with its small population and young industries, Canada was in any case unable to afford. Although the government took powers in 1944 to set up a general system of price supports, comparable with that of the U.S.A., it was only by the Agricultural Stabilization Act of 1958 that it actually did so. It is true that in the interval the Canadian government had supported the nation's leading crop, wheat, but it is noteworthy that the United States support price has been from one-third to a half as much again as the Canadian, and has in general been *above* the price obtainable in the international market, while the Canadian guarantee has been well below it. Furthermore, the limited Canadian support has been paid to the farmer only when his crop can be sold, and this proviso, as Section 5 of this chapter explains, is an important one. Thus, whatever its sympathies, the Canadian government has left the farmers to fend largely for themselves, winning markets by their own efficiency, and they have not been able, like their American neighbours, to enjoy the luxury of producing 'for the government'.

3. *American Agriculture in the 1960's*

So far, we have been concerned with some of the long-standing realities underlying the agriculture of North America. But no feature of the American farm business is of longer standing than rapid change. Technical developments bring with them economic and social changes, and these in turn affect the distribution and character of the farm population.

If we examine these changes, we find that the progress on the farms is due to two basic processes. One is mechanization, and the other is the increasing application of science and research to agriculture.

Mechanization began in earnest with the automatic harvesters of the 1830's, took a long step forward with the introduction of the tractor, and is today in evidence all over the farm—in the cotton-picker, the combine and the belts which carry food into the cowshed and carry refuse out. And mechanization is linked in turn with other developments.

1. It has released for other uses millions of acres formerly needed to provide feed for horses and mules.

2. It has had the effect of greatly enlarging the area that one man or one family can farm. In theory, therefore, mechanization should lead to fewer and larger farms. In practice, of course, this can only happen if holdings are amalgamated and some of the farmers find other work. In North America, although the average size of farm has doubled since 1935, this increase has still not been rapid enough to give the farmer the full advantage of his machines. Although many farmers have left the land, those who remain are constantly achieving higher output: in fact, there are still too many of them.

There is, however, a side-effect of mechanization which is not a benefit at all. It is that the use of machines may enable a farmer to make a living by cultivating a large area of poor land with a very low return per acre. Without machines it would not yield a livelihood, and very probably it ought not to be cultivated at all.

3. Mechanization has altered the character of farm work, by raising the level of technical skill required for it. The old casual labourer is no longer in demand; his place is taken by the machine, and such labour as is required usually demands training and education.

Scientific agriculture, thanks to the work done in the laboratory and on the seed plot, is obtaining higher yields per acre, and at the same time taking less out of the land, than at any time since white settlement in North America began. In economic terms, the drain on the capital asset—the land—is lower, and the interest rate is higher, in today's conservation farming, than they have ever been before.

How has this come about? There are three main ways.

1. Probably the most important single factor has been the breeding of new strains of crops. Half a century ago, the main problem was to produce strains which would stand the rigours of drought and frost. More recently, the emphasis has been on breeding to raise yields. An outstanding example of this has been the development of hybrid corn. In 1937, when the new hybrids were just becoming available, the average American

corn yield was about 25 bushels to the acre. It is now well over 60, and as much as 80 in favourable areas. The case of sorghum is even more remarkable—the average yield actually doubled during the single decade of the 1950's. Higher yields naturally mean that the crop can be concentrated on the best lands, and the inferior lands can be used in other, more suitable ways.

2. In part the progress is due to a greater input of fertilizers. For the American farmer, fertilizer use is a recently acquired habit: the more old-fashioned habit was to move on to new land when the old soil was exhausted. But there is no longer space to do this, and fertilizer use has increased almost fourfold since 1938.

3. In part, too, progress has come with the development of selective weed killers and insecticides. In so far as they both reduce labour needs in weeding and give the cultivated plants a better chance, the effect of these chemicals is to increase the all-round efficiency of the cropping, to combat the spread of worthless plants that readily invade overworked fields, and to increase the stock-carrying capacity of the land.

The scope of this technical improvement has already been stated: agricultural output has been increased by 70 per cent. in 30 years, and can undoubtedly be raised still higher, merely by applying to more farmland the lessons already learned. Meanwhile, profound economic and social changes have accompanied these advances. The greatest of these has certainly been the migration away from the farms. Mechanization has been responsible for a part of this movement, since it cuts labour requirements; but the opposite is also true—that the drift to the towns has made farm labour expensive to hold, and so encouraged farmers to employ machines. In Canada, in spite of an increase of more than 100 per cent. in total population during the period, the farm population was smaller in 1961 than in 1911. In the United States, it was actually less than half as large as in 1911, and during the single decade of the 1950's the farm population lost more than 10 million persons through migration. Yet the United States Department of Agriculture asserts that 'underemployment is a serious problem in agriculture' and 'concluded that if such underemployment were suddenly ended, 1·4 million workers would be added to the list of unemployed'.[1]

[1] *After A Hundred Years*, U.S. Dept. of Agriculture Yearbook, 1962, p. 510

For those who remained, however, other changes were taking place. If the technical aids to farming are making it, as a profession, more profitable and more attractive, they are also responsible for increasing the capital investment necessary for success. In order to succeed in the competitive, surplus-producing agriculture of today, it is necessary for the farmer to make use of every labour-saving device available. But so great a capital investment does this involve that many a farmer's son, who in a previous generation would have set up in his turn as an independent farmer, is unable to afford such a step, and must leave the land to seek work as a wage-earner instead. It would seem true to say that, whereas the formative factor in the American farm economy was once cheapness of land, it is now expense of equipment—an investment of over $20,000 per farm employee.

It is not only between the country and the towns that there has been a movement of population; the pattern is changing within the farm areas themselves, and that in three ways.

1. Use of the motor-car encourages increasing numbers of farmers to live, not in isolation on their holdings, but in a nearby village or town, from which they motor to work each day.

2. The needs of today's farms are more varied than in the past; they include machine spares, chemicals and fuels, and the widening range of purchases that accompany a rise in the standard of living. The effect of this is that, whereas he could formerly satisfy all his day-to-day needs at a local crossroads store, the farmer now tends to transact his business in the nearest town, where a wider range of shops and services is available. In consequence, the smallest form of rural settlement is moribund, and is being replaced in importance by the local supply centres, with their greater capacity for catering to the modern farmer's needs.

3. While the rural population is leaving the farms, there is a reverse movement which, particularly in the vicinity of the big cities, is doing something to balance the trend. City people move out into the old farm homesteads, which become country residences. In many cases the newcomers practise a little farming, without either needing or attempting to make a living from it. In New England, and elsewhere on the marginal lands of the

east, such part-time farming occupies a considerable area.
If the patterns of production have changed, so also have
those of demand. As the standard of living within a country
rises, there occur changes in the kinds of food which the population consumes. In North America these changes have resulted
in a decline in the consumption of bread and potatoes, and an
increase in that of the higher-priced livestock products—meat,
milk, and butter. It is partly in response to this changing
structure of demand, and partly as a consequence of the modern
stress upon scientific land use, that there emerges one further
trend of which we must take note. It is a trend away from the
old regional specializations of the agricultural 'belts', with their
unhealthy tendency to monoculture, and towards diversity
within regions. This diversity is usually taking the form of an
increase in the area under pasture, and the development of
livestock farming. While the trend is most marked in the old
cotton and wheat areas, it is interesting to notice that the plans
for the development of reclaimed lands in the Columbia Basin
and the Central Valley of California were equally emphatic
about the part which it was hoped livestock farming would
play. In all these regions a rising demand for livestock products is assumed, although, to judge by present appearances,
this rise is being over-estimated.

Whether or not this is the case, however, the laying down to
fodder crops of overworked fields, and the encouragement of
livestock farming as a restorative for the land, must certainly
be approved by all those who are concerned for the best
interests of North American agriculture.

4. Farming the Dry Lands

Over much of western North America the rainfall is too
slight, or too unreliable, to permit the growing of crops by the
ordinary methods adopted farther east. This vast, dry west has
for long, therefore, been a region of extensive grazing, much of
it useful, even so, for only a few months in the wetter season of
the year. In these circumstances, the region was producing in
the 1920's an average annual output equivalent to only 35 cents
per acre, or roughly the cost of keeping one head of cattle on the
ranges for one month. The basic problem of the region, then

and now, is somehow to increase this dismally low figure.

Higher output per acre can be obtained either by planting crops or by increasing the numbers of stock carried on the range. Since neither of these things can be done as the natural conditions stand, special methods must be introduced. The two methods which are most widely adopted are dry farming and irrigation.

DRY FARMING

On millions of acres too dry for ordinary cultivation—notably on the Great Plains—cropping is, nevertheless, carried out by the use of techniques which are known collectively as dry farming. The principles underlying these techniques are simple. They are (1) to conserve by every means possible the scanty amounts of moisture available in the soil, and (2) to practise the form of cropping which will make the least demand upon these scanty supplies.

To achieve these objects the farmer generally plants crops with low water requirements, and spaces them more widely than would be normal in the wetter east. The land is usually cropped only in alternate years, and the fallows are so treated as to conserve the moisture of the fallow year for the following crop year.

When we come, however, to the question of how the fallows should be treated, we find that even since the 1930's there has been a marked change of opinion as to the methods to be adopted. The earlier method is well reflected in W. P. Webb's book *The Great Plains*, published in 1931, and dealing with the adaptations of farming technique which were forced upon the early settlers of the region. This method consisted, briefly, of reducing the surface of the fallow land to a 'dust mulch'—a finely powdered surface layer which, it was argued, would reduce loss of water through evaporation. But the drought years of the 1930's all too effectively showed that there was little point in retaining the moisture while losing the soil, which blew away in clouds. Today a different method is commonly used. The field surface is left rough, not powdery, and while the fallows are weeded to ensure that no water is lost to worthless vegetation, the soil is covered with a layer of trash and straw, spread to protect it from the action of both sun and wind.

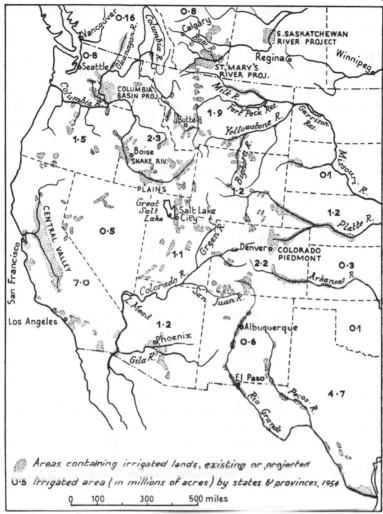

FIG. 21. Western North America: Principal Irrigated Areas.

That moisture can be conserved, and crops grown, by this means seems clear. A large proportion of all North American wheat and sorghum is grown in this way. However, the main question raised by dry farming is one not so much of technique as of desirability. The fact that crops *can* be grown beyond the margins of ordinary cultivation may merely encourage farmers to rash expansion into the climatic danger zones; in other words, it may simply make dangerously possible what ought not to be done at all.

IRRIGATION

The alternative, and much more spectacular, method of extending the farm frontier into dry lands is by irrigation. By 1959 there were some 33 million acres under irrigation in the U.S.A., and over a million in Canada, the bulk of them in Alberta. In the eleven western states of the U.S.A., this irrigated area represents some 30 per cent. of the acreage under crops, and thus plays a part of real importance in the region's life.

Not all of this irrigated area, however, is land reclaimed from desert or semi-desert. In fact, irrigation has been applied in three quite different situations: (1) to bring into use completely waste, arid areas; (2) to increase crop yields in areas where cultivation is already possible, but where scanty rainfall limits growth; and (3) to give security to farmers in areas where rainfall is unreliable, and drought is a menace. Making the desert blossom is only one of the functions of irrigation and therefore, as the next section of the chapter suggests, it is probably an overrated one. Irrigation is of vital importance outside the desert areas, in a *supplemental* role, giving security to the agriculture already carried on there.

Great as has been the contribution of irrigation farming to the development of the west, those who pioneered its use envisaged for it a still wider application. With 34 million acres already irrigated, the present estimate of the additional irrigable area amounts to some 15 million acres. But early estimates were at least double this figure. That a scaling-down of the estimates has been necessary over the past seventy or eighty years is due to a growing appreciation of the fact that irrigation is not a panacea for all the ills of a dry region, but a specialized technique, of limited usefulness and limited application.

The limitations are, in the first place, a product of physical conditions. Apart from the obvious consideration that only the reasonably level areas of the dry west are irrigable, there are three principal factors that restrict the usefulness of this solution.

1. The character of the soil must be suitable for applying irrigation water. If it is too porous or too light, the water will

drain through it too rapidly. On the other hand, a heavy, badly drained soil (or an area so level that there is no natural slope to carry the water off) may become waterlogged. In a number of western projects this has, in fact, happened. The result is serious; not only does the soil become difficult to work, but in areas such as these, where the evaporation rate is high, the moisture is drawn up to the soil surface, and there deposits a salt layer, a 'black alkali' crust, that ruins the land for crops and often can only be removed by expensive flushing with fresh water.

2. Another physical limitation on the size of the area that can be irrigated is the large amount of water needed for the process, whether pumped from wells or diverted from streams. Since most irrigation projects, by their very nature, are in hot, dry areas, the water requirements of the crops grown on them are at a maximum. Furthermore, owing to losses which occur through seepage from the irrigation channels or through evaporation, only about one gallon out of every three that are diverted or pumped to the fields actually reaches the crop roots.

It was this factor of loss *en route* which was overlooked by the early planners, and which led to over-estimates of the irrigable areas that sometimes left them with canals prepared but without water to fill them. Downstream users might find the entire flow of a river diverted to supply irrigation projects farther upstream. In other areas pumping of underground water for irrigation has so lowered the water table that lands which were by nature fertile have become sterile. In Arizona, in California, and in parts of the Dakotas, the water requirements, even of the irrigated lands so far developed, greatly exceed the rate of underground replacement.

3. The third factor is that irrigation possibilities are governed by the *nature* of the water-supply. To be serviceable, the supply must be dependable from year to year, and must be available during the season of greatest need, generally from April to August. But the majority of projects depend upon the flow of streams, and few of the western rivers have a régime that meets these requirements. Not only does their flow vary widely from year to year, but in most cases it reaches its peak in the spring, dwindling away by the late summer to little or nothing.

It therefore becomes inevitable that if these rivers are to be used for irrigation they must be controlled. Storage must be

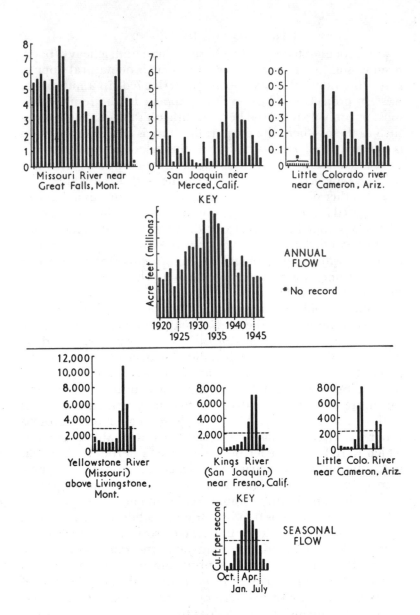

FIG. 22. The Dry West: River flow in the west, showing annual and seasonal variations, illustrated by examples from the San Joaquin, Colorado, and Missouri River systems, at the points indicated. (From *Irrigation Agriculture in the West*, U.S. Dept. of Agriculture Misc. Pub. No. 670, 1948, pp. 25 and 27.)

PLATE V

Cotton Picking: The old (*above*) and the new. The workers in the upper picture can pick about 175 pounds per day: the machine can pick 15,000 pounds

PLATE VI

The Western Ranges—The case for conservation farming. These two photographs, taken in Arizona in 1903 (*above*) and 1943 (*below*), show the same area and the effects on it of overgrazing by livestock. In the later scene, the grass cover has been removed, and the area has been invaded by valueless mesquite provided, both to counter the late-summer shortages and to eliminate year-to-year fluctuations. The necessity for storage further reduces the number of areas to which irrigation can be applied. It also brings into consideration a new and more drastic limiting factor—cost.

The earliest American irrigation projects were simple stream diversions, constructed by a few farmers and costing little but their own labour. Today's projects involve dams, reservoirs, and canals; and the cost may run into billions of dollars as more elaborate schemes are constructed, involving a million acres or more. Since the simplest projects were generally undertaken first, it is probable that any further extensions of the irrigated areas will involve higher, rather than lower, costs.

This change in the nature of the typical irrigation project was given expression when the North American governments recognized that irrigation had become a matter too big to be left entirely to individual initiative. In 1902 there was founded, within the United States Department of the Interior, a Bureau of Reclamation, charged with bringing into use suitable dry lands on the federal domain, and although, in quantitative terms, the bulk of the irrigated acreage is still on private projects, it is the huge Bureau of Reclamation schemes of recent years that have caught the public eye. In Canada the federal government was drawn into the field of irrigation finance by the distress of the Prairie farmers in the depression-and-drought years of the early 1930's, from which resulted the Prairie Farms Rehabilitation Act of 1935.

Not all the costs involved in a new project arise directly out of the irrigation works, but it seems fair to say that, on the large-scale projects which have added most to the irrigated acreage of the west in recent years, the costs have been running at $500 per acre and upwards, with responsible 'all-in' estimates for the Columbia Basin Project as high as $1,000 per acre. For the future, in any case, it is in terms of this kind of project, and this level of expenditure, that the west must think.

As has already been suggested, the financing of such projects is almost inevitably a matter for the government, which undertakes the development of a whole valley or region at a time. But even if the government provides the capital and does so interest-free, the farmer is still burdened by the tremendous cost of repayment and of maintenance. This burden can in practice be reduced by adopting the solution of the multi-purpose project, in which irrigation is not developed alone, but in combination with water power, recreation, or flood control. Part of the cost of constructing the irrigation works can then be set against the other users, and either be paid for by the consumers of electricity, or else be absorbed as a social cost upon the public who benefit from the parks or the flood control. On the Columbia Basin Project, for example, the Department of the Interior decided upon the following allocation of costs and repayments:

Total costs (estimated)—$455 million[1]

Costs attributable to			But repayment called for	
irrigation	.	.	$342 million	from irrigation users	.	$86 million
Costs attributable to			But repayment called for	
power plants	.	$113 million	from power users	$369 million
	$455 million			$455 million

Such a method of developing the dry lands raises questions of first importance, and some of these are discussed in the next section. For the moment, let us return to the original problem—how to raise the basic output of the dry ranges from its pre-war average of 35 cents per acre. That this can be done in places by cultivation, using either dry farming techniques or irrigation, is apparent. But the great bulk of the dry west will never be anything but rangeland, and the particular value of the cultivated patches is not so much that they grow exotic crops, but that they provide a firm agricultural base for the extensive ranching that must always be the dominant agricultural activity of the area. In other words, the simplest, and almost certainly the cheapest, way of increasing western productivity is by using the arable lands not to produce export crops, but to guarantee the well-being of a greatly increased livestock population. But this generalization must now be related to a wider consideration of an agricultural policy suited to the needs of the North American nations as a whole.

[1] The actual costs were, as might be expected, much higher than this by the time the scheme was opened. Almost the whole extra burden of cost was either allocated to power users or absorbed by the federal government, so that the final share of irrigation users was little more than 15 per cent.

5. An Agriculture Policy for the Future

The changing fortunes of the American farmer in the past thirty years have focused attention on the need for a clear policy for agriculture, and so have made the attitude of the government a major factor in the farm economy. The two policy questions which both North American governments have to face are: what help, if any, should be given to the farmers, and how much land is needed for agriculture? In this section, we shall consider the answers of the Canadian and United States governments to these two questions.

CANADA

(a) *Assistance to the farmers.* We have already seen that the two principal, but conflicting, influences on the Canadian government's agricultural policy have been the importance to the nation of agricultural exports and the limited resources of the federal government. While, therefore, it has repeatedly intervened to ensure the smooth flow of agricultural exports, it has been obliged to find ways of doing so which would cost less than those open to its populous neighbour south of the border. In these circumstances, the government has concentrated its attention primarily on aiding the farmers in shipping and marketing, rather than on giving them high price supports. Only with the 1958 Stabilization Act was such a system of guarantees (with a 'floor' of 80 per cent. of the base price) brought into being.[1] Before that date, the government's policies were focused on one particular commodity—wheat—and on the principal area where wheat is grown—the Prairies

1. *Canadian wheat* We have already seen (p. 77) how, as long ago as 1897, the Canadian government intervened with the Canadian Pacific Railway (in the Crow's Nest Pass Agreement) to secure for western farmers low freight rates on wheat exports. Since that time this special consideration for the wheat farmer has continued. In 1912 a Board of Grain Commissioners was set up, with powers to control the grading and handling of wheat. Alongside this control of *shipments* there ran, from 1914

[1] That is, the government sets a 'base price', which is the average price during the preceding 10 years, and guarantees the farmers that, whatever happens to the world market prices, they will not receive less than 80 per cent. of the base price for their produce.

I

onwards, a series of measures controlling wheat and grain *prices* and these culminated, in 1935, in the establishment of the Canadian Wheat Board.

The Board is empowered to buy and dispose of all the wheat —and other grains—that farmers choose to sell to it. It controls the export of all grain from Canada. Its particular importance, however, is that in doing this it sets a price each year which holds good all the year and thus serves as a guaranteed minimum for the crop. Since 1935, therefore, Canadian farmers have had the security of a semi-formal support arrangement which places a floor, but only a low floor, under the prices they receive; the Canadian government, on the other hand, has avoided the vast expense involved in the more rigid price support system used in the U.S.A.

Just because the Canadian price support system has been only a limited one, however, it cannot completely insulate the wheat farmers against the fluctuations in the level of world prices. The primary cause of the trouble is simple: over a series of years the Prairie farmers have harvested bumper crops for which the Board's salesmen have been unable to find markets. Since the Board is only a sales agency and does not buy up surplus crops (as does the United States government), it can help the farmer only to the extent that it can dispose of his grain, while the 1958 support scheme does not apply to grain sold within the Board's jurisdiction. In some years, however, the stocks remaining in the carry-over from the previous crop-year are very large, and then the Board has to buy the new crop on a strict quota basis, which may mean financial difficulty for the wheat farmers, and which has forced the government to introduce a system of loans and advances against the crop.

Canadians may well feel, however, that in this situation they are the victims of the virtues of others—specifically, the government of the United States. In order to dispose of its own huge wheat surpluses, the U.S.A. has used them to strengthen its position abroad and to relieve distress under its aid programmes. But each bushel of wheat that is either given away or sold on easy terms to a country in need has the effect of reducing the size of the genuinely commercial wheat market. To the U.S.A., this is not a matter of the first importance, since the *main* market of its wheat farmers, as we have seen earlier, is at home. But to the Canadian wheat growers, whose prosperity depends upon the sale of wheat on a strict business basis, this international generosity can be a serious threat, just as the sale of surplus United States cotton at less than current market prices undercuts the producers in Egypt or Brazil. Thus the different position occupied by wheat production in the economies of the two countries means that, while both export wheat, their policy interests are quite different.

2. *The Prairies.* The government's concern for agriculture can also be traced in its activities in the Prairie Provinces (which form, of course, the main wheat-producing area). In common with the rest of the Agricultural Interior, the Prairies suffered severely in the years of depression and drought from 1929 to 1934. In 1935, therefore, the government passed the Prairie Farms Rehabilitation Act, under which it took wide powers to restore prosperity to the region. Soil erosion was checked, marginal lands were taken out of cultivation, scientific farming was encouraged, and irrigation schemes were either assisted or developed, to bring security to farmers on the dry margins. Over the years, the P.F.R.A. has been used in so many different settings that it has become a kind of governmental Aladdin's Lamp for the Prairies.

(*b*) *The planning of land use.* The other principal aspect of agricultural policy concerns the planning of future land use and, in the case of Canada, especially the question of opening up new farmlands. Here it is necessary to notice that, in spite of the strenuous efforts that have been made by various agencies, the rate of immigration to Canada's farms is slow; today's newcomers make for the cities. This means that the total area in farms is unlikely to increase greatly over the next few years, and that consequently the expansion of the area in farms, whether by northward penetration or by irrigation of dry areas, should be cautious. On the other hand, some of the present farmlands should never have been farmed at all, and this, coupled with the regional shifts of population that are taking place, may well lead to the abandonment of lands in the east or in the dry Prairies, with a balancing expansion in British Columbia and northern Alberta. Among the questions which the federal government and the provinces must decide is whether they should encourage the marginal farmers to remain where they are (and spend money, if need be, to secure them there), or whether they should sponsor the opening of new lands where resettlement can take place, free from some of the natural and economic handicaps of the old.

THE U.S.A.

Agricultural policy in the United States differs in several respects from that in Canada. The situation of government and farmers in the early 1930's was much the same in both countries —prices were ruinously low, while the farmers kept producing more to try to balance their accounts—but over the past thirty years the policies of the two governments have diverged.

(a) *Assistance to the farmers.* In the 1930's, what was needed was to raise farm prices and to curb farm output, and the New Deal legislation of 1933 sought to do this by a system of acreage quotas—that is, the farmers were offered payment if they would undertake *not* to plant crops. Thirty years later, a version of this same system still operates; the government fixes a 'parity' price for each farm commodity and buys, at a stated percentage of the parity price, the output of farmers who cannot find a market and who abide by their acreage quota.

Over the years, this sytem of support has revealed some weaknesses. One is that a quota system which limits acreage and not output is undermined by the constant rise in agricultural productivity. This simply means that the surpluses (which the whole scheme was designed to eliminate) can be produced from a smaller acreage than previously, but are produced just the same. A second weakness is that, by accepting their acreage quotas, the farmers have cropland to spare; they plant this with alternative crops, and so have built up a succession of new surpluses, which have to be disposed of in their turn. A third weakness is that, even though the surpluses continue to pile up, and cost millions of dollars a week just to store, every effort to reduce the level of price support has been opposed by the farm interests. Yet only such a reduction in the support level can remedy the situation—that, or a degree of government control over the farmers which, politically, would be just as unacceptable to them. But considering that the United States' support system was created originally to rescue farmers from destitution, it is not at all surprising that it fails to work smoothly in a period of much greater national prosperity. An alternative remedy, originally suggested in the 1930's and now revived, is that of the 'soil bank'. Under this scheme, the government makes payments to farmers who rest their land by withdrawing it from cultivation. The land is benefited and the crop acreage is reduced, both without loss to the farmers, whose problem has always been how to carry the *initial costs* of conservation farming, over the period when their crop area is reduced but their yields have not yet begun to rise.

(*b*) *The planning of land use.* The price support programme is the result of a long campaign by the American farm interests to secure their position and to safeguard their future. The same atmosphere of struggle surrounds the other great policy issue of the post war years: the issue of land use and future development. As original owner of 1,400 million acres of land, and as present landlord of 400 million acres, the federal government has from the first been vitally concerned with land policy. A bewildering array of government agencies play a part in carrying it out, and it may be useful to give here a list of those most concerned with problems in this sphere. The Department of the Interior has overall control of the public domain. Under it, the Bureau of Land Management administers 180 million acres of grazing lands, and the Forest Service some 130 million acres of national forests. The Bureau of Reclamation, founded in 1902 for the purpose of bringing into use irrigable dry lands, now administers about 10 million acres. The Bureau of Indian Affairs is another branch of this Department, and has charge of some 55 million acres of Indian Reserves. Other agencies involved are the Department of Agriculture, with its branch, the Soil Conservation Service; the Corps of Engineers, whose tasks of flood control and navigation improvement make it the partner—and sometimes the rival—of the Bureau of Reclamation in building dams; and the Geological Survey, which is responsible for much of the survey and classification of the nation's natural resources.

Briefly, there are two main policy issues. The first is: what should be the attitude of the federal government towards ownership and disposal of the public domain? The second is: if new farmlands are required, to support a growing population and a rising standard of living, where are they to be found?

We have already see in Chapter III how the attitude of the federal government towards the empty lands it owned has changed with the passage of time. Originally viewing these lands as a source of revenue, the government came in time to regard them, in a more ideological light, as providing homes for future generations of Americans. More recently still, the declared policy has been to regard the remaining areas as a source of food and recreation for an expanding population, and to return to the materialistic task of conserving resources.

All three of these attitudes are perfectly legitimate, provided that the government is clear about which object it is pursuing, and frames its legislation to suit the purpose, for the three are not compatible. The mid-nineteenth century was the heyday of the 'homes for Americans' outlook. It was symbolized by the Homestead Act of 1862, which made available 160 acres of public land, at a nominal price, to anyone who would settle on them. It was furthered by the system of railway land grants, under which the government would subsidize the construction of a railway by giving the company title to large areas along its course. The assumption was that the railway company, in order to provide itself with traffic, would promote rapid occupation of its lands so that, by this means also, settlement of the west would be accelerated.

If the policy direction of the nineteenth century was clear, however, that of the twentieth century has been much less so. The rate of immigration into the U.S.A. has been reduced; the best portions of the public domain have been taken up; a conservation movement has developed as a reaction against nineteenth-century carelessness, and as a result of the policy of reservations (see p. 81) the public domain has been closed. Necessarily, this means the end of the 'homes' policy. The present emphasis is, as we have seen, upon America's increasing demand for food and open space, and the role of these lands in their provision. But the framework of the law is still that of the Homestead period, a framework adapted, moreover, to the sub-humid eastern plains rather than to the dry west (of which the remaining part of the domain consists) with its thinly scattered resources of water and grass.

Fifty-four per cent. of the eleven western states is still owned by the federal government. There are many Westerners who accuse the government of neglecting its domain, particularly since 1935, when the Democratic administration closed it. 'Thenceforth the pattern was plain: the public domain was for the Government, not the public' (*Time*, 23 August 1954). There is strong western support, needless to say, for the demand that the domain should be made over to private owners. This is almost certainly unsound, both because private ownership has all too frequently been associated with careless use in the west, and more especially because of the necessity of using most of these areas in a multi-purpose role. There must in that case be some managing agency, for conflict of interest is inevitable: 'Grazing is reduced in the interest of watershed protection and water yield, and the grazier understandably objects. Why should we expect him to do otherwise unless he is motivated by a larger fund of "social consciousness" than are most of us?'[1] In this conflict of interest it seems improbable that there is a better referee than the government.

But while there is no apparent justification for selling out the public domain, there is a strong case for expecting the government to review its policy in the light of present conditions, for conservation is not to be regarded as an alternative to develop-ment (there are Americans who will cry 'Give away' at the least sign that the federal government is encouraging private enter-prise in the west), but as a sensible speed limit on rate of progress. New objectives may make changes desirable. In par-ticular, the acreage limitations[2] imposed on settlers in the Homestead days (when the object was to help bona fide settlers and to thwart the speculators and combines) seem inappropriate in an era concerned primarily with food production.

This, however, merely begs the larger question: is there a need for increased food production and, if so, what lands should be used for the purpose? Here is the last, and probably the most important, policy issue to be discussed in this section.

The population of the U.S.A. is rapidly increasing, and it is estimated that, by 1960 standards, the equivalent of 30 million

[1] M. M. Kelso, 'Current Issues in Federal Land Management', *Journ. Farm Econ.*, vol. xxix, p. 1301.
[2] The principal limitations were: under the 1862 Homestead Act—160 acres; under the 1877 Desert Land Act and the 1916 Homestead Act—640 acres; on Bureau of Reclamation schemes—not more than 40 acres of *irrigated* land per settler.

acres of new cropland will be required by 1975 to feed this larger population. During the past decades, however, as we have already seen, the additional food supplies required for a growing population have come not by increasing the area of farmland, but by raising the yields. There is probably no need, therefore, to bring new land into cultivation in order to produce the *equivalent* of 30 million acres of crops.

But in practice it is quite certain that new areas will be brought under the plough. It is certain, firstly, because new lands are needed to replace worn-out or marginal farmlands, which should be retired from cultivation. It is certain, secondly, because today's higher yields generally involve concentrating on the best areas available, and some of these may not at present be under cultivation. And it is certain, in the third place, because of the way in which farmland is being swallowed up every day for non-agricultural purposes—housing, roads, air-fields, and factories.

The first and second of these points need no special comment: what they amount to is a *rearrangement* of the nation's agricultural areas. It is estimated that there are probably 40 million acres of farmland which should be withdrawn from cultivation, and the soil bank offers farmers an incentive to retire them. They can be replaced by areas more favoured in their topography and soils, but at present needing irrigation, drainage or clearance of forest cover. On these favoured lands, farming will be efficient and productive.

The third point calls for fuller comment. It is calculated that the U.S.A. is now losing agricultural land at the rate of 2 million acres a year. Judged even by the standards of twenty years ago, today's developments in housing, commerce and transport—the homes, the car parks, even the crossroads—all consume space on a gigantic scale. And most of this 'space' represents agricultural land now converted to other uses. Of course, only in a very large country could such a rate of loss be sustained. Not only does the U.S.A. sustain it, but it does so without any particular concern for the farming displaced by the new roadways or factories.

To understand this attitude of unconcern, we must recall not only the traditional American confidence that there is plenty of room for all, but also the hard fact that, in the scale of land values, almost any other form of land use—say a car park for a supermarket—stands higher than farming. Acre for acre, most areas yield a higher return when they are converted from agriculture, regardless of what they are converted to. With so much space available in the U.S.A. we find, therefore, that areas which *can* be used for anything but agriculture will be developed for those other purposes; that agriculture is a kind of residuary legatee; and that there is in progress in the United States what might be described as a game of 'Last-across-the-road-grows-food-for-the-rest'.

This is easily seen in the way in which the eastern seaboard has left the business of food supply to the less crowded lands farther west. As a matter of fact, the north-east is rapidly getting out of the farm business altogether, as Chapter VIII explains. But it comes as something of a shock to find that it is now being seriously suggested that California, the largest food producer among the fifty states, should do the same: that since so many people want to live there agriculture, already being driven away from several hundred thousand acres each year, should take a subordinate place in the state's economy. In other words, the business of agricultural supply, having moved westwards from the crowded east, now promises to rebound from the crowded west coast into the area where, after all, it most naturally belongs—the Agricultural Interior.

For all these reasons, we can assume that new land will be required for agriculture. It can be brought into use by two main methods: reclamation by irrigation in the dry west, or reclamation by other means in the humid east and north-west.

Of these two methods, it is undoubtedly irrigation which has occupied the limelight, particularly during what J K. Galbraith has described as 'the vast post-war boom in our great nationalized industries of dam-building and ditch-digging'.[1] As a method, it has the advantage of producing spectacular results. But in view of the enormous cost of recent schemes, it is necessary to overlook the spectacular, and to be quite clear that this is in fact the most economical way of adding to the food reserves of the nation.

That Westerners are themselves enthusiastic about federal irrigation projects need surprise no one, for the local benefits

[1] J. K. Galbraith, *American Capitalism*, H. Hamilton, 1952, p. 187.

conferred by such a project are great. The government makes the community what is in fact a large interest-free loan; taxable values are much enhanced; and the basis is provided for compact, intensive land use, with all the advantages of concentrated settlement, such as lower costs of services. But on the national level the advantage may be much less distinct. There seems some reason to fear that the decisive factor in government reclamation planning may have been not a clear concept of *national* need, but rather a sectional political influence.[1] This is particularly likely when, as is usually the case, irrigation is linked with the development of electric power, for power supplies in their turn can provide a basis for industrialization, by which the whole region will be enriched.

According to present government estimates, increased crop acreages for the future could be provided by 15 million acres of irrigable lands, 20 million acres that could be made productive by drainage, and 42 million acres which, if cleared of forest or brush, would provide good (Class I or II) arable land. In addition, there are large areas at present under grass that could, if necessary, be cultivated. If the national need is simply for more cropland, then there are millions of acres in the humid east which either are lying idle, or could yield much larger returns if improved. One comparative study[2] has suggested that, for every acre of cropland reclaimed by irrigation in the Columbia Bend, not less than $7\frac{1}{2}$ could have been reclaimed in the southern Piedmont at the same cost. While it is true that many of these idle areas in the east need both drainage *and* clearance, and while it is reasonable that a *part* of the additional cropland required should be obtained by irrigation in the west, it is also true that, in the words of a Department of Agriculture bulletin, 'more of the physically feasible irrigation projects in the West than of the physically feasible drainage works in the South and East are now authorized'.[3]

Here, clearly, is a matter involving the use of federal resources which should be decided by national considerations alone. Where the benefits derived from reclamation works are local benefits, then taxpayers elsewhere are entitled to argue

[1] On this point, see V. W. Johnson and R. Barlow, *Land Problems and Policies*, McGraw Hill, 1954.
[2] R. Ulrich, in *Journ. Farm. Econ.*, vol. xxxv, pp. 62–73.
[3] *Agricultural Land Resources in the United States* (see Further Reading, p. 125), p. 89.

that the financing of such projects should be local too. The two arguments which can legitimately be advanced in favour of western, rather than eastern, development are (1) that in view of the marked growth of population in the west, that is where additional food supplies are likely to be needed, and (2) that the west needs in any case to exploit its water-power reserves, and that irrigation may as well accompany the development and be subsidized by power users. To both these arguments, especially if they are used to justify federal participation, there are clear rejoinders. Upon the merits of each side of the case, and not upon political sectionalism, must depend the future policy of the government.

FURTHER READING

THE Department of Agriculture of both the Canadian and United States governments have issued a great variety of publications, both statistical and descriptive, and their catalogues give details of these. In addition, each state and province, through its Agricultural Experiment Station or equivalent organization, publishes bulletins dealing with local agriculture, and most of them have issued a bulletin with a title like *Types of Farming in . . .* which gives an excellent detailed description of their agriculture. Among specific publications, O. E. Baker's series on 'Agricultural Regions of North America', *Econ. Geog.*, vols. ii–ix, have only recently and partially been superseded by L. Haystead and G. C. Fite's *The Agricultural Regions of the United States* and E. Higbee's *American Agriculture: Geography, Resources, Conservation.* An excellent series of distribution maps are included in *The Agricultural Resources of the World*, by W. Van Royen. For a specifically Canadian reference, see *Canadian Agriculture in War and Peace, 1935–50*, by G. E. Britnell and V. C. Fowke. On the impact of technical change on farming, see E. Higbee's *Farms and Farmers in an Urban Age;* 'Agricultural Production in the United States: The Past Fifty Years and the Next', by C. Harris, *Geog. Review*, vol. xlvii, pp. 175–93, and the 1962 Yearbook of Agriculture, *After A Hundred Years.*

On the subject of dry land farming and agricultural policy there is a vast literature, only a few items of which are by geographers. Perhaps the three most useful books are *Western Land* and *Water Use*, by M. H. Saunderson, *The Federal Lands*, by M. Clawson and B. Held, and *American Resources*, by the geographers J. R. Whitaker and E. A. Ackerman. Forecasts of future development are given in *Agricultural Land Resources in the United States*, U.S. Dept. of Agriculture, Ag. Information Bull. No. 140, June 1955. See also *Land Use and Its Patterns in the United States*, by F. J. Marschner, U.S. Dept. of Agriculture Handbook No. 153, 1959, and the 1963 Yearbook, *A Place to Live.* Among the periodicals, the *Journal of Farm Economics* and *Land Economics* contain valuable materials.

V
INDUSTRY

1. *Introduction*

I T is estimated that a half of all the world's manufactured goods are produced in the U.S.A. In relation to its small population, Canada's share in world output is also high. That North America should thus have taken over the role of nineteenth-century Britain as world manufacturer is to be explained only partly in terms of rich natural resources. Great as these are, another part of the explanation must be sought in outlook and in organization, without which the resource base might have lain as valueless as in the days when the Indians roamed the continent.

There are certain impressions of American industry traditionally held by Europeans—that it is made up of huge combines operating equally huge plants; that the Americans have invented a machine to do everything in life; and that American industry possesses an almost miraculous efficiency, when judged by such standard criteria as output per worker or output per hour. Although few aspects of American life are more widely misunderstood, these crude impressions do serve at least to call attention to the factors which have been decisive in establishing North America's industrial supremacy.

(*a*) *Size of units.* While there are thousands of plants in both Canada and the U.S.A. which employ only a handful of workers, it is true that in most industries output is dominated by a few large corporations, and that these tend to spread between the two countries without much reference to the international boundary. Far from finding such a situation undesirable, most Americans contend that there is no reason to be afraid of bigness as such, and that the ever-increasing complexity of modern industrial processes, together with the need for more costly research, absolutely requires the creation of larger industrial units. Further, it may be pointed out that it is only in the past few years that the control of such huge business units has been made possible—by devices like the electronic calculator, or by telephonic and radio communication—and that the larger units are merely taking advantage of these advances. Only when the leadership of an industry falls into the hands of *too* few firms does the equally strong, and often conflicting, American fear of monopoly overcome the widespread belief that bigness and goodness are somehow allied. Then the Anti-Trust Laws are invoked against the monopolist, but often in a manner sufficiently uncertain to emphasize, rather than resolve, this basic dilemma in the American mind. Meanwhile the industrial corporation, with its billions of dollars in capital assets and its vast expenditures on scientific and social work, has become a profoundly influential element in the life of the nation.

(*b*) *Mechanization.* The widespread mechanization in both factory and home in North America is perhaps best accounted for in two ways. On the one hand, the general level of American labour costs (which finds its best-known modern expression in the price of American haircuts) has always been high enough to encourage manufacturers to seek ways of replacing men by machines. On the other hand, a high standard of living makes available surplus income that can be spent on removing the drudgery from life by the installation of machinery. To these two considerations may be added a third, the size of the North American market is sufficient to encourage large-scale production techniques, based upon the classic American industrial device of moving-belt construction and the more recently established control methods of automation.

(*c*) *Productivity.* Part of the explanation of the great productivity of American industry lies in what has already been said about mechanization. But it would be a mistake to attribute high productivity solely to this factor, as was clearly recognized by the productivity teams from Britain which visited their industrial counterparts in the United States between 1949 and 1952. In their reports the teams constantly referred not so much to the number of machines as to the attitude of the workers and the skill of the management. While North America has its share of labour disputes, there is on the whole a carefully preserved industrial climate which encourages the worker to maximum effort and which is the product of planning, based on detailed research, by a trained management. To these joint factors of managerial ability, and of huge expenditures on research into both the technical and the human aspects of industry, America owes much of its present industrial advantage.

Such elaborate research programmes are only made possible by the basic condition that underlies all American industrial development and that multiplies whatever advantages of technique or skill the American worker may possess—the great size of the internal market. The manufacturer who anticipates sales in terms of millions can spend far more on research—or for that matter on any of his other overheads—than the manufacturer whose sales will number only thousands, without incurring extra cost per unit. Here then lies another secret of American industrial success.

All these circumstances have their effect on the changing geographical patterns of the continent's manufacturing, and it is now time to make a brief survey of the industrial areas.

2. *The Distribution of Industry*

While one of the features of modern industrialization in North America has been the tendency for industry to spread into rural districts, there remain certain major concentrations. These are:

(*a*) *The Middle Atlantic Region*, stretching along the Atlantic coast from New York to Baltimore and inland to such towns as Reading and Bethlehem. As a 'funnel' for many of the United States' imports and exports, this well-established area attracts a major share of the nation's processing, with a full range of industries from the heaviest to the lightest.

(*b*) *The Northern Appalachians*. In the valleys round Scranton and Wilkes-Barre there is a small industrial area, located on the Pennsylvania anthracite field. Suffering today from problems of accessibility and from the decline in anthracite production (see p. 133), this old industrial area faces an unpromising future.

(*c*) *Southern New England*. In the three states of Massachusetts, Rhode Island, and Connecticut, where manufacturing is widespread, lies North America's oldest industrial area. There are marked local specializations, among them textiles and leather goods, with a growth of new industries introduced to relieve dependence on older ones whose fortunes are declining. Boston is the largest manufacturing centre and the commercial hub of the area today, as it has been throughout New England's era of industrial development.

(*d*) *The Mohawk Valley*, a linear industrial belt stretching from Albany to Rochester, N.Y. Benefiting by their unrivalled location on one of North America's natural 'connecting links', a number of manufacturing towns have grown up, each with its own specialities.

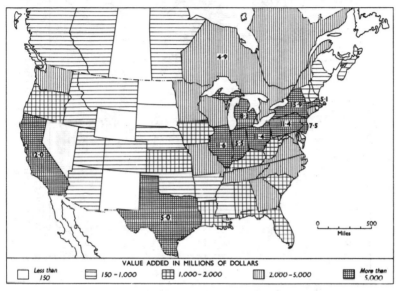

VALUE ADDED IN MILLIONS OF DOLLARS

☐ Less than 150   ▤ 150 – 1,000   ▦ 1,000 – 2,000   ▥ 2,000 – 5,000   ▦ More than 5,000

FIG. 23. North America: Value added by manufacture, by states and provinces, 1958.

(*e*) *The St. Lawrence Valley*, for long the industrial core of Canada. This area is focused upon the great centre of Montreal, which contains some 13 per cent. of Canada's manufacturing workers and has a wide range of industries. Elsewhere the processing of forest products predominates. The use of hydro-electric power is basic to the valley's industrial development.

(*f*) *The Industrial Eastern Interior*. Throughout a wide region that includes the Ohio Valley, the eastern Corn Belt and southwestern Ontario, industry has everywhere penetrated into what is still basically an agricultural section and has created such large industrial centres as Toronto and Cincinnati. While industry's original business in this area was the supply of farm requirements and the processing of farm products, the region

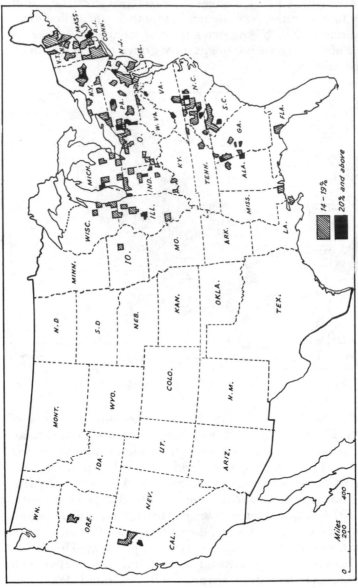

FIG. 24. U.S.A.: Intensity of manufacturing activity. The map shows those counties where, in 1947, more than 14 per cent. of the total population was employed in manufacturing. (Compiled from the U.S. Census of Manufactures, 1950.)

has attracted many other industries spilling over from the more crowded parts of the old manufacturing regions.

Geographically a part of the *Eastern Interior*, but functionally distinct, are three of the most intensively industrialized areas of the continent.

(*g*) *The Pittsburgh–Lake Erie Region*, stretching along the coal and iron routes of the Great Lakes and Appalachian area from Toledo to Hamilton, Ont., and southward into Ohio and western Pennsylvania. This is the core area of American heavy industry.

(*h*) *The Chicago–Lake Michigan Region*. This has many of the characteristics of the Lake Erie steel area, but it also fulfils the supply and processing functions typical of the Eastern Interior as a whole. In both roles Chicago dominates the Interior, with more than 5 per cent. of United States industrial employment.

(*i*) *Michigan*. Although Michigan, too, is geographically a part of region (*f*), it is treated separately here because the state's manufacturing is so dominated by the automobile industry. Nearly 30 per cent. of Michigan's industrial workers are associated directly with it, and in Detroit this figure rises to over 30 per cent. Branches of the industry are to be found scattered widely throughout the state.

(*j*) *The Cities of the Western Interior*, among which the most important are Winnipeg, Minneapolis–St. Paul, Omaha, Kansas City, and St. Louis. These cities, and scores of lesser centres, perform in nearly every case the same double function. They serve as regional supply points, and they participate in the Midwest's basic industries—meat packing, flour milling, and the production of agricultural machinery.

(*k*) *The South-Eastern Region*, a wide horseshoe round the southern end of the Appalachians. An area of scattered industry rather than of great manufacturing centres, it has been the scene of much recent development, powered by hydro-electricity and Southern petroleum, and has specializations in cotton textiles, tobacco, chemicals, and plastics.

(*l*) *The Texas and Gulf Coast Region*. This industrial area is of recent growth, and its resources and facilities have already attracted a wide variety of plants to the coast and to the inland oilfield regions, which are dominated by Houston and by the

K

Dallas-Forth Worth conurbation respectively.

(*m*) *The Pacific Coast*. Here, industry is concentrated in four or five nodes—the Vancouver area, the lowlands of Puget Sound and the lower Columbia, the San Francisco Bay Region, and the Los Angeles–San Diego lowland. As another new industrial area, the Coast has developed a wide range of products for both local and national markets, with a long statistical lead for three types of industry: food processing, lumber manufacturing, and transport equipment.

Of the factors of location that influence this industrial pattern, some—the classic forces of proximity to coal supplies, to means of transport, or to markets—are common to all industrial communities. But what may be regarded as a peculiarly North American phenomenon is the influence on distribution of the force of local competition.

In a great free-trade area like Canada or the U.S.A., where space is usually plentiful and both resources and markets are widely scattered, the manufacturer generally has the choice of a number of equally suitable locations for his plant. Where this is the case, he can base his final decision not merely on broad considerations of markets or transport but on a detailed study of social conditions in the rival locations he has in mind. That is to say, being assured of a number of reasonably suitable sites, he can pick the one which will give to his plant and his workers the pleasantest possible surroundings and the richest community life. The kind of factor upon which he will ultimately make his decision may well be: what recreational facilities will this community afford the workers? Are the schools good? Does the appearance of the town show the citizens to be progressive and house-proud? How efficient are the public services? That these social considerations should bulk so large in the manufacturer's mind may upset the geographer's explanations, but the prominence given to them betokens a high standard of living, a mobile labour force, and a concern for the industrial worker that would have been welcome in earlier phases of industrialization.

The opposite side of the matter—the community's approach —is equally significant. State with state and city with city, the communities of North America compete with each other to attract to themselves new business, business which will increase their tax incomes and provide new sources of employment. Most self-respecting communities want to expand, and will seek in doing so to maintain a balanced employment structure and to attract desirable forms of industry—those that will be clean to live with or that will bring to the community a skilled type of worker with high wage rates. If a manufacturer is planning for this type of industry, he will probably be wooed by the local Chamber of Commerce; he may perhaps be offered bargain tax rates as an added inducement. If his coming would harm the social environment of the community, he will be discouraged.

This form of competition has been particularly evident where the federal government has been building industrial plant for military purposes. Government investment of this kind is usually a valuable addition to the assets of an area, and competition to secure contracts is keen. What atomic power has meant to Tennessee, or missiles to California and Florida, can never be fully assessed, but it amounts to hundreds of millions of dollars of additional income for the state.

3. Coal, Iron, and Steel

COAL

The backbone of North American industry is formed by a continental coal production of between 400 and 450 million tons and a steel-making capacity in excess of 140 million tons. Upon the movements of these huge quantities of primary industrial materials depends the whole pattern of an industrial structure of unparalleled magnitude.

By far the greatest part of the coal output comes from the Appalachian region. Virtually all of North America's anthracite is produced on the Pennsylvania fields, where today's output of this once-popular fuel (less than 20 million tons) is far below the 1916 peak of 98 million. Of the continent's bituminous coal, some 70 per cent. of the annual production is mined in the great Western Appalachian field. Underlying the plateau section of the Appalachian System, this remarkable gift of nature provides wide areas of good coking coal that are often aligned in thick horizontal seams which outcrop on valley sides and afford the easiest possible conditions for mining. The earliest development occurred in the northern end of the field, in southwestern Pennsylvania, and with the passage of time mining has spread south through West Virginia and into eastern Kentucky.

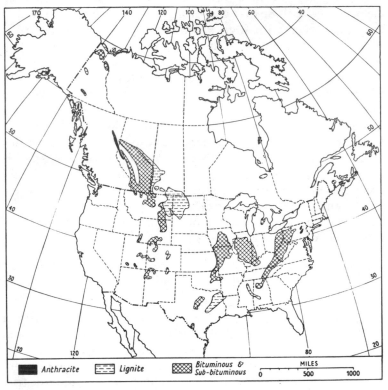

FIG. 25. North America: Coalfields.

Meanwhile, far to the south, the field has been developed around Birmingham, in Alabama, where it is partnered by iron ore deposits. Today, Appalachian coal supplies a continent-wide market, moving not only north to the steel mills but eastward and westward to the ports of Hampton Roads and the Great Lakes, whence it is distributed by water.

Far behind the Appalachian region in importance rank the Eastern Interior fields of Indiana, Illinois, and Missouri. Nevertheless, their total output is considerable, and they supply a wide area of the Midwest. But their usefulness is limited by the fact that their coal is not generally suitable for coking.

In the western half of the continent there are vast scattered coal reserves, many of them low-grade. They are mined in places as various as Alberta, Wyoming, Utah, and Colorado in order to supply local requirements, but their further exploitation is hampered by two factors. (1) There is no large market within economic range of these deposits; and (2), as we shall later see, in these western and south-western parts of the continent, coal is climbing the economic gradient of competition against oil and natural gas. Western coal production in both Canada and the U.S.A. has generally proved profitable only in relation to local needs: many of the early mines were operated by the railways primarily for coaling their own locomotives.

Coal production in North America today is well past its peak: in 1961, it amounted to some 420 million tons in the U.S.A. and 10 million in Canada. This has been mainly due to the competition of other fuels, the effect of which is shown by the following figures:

Energy Consumption in the U.S.A., 1930–60

(*Percentage of total consumption supplied by various sources*)

| | Coal | | | Natural | Water |
	Anthracite	*Bituminous*	*Petroleum*	*gas*	*power*
1930	7·7	53·5	25·1	9·9	3·5
1940	5·2	47·2	31·4	12·4	3·8
1950	3·0	34·8	37·2	20·3	4·7
1960	1·0	22·2	41·4	31·5	3·9

The coal industry, recognizing the weakness of its position, has fought back well. It has modernized equipment, mechanized production and succeeded in stabilizing total output. However, the price of success must not be overlooked—it has been achieved by replacing miners by machines. In 1939, coal mining employed almost half a million persons. By 1954, the figure had been exactly halved, and in 1960 it was only a little over 200,000. (On the Pennsylvania anthracite fields, employment fell from 180,000 in 1914 to 20,000 in 1960.) Whatever comfort production figures may give to the industry as a whole, these have been times of deep distress in the unemployment areas of West Virginia and Kentucky. The importance of the coal industry to these states is best seen in one simple fact:

before the war, the term 'depressed area' in the U.S.A. applied almost by definition to the Old South. Now it refers to a region which has the same name as the coalfield—Appalachia.

IRON ORE

Over the past hundred years North America's iron ore production has been just as markedly dominated by a single source as has its coal production. This source is the vast ore bodies on the shores of Lake Superior, first made accessible to industry by the opening of the Soo Canal in 1855, and reaching full development with the opening up of the Mesabi Range in the 1890's. From this wilderness area, where the main ore bodies lie almost ideally accessible for working, there has flowed a century's supply of high-grade ore for Canada and the U.S.A. alike.

The future prospects for Superior ore, however, are less encouraging. The tremendous drain of the past decades, and especially of the period since 1940, has removed the most accessible and most valuable ores. Huge quantities of lower-grade ore remain, but the situation confronts the steelmen with two alternatives. One is to process, or 'beneficiate', the low-grade ore at plants in the vicinity of the mines, in order to reduce the bulk of the material that has to be carried across the Lakes, and to supply the industry's furnaces with the same grade of material as they are at present adjusted to consume. Such plants have already been established on the Lake Superior shore, and low-grade taconite deposits are being treated in this way. Inevitably, however, a new item of cost is involved in this extra processing stage. The other alternative is to seek new sources elsewhere.

Around Birmingham, Ala., there are deposits of ore which have been worked for a century and which, in conjunction with the adjacent Appalachian coal, form the basis of a well-established and low-cost steel industry. But, for the quantities of ore they require, the northern steelmen are at present looking to two other sources—Labrador and Latin America.

The story of the discovery of iron ore in the forested wilderness of Labrador, 300 miles north of the St. Lawrence; of how the concession holders battled with the elements, and of how at length the ore fields were linked by rail with tidewater, has lost nothing in the telling. More prosaically, the companies involved—in which Great Lakes interests are prominent—are now shipping some 15 million tons a year from Sept Iles (Seven Islands) and Port Cartier. Some of this is low-grade ore which has already been beneficiated like that from Lake Superior. This Labrador ore is now available to replace Mesabi ore throughout the Lake Erie–Pittsburgh area and on the Atlantic coast. About half of it moves west by the St. Lawrence Seaway (p. 165); with the present freight rate structure, the costs of moving it to Pittsburgh via the Seaway and via the Atlantic coast ports are roughly equal.

Imported ores from Cuba, Venezuela, or Chile are widely used by the east coast steel mills, and both the largest companies—United States Steel Corporation and Bethlehem—have made big investments in Venezuela. In view of the prospects for Mesabi, it is significant also that when, in the early 1950's, U.S. Steel was seeking a site for its newest integrated steel-mill, it chose an Atlantic seaboard location—Fairless, near Trenton, N.J.—where it uses Latin American ores almost exclusively.

THE STEEL INDUSTRY

The assembly and dispatch of the great quantities of heavy materials with which a modern steel mill deals are problems of such dimensions as to make the steel industry 'transport-orientated'. In terms of quantities involved the ore presents the biggest problem, but in terms of cost the most expensive item is the shipment of the finished product. In practice, therefore, the decisive location factor in the modern industry is likely to be proximity to markets. However, such is the capital investment represented by an integrated mill (U.S. Steel spent $400 million on the Fairless Works), that another feature of the industry is its high degree of inertia. The giant corporations which alone can afford to compete in such circumstances will accept higher costs for a period, in unfavourable locations, rather than have to build afresh.

Bearing in mind these factors, we can now briefly consider the industry's distribution. There are, firstly, several plants on the Atlantic coast. They receive most of their ore from abroad and their coal from the Appalachians; it generally travels by rail to Hampton Roads, and by water from there. The strength of their position lies in their access, by water or by land, to the great Middle Atlantic market area. It is, in fact, a position strong enough to enable them to supply New England as well and to give to the oft-proposed New England steel works (which would be much farther from its coal supplies) only a slender chance of competing successfully.[1]

The largest part of the steel industry, however, is to be found in the central region, between Chicago and Milwaukee in the west and Buffalo and Hamilton, Ont., in the east. The centre-line of this region is the Great Lakes routeway by which Superior ore—in recent years, some 60 million tons per annum—moves eastward (see Fig. 50). Originally, the movement was a simple one: ore from Superior was carried to meet Appalachian coke at Pittsburgh. Since the 1890's, however, the pattern has grown more complex, for a reverse flow of coal shipments has developed, amounting to about 40 million tons per annum, and with coal and ore moving in opposite directions between Duluth and West Virginia, the flow could clearly be interrupted not only at Pittsburgh but equally at any other point *en route*. In practice, the most suitable place at which to interrupt it is at the lake-shore ports where trans-shipment takes place. Thus the industry has spread from its Pennsylvania–Ohio nucleus back along the centre-line, with concentrations in the first instance at the ports along the Lake Erie shore and then at other Great Lakes ports like Chicago and Hamilton, which are not on the direct Duluth–Pittsburgh route but are equally accessible to the ore carriers. Indeed, the industry spread the whole distance to Duluth, where a large steel mill was opened in 1915, but this proved to be an over-optimistic extension of the process, owing to the remoteness of the plant from its markets.

Three other groups of steel works must be briefly mentioned. One is that around Birmingham, Ala., at the southern end of the Appalachian coalfield. Here the juxtaposition of fuel and ore makes for low production costs and gives the industry a dominant position in the expanding markets of the south and south-west. The second location is in the Maritime Provinces

[1] This is the calculation, at least, of W. H. Isard and J. H. Cumberland in 'New England as a Possible Location for an Integrated Iron and Steel Works', *Econ. Geog.*, vol. xxvi, pp. 245–59.

of Canada, where local coal supplies are used in conjunction with ores imported from Newfoundland. Output is small and remoteness hampers development.

The other group consists of the scattered plants of the west. While a few of these, such as that at Pueblo, Colo., are of earlier date, most of them are a product either of military supply programmes in the Second World War or of post-war expansion by eastern firms into the new western markets. Thus each of the major industrial centres of the Gulf and Pacific coasts—Houston, Los Angeles, San Francisco–Oakland, Seattle—is a steel producer, although not one of them is well situated in terms of raw material supply. In addition, the United States government constructed, and U.S. Steel now owns, the Geneva Works near Salt Lake City, a plant with reasonable access to ore and coal (100 to 200 miles of movement in each case), but remote from the market it was built to serve, on the Pacific coast. In one way or another, therefore, all these western plants operate under considerable handicaps.

This distribution pattern of the steel industry was for a long time stable. Before the Second World War it was maintained by a number of factors, among them the power of the great corporations, which found expression in the price system known as 'Pittsburgh Plus'. Under this system, all steel sold was, by agreement within the industry, priced as if it had been produced in Pittsburgh and shipped from there, even though in reality the purchaser fetched it himself from a mill in his own city. The object of this device was to discourage the spread of production into outlying market areas and thus to protect the steelmakers' huge investments in the central region. It was a kind of stage-managed industrial inertia, enforced by the overwhelming power of the U.S. Steel Corporation.

But the pattern is now changing. In 1924 Pittsburgh Plus was declared illegal, and in 1948 its successor, the basing point system, was also abolished, freeing the industry from artificial restraints upon relocation. At the same time other, technological, changes are taking place. The industry is using less iron ore and more scrap metal in its furnaces. To the extent that this occurs (and on the west coast 85 per cent. or more of the furnace material is scrap), it lessens the importance of access to ore and increases that of access to scrap—which is found in areas of greatest steel use, that is, in the market areas. The industry is using less coal too, as plant efficiency increases, and especially because of the tendency to integration, by which the metal is heated only once and goes through all the stages of production in one continuous process. To these technological and pricing changes must be added the effects of the decline in the Lake Superior ores and of the government's policy of encouraging industrial decentralization. All these influences combine in support of the view that, if further expansion of the industry takes place, it will be in those market areas—the Atlantic and Pacific coasts and the Detroit and Chicago areas—which are at present deficient in capacity, and that it will occur at the expense of the old nuclear area around Pittsburgh which has for so long dominated American steel production.

4. *Petroleum and Natural Gas*

We must now consider briefly North America's other sources of power for industry. The first of these are petroleum and natural gas, of which the U.S.A. is both the largest producer and the largest consumer in the world. In 1961 its output was 2,600 million barrels of crude petroleum (or half the total world output) but the country was, nevertheless, a net importer. The production of natural gas was in excess of 13,000,000 million cubic feet.

The rise of the United States petroleum industry has been one of the great economic phenomena of the past century. It is only about a hundred years since an oil strike in western Pennsylvania ushered in the era of commercial exploitation. The early days of the industry were marked by savage competition, from which John D. Rockefeller's Standard Oil Trust emerged in 1882 with a virtual monopoly of the continent's refining and pipeline facilities and so a stranglehold upon the producers who depended on these facilities. The early Pennsylvanian fields were soon eclipsed by those of California, opened in the 1890's, and much more so by the south-western fields which came in after 1901. New fields were discovered and new wells were drilled in such numbers that production far outstripped demand and untold wastage occurred. The wastage and accompanying fluctuations in price gave to the oil states and the oil companies alike an interest in controls, and in the 1930's quota systems were introduced. In the Second World War the federal government intervened in the national interest with a nation-wide quota scheme, which the industry has, since the war, voluntarily applied. Thus, after 80 years of competitive exploitation, a self-imposed sobriety has come to mark the industry. Today the leading producer-states are Texas, California, Louisiana, and Oklahoma, while Kansas, Illinois, Wyoming, and New Mexico play a smaller but still significant part.

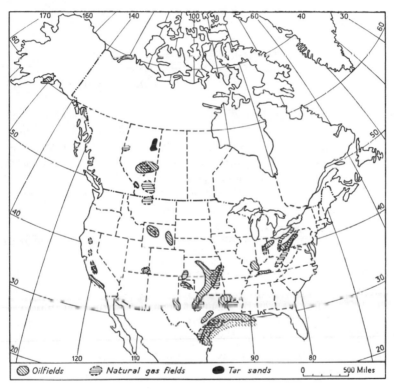

Fig. 26. North America: Petroleum and Natural Gas. (For a more detailed map of the Alberta oilfields, see Fig. 64.)

As the petroleum industry has grown over the past century, so too has its market. In the early days the product in demand was kerosene, for lighting and heating. Then at the turn of the century the advent of the internal combustion engine created an entirely new market, which was the prime cause of the great increase in exploration and production in the period 1900–40. Today 75 per cent. of the total petroleum output is converted into motor fuels. The next development was the emergence of the petro-chemical industries, which provided a market for the by-products that had formerly gone to waste in the process of petrol production. Finally, there has been the growth of a market for natural gas as a fuel. This gas, present in many oil wells, was for long regarded as a nuisance and was either burnt or allowed to escape. Only recently has natural gas come to be appreciated as a fuel in its own right, and been piped away to the factories and homes of almost the whole continent. Since 1925 United States production has increased sevenfold. Thus, with the passage of time, the industry has achieved an ever fuller use of its raw materials and reached a widening circle of market outlets.

In Canada the industry's development is far more recent. As lately as 1936, the country produced only one and a half million barrels of oil and 28,000 million cubic feet of natural gas. The comparable figures for 1962 were 244 million barrels and 955,000 million cubic feet. A long period of intensive but almost fruitless search was crowned by the strike at Leduc, near Edmonton, in 1947. This was followed by a series of other discoveries in Alberta and later in Saskatchewan.

Today, under the watchful eye of the provincial governments, production is increasing as fast as new outlets for the oil can be found. Pipelines connect the Prairie fields with both the cities of Ontario and the Pacific coast. However, the most significant feature of the new oil area is not its production— which by United States standards is at present small—so much as its location within the continent. The north-west has up to now been largely dependent on outside oil supplies, and from a stragetic point of view the opening of the Alberta field was most timely.

The petroleum industry has three phases: production, transport, and refining. But such is the nature of the commodity that the producer is almost inevitably dependent upon the transporter and the refiner. It was appreciation of this truth that was the secret of Rockefeller's early success in oil, and his refusal to enter the sphere of production finds its modern counterpart in the fact that while the petroleum industry, like the steel industry, is dominated by a few corporations—the 'majors'—this dominance is more marked in transport and refining than in production. The majors in the United States control over 90 per cent. of the refinery capacity and most of the pipelines, but only 35 per cent. of the producing wells. (Even this low percentage is a comparatively recent development. It is the need for, and the creation of, more involved techniques of prospecting that has brought the majors into this field, and largely replaced the lone prospector by the team of oil company scientists with their costly research methods.) Thus the control of the large industrial units over the small units and individuals engaged in production is indirect, but nevertheless real.

The network of transmission pipelines for various petroleum products that has grown up over the years now forms a vitally important element in the continental communication system. While the trunk lines run from the south-west to the Middle Atlantic region and the Chicago and Detroit areas, few settled parts of the continent are today isolated from the network. Alternative routes to northern markets are provided by the pipelines to the Pacific and Gulf coasts, from which a fleet of tankers carries both crude and refined products to the Atlantic coast and to foreign ports.

The refining phase of the industry may in principle be located anywhere between the well and the market, but for technical reasons the refineries are usually either in the market areas or at the ports of shipment from the oilfields. Refinery towns are dotted along the coastline of Texas, Louisiana, and southern California, while important concentrations are also to be found on the New Jersey–Chesapeake Bay shore, adjacent to the great eastern cities, and at points along the Great Lakes and Mississippi waterways.

Since the Second World War petroleum and gas have made great strides in competition with coal as a domestic and industrial fuel. The railways have changed from steam to diesel traction (see p. 169). Road and air traffic consume increasing quantities of the industry's products. On the domestic side, a large proportion of America's housewives now cook with gas from Texas or Oklahoma and not from a local gasworks. But the progressive substitution of oil fuels for coal and the constant rise in consumption are a cause of much anxiety, since they raise, at least for the oil states and certainly for the nation's strategists, the profoundly important question of the correct rate of use of oil reserves. The cost advantage at present enjoyed by petroleum products may be replaced in a generation or two by an absolute shortage of oil. Thus the question at issue is whether North America should slow the rate of oil extraction and import more for the present, or whether exploitation should continue at maximum rates, whatever the risk for the future.

Needless to say, the issues raised by such a question are of the first importance. From a strategic point of view, it would seem best to husband the continent's oil supplies against an emergency when Latin American or Middle East oil might be inaccessible, and to increase imports to meet present needs. The United States government, however, has actually issued recurrent warnings to the oil companies to *reduce* imports, on the ground that nothing should be done to discourage or lessen the efforts of the home producers in maintaining the search for new oil supplies.

But there is a further consideration, to which we must now turn—that there are other sources of power likely to be available, alternative to both coal and petroleum: electricity and atomic energy.

5. *Electric Power and Atomic Energy*

The rivers of North America provide the continent with a valuable potential source of power. This the two nations have exploited to such good purpose that the U.S.A. and Canada rank first and second respectively among the countries of the world in terms of installed hydro-electric generating capacity.[1] Even so, the present development represents only about one-quarter of the continental potential.

The U.S.A. is favoured by the fact that, although many of its power sites, both developed and potential, are in the remote

---

[1] It must be added, however, that while virtually all Canada's electricity is water-generated, hydro-electricity accounts for only one-fifth of the total electricity output of the U.S.A.; the remaining four-fifths are steam- or petrol-generated.

Mountain West and on the Pacific coast, yet the Industrial East and the Midwest also possess tremendous resources in the New England rivers and the Mississippi Basin. Canada's potential is concentrated in two areas—the southern half of the Laurentian Shield and the mountains of British Columbia. In the first of these areas, it is well placed to power the industries of the St. Lawrence Valley, and has played a vital role in their development. A good deal of the potential, however, is in remote areas, and its use involves either long-distance transmission or the location of plants at the power sites, as in the case of Kitimat (p. 454).

Almost every major river in the United States has now been 'put to work', though not all of them as spectacularly as the

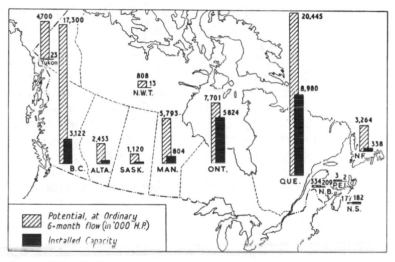

Fig. 27. Canada: Hydro-electric resources and development, by provinces, 1957.

now-famous Tennessee. Of the potential remaining undeveloped—some 110 million kilowatts—over half is in the Mountain and Pacific regions, with about one-sixth in the state of Washington alone. Here it is the Columbia River, already harnessed by such giant works as the Grand Coulee and Bonneville Dams, that represents the principal source for future development.

The three areas of the continent in which hydro-electricity
has been particularly important in industrial development are
the Pacific North-West, the Tennessee Valley, and eastern
Canada. The first of these, remote from supplies of either coal
or oil, could never have responded as it did to the demand
created by war in the Pacific without drawing upon its one
local source of power. The Tennessee Valley, although close to
the Appalachian coalfields, has found an altogether new prosperity in power development and has been the scene of a new
type of rural industrialization, made possible by the use of
electrical energy. In the St. Lawrence Valley and southern
Ontario, another area situated none too favourably in relation
to coal and oil, electric power supplies have been sufficient not
only to support Canada's industrial core,[1] but also to permit of
a considerable export of power across the border to the heavy-
consumption areas of the north-eastern United States. Completion of the St. Lawrence Seaway made a further 2 million
kilowatts of generating capacity available for the expanding
industries of the valley.

Despite the rapid increases in generating capacity brought
about by the construction of large numbers of dams in recent
years, many parts of the continent are suffering from shortage
of power. Even the Pacific North-West, for all its Columbia
Basin development, suffers in this way and the T.V.A., with
heavy power commitments to atomic energy plants, now produces far more electricity from thermal power stations it has
had to build than from turbines at the dams for which it is
famous.

Apart from the material problems to be met in increasing
capacity to meet present demand, there has been another, political, hindrance to expansion in the U.S.A. This is the question
whether the new power schemes should be in government or
private hands. The emergence of the T.V.A., followed by the
Bonneville Power Administration, as federal agencies selling
electricity in competition with private companies, touched off a
political dispute that is still a burning issue wherever new con-

[1] Thus R. L. Hearn writes, in 'Ontario Hydro—A Pattern for Progress', *Can.
Geog. Journal*, vol. l, p. 217, 'The economic history of Ontario over the past 50
years is inextricably interwoven with the progressive pattern formed by the power
transmission lines. . . . As "trade followed the flag", so industrial development and
population congregated along the power lines.'

struction is projected, be it on the Columbia, the Snake, the Colorado, or the Missouri. While the co-ordinating role of the government is generally accepted, there seems no need for the government therefore to assume responsibility for all construction, nor indeed any likelihood that Congress would vote the funds necessary. In spite of this, the government has not always encouraged private development, with the result that between the two contestants the rivers have flowed on unharnessed.

The impact of atomic energy upon American industry is a subject about which it is still too early for the geographer to make any prediction. Suffice it to say that the determination of the North American nations to find peaceful applications for this new source of power makes it certain that changes will be taking place in the organization and distribution of industry, just as charcoal, coal, and electricity have in their turn created each its characteristic industrial landscape. In so far as the initial application of atomic energy is likely to be in the generating of electricity, we may expect the appearance of the same geographical features as have already emerged in areas where industry relies largely on electric power, and especially we may expect industrial decentralization. That power will become rapidly cheaper seems unlikely at present; the atomic pile will simply replace bulkier fuels. Perhaps, therefore, the newly industrialized areas of the south-east and north-west provide the geographer with the best foretaste of the effect of this mightiest of all industrial resources.

6. *Two Sample Industries—Automobiles and Textiles*

It is clearly impossible to describe here all of the major industries of North America; space permits the discussion only of samples. In choosing these samples, we may well turn our attention to the manufacture of automobiles and of textiles. Not only have these two industries undergone interesting recent changes, but they represent the two sides of consumer goods production—the durable and non-durable categories—and so, taken together with the steel industry (the backbone of capital goods production) which has already been described, they form a small but balanced cross-section.

L

THE AUTOMOBILE INDUSTRY

Although it is barely 50 years old, this is a record-making industry. In the United States it ranks first in terms of value of output among all industries making a single product. It is the largest customer of the American steel industry. It contains the world's largest manufacturing corporation—General Motors of Detroit. Its output of private cars alone in 1960 was 7 million (some 320,000 in Canada and the remainder in the U.S.A.). In 1961 it was employing nearly 650,000 workers.[1]

A strictly geographical explanation of the fact that half of these were concentrated in Michigan, and 30 per cent. of them in the Detroit area alone, would be difficult to supply. The state has little mineral wealth to attract industry, and lies midway between the two older-established industrial areas of Pittsburgh–Lake Erie and Chicago. While it might have been predicted that an industry using so much steel would be drawn to a location somewhere on the Great Lakes coal and iron route, and while the main market in the early days was in the Midwest, the decisive location factor seems to. have been the whereabouts within this general zone of a few successful producers, and especially the whereabouts of Mr. Henry Ford.

To understand what has happened to this industry, it is necessary to recall its early history. In its beginnings, it was an industry of hundreds of small, independent producers, and each car was regarded as a separate construction task; indeed, many of the early car manufacturers were former coachbuilders, with the mentality of their earlier trade still unaltered. But between 1908 and 1914 came the vital change in the industry's character. Henry Ford of Detroit applied to car manufacture the techniques of standardized parts and the assembly line, and so ensured that in the future all the advantages would lie with the mass producer.[2] The effect of this

---

[1] Not even these facts, however, give a true impression of the importance of the automobile industry in American manufacturing. According to statistics quoted by J. H. Glasgow in *The North American Midwest*, ed. J. D. Garland, Wiley, 1955, p. 131, 'Of the total supplies available in the United States, either through production or import, the automotive industry of this country uses the following percentages: Rubber 75, Plate Glass 73, Lead 32, Nickel 30, Steel 20, Copper 16.'

[2] The way in which the industry has become centralized since it began in 1895 is traced by C. W. Boas in 'Locational Patterns of American Automobile Assembly Plants, 1895–1958', *Econ. Geog.*, vol. xxxvii, pp. 218–30.

change from small-scale to large-scale production has been to reduce the number of manufacturers from hundreds to half a dozen, and to give the 'Big Three'—General Motors, Ford and Chrysler—all but 1 or 2 per cent. of the total output.

Both the changing organization of the industry and the nature of the finished product, which is an assembly of thousands of parts—metal, cloth, plastic, and glass—have their effect on the location pattern of car manufacturing. Around the main Detroit assembly plants, there has grown up a ring of industrial towns in which vehicle parts are manufactured. The great corporations, each controlling numbers of these parts producers, can distribute their activities in the most economical way, and it is by this process that the whole of southern Michigan has become involved in the industry.

On the other hand, vehicle assembly is not confined to Michigan. All the firms now producing do so for a national market. But to distribute such bulky objects as complete cars to all parts of the continent from one small producing area is clearly uneconomical, and there are now assembly plants in outlying market areas in half the states of the U.S.A. (although the Canadian industry remains concentrated almost exclusively in Ontario). Only the essentials of the vehicles are shipped from Michigan, which greatly reduces freight costs; the accessories are produced and the car is assembled in the market area. Thus there grows up around the assembly plant, in California, or Georgia, or New Jersey, a ring of parts producers supplying the branch plant just as the suppliers in Michigan serve the main works at Detroit.

THE TEXTILE INDUSTRY

For many years after the introduction of factory production, the bulk of North America's woollen and cotton cloth was made in southern New England; and the manufacture of garments from the cloth was centred in much the same area—the north-eastern states. The cotton used came from the southern states, and the wool largely from the Far West, to be processed in the north-east and sent on its long return journey to the consumer, in much the same way as England herself was drawing upon the raw material supplies of her colonies and exporting her manufactures to them. The strength of New England's position lay in

its early interest in commerce and industry, and in its water
power, capital resources, and labour force. The north-east, with
the main stream of immigration running through it, was able
to maintain a cheap yet skilled supply of tailors and garment
makers.

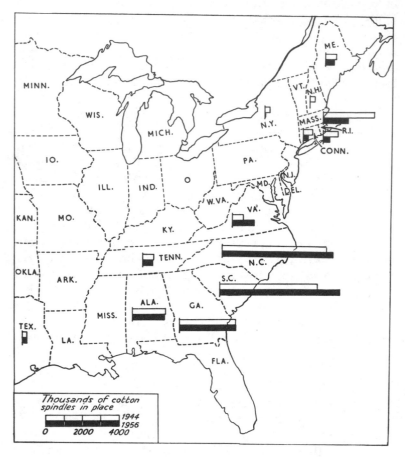

FIG. 28. U.S.A.: The cotton textile industry. Cotton spindles in place, by
states, 1944 and 1956.

Today the Middle Atlantic region still retains a large share of
the nation's clothing industry; more than one-third of the industry's workers are to be found in the New York–New Jersey

metropolitan area alone. But New England has lost its dominance in textiles to the South.

Significant development of the textile industry in the
southern states dates from about the year 1880. It was in the
early 1920's that the new area drew level with the old, in terms
of employment and numbers of spindles operated, and by 1958
the twelve south-eastern states were employing 566,000 textile
workers compared with only 124,000 in New England. After
beginning, not surprisingly, with the manufacture of cotton
cloth, the southern mills have now captured a share of woollen
textile production also, and at the same time have pioneered
the development of new, synthetic fibres derived from the
forest and mineral resources of the region.

The general decline of New England's industrial advantages
is discussed in Chapter IX, and the recent industrialization of
the South in Chapter XIII. These accounts provide the background, and we are concerned here only with the migration of
a particular industry. Among the many possible causes of the

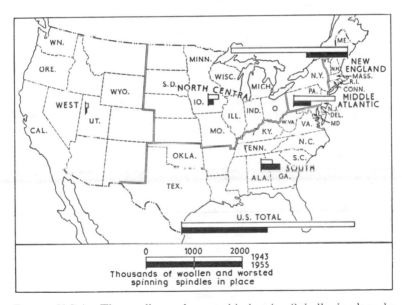

Fig. 29. U.S.A.: The woollen and worsted industries. Spindles in place, by
regions, 1943 and 1955. Notice the marked decline in the total for the
country as a whole (in face of competition from other fabrics), as well as
the regional shifts.

movement, those most commonly cited are (1) the greater enterprise of the southern mill owners, (2) the greater efficiency of southern labour, based primarily on the use of modern machinery, (3) restrictive legislation in New England governing conditions of employment, shift working, &c., (4) the structure of taxation, and (5) though given less prominence than might be expected, the southern advantage of proximity to raw materials.[1]

It seems probable that in time the woollen industry, like the cotton industry, will desert New England, if only because of the increasing competition offered to both these long-established industries by the new fabrics whose history and whose production belongs to other parts of the country. With the departure of textile manufacture, the north-east's clothing industry may also be affected, but although this industry has indeed grown up in numerous market areas farther west, the great concentration in the Middle Atlantic region seems, at least for the present, to be maintaining its importance.

7. American Industry Since the War

For American industry the Second World War meant expansion on an unprecedented scale. Between 1939 and 1947 employment in industry rose by 52 per cent. in the U.S.A. and by 72 per cent. in Canada. In the same period the industrial output, measured in terms of value added by manufacture,[2] rose by 200 per cent. in the U.S.A. and by 180 per cent. in Canada.

In Canada the percentage increase in the number of industrial workers was spread very evenly among the provinces, but because in both 1939 and 1947 the two provinces of Ontario and Quebec had, between them, 80 per cent. of the Canadian

---

[1] In 1948 the closure of a textile mill at Nashua, N.H., represented so serious a threat to the city's employment than an official investigation was made of the necessity for so drastic a step. The reasons given by the mill owners were: that southern plants could produce more cloth per hour with less workers; that New Hampshire law prohibited the working of a 3-shift system; that power costs were much higher in the north-east than in the south; that freight rates increased the cost of cotton used above the southern level; and that property taxes per spindle were five times as high as in the south.

[2] Calculated by subtracting the cost of materials, containers, fuel and contract work from the total value of shipments.

total, the absolute increases were much greater there than elsewhere. In the United States, on the other hand, there were marked regional differences in the rate of industrial expansion. The westward movement of the population was reflected in a corresponding increase in the employment figures for the western, and especially the south-western, states, over against the older industrial areas of the north-east. Yet, as in Canada, the percentages were misleading; in actual numbers of workers, the major part of the industrial population remained concentrated in the north-east. Of the eight principal industrial states, only California lay outside the area traditionally known as the Manufacturing Belt.

The war-time increases were by no means evenly spread among all types of industry. In the U.S.A. the number of workers in the metal goods industries rose by 93 per cent., in rubber goods by 77 per cent., and in chemicals by 69 per cent., while employment in textiles increased by only 15 per cent. and in leather goods industries by 6 per cent. In Canada the greatest increases were again registered by the metal goods industries, and the least by textiles.

POST-WAR CHANGES

After the war, there was a period of adjustment to peace-time conditions. Since the late 1940's, however, there have been several long-term changes taking place in North American industry, and it is the main purpose of this section to notice what these are. They comprise changes in (a) types of industry, (b) total employment, (c) nature of employment and (d) distribution.

(a) *Changes in type of industry.* Once the over expanded war industries had contracted to peace-time size, there were three main factors responsible for changes in the type of industry being carried on in North America. One of these was the introduction of new materials, some of which replaced older materials—as in the case of nylon, plastics, and light metals—while others were responsible for the creation of whole new industries; perhaps the best example of these is the group known as petro-chemicals. Such changes in raw material base naturally result in changed industrial locations, and so in the growth of new industrial areas.

The second factor was advancing technology, which meant that some types of manufacturing were growth industries on a big scale. Chemicals and electrical engineering are probably the best examples of this trend; they have expanded as the research frontier advances.

The other main influence has been the rising standard of living, which has increased demand for some types of goods— cars, household gadgets, newsprint—without much affecting others. In today's affluent society, it is the 'durable consumer' goods which have become the mainstay of industrial demand— these, and the military equipment produced by private industry for the government.

In this situation, American industry has enjoyed almost unbroken prosperity since the war, but it is a situation which has its dangers. Changes in military policy and demand may have serious effects on areas (like southern California) where defence spending is high. And the demand for durable consumer goods like cars and household appliances inevitably varies with the prosperity and the whims of the whole nation: to a large extent, it is a social demand that industry has itself created by its own salesmanship.

(b) *Changes in total employment.* The total employment in industry in North America reached an all-time peak in 1956 or 1957. Since that time, the total has been declining, although the index of output has continued to rise. That industry is producing more with less labour is explained by the spread of automation—the replacement of workers by machines. The numbers employed in a particular industry give, therefore, a less and less precise guide to its growth. Some of the largest industrial plants today, such as the oil refineries, operate with only a handful of men to control them.

(c) *Changes in the nature of employment.* This second type of change leads on to a third—in the kind of work for which labour is required. This is a change from 'blue-collar' to 'white-collar' work, and it is reflected in the fact that the ratio of 'production workers' to total employees is steadily falling; that is, more and more of the employees are office, planning or sales staff. In today's industry the demand is more for training and less for either stamina or manual skill than in the past.

(d) *Changes in the distribution of industry.* All these changes have

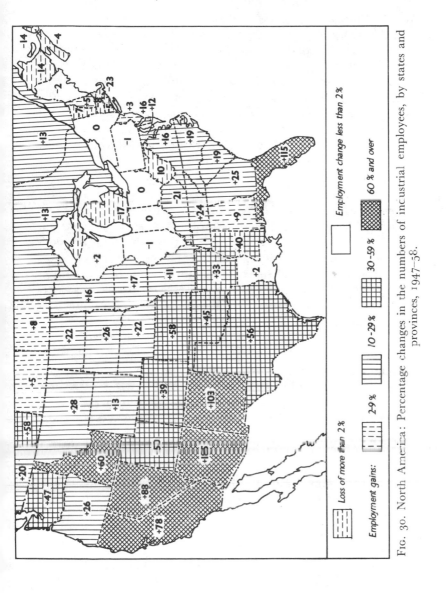

FIG. 30. North America: Percentage changes in the numbers of incustrial employees, by states and provinces, 1947–58.

contributed to shifts in the location of industry and so, too, have other forces in North American life which we must recognize. Among these are:

1. *The dispersal of industry.* Manufacturers are moving out of the older, crowded industrial areas. This is partly a security move, produced by the realization that American industry is highly concentrated geographically and thus vulnerable to attack. Dispersal is therefore officially encouraged. It is partly, also, a move to new sources of power: electricity, oil, and natural gas. Just as the old Manufacturing Belt was an expression of the influence of coal fuel upon industry and transport, so there are growing up new industrial areas whose character is a product of the newer fuels.

Here it is worth noting that, compared with coal, all of these newer power sources tend to exercise a 'liberating' effect on industry. For several decades the motive power in factories was supplied by coal-produced steam, and the movement of goods was based upon railway transport. The effect was to crowd plants together around their boiler-house, and to tie them to sites along the railways. From these technical circumstances emerged the 'dark satanic mill' landscape of nineteenth-century industry.

Today such a layout is unnecessary. Use of electricity or natural gas permits the dispersal of plant operations, while the coming of the petrol-driven road vehicle has reduced the significance of the railside location. Moreover, what has become technically possible has also become socially desirable. In a continent where labour is notably mobile, and where it is axiomatic that the worker will usually move rather than put up with unsatisfactory working conditions, it is not surprising to find that new industrial communities are springing up, generally small by contrast with the great concentrations of the steam age, but less crowded and better adapted to the living standards of the modern American worker.

2. *The influence of freight rates.* The changing structure of both the Canadian and United States freight rate systems has already been mentioned in Chapter III. Both governments are committed to a policy of making freight charges standard throughout all regions of the country, and of eliminating the differentials which formerly placed a city or an area at a dis-

advantage in relation to its neighbours. Like the abolition of the basing point system (see p. 139), this policy will free industry from artificial restraints upon its location, and allow manufacturers everywhere a chance to compete with each other.

3. *Government contracts.* Much of the industrial development which has occurred was financed by the federal governments. In placing their orders they were under a political obligation to spread these orders fairly between all the regions of the country, since the contracts meant job opportunities for the region. In the event, this construction for war and defence purposes has contributed to the westward shift of industry, for in relation to the pre-war position, the north-east obtained less than its fair share of the new industries.

4. *New markets.* The most basic cause of recent changes in distribution has been the growth of new market areas. Formerly both population and purchasing power were heavily concentrated in the old manufacturing regions themselves. Owing, however, to the general westward drift of the population, to the prosperity of some farm regions, to the minimum wage legislation, and to such local factors as the development of the Texas and Alberta oilfields, the purchasing power or potential market for the manufacturer in the outlying regions has greatly increased.

Manufacturers who cater for the national market have responded to this situation by establishing branch plants in the new market areas. While this trend is, perhaps, most marked in the automobile industry, it applies equally to agricultural machinery or soft drinks. Thus a growing industrial maturity characterizes the Pacific coast, the Canadian Prairies, Texas, and the south-east.

All these factors have produced a movement of industry into *rural areas* and into *the west and south*. They have led to a decline in the relative importance of the older industrial towns of the east, and to a distribution of industry more in keeping with the distribution of population. A spectacular new 'manufacturing belt' has grown up along the Gulf coast, an area which offers oil, gas, labour, capital, and space for expansion. Southern California is now a great industrial area, and so, in their way, are the Appalachian Piedmont and south-western Ontario, all

of them basically different in character from the older manufacturing areas.

CANADA'S PROBLEMS

Canada has its own industrial problems. Until very recently
the principal one has been that Canadian industry, producing
for a small home market (very little of the output of secondary
manufactures is exported), and unwilling simply to import
manufactured goods from the U.S.A., has lagged seriously
behind the latter in industrial efficiency.[1] There appeared to
be a real danger that the country might become over-industria-
lized in relation to national demand and the availability of
cheap United States manufactures, so that to maintain the
structure it would be necessary to protect Canada's own
industries and raise the price level.

In a number of industries, this danger is still present. On the
other hand, the Canadian economy expanded at a high rate
throughout the 1950's—higher than that of the U.S.A.—and
industrial efficiency has been improving. Consequently, there
should be no question of Canadian industry as a whole running
out of markets for its goods, although particular branches may
find that they have expanded too ambitiously, and be obliged
to contract again.

One reason why the 'efficiency gap' is being closed, however,
itself constitutes a major problem for Canadians. Part of the
reason for the statistical increase in industrial efficiency is to be
found in the large share of Canadian industry now owned or
controlled by interests in the U.S.A. Either by share purchase
or by the establishment of branch plants in Canada, individuals
and corporations from the United States have come to hold a
share in the capitalization of Canada's industry that may be as
much as 40 per cent., and in certain strategic industrial groups,
such as chemicals and non-ferrous metals, may be more than
50 per cent., according to estimates by the Dominion Bureau of
Statistics.

In such an arrangement there is much that is beneficial; the
United States corporations can apply in Canada the fruits of

[1] The Royal Commission on Canada's Economic Prospects estimated in 1957 that
real output per man-hour in secondary manufacturing was 35–40 per cent. below that
in the U.S.A.

research financed by their much larger American operations, and can afford costs of modernization or automation which might lie beyond the resources of a small, all-Canadian firm. At the same time, Canadians see in these developments some cause for concern: (1) because the dividends paid out by Canadian industry are leaving the country in such quantity (normally, more than a half do so); (2) because control by American interests tends to divert Canada from her traditional economic connexions with the British Commonwealth; (3) because it is felt that such an arrangement denies Canadians full access to the higher technical positions in their own industry; (4) most basically, perhaps, because of the challenge presented to a young and vigorous nation by the foreign ownership of nearly half its industry. For all the country's present vitality, and for all the differences in form, Canada shares with the older lands of Western Europe a common problem: that of living with the U.S.A. The solution of this problem is a matter of serious concern to Canadian governments and industrialists alike.

Manufacturing in the U.S.A.—Numbers of Industrial Employees, and Value Added by Manufacture, 1958

(*By industry groups, according to the U.S. Bureau of the Census Classification*)

Industry Group	Number of employees	Value added by manufacture (millions of dollars)
Food and kindred products	1,698,814	17,532
Tobacco and manufactures	84,467	1,413
Textile mill products	901,677	4,857
Apparel and related products . . .	1,180,517	6,004
Lumber and wood products	581,302	3,176
Furniture and fixtures	347,599	2,349
Paper and allied products , , .	555,390	5,707
Printing and publishing	864,101	7,923
Chemicals and allied products . . .	699,166	12,270
Petroleum and coal products . . .	179,166	2,518
Rubber and plastics products . . .	347,842	3,276
Leather and leather products . . .	349,050	1,897
Stone, clay and glass	554,042	5,529
Primary metal industries	1,096,359	11,671
Fabricated metal products	1,057,986	9,412
Machinery, except electrical	1,348,245	12,391
Electrical machinery	1,122,284	10,395
Transportation equipment	1,557,759	15,283
Instruments and related products . .	296,558	2,906
Miscellaneous manufacturing . . .	571,434	4,754
U.S.A. total	15,393,766	141,270

THE historical background of the subject is covered by *The Development of American Industries*, by J. G. Glover and W. B. Cornell, or *The Epic of American Industry*, by J. B. Walker, while E. B. Alderfer and H. E. Michl's *Economics of American Industry* and E. L. Allen's *Economics of American Manufacturing* are valuable sources on present patterns. Interesting attempts to delimit the manufacturing regions of the continent have been made by Sten De Geer, *Geografiska Annaler*, vol. ix, pp. 233–59; R. Hartshorne, *Econ. Geog.*, vol. xii, pp. 45–53, and C. F. Jones, ibid., vol. xiv, pp. 217–22, while wartime and post-war changes are recorded by A. J. Wright in *A.A.A.G.*, vol. xxxv, pp. 144–66, J. W. Alexander in *Econ. Geog.*, vol. xxviii, pp. 128–42, and V. R. Fuchs in *Changes in the Location of Manufacturing in the United States since 1929*. See also C. D. Harris, 'The Market as a Factor in the Localisation of Industry', *A.A.A.G.*, vol. xliv, pp. 315–48.

A selection of useful general references on coal, iron, and steel is: R. E. Murphy and H. E. Spittal, 'A New Production Map of the Appalachian Bituminous Coal Region', ibid., vol. xxxiv, pp. 164–72; R. E. Murphy, 'Wartime Changes in the Patterns of United States Coal Production', ibid., vol. xxxvii, pp. 185–96; 'Some New Maps of the Underground Bituminous Coal Mining Industry of Pennsylvania', by G. F. Deasy and Phyllis R. Griess, ibid., vol. xlvii, pp. 336–49; 'The Great Lakes Coal Trade,' by A. G. Ballert, *Econ. Geog.*, vol. xxix, pp. 48–59; 'Some Locational Factors in the Iron and Steel Industry', and 'The Future Location Pattern of Iron and Steel Production', both by W. Isard, *Journal of Pol. Econ.*, vol. lvi, pp. 203–17 and vol. lvii, pp. 118–33, respectively, and A. Rodgers's article on industrial inertia in the steel industry, in *Geog. Review*, vol. xlii, pp. 56–66. Articles dealing with specific regions and their industries will be found in the Further Reading of the regional chapters.

On the textile industry, see Alderfer and Michl (above) and the Further Reading for Chapter IX.

Petroleum and gas are dealt with in *World Geography of Petroleum*, by W. E. Pratt and D. Good; *Our Oil Resources*, by L. M. Fanning; 'Natural Gas in North America', by J. Davis, *Can. Geog. Journal*, vol. xlvi, pp. 182–200, and 'The Geography of Natural Gas', by J. J. Parsons, *Econ. Geog.*, vol. xxvi, pp. 162–78.

Figures of industrial production for the U.S.A. are given in the *Census of Manufactures*. The latest census available is that for 1958.

Many of the above deal directly or by implication with Canada as well as the U.S.A. For a specifically Canadian survey, A. W. Currie's two books, *Economic Geography of Canada* and *Canadian Economic Development* are valuable, although now somewhat out of date. A series of articles on individual industries—paper, aircraft, automobile, &c.—have appeared in the *Canadian Geographical Journal*. See also 'The Geography of the Canadian Iron and Steel Industry,' by D. Kerr, *Econ. Geog.*, vol. xxxv, pp. 151–63. Canada's oil development is described in 'Oil and Canadian Geography', by J. R. White, *Can. Geog. Journal*, vol. lx, pp. 144–52, and industrial and mining statistics are found in the *Canada Year Book*. On Canada's industrial prospects, see *The Canadian Economy; Prospect and Retrospect*, by R. Caves and R. Holton, and the *Report of the Royal Commission on Canada's Economic Prospects*.

PLATE VII

Chicago: The city centre from the south-west. This photograph, which covers the same area as Fig. 51, shows The Loop, the Chicago River, the concentration of railway tracks, and the general congestion of a city centre which has grown too small for its modern role as regional capital. At the lower left, a new through highway was being constructed when the photograph was taken, to reduce some of this congestion

PLATE VIII

The St. Lawrence Seaway: Iroquois Lock

VI

TRANSPORT

1. *Introduction*

THE most important early routes into the North American interior were along the waterways. It was by means of the St. Lawrence, the Great Lakes, and the Mississippi that the French made the swift westward penetration in the years before 1763 that almost succeeded in closing the ring round the English colonists farther south and east. It was by the water routes that the English thrust more slowly west through the mountains until, crossing the portages, they reached the Ohio River and made of it the main road to the west. And it was largely by water that Mackenzie made the first transcontinental journey, from Upper Canada to the shores of the Pacific, in 1793. There were few land routes, and those that existed— the Wilderness Road to Kentucky via the Cumberland Gap, and Zane's Trace through Ohio, for example—were so full of hazards that, until the opening of the Erie Canal (1825), the safest and most economical freight route to and from the interior was a one-way circuit, whereby goods travelled down the Ohio with the current, and returned by way of the Mississippi, the Gulf, and the Atlantic to the east coast cities.

Only in the lands beyond the Mississippi, where the rivers were, and are, mostly unsuitable for navigation, did land routes from the first possess a comparable importance. Here the historic trails struck out across the plains and mountains—the Santa Fe, linking the east with the Spanish settlements in New Mexico; the Gila, the Spanish route to California; the Oregon Trail that carried the early emigrants to the north-west, and its branch, the California Trail, leading (after 1848) to the gold-fields. Later, when the first railways came to the west, they followed much the same routes.

If the opening of the Erie Canal, as a two-way route for freight, revolutionized travel in 1825, the changes brought about by the railways were even greater. In determining the regional balance of power within the continent, and in the settlement of the west, the role of the railways was of the utmost importance. It was in the late 1840's that a crude network of lines reached as far west as the Mississippi. Before that time the all-important river traffic on the Mississippi had linked the new Midwest with the South. With the coming of the railways, this link was replaced by a far stronger one between the Midwest and the north-east, whose significance was quickly demonstrated. As J. T. Adams writes: 'When civil war at last came, and the South counted on the West joining with it on account of their being bound together by the arms of "Ol' Man River" and an outlet on the Gulf, it was the newly completed railways between West and North that enabled those sections to hold together, instead of South and West.'[1]

But it was west of the Mississippi and on the Canadian Prairies that the railways exerted their maximum influence. We have already seen, in Chapter III, how both the United States and Canadian Governments made the railway companies their agencies for settling the west, giving them in return land grants with which to finance their operations. Equipped with millions of acres for disposal, the railways set out to colonize the lands along their right of way, and in doing so became the greatest single factor in fashioning the cultural landscape of the west.

For the western railway was so much more than just a pair of tracks. It was a whole economic system in itself. It had first to find its settlers. To do this, it conducted recruiting campaigns throughout Europe and eastern America, and indulged in propaganda sufficiently fanciful to earn the name of 'the Banana Belt' for one railway's lands. It then carried the settlers and their goods, free of charge, to their new homes, and established them with tools and grain or stock. In years of drought it gave relief supplies to tide the farmers over, and it maintained agricultural advisory services to increase output. It was buyer and shopkeeper to the settlers, and sometimes it abused its monopoly. Finally, it was responsible for the location and layout of the towns and villages, itself deciding which cluster of huts and tents should become a city, and which should disappear from the map. Along the western railways today it is common to find that, while one half of the settlements may have Spanish or Indian names, the other half are either called after railway engineers, or were named by them.

In eastern North America the heyday of rail transport lasted

1 *The Epic of America*, Routledge, 1945, p. 244.

until the First World War; in the west until the 1920's, for there
the network of all-weather roads is of very recent date. (In the
north there are areas whose transport has, from the first, been
based upon the aeroplane, where neither railways nor roads
have penetrated.) Not long after road transport came to challenge the railways' monopoly of heavy freight haulage, the
commercial airlines began to capture the railways' business at
the other end of the scale—the carriage of mails and packages.
In the field of passenger traffic, while the motor bus provided
alternative transport for the less well-to-do traveller, the aeroplane catered for the more wealthy, both at the expense of the
railway.

Thus the railways' share of the national transport business
has markedly declined. By 1960 their passenger traffic in the
U.S.A. (calculated in passenger-miles) was only slightly larger
than that of the bus services and less than the airlines; in any
case, an estimated 90 per cent. of all passenger-miles were
covered by private car. The position regarding freight traffic is
set out in the table which follows. Here again the share of the
railways has considerably declined (by 21 per cent. since 1939),
but the volume of traffic they handled in 1961 was 60 per cent.
greater in quantity than in 1939. This is not surprising when we
recall the great increases in industrial and agricultural production that have taken place in the interval.

U.S.A., Domestic Freight Traffic, 1939, 1950, and 1961

(Unit—1,000 million ton-miles (T-M))

	Railways		Inland Waters		Motor Trucks		Oil Pipelines		Air Carriers	
	T-M	%	T-M	%	T-M	%	T-M	%	T-M	%
1939	370	64·4	96	16·7	52	9·2	55	9·7	0·012	..
1950	628	57·6	163	15·0	170	15·6	129	11·8	0·318	0·03
1961	584	43·8	209	15·7	304	22·8	233	17·5	0·895	0·06

2. Waterways

North America possesses a system of inland waterways which
is extensive and, thanks to a century of engineering improvements, well integrated. In 1961 some 210,000 million ton-miles
of freight were carried over this system. Its two major compo-

M

nents are the Great Lakes and the Mississippi River with its tributaries, which together accounted for some 85 per cent. of the freight movement mentioned.

Although its relative importance in the nation's transport system has greatly declined since the river-boat era before the Civil War, the Mississippi System has been much extended and improved since that time. From the ocean traffic terminals at New Orleans and Baton Rouge, 9-foot channels now extend up the main stream as far as Minneapolis, up the Ohio and Monongahela beyond Pittsburgh, and up the Tennessee to Knoxville. The Missouri, perennially a navigator's nightmare, has a 9-foot channel as far as Sioux City, and fulfilment of the Missouri Valley Project (see p. 363) will mean that this can be extended. The Arkansas River is to have a 9-foot channel up into eastern Oklahoma by 1970. The whole system connects at New Orleans with the Intra-coastal Waterway and, by way of the Illinois River and a canal across the low divide south of Lake Michigan, with the Great Lakes at Chicago.

The St. Lawrence and Great Lakes provide a natural route to the heart of the continent, but one whose present usefulness is based on improvements made by the governments of both the U.S.A. and Canada. In the west is the Sault Ste Marie (Soo) Canal, opened in 1855 to clear the way from Lake Superior to Lake Huron, and now the continent's busiest artificial waterway. While significant amounts of western grain and timber are shipped through the canal, the bulk of this tremendous movement is represented by iron ore on its way from the Superior mines to the steel regions. In the east the Welland Canal, completed in its present form in 1933, serves to by-pass the Niagara Falls on the Canadian side, and shares the strategic importance of the Soo Canal, although at present it carries a far smaller volume of traffic.

As a result of these improvements, most of the Great Lakes route was open for ships 600 feet and more in length and with a draught up to 30 feet. The weak link in the chain, however, was the section of the St. Lawrence itself between Kingston, Ont., and Montreal, where there was still only a shallow channel and short (300-foot) locks. To open the great deep-water system farther inland to ocean-going vessels was the object of the St. Lawrence Seaway, opened in 1959. Begun jointly by the

Canadian and United States Governments in 1955, the scheme
provides, besides hydro-electricity for both countries, a 27-foot
channel from the lakes to the sea, thus making Chicago and
Duluth as truly ocean ports as Montreal or New York.

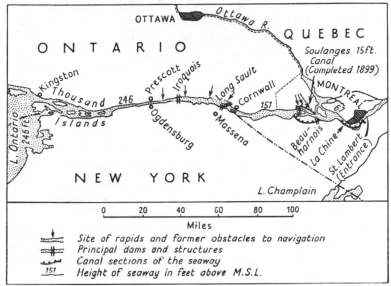

FIG. 31. The St. Lawrence Seaway.

The St. Lawrence–Great Lakes route is available for only
seven to eight months in the year, owing to winter ice in the
canals and along the lake shores. The actual terminal dates of
the navigation season[1] are effectively set by the insurance
companies rather than by nature. During these seven months,
however, this shipping route performs a function of singular
importance in the economy of North America.

After the Seaway was opened in 1959, traffic built up rather
slowly at first, but from 1961 onwards there has been a steady
rise, to over 30 million tons of cargo carried in 1963. Of this,
about one-quarter is movement to and from countries outside
North America, and this foreign trade is largely handled by
two ports—Chicago and Toronto. Of the cargoes carried on the

[1] Over the period 1930 to 1950 terminal dates of the season have been as follows:
Soo Canal—closure varied between 14 Dec. and 14 Jan., opening between 22
Mar. and 20 Apr.; Straits of Mackinac—closure varied between 9 and 20 Dec.,
opening between 23 Mar. and 26 Apr. Source: Haming, *The Port of Milwaukee* (see
Further Reading, p. 294), p. 14.

Seaway, grain from the west and iron ore from the Lower St. Lawrence make up two-thirds of the total. This grain traffic, which formerly came down the Lakes and then moved overland to the Atlantic coast ports represents the Seaway's one major 'capture' so far. It is possible that others may follow.

In terms of tonnage of goods carried, no other section of the waterway system can compare with the Great Lakes and the Mississippi. Nevertheless, some other rivers and canals have great local importance, especially those of the Gulf coast. A number of the manufacturing and refining cities of the coastlands—Houston, Beaumont, Lake Charles—are linked with the sea by ship canals,[1] and cross-linked, in turn, by the Intra-Coastal Waterway, a route designed, when complete, to provide a sheltered 12-foot channel from New Jersey to the Mexican border. Some parts of this waterway are canals in the accepted sense, while others make use of the lagoons and sheltered water behind the long line of off-shore sand bars in the Gulf. The Intra-Coastal has become a lifeline for the booming industries of the 'golden crescent' on the Gulf coast; it now carries as much traffic as the Ohio River, and the number of industrial plants choosing a location on its banks is continually increasing.

In the north-east water transport plays an important part in the movement of goods between the great manufacturing cities. This water movement, however, is now essentially coastal, making use of such 'short-cut' canals as that at Cape Cod, or the Chesapeake and Delaware between Baltimore and Philadelphia. The historic canals of the interior, such as that from the Hudson to Lakes Ontario and Erie, whose opening revolutionized transport a century and a quarter ago, have greatly declined in importance in comparison with the railways and roads that now parallel their course.

3. Railways

Anglo-America has a railway mileage almost identical with that of Europe-with-Russia—270,000 miles, of which some 225,000 miles are in the U.S.A. and the remainder in Canada.

---

[1] A project for a ship canal from New Orleans to the sea, which will by-pass the tortuous delta course of the Mississippi, is under construction.

The standard (4 ft. 8½ in.) gauge prevails over almost the whole of this system; the only important exception being the 700 miles of 3 ft. 6 in. track in Newfoundland.

While the system of railway-operating in the two countries is virtually identical, and traffic movement takes place freely across the border, subject only to customs check, the patterns of railway ownership are quite different. In the U.S.A. no less than 400 companies operate parts of the system, of which about 100 are Class I railways (defined as railways with an operating revenue of more than $1,000,000 per annum). In Canada, on the other hand, the bulk of the system is controlled by two great companies—the Canadian Pacific and the Canadian National. The Canadian Pacific is the product of private investment backed by a government land grant (see p. 84); the Canadian National represents a consolidation, made in 1923, of a number of earlier companies, and is operated by the government. Since the Canadian National was in reality formed to save a number of financial lost causes, it is considerably handicapped in competing with its privately owned rival.

The railway network as it appears today is a product of intense competition in the great railway-building era of the second half of the nineteenth century. On the one hand, cities fought to secure railway connexions and, having succeeded, to use them to extend their spheres of economic influence. On the other hand, the railways fought among themselves to attract the traffic. A large part of the struggle was financial rather than technical, and by the time that the scandals of the Railroad Era had brought down on the railway promoters the attentions of federal and state governments, the continent had been criss-crossed with lines, many of which could never be economically justified or, even if they could, had been built under conditions that crippled the line's working, wasted the investor's money, and enriched no one but the promoter.

In North America today, as in Europe, the railways are suffering from the competition of other transport services—road, air, and water. And as in Europe, they have attempted to meet this situation by two means: to get rid of services which do not pay, and to improve those which do.

Since they lose money steadily on their passenger services the railways, after a post-war effort to attract travellers by fast luxury expresses, have largely abandoned the attempt. Services have been cut, and non-paying branch lines and stations closed. In some larger cities, where the old passenger station stood at the centre of affairs on a valuable site, the ground has been sold and the small remaining business transferred to a suburban station—where it becomes smaller still.

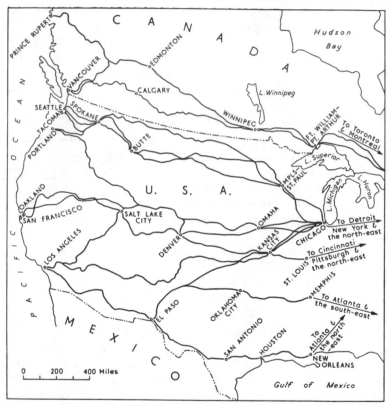

Fig. 32. Transcontinental Railways of Western North America. Notice how the convergence of lines at certain centres (e.g. Kansas City and Spokane) gives particular importance to these cities.

But to keep their freight services the railways have fought hard and well. They have accepted the fact that road and pipeline transport have come to stay, and have produced integrated services—as in the 'piggy-back' trains that carry road trucks by rail. They have improved their own tracks and signalling (a very necessary step since most North American railways are single-track). They have switched completely from steam haulage to diesel for greater speed and efficiency (although a few sections of line are electrified.) And the railway companies themselves have sought, by mergers for greater efficiency and by financing their own road haulage and pipeline operations, to beat their competitors by joining them.

The density of the railway network corresponds very fairly with the distribution of population, with the same marked change, about the 98th meridian, from a closely covered east to a sparsely covered west, that we have already noted in other connexions. Crossing the emptier west, there are nine transcontinental routes, two in Canada and seven in the U.S.A. The focus of the United States' seven routes, and the unchallenged railway centre of the country, is Chicago. While other cities may be more exclusively concerned with railroading, none can rival the tremendous concentration of 22 major railways and 7,800 miles of track that characterize the Chicago 'terminal district'. Indeed, so much a focus of routes is Chicago that to travel through it without changing trains is one of the traveller's rarest experiences.

From both Canada and the United States railway ownership and operation extend across the border into the neighbouring country. The U.S.A.'s New York Central Railroad, whose main line runs south of the Great Lakes from Chicago to Toledo and Cleveland, has an alternative, Canadian route via Detroit and the northern lake shore to Buffalo, over which its trains pass in bond. From the Canadian side, in order to reach an ice-free port for winter use, the Canadian National Railways own a line that cuts across the U.S.A. to the Atlantic coast at Portland, Maine.

4. Roads

As North America has taken the lead in the production of motor vehicles, so it has been also the first continent to create a network of roads designed specifically to take advantage of this new form of transport. With vehicle registrations in the two countries reaching a total of well over 60 millions (there is one private car for every seven persons in Canada, and for every four in the U.S.A.), the task of providing for and controlling this huge volume of traffic becomes a problem of the greatest national importance. Its proportions can best be judged by the fact that in 1962 more than $7,000 million were spent on road construction in North America.

Responsibility for this great network and its maintenance is divided, as in Europe, among various bodies. In Canada virtually the whole responsibility lies with the provinces, or, in the case of city streets, with the municipalities. In the U.S.A., however, the federal government has established a basic network of principal routes for which it is responsible—some 200,000 miles in all. The states develop their own systems within this framework, and, as in Canada, the municipalities are responsible for the upkeep of their streets.

The establishment of this network has been no easy task, considering the natural hazards involved—the lakes and muskegs in the north, the mountains and deserts in the west, the swamps of the southern coasts, and the extremes of heat and cold that break up road surfaces. There could be no better expression of the economic meaning of federalism than the hundreds of miles of expensive roads that criss-cross the empty west and the Great Plains, roads that have little local use, but are justified by and built for the through traffic which they carry across the nation.

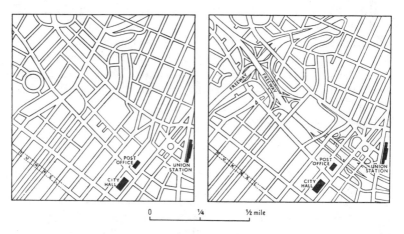

0   ¼   ½ mile

Fig. 33. Los Angeles, 1948 and 1958. The maps show how, during these years, an increasing volume of traffic moving through the city centre has required the construction of a new system of 'freeways' to handle it.

The network is not yet complete. There are still several links missing in the United States network, and in Canada there is much to be done. The Trans-Canada Highway was only completed in 1962, and in the north the 'Roads to Resources' programme (p. 455) has a wilderness to conquer. Besides this, only a small proportion of Canadian roads are surfaced with bitumen or concrete.

But in a wider sense this road network is incomplete because the volume of traffic is constantly overtaking the rate of construction. Highways built a decade ago are already superseded by super-highways with double the traffic capacity. Around such cities as New York and Los Angeles, the congestion of arterial roads is becoming intense, and finding space for these broad highways is a problem that is often solved by carrying the new artery above or below the old street level. But to a visitor returning to America after an absence of ten or fifteen years, the progress of road building during the interval is quite the most striking feature of the landscape.

Recognizing this situation, the United States government has undertaken the building of a completely new network of Interstate Expressways, 41,000 miles in length, and costing $1 million per mile, by 1972. In the meantime, the car has placed its mark on North American life, in that parking space has become all-important, and so business has moved out, as much as possible, from the crowded centres of cities to suburban locations, where space is available. In other words, something of the same dispersal that we have noticed taking place in industry is occurring in retail services also, and once again in the changing pattern motor transport is playing a part. With the strain of traffic on it reduced, it is then possible to redevelop the city centre, and so to adapt it to the requirements of the motor age.

5. Airlines

From the time that air travel first became a commercial possibility, conditions in North America have favoured its development. This method of travel is well suited to two countries whose area is enormous, whose parts are separated from each other by considerable natural barriers, but whose administrative and commercial structure makes rapid communication between regions essential. Once a network of principal routes had been created, no city of any size could afford to be isolated from it, so that municipal airport construction was pushed ahead, and 'feeder' lines to the main routes were developed.

In three particular fields, however, the use of air transport has had especially significant results.

1. The development of cheap 'coach' travel by air has greatly increased the airlines' passenger traffic by reducing fares to the level of railway rates.

2. In the opening up of areas of the remote Canadian Northlands, both the initial surveys of the region and the supply of the pioneer settlements have been entrusted to air services. Before the opening of the railway to Seven Islands (see Fig. 78), the whole development of the Labrador iron-ore field was based on air supply.

3. In industry, use of company planes facilitates control of a concern, even if, as we have seen in Chapter V, it is dispersing its operations to a number of regional plants. Likewise on the farm, aircraft are used not only to spray crops or sow seed, but also to carry the farmer from point to point to control operations. These private movements by air, when added to the scheduled flights that carried some 60 million passengers over internal routes in 1960, make up a formidable volume of traffic, which is already causing serious handling problems—problems that will become increasingly acute as time goes on.

FURTHER READING

Waterways. Books dealing with the picturesque early phases of water transport are legion; special mention may perhaps be made of the Rivers of America series, published by Hodge & Co. For the present significance of waterways, see 'The Traffic Pattern on American Inland Waterways', by D. Patton, *Econ. Geog.*, vol. xxxii, pp. 29–37, and 'A Comparative Analysis of United States Ports and Their Traffic Characteristics', by R. E. Carter, *Econ. Geog.*, vol. xxxviii, pp. 162–75, and the Further Reading of Chapter XII. The St. Lawrence Seaway project produced an enormous literature while it was under discussion: since its opening, both T. L. Hills and L. Chevrier have published books entitled *The St. Lawrence Seaway*. In this context, see also 'Opening of Navigation in the St. Lawrence', by W. H. Van Allen, *Can. Geog. Journ.*, vol. lxiv, pp. 150–9.

Railways. A great deal of information is published and readily supplied by the Association of American Railroads. A number of the railways have published histories, such as that of the C.P.R., *Steel of Empire*, by J. M. Gibbon. For more general coverage the books of G. C. Quiett and L. Beebe may be mentioned. For an up-to-date survey, see E. L. Ullman, 'The Railroad Pattern of the United States', *Geog. Review*, vol. xxxix, pp. 241–56, and W. H. Wallace, 'Railroad Traffic Densities and Patterns', *A.A.A.G.*, vol. xlviii, pp. 352–74.

Roads. There is little literature produced by geographers that deals with road transport in general terms; a few textbooks on economic geography deal with the subject briefly. One or two regional studies of road routes are listed in the chapters dealing with the regions concerned. The opening of the Trans-Canada Highway was covered by E. J. Marten in *Can. Geog. Journ.*, vol. lxvii, pp. 75–91.

Airways. Little has so far been written by geographers in this new field, but E. J. Taaffe has written 'Air Transportation and United States Urban Distribution', *Geog. Review*, vol. xlvi, pp. 219–30, and 'The Air Passenger Hinterland of Chicago', *Univ. of Chicago Research Papers in Geography*, No. 24, and reference may also be made to 'Patterns of Air Service Availability', by G. E. Pearcy and L. M. Alexander, *Econ. Geog.*, vol. xxvii, pp. 316–20.

For a general study of the patterns created by transport development, see *Transportation and the Growth of Cities*, by H. W. Gilmore.

VII

FOREIGN TRADE

1. *Canada*

THE economy of Canada has matured rapidly since the beginning of the Second World War, but her foreign trade is still that of a primary producer, which exports food and raw materials, and imports, in the main, manufactured goods. Within this framework, Canada ranks fourth among the world's trading nations—a remarkable placing considering her small population.

In recent years the list of Canada's principle exports has been headed by the forest products group—newsprint, wood pulp, and sawmill timber—for which the U.S.A. is by far the largest customer. The two other main groups of exports are (1) grain and flour and (2) minerals, chief among them aluminium, nickel, copper, zinc, iron ore, and asbestos. Together these three groups make up over 70 per cent. of the volume of exports. The principal imports are machinery of various kinds, raw materials for textile production, coal, and warm-climate foods—sugar and coffee. The only recent change here has been the decline in importance of petroleum imports, following upon the development since 1947 of Canada's own Prairie oilfields.[1]

While these lists of the commodities involved in Canadian trade have not greatly altered since the 1930's, there has been a definite change in the *direction* of trade. Over this whole period, 75 per cent. or more of Canada's trade has been conducted with two countries—Great Britain and the U.S.A. But Britain's share has been diminishing, while that of the United States has increased by about the same amount. This process has been most marked as it applied to Canadian exports, of which 36 per cent. were sent to Britain in the early 1920's, but only 16 per cent. in 1951 and 14 per cent. in 1962. Meanwhile the United States' share rose from 40 per cent. in the 1920's to 58 per cent. in 1951 and 1962. Changes in import sources have been less marked: the United States supplied a steady 68–70 per cent. at both ends of the period 1920–60, but Great Britain's contribution dropped from 15 or 16 per cent. to less

[1] See also the table on p. 182.

than 10 per cent. Although Canada's cultural attachment to Britain and France remains strong, the economic connexion has grown weaker.

The explanation of this trend involves a number of factors. Changes in the destination of Canada's exports have been due, on the one hand, to the increase in demand for industrial raw materials that has accompanied the great expansion of production in the U.S.A. They have been due, on the other hand, to Great Britain's post-war difficulties in paying for Canadian goods. From Canada, as from the United States, Britain has been wanting to buy more than she could sell in return. Since, in spite of political ties with the Commonwealth, Canada lies outside the Sterling Area, trade with her presented Britain with a 'dollar problem' less in degree than, but similar in nature to, the problem of trade with the U.S.A.

The change in Canada's sources of imports is readily explained. In the mid-nineteenth century Great Britain was the chief source of manufactured goods for both Canada and the U.S.A. But as industry developed in the United States, the American manufacturer entered into competition with the British. He possessed at least two immediate advantages: (1) a great advantage of proximity to his market in Canada, and (2) a similarity of conditions and needs between Canada and the U.S.A. This meant that, to the American, the Canadian market was merely an extension of the home market: the combine harvester or motor-car developed to meet the needs of one country was suited to the other also, whereas to the British producer North American conditions were foreign, and British goods were less well adapted to them.

The present century has witnessed what can be called the Americanization of the Canadian consumer. That this process is not complete is due partly to the unrivalled quality of some classes of British goods, but also partly to sentiment, to a continuing Canadian preference for British goods because they are British.

There are in Canada's trading position two obvious weaknesses. One is her degree of dependence upon one trade partner, the U.S.A. Whatever fluctuations may occur in the level of business activity in the United States will be felt with even greater intensity in Canada, in her role as supplier of raw materials to American industry. This trading position, together with the strong influence of United States' interests in Canada's own production (see p. 158), has long implied, for some Canadians at least, a real danger of being reduced, economically, to 'colonial' status *vis-a-vis* the U.S.A.

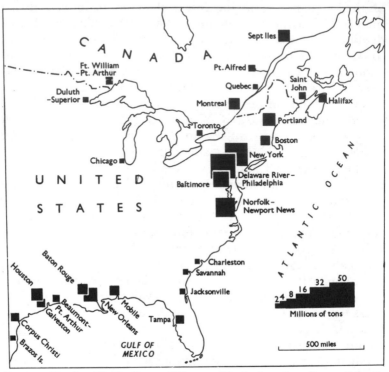

FIG. 34. Foreign Trade Ports of Eastern North America. Ports of the St. Lawrence, the Atlantic Coast, and the Gulf of Mexico, and the volume of foreign trade (figures in millions of tons) handled by each in 1961.

The second weakness lies in Canada's dependence on exports of primary products, providing as they do a notoriously unstable base for a national economy. The fact that Canada has achieved, for a primary producer, an exceptionally high standard of living merely underlines and intensifies the problem of maintaining stability at so high a level. Of the dangers of this position Canada has long been aware; if she had not been, the difficulties of disposing of her wheat crop, year by year in the 1950's, would have called attention to the problem.

It can be solved in two ways. (1) The Canadian Government
has, as we saw in Chapters III and IV, taken special precau-
tions to safeguard the output of agricultural export products, so
that her farmers may be as far as possible insulated against
fluctuations of price and demand. (2) Canada's own secondary
production can be encouraged, in order to make the nation
(whose resources are enormous) more self-sufficient—that is,
less dependent on the imports of manufactured goods which her
exports buy. This is, of course, what has happened in the
U.S.A.; starting from the same trading position as Canada
occupies, the United States economy has developed to a stage
where, far from importing manufactures, she exports them in
quantity, and where, as we saw in Chapter IV, many of her
exports of primary products are only marginal; the bulk of her
primary production is sold at home.

It is unlikely that the Canadian economy will follow to this
stage the course of development in the U.S.A. There will
always be a large grain surplus to dispose of, and there are unlikely to be, in the foreseeable future, large quantities of
Canadian manufactures competing in world export markets
with those of the United States, Great Britain, or Germany.
Within limits, however, the Canadians can certainly succeed,
as they have already in measure succeeded, in reducing their
dependence on their over-simple foreign trade, by a fuller
exploitation of the manifold resources within their own borders.

2. The U.S.A.

The years of her nationhood have seen the transition of the
U.S.A. from a series of colonies, shipping raw materials to the
mother country in exchange for manufactured goods (which
they were hindered by various regulations from making for
themselves), to a great manufacturing nation, importing raw
materials and exporting the products of its industries. Something of this great transition can be seen in the table of exports
and imports shown on the next page.

At the end of the century covered by this table, among the
principal exports of the U.S.A. were motor vehicles, industrial
and electrical machinery, and other steel goods. But it was not
only industrial products that were exported; for, thanks to the

Exports and Imports of Merchandise, by Economic Classes, in Selected Years, 1851–1960

(Percentage of total in each class.)

	Crude materials	Crude foodstuffs	Manufactured foods	Semi-manufactures	Finished manufactures
			Exports		
1851–60	61·7	6·6	15·4	4·0	12·3
1881–90	36·0	18·0	25·3	5·1	15·6
1921–5	27·5	9·7	13·9	12·5	36·4
1946–50	14·0	8·3	10·3	11·1	56·3
1956–60	12·9	7·4	6·0	15·0	58·7
			Imports		
1851–60	9·6	11·8	15·4	12·5	50·7
1881–90	21·4	15·3	17·8	14·8	30·7
1921–5	37·4	11·1	13·0	17·6	20·9
1946.50	30·3	18·8	10·7	22·3	17·9
1956–60	22·3	14·0	10·5	22·1	31·1

application of some of this same machinery to agriculture, the United States had achieved industrial maturity without ceasing (in marked contrast with nineteenth-century Britain) to be an agricultural producer and exporter. Grain and cotton figured as prominently among the exports at the end of the period as at the beginning, although an earlier export of meat had been curtailed by greatly increased demand at home. The U.S.A. is, in fact, an exporter of *both* agricultural and industrial products, as well as of coal and petroleum.

The list of imports has changed a good deal in recent years. One group of commodities, however, has retained its place—tropical products, mainly coffee and sugar. Several items have lost prominence because replacements for them are now available—rubber, jute, wool. Meantime, two items have established themselves at or near the head of the list. One is petroleum products. Since the U.S.A. is the world's largest producer, and since it also exports petroleum, this item is perhaps a surprise. But the country finds it convenient to draw on Caribbean supplies to supplement its own, and is a net importer, so great is United States' demand. The other item, whose importance has steadily increased, is the paper–wood pulp group. Most of these imports come in from Canada, where the forests are being exploited for the benefit of newspaper readers in the U.S.A.

It is not surprising that this great change in the nature of United States' foreign trade has been accompanied by a change in its direction. The table shows how trade with the industrialized countries of Europe has been replaced by trade with the primary-producer, non-industrial countries of America and Asia, leaving Canada as the chief trade partner at the present day.

Exports and General Imports, Distribution by Continents in Selected Years 1850–1956

(Percentage of total represented by trade with each continent.)

	North America		South America	Europe	Asia
	*Northern****	*Southern†*	*America*	*Europe*	*Asia*
Exports					
1850	6·6	9·9	5·4	75·2	2·1
1891–1900	6·3	6·2	3·4	77·9	3·2
1921–25	14·3	10·1	6·8	52·7	11·3
1917	14·7	11·9	16·3	35·9	13·3
1956	20·9	10·4	10·1	27·1	14·1
Imports					
1850	3·0	9·3	9·2	71·0	7·2
1891–1900	4·8	13·4	14·1	51·6	12·7
1921–25	11·5	14·9	12·2	30·4	27·3
1947	19·6	17·6	21·8	14·2	18·3
1956	23·0	11·4	19·9	23·5	15·9

* In practice, Canada.
† Includes Mexico, the countries north of Panama, and the West Indies.

The changes shown in this table may help us to understand why, for the nations of Europe, trade with the U.S.A. has become such a problem. The old economic relationship between the two sides of the Atlantic has been completely reversed, and at the same time Europe has been left with the reality that the American capacity to produce has outstripped that of the rest of the world.

What was this old relationship? In the formative years of the American economy, and especially after the Civil War ended

N

in 1865, great sums of money and quantities of goods were supplied by Europe for industry, railway construction, and land development in the U.S.A. Europe provided, in fact, much of the capital for the great westward expansion. In the 1860's, although the United States had been independent for nearly a century, in an economic sense she was still a colony of Europe, and paid her way by the export of raw materials to her creditors.

But between 1865 and the war of 1914–18 this situation was changing, and by the time the war ended in 1918 it was completely reversed. The U.S.A. was now a leading industrial nation, her goods in great demand, and the European nations were heavily in her debt for war supplies which they had bought. Faced with the necessity of selling their own goods to the U.S.A. to balance their accounts, the foreign debtors then found their efforts thwarted by the United States' tariff policy. A high tariff wall, which had long since outgrown its original economic justification, surrounded the American market, and hindered the entry of foreign goods.

Ever since 1918, therefore, there has been a 'dollar gap' in Europe's relations with the U.S.A.—the European countries (and especially Great Britain) have imported more from the United States than they have exported to it. During the Second World War this gap was bridged by the 'Lend-Lease' arrangement; after the war it grew immeasurably wider, as war-shattered European countries tried to obtain the supplies necessary to rebuild. The American reaction to this situation, startling in its generosity, was to launch the programme of international gifts which has become known as Marshall Aid, and which made available some $13,000 million for economic revival in Europe between 1948 and 1950. But even this seems small beside the total sum of American non-military aid in the years since 1945, which is now in excess of $60,000 million.

In 1950, it looked as if this immense dollar gap could never be bridged. But by 1960 the situation had completely changed once again. The debtor nations had recovered and made determined, and successful, efforts to sell to the U.S.A. The United States, for its part, had greatly reduced its tariff levels, and had given away or loaned so much under its aid programmes that the dollar gap had actually reopened—in exactly the opposite sense. It was now the U.S.A. whose trading position was a source of anxiety to it, and the European nations which had stabilized their own position.

Nevertheless, no one doubts that the United States, with its tremendous productive capacity and immense resources remains a formidable competitor in world trade, and one which will always challenge other nations by its standards, skills, and will to work. Some at least of the stimulus for the formation of the European Economic Community is due to the example and challenge of the great free trade area across the Atlantic which forms the United States of America.

A very high proportion of the foreign trade of the U.S.A. is handled by the ports of the Middle Atlantic coast, from Portland in Maine to Hampton Roads (see Fig. 34). The value distribution of foreign trade is even more marked than the distribution by weight: New York handles 40 per cent. of the national total, and outside the Middle Atlantic Region only New Orleans and San Francisco have a long career as important foreign trade ports.

However, the changes which we have just been considering in the nature and direction of that trade, together with developments within the U.S.A. itself, have altered this situation considerably. For one thing, as we have seen, Europe's share in the United States' foreign trade has declined, and that of Asia and Latin America has increased. The first effect of such a change is to increase the importance of the Pacific and Gulf coast ports, which are best situated to handle this trade—San Francisco, Los Angeles, Houston, Galveston, and New Orleans. By 1960, the ports of these coasts exported half as much again by weight as those of the Atlantic coast, although their imports were still considerably less.

Developments within the U.S.A. have also caused changes. Expansion of the regional economy in the south and west— increasing population, oilfield development, industrialization —means that a much larger proportion of United States goods is now being produced in areas adjacent to the Gulf of Mexico and the Pacific. These goods naturally move to nearby outlets, and so reduce the flow which has traditionally passed through the ports of the north-east. In the Midwest, the St. Lawrence Seaway has created a kind of 'Great Lakes coast' which has the same effect on trade. As we have seen, goods destined for overseas markets which formerly moved through New York or Baltimore are now shipped direct from Duluth or Chicago. All these factors threaten the long-standing pre-eminence of the ports on the Atlantic Seaboard, especially the smaller ports which are, and always will be, overshadowed by the nation's principal and historic door to the world—New York.

U.S.A. and Canada—Leading Exports and Imports By Value, 1961

(According to the official classifications. All figures are in millions of dollars.)

U.S.A.

Exports	Value	*Imports*	Value
Industrial machinery . .	2,747	Petroleum and products .	1,643
Grains and preparations .	1,894	Non-ferrous metals and ferro-	
Chemicals and related products	1,725	alloys	1,253
Automobiles and parts . .	1,136	Paper and pulp . . .	1,093
Cotton unmanufactured .	884	Coffee	961
Electrical machinery . .	877	Textile manufactures . .	864
Fats and oils . . .	722	Machinery, electrical, &c. .	790
Non-ferrous metals . .	698	Automobiles and parts . .	588
Textile manufactures . .	683	Sugar	508

CANADA

Exports	Value	*Imports*	Value
Newsprint paper . . .	761	Machinery (non-farm) . and	
Wheat and wheat flour . .	724	parts	611
Lumber and timber . .	355	Aircraft and parts . . .	312
Wood pulp	346	Automobile parts, except	
Nickel, primary and semi-		engines	304
fabricated . . .	342	Petroleum	291
Aluminium, ditto . . .	250	Electrical apparatus . .	257
Copper, ditto . . .	202	Automobiles, passenger . .	157
Petroleum	152	Tractors and parts . .	136
Iron ore	136	Plastics and products . .	105

FURTHER READING

FULL statistics of Canadian and U.S. foreign trade are available in the *Canada Year Book* and *Statistical Abstract of the United States* respectively. These cover both type and direction of trade. See also 'A Comparative Analysis of United States Ports and Their Traffic Characteristics', by R. E. Carter, *Econ. Geog.*, vol. xxxviii, pp. 162–75.

On the problems of trade between North America and Europe there is a large literature, mostly in periodicals dealing with economics and current affairs. Some of the best, yet the least technical, discussions are in *Foreign Affairs*. See also R. Marjolin's *Europe and the United States in the World Economy*.

VIII

THE MIDDLE ATLANTIC REGION

1. *Introduction*

THAT a survey of the regions of Anglo-America should begin with the Middle Atlantic region is entirely appropriate. Whether judged by its share of the population, industry, or foreign trade of the continent, or by its wide control of the nation's business, this region's primacy is abundantly evident. In this small section of the continent are found the world's greatest urban concentration and three other metropolitan areas with populations of over a million. Its ports handle a high proportion of all the United States' foreign trade and it has—partly as a result of this fact—a full range of manufactures, from the heavy industry of Trenton or Baltimore to the luxury goods of New York City. From its beginnings as an assortment of English, Dutch, Swedish, and German settlements, the Middle Atlantic region has achieved its primacy with the help of few geographical advantages other than the all-important one of position.

For present purposes, we shall consider the region to stretch from the Hudson River in the north to the Potomac in the south, and inland to include the Appalachian Plateau, although this Appalachian hinterland is included largely for purposes of contrast. Defined in this way, the region divides into several physical sub-sections. In the east lies the Coastal Plain, cut by the deep indentations of Delaware Bay and Chesapeake Bay, and diminishing rapidly in width as it stretches northward. In character, much of it is a sandy, infertile area, covered in large part by pine barrens. The long line of coastal sandbars and lagoons that extends north and south from Cape Hatteras and Pamlico Sound continues all the way to Sandy Hook at the entrance to New York Harbour, and fringes the coast of Long Island; but to compensate the sailor for this inhospitable shore the drowned valleys of Chesapeake and Delaware Bays and the lower Hudson carry shipping far inland to magnificent natural harbours.

On the landward side the plains end at the Fall Line. Along this line the recent formations of the Coastal Plain meet the older rocks of the Piedmont at a point where the erosion slope of the latter steepens and where, consequently, there are falls in the rivers flowing off the Piedmont. Representing as it did both head of navigation and source of water-power for early industries, the line became the site of a string of settlements stretching from Trenton in the north, southward into Alabama.

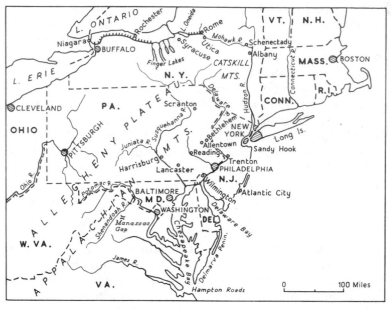

FIG. 35. The Middle Atlantic Region: Location Map.

West of the Fall Line lies the Appalachian System, with its four component parts. But in this middle section of the system altitudes generally decline from south to north, and indeed in southern Pennsylvania the Blue Ridge virtually disappears for a short distance, to reappear in muted form in northern New Jersey. Elsewhere, the mountains are pierced by water gaps— notably those of the Potomac, Susquehanna, and Delaware— as well as by dry gaps like that at Manassas that presumably result from river capture. In peace as in war, to the railway engineers as to Lee and Stonewall Jackson, the position of these gaps has been a matter of constant and decisive significance. Beyond them, in this section, lies the Great Valley of the

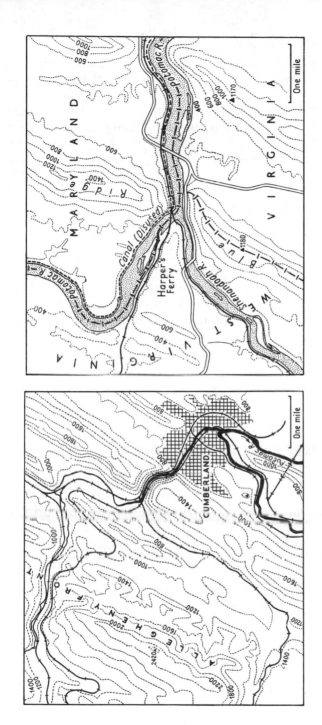

Fig. 36. Appalachian Topography. The Potomac River is shown (left) below the Allegheny Front, the line of junction of the Appalachian Plateau and the Ridge and Valley section, and (right) joining with the Shenandoah River, which is flowing (with the grain) of the Appalachian System, to cut through the subdued northern section of the Blue Ridge, at Harper's Ferry, West Virginia.

Appalachians, notable both for its fertile farmland and as an important routeway giving access, through further gaps, to the interior.

Between the Susquehanna and the Hudson the Piedmont also changes its character somewhat, thanks to the presence among its hard, crystalline components of a belt of softer Triassic formations (which incidentally reappear both in New England and in the Maritimes). The Triassic area lies, on the whole, well below the Piedmont surface level, but included in it are several bands of trap rock—igneous intrusions that form ridges in northern New Jersey.

Throughout this region, soils that encourage the farmer are found in only limited areas. The climate, however, is a factor generally in his favour. The presence of the ocean, here warmed by the Gulf Stream, and the deeply indented coastline give the area a long growing season and serve to moderate temperature extremes. On the other hand, the farmer's gain is the city-dweller's loss, for in the region's great urban centres the hot, humid summer weather makes heavy demands on the workers.

2. Agriculture

Like the settlers of New England and of Virginia, the early inhabitants of the Middle Colonies had of necessity to look to the land for the supply of most of their needs. They were, however, more favoured by natural conditions than the New Englanders and were, on the other hand, free from the commercial link that tied early Virginia's economy so firmly to tobacco production. There were Dutchmen on the Hudson, Swedes on the Delaware, and Germans in Pennsylvania, besides the British colonists who quickly became the dominant element. Each group developed its own agricultural methods, and farming was more mixed than in the colonies to the north and the south.

The semi-feudal conditions of land tenure in some of the early settlements, and the pressure upon the land of an increasing immigrant population, soon produced a drift westward towards the mountains. Here in the rougher terrain of the upper Piedmont and, later, of the Appalachian valleys, independent farmers carved out their holdings, accepting the handicaps of infertility and remoteness in exchange for liberty of action. To

the eighteenth-century farmer the exchange seemed a reasonable one; his twentieth-century descendant, occupying the
same hill farm, suffers the handicaps without the same
compensation.

The present agricultural pattern of the Middle Atlantic
region is the product of one overwhelmingly important factor:
the rise of the seaboard cities. In the general discussion on
agriculture we saw how western competition has limited the
range of products with which the eastern farmer can succeed
and how, even so, he needs excellent transport facilities to
market in order to compete. In the Middle Atlantic region these
circumstances combine to create a dairying and truck-farming
area, based on the supply of milk and vegetables to the huge
urban populations of the region, and marked by wide variations in farm prosperity between the areas adjacent to the cities
and the remoter hill farms.

The importance of cattle rearing, especially in the states of
Pennsylvania and New York, is clearly revealed in the agricultural statistics. In Pennsylvania the crops of the classic 'Pennsylvania Rotation'—corn, oats, wheat, and hay, most of which
are fed to cattle—occupy over 80 per cent. of the state's cropland, while in New York State dairying accounts for nearly a
half of the 'total productive farm work'. It is mainly to the
urban demand for fluid milk that the region caters.

On the sandy soils of the coastal plains, however, dairying is
unimportant. Its place is taken by truck farming. Among the
pine barrens of New Jersey and the Delmarva Peninsula,[1] and
on Long Island, there has developed the world's largest concentration of this intensive and highly specialized type of farming. The whole range of kitchen vegetables is grown, and one
crop follows another on each plot throughout the long growing
season.

Within the coastal region, potato growing is concentrated
in two areas: eastern Long Island and the southern tip of the
Delmarva Peninsula. Here, the distinctive potato barns show
that the farmers specialize in the crop. Potatoes have, in fact,
become increasingly a specialist crop through the years. The
days are long gone when every farmer in the east grew them;

[1] The peninsula enclosing Chesapeake Bay and forming parts of Delaware,
Maryland, and Virginia.

today, there are four or five specialist potato areas in the U.S.A. which account for almost the whole crop (Fig. 19).

This remarkable concentration of truck farming is due partly to the genuine suitability of the light soils for fruit and vegetable production, but partly also to the fact that these crops grow in a topsoil that is in any case so largely man-made that the nature of the subsoil is relatively unimportant. Thus the otherwise almost useless pine barrens find in truck farming an ideal function. Lying within 50 or 60 miles of New York or Phila-delphia, and possessing an unrivalled road network, as well as various rail and water routes, the northern end of the coastal plains provides the truck farmers with an unassailable position from which to market their output. So intensive is production that, in spite of the huge urban demand within the region, a large proportion of the output is sold under contract to the numerous canneries for shipment elsewhere—and even so the truck farming is by no means occupying all the space available to it.

No other farm product has the region-wide importance of milk or truck crops, but several are of local significance. Poultry raising, like vegetable growing, is well adapted to the pockets of agricultural land that lie between the cities: it requires little space and caters for the urban markets, so that in Delaware, New Jersey, and Long Island it plays an important part in the farm economy. Two other specialities beloᴴᵍ ᴵᴷ ᵗhe lower Piedmont, where, on the better soils, the farme   introduce a cash crop into their rotation—either tobacco or apples. While the main tobacco areas lie farther south, the products of southern Pennsylvania and Maryland find a ready market. Apple growing, which similarly has its centre farther south, in Virginia, belongs especially to the southern and south-western edges of the region.

From a survey of the chief farm crops, we may now turn to the pattern of agricultural subdivisions within the region. They are listed in sequence as they would be noted by a traveller making a traverse from the coast to the Great Valley, and then either west to Pittsburgh, or north to the shore of Lake Ontario. On the coastal plains, as we have seen, truck farming covers a large part of the agricultural land of Long Island, Delaware, and eastern Maryland, and all that of New Jersey except its north-western edge. Over this area vegetable plots alternate with waste lands. Inland across the Fall Line, the lower Piedmont reveals a marked contrast. Here, with its focus in south-eastern Pennsylvania and its heart in fabulous Lancaster County (which produces one-tenth of the entire agricultural

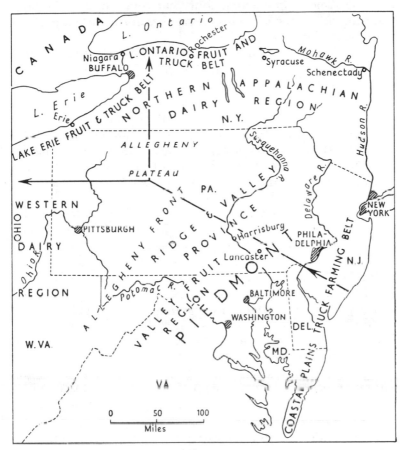

Fig. 37. Agriculture in the Middle Atlantic Region. The arrows pointing inland from the coast indicate the approximate line of the traverse described on pp. 188–91.

output of Pennsylvania), is one of North America's most prosperous farm areas. The farms average less than 100 acres in size, but their handling by successive generations of the Pennsylvania Dutch (the best farmers of whom were German

Mennonites by origin) has been scrupulously careful. It is indeed the skill of the farmers, together with the proximity of the Philadelphia market, which underlies this remarkable prosperity; for although, on the good soils of the area, tobacco, mushrooms, apples, and poultry are all raised as money crops, it is the same unspectacular four-year rotation, and the same dairying as is practised elsewhere, that form the basis of the farm operations.

As the traverse continues across this prosperous lower Piedmont and approaches the hills, the situation changes. Natural conditions become less favourable: the terrain rougher, the soils more patchy, and the growing season shorter. Distance to market increases. The effects are: (1) the land in farms becomes more scattered; (2) the cash crops of the lower Piedmont disappear; (3) the farmers no longer concentrate on dairying, for they cannot market their milk, except in smaller centres like Harrisburg or Scranton; and (4) prosperity varies markedly with access to such local centres.

Beyond the Great Valley, with its fertile bottom lands, these tendencies become rapidly more pronounced. They reach their end-point in the deeply dissected forest country of the Appalachian Plateau, in the hill farms whose isolation and meagre natural endowment prevent the practice of anything other than subsistence farming. Operating much as their eighteenth-century predecessors did (and enjoying a standard of living not greatly different), these farmers and their holdings have represented an anachronism in the system of commercial agriculture of twentieth-century America, and afforded the clearest illustration of the dependence of eastern farmers on market outlets. Each year that passes now sees the abandonment of more of these plateau farms, and the return of the land to the forest that used to cover it.

Beyond this agricultural 'dead heart' of the region, both westwards and northwards, we can trace in reverse much the same sequence as that observed across the Piedmont. To the west the market for milk recovers with the approach to Pittsburgh and the coal and steel towns, while on the north side of the plateau the industrial cities of the Mohawk Gap and the lake shore provide a similar stimulus. Thus there are in western Pennsylvania and New York State dairy regions similar to, if less prosperous than, that of the Piedmont. On the north, indeed, there is even a counterpart of the coastal truck farming belt, where market gardens, vineyards, and orchards extend along the Niagara Peninsula and the slopes south of Lake Ontario.

In all the states in this region, the area in farms is steadily decreasing. Between 1940 and 1959 Pennsylvania lost $2\frac{3}{4}$ million acres of agricultural land, and in New York the current rate of loss is calculated at 100,000 acres a year.

What are the causes of this decrease? The first is the expansion of urban and industrial settlement over former farmland. This is a natural result of population growth, but a result intensified by today's social concepts and ideals—the concepts of building 'out' rather than 'up', which tend to spread the suburbs of cities over huge areas of low-density housing. Many American communities have by-laws enforcing a *maximum* housing density of 2 acres per house. Small wonder, then, that the cities of the Atlantic Seaboard have overrun both agricultural land and smaller towns and villages many miles from their original centres.

The second cause of decline, however, is due to the action of the farmers themselves, in abandoning marginal lands. In some whole sections of the region, such as the Watertown Plateau in upper New York State, and very generally above the 1,000-foot contour, farming has ceased altogether. In today's farming, the poorer and remoter lands simply will not yield a worthwhile living. So strongly is the trend towards farm abandonment running that the planners can forecaste closure and re-plan land use even before the farmer has actually made his decision to give up. Only the better farmlands, like the Pennsylvania Piedmont and the truck areas of the coastal plain have held their own, agriculturally, in the national setting.

What of the future? To all appearances, both of these trends will continue. In New York State, it is expected that the urban areas will more than double their population in the next fifty years. An extra 15 million people will be wanting homes, mainly on the fringes of the present suburbs. To provide these will mean extending the New York built-up area eastwards on Long Island (the eastern half of which is at present almost empty) and into the hills to the north and west. The cities of the Hudson–Mohawk lowlands and the Lake Ontario shore will spread further, to overrun some of the best of the state's remaining farmland.

From an economic point of view, as we saw in Chapter IV, there is little reason to regret the passing of low-value agricultural land. However, there must be some sensible limit imposed on the spread of built-up areas, and so there arises the question of other uses for abandoned farmland. In the Middle Atlantic Region there are two such uses. One of these is forestry. The original farmers, when they cleared the land, left patches of forest which they used in relation to their fields—for fencing timber or as shelter for their stock. Today, forests are planted for their own sake, either to control run-off and improve the catchment areas of the big city reservoirs, or to produce commercial pulp for the ever-expanding newsprint market. In this way, rather ironically, the land acquires a new value when man plants new forests and completes the cycle which began when he first cut down the old forests, 200 years ago.

The other use for these lands is recreational. So large an urban population as the region possesses must find an outlet, and as the land empties of farmers, much of it is enclosed in state forests and parks, and so is secured as open space in perpetuity. In this way, the whole mass of the Adirondack Mountains has been set aside and so, too, has a large section of the Catskills. In face of the advancing tide of urban sprawl, the states will be well advised to make many more reservations yet, in order that the cities of the future may be able to provide their inhabitants with space to breathe and relax.

3. Industry

The growth of industries in the Middle Atlantic region has been favoured by circumstances of both location and history. When the revolt of the colonies threw the U.S.A., in a new sense, upon its own resources, it gave a powerful stimulus to industrial production in the communities of the Atlantic seaboard. Local deposits of iron ore in eastern Pennsylvania and charcoal from the Appalachian forests formed the basis of early iron working, and skill in a host of crafts that later became factory industries was brought into the coastal cities by immigrants from Europe. This immigrant stream also ensured that, when the factory phase of industry opened, there was a constant supply of cheap labour. Then, as the settlement of the west began in earnest, the east coast states served as a supply base, providing the migrants with manufactured goods for their westward penetration, much as Europe had served as a supply base for the earliest colonists. Throughout three centuries during which North America's most important connexions, both cultural and economic, were with Europe, the Middle Atlantic region profited by the constant passage of people and goods between the Old World and the expanding frontier of the New, to secure for itself a large share of the processing and shipping services required by both east and west.

Today the strength of the region's industries depends partly on a continuing exploitation of this position in relation to foreign trade, and partly on the huge size of the local market which the position has in turn created. This has permitted the development of a full range of manufactures, and 95 per cent. of the 500 types of manufacture recognized by the census are represented in the state of New York alone.

In relation to industrial employment, however, two materials are of special significance. One of these is cloth. The two industrial groups of textile mill products and apparel account for a quarter of the industrial employment in the New York–New Jersey metropolitan area, and for one-sixth of that of Philadelphia. Although the region possesses numerous woollen textile and knitting mills (Philadelphia is an outstanding mill centre), it is overshadowed in this respect by New England, and concentrates rather on the manufacture of clothing. Although it is commonly found in any large city, this clothing industry has its focus in a remarkable area occupying only a few city blocks on Manhattan Island, New York, where several thousand small factories employ some 30 per cent. of the nation's garment makers, and produce nearly three-quarters of the United States' output of women's clothing.

The region's other principal industrial material is steel. Before the Civil War the centre of the nation's iron industry was in eastern Pennsylvania, where local ores were smelted, first by charcoal and later by anthracite from the Scranton area. After the war, however, the greatly increased demand, the change to steel production, and the introduction of new furnace techniques meant both that the Pennsylvania ores were quite inadequate to supply the industry, and that access to coal became relatively less important than access to ore and to market. The result was that the bulk of the steel industry moved westward to Pittsburgh and the Great Lakes. Part of it, however, either remained in eastern Pennsylvania, where there are still a number of small mills, or else moved eastward from the mountains into the coastal plains. Here, coal that had come by rail over the Virginia mountains to the ports of Hampton Roads, and thence by water, could meet ore from Central and South America, and the seaboard cities provided an unrivalled market. This eastward movement was exemplified by the transfer of the Bethlehem Steel Corporation's main plant from its former interior location in the Lehigh Valley to Sparrows Point, Baltimore, where a small mill was acquired, enlarged, and reopened in 1916, as the first American steel works to rely almost exclusively on imported ores. The advantages of a tidewater location were re-emphasized in 1950 by the decision of the U.S. Steel Corporation to build its great Fairless Works (see p. 137) on the Delaware south of Trenton.

Accompanying the primary steel production of the region are a host of steel-using industries—shipbuilding in the port cities, construction of railway stock and machinery, and the manufacture of tins for the canning industry. Apart from these, two other groups of manufactures deserve mention. One of these is the chemicals group, well represented in both its heavy and light branches, in both agricultural chemicals and in pharmaceuticals. Apart from numerous plants in the New York–New Jersey area, the region contains the headquarters, though by no means all the components, of the great Dupont concern at Wilmington, Delaware.

The other, and closely associated, industry of note is oil refining, whose presence here is related both to regional markets and to export. By pipeline and by tanker, the crude or semi-refined products are brought from the south-west to the Middle Atlantic coast for processing and distribution. Since sea transport is involved in both receipt and shipment, most of the refinery sites are on tidewater, frequently on reclaimed marshlands that afford the most suitable sites for this industry within the vicinity of the cities.

The Middle Atlantic region is one of the greatest industrial areas of the continent. During the Second World War, it suffered a slight decline relative to the faster-growing areas in the west; most of its indices of expansion were below the national average, and the government's construction programme allotted the region rather less than its share of new industry in proportion to its existing plant. But the decline was *only* relative and was less than might have been expected, considering that this is an old industrial region, in which population is increasing less rapidly than in other areas, and that it is already, industrially, a surplus producer. Since 1945 the wartime trend has been continued, thanks to the national policy of decentralization (see p. 156) and to industry's need for more space than the crowded surroundings of the seaboard cities can offer. In spite of this, the region which provides American manufacturers with their most highly concentrated market is not likely to suffer neglect, and any loss in industrial status is, in any case, more than compensated by the growth of the service functions that give this region, through its banks and insurance companies, financial dominance in so much of the nation's life.

4. *The Seaboard Cities*

This is, before all else, a region of great cities. Nearly 15 million people live in the urban area that sprawls across the mouth of the Hudson, and has its dramatic focus on Manhattan Island, New York. To the south, and dwarfing such intermediate centres as Trenton (266,000) and Wilmington (366,000), are Philadelphia, which has some 4·3 million inhabitants within its metropolitan area, Baltimore with 1·7 millions, and Washington, the federal capital, with 2 millions. Diverse in character, all four of these great centres have their distinctive functions, the first three as ports, manufacturing cities, and commercial centres, the fourth given over to the business of government.

When the end of British rule in the U.S.A. and, later, the Louisiana Purchase opened the era of widespread settlement beyond the Appalachians, there rapidly developed among the Atlantic coast ports an intense rivalry to secure a share in

o

the lucrative supply and transit business with the west. From the first the decisive factor was transport; as communications developed, stage by stage, so the advantage swung from one city to another. In the first stage, up to 1825, Baltimore held a slight advantage. It was the newest of the ports, but it lay closest to the eastern end of the first main route across the Appalachians —the National Pike authorized in 1806. Then, dramatically, the situation changed: New York was linked by the Erie Canal with the Great Lakes. Both Philadelphia and Baltimore responded with canal projects, but it was one thing to cut through the low Mohawk–Lake Ontario divide, and quite another to cross the main Appalachian barrier, with the Philadelphians reduced to hauling their canal boats up a cable incline to climb the Allegheny Front. Baltimore interests turned to other expedients, and in 1828 began work on America's first railway, the Baltimore and Ohio. A new phase in the struggle opened. Philadelphia responded with the Pennsylvania Railroad, New York with the New York Central and some lesser lines. The southern routes were shorter, but the northern were less heavily graded, and construction went ahead much faster. Competition was intense, and the last stage of the rivalry developed as a struggle for advantageous freight rates. This was won by Baltimore. With its shorter route to the interior, it secured in 1877 an advantage over New York and Philadelphia which it held almost up to the present time. Since the freight rates on most commodities being shipped to Europe are the same for all ports between Hampton Roads and Maine, Baltimore was able to use this rail differential to good effect in building up its export trade, especially in grain.

It was, nevertheless, New York which outstripped its rivals in the end, for although the canal era passed, the Hudson River routeway proved a permanent and decisive advantage to the city at its entrance. To this advantage of strategic location New York could add that of its splendid harbour, opening directly on to the Atlantic (both Philadelphia and Baltimore face southeastwards down their bays) and its maritime and commercial links with Europe. Once New York established its leadership, it grew with increasing momentum, until today few American concerns doing business on a national scale can afford *not* to have a New York address.

To this story of inter-city rivalry on the Atlantic coast there is a tailpiece to add. In 1959, there appeared a new threat to the trade of all these cities—the St. Lawrence Seaway. Ever since 1825, the main trade route from the Great Lakes eastward had run overland to these Atlantic ports. Midwestern grain exports, in particular, were handled there, especially at Baltimore. But the Seaway has cut very deeply into this transit trade, and grain handling facilities at the Atlantic ports now stand idle, in spite of reduced rail rates granted by the I.C.C. The Seaway has done for Montreal, Toronto, and Chicago what the Erie Canal did for New York and Buffalo in the early days of the rivalry between the Atlantic coast cities, and this time on a far larger scale.

NEW YORK

The mouth of the Hudson seems a place foreordained by nature as the location of a great city. As we have seen, its position here enabled New York to outdistance its nineteenth-century rivals. Yet, paradoxically, it is far from providing an ideal *site* for the kind of city that has grown up there. Few of the world's major centres can be so surrounded by geographical restraints as New York. Its core is on an island—Manhattan, 12 miles long, but in general only 2 miles wide—which, while it more than served the purposes of the original Dutch settlers, is today hopelessly overcrowded. Its suburbs lie either on adjacent Long Island or on the mainland, and formidable water-barriers interrupt the movement of workers and goods on all sides except the north. Furthermore, it is essential to New York's port function that these waterways be left free of obstructions. Especially is this so on the west—Hudson River—side of Manhattan, where the largest ocean liners dock. But it is precisely from this western side that most of the freight movement into New York occurs. Even beyond the Hudson, the roads and railways approaching New York from the west (see Fig. 38) have to cross a series of inlets and marshes, and these form further constrictions, hampering the development of an adequate transport network.

Manhattan's links with east and west consist of six bridges, four road tunnels, and a swarm of ferries. Of the seven or eight railways which approach the Hudson from the west only one, the Pennsylvania, penetrates (by tunnel) to Manhattan, and even so its main freight terminal is west of the Hudson. The terminals of the other railways line the New Jersey shore, and passengers using their services begin the journey by ferry boat. Only to the northward, across the narrow Harlem River, is it a simple matter to leave New York. This fact goes far to explain the important part played in the life of the city by the underground railway network which links the sections of this traffic-bound metropolis, by tunnelling under the obstacles.

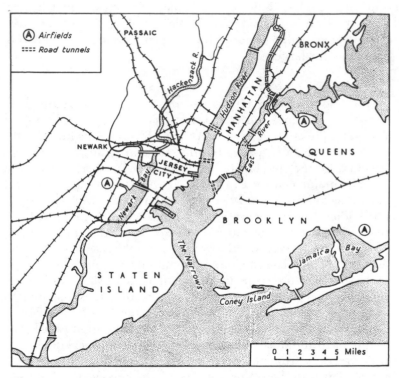

FIG. 38. New York City: The western approaches and the bridges. A road bridge has now been opened over The Narrows also.

Yet in spite of congestion and trans-shipment costs, New York has become the world's greatest port. With over 700 miles of waterfront available within the harbour area; with its deep channels and a small tidal range; with its access routes to the interior, it has come to dominate the Atlantic coast. In 1956 the New York Customs District handled nearly 40 per cent. by value of the country's foreign trade. In terms of total tonnage handled—imports, exports, and coastwise trade—only the Philadelphia area and Baltimore handled even as much as one-third of the amount (90 million tons) that passed through New York.

As with commerce and trade, so with manufacturing, New York has grown to dominate the continent. The pressure on space in the central districts of the city, which is epitomized by the skyscrapers, has driven all but the lightest industries (such as the garment manufacture already mentioned) down to the waterfronts and out to the fringes of the urban area. Much of the heavy industry is to be found on the New Jersey shore, while many industries newly arrived or recently expanded—such as petroleum refining—have had to take up sites on reclaimed marshlands at the heads of coastal inlets in the Jersey City–Newark area.

Within metropolitan New York the zonal differences in land use, culture, and even language are a source of constant interest to the visitor, for New York is a series of cities within a city. For a century and a half it has been the funnel through which has flowed the greatest tide of immigration known to modern history, and it has acquired in the process a huge foreign-born population. Since these immigrants so often arrived with little knowledge of the ways of the New World, and without even the rudiments of its language, it is not surprising that groups of the same nationality have tended to congregate in specific areas of the city, in Little Greece or Little Italy, where they could do business in the language of their homeland and find the re-assurance of at least some vestiges of a familiar culture. Within the narrow limits of Manhattan Island, these cultural divisions are clear and abrupt. The largest groups in the city with their own individuality are the Negroes (15 per cent. of the population in 1960) whose focus is Harlem in upper Manhattan, and the Puerto Ricans, who form the newest of the immigrant groups. New York also contains 2 million Jews, nearly half of whom live in Brooklyn.

Around the Central Business District on southern Manhattan Island stretch the suburbs, interrupted and elongated by the water barriers that surround the city. The average worker in

Manhattan requires exactly an hour to reach home.[1] In its outward spread, New York has overrun or overshadowed other cities which, in a different setting, would be sizeable in themselves, like Newark (405,000) and Paterson (143,000), and which had their own origins. The only way to slow down this outward spread is to build upward—to increase the number of skyscrapers and apartment buildings within the central areas and, of course, to increase the congestion there by doing so.

Although the canal link between the Hudson River and Lake Erie, which wrought such a revolution in transport in 1825, has now faded into insignificance, the Hudson–Mohawk route as such has retained, in the railway and road eras, its importance both to the city of New York and also to the series of towns that lie along it. Followed by the New York Central Railroad and by a multiple road link, this route has been the main channel by which the output of the Midwest reaches its markets, and is an admirable location for industries which tap this flow of goods to obtain their materials. At the eastern end of the corridor, where the Mohawk joins the Hudson, lies the Tri-City area (Albany, Troy, and Schenectady) with a population of half a million. Schenectady, 'the electric city', is the home of General Electric Corporation, and the district also manufactures railway stock, machinery, and textiles. West of here lie a number of smaller centres, and then in the neighbourhood of Lake Oneida on the low Mohawk–Erie watershed are the three cities of Utica, Rome, and Syracuse, each with its own industrial emphasis.

Owing to the configuration of the river gaps to the north of the city, New York's sphere of influence extends far inland. Moreover, New York draws off, as we shall later see, a large part of the traffic of southern New England. By contrast, the hinterland of *Philadelphia* is more circumscribed. The city itself, carefully sited and planned by Penn on his arrival in 1682, lies between the Delaware and Schuylkill Rivers just above their junction. This site gives the modern city advantages of location far beyond either the purposes or the imaginings of its founder:

[1] E. M. Hoover and R. Vernon, *Anatomy of a Metropolis*, New York Metropolitan Region Study, Vol. i, 1962 edn., p. 143.

40 miles of navigable waterfront on the two rivers, deep channels, and room to expand. On the other hand, the lack of a natural route to the continental interior, of which Penn took little account, is a permanent problem. The Pennsylvania Railroad, Philadelphia's main link with the west, winds its tortuous way up the Susquehanna and the Juniata, until with a final contortion it conquers the Alleghenies by means of the famous Horseshoe Curve. Of recent years, the situation has been improved by the construction of the Pennsylvania Turnpike, a through route from Harrisburg to Pittsburgh, as the principal road route across the Appalachians. But the pronounced southwest to north-east grain of the country behind Philadelphia, with its influence on the direction of railway routes, has the effect of bringing within the sphere of New York much of the industrial country of eastern Pennsylvania which would otherwise be tributary to Philadelphia.

As a manufacturing centre, Philadelphia has a range of industries second only to that of New York, with machinery and textiles as the two leading groups. Among the city's specialities are radios, children's clothes, and knitgoods, while across the Delaware, in the east bank suburb of Camden, products from the truck farms of the coastal plains are canned.

As a port also, Philadelphia ranks as a lesser New York. It possesses a major share of the nation's shipbuilding and ship repair industries (claiming among other distinctions the continent's largest dry dock), and both banks of the Delaware are lined with piers and wharves. In the business of the port, coastwise traffic plays an important part, especially the receipt of crude oil for refining and subsequent reshipment.

Behind the city, across the gently rolling Piedmont, stretches a spread of suburban settlement that is virtually continuous from Trenton on the north-east to Wilmington on the southwest. Beyond the suburban ring, between 40 and 80 miles from Philadelphia, lie a number of smaller industrial centres such as Reading, Lancaster, and the Lehigh Valley towns of Allentown and Bethlehem, each possessing significant manufactures, with the steel goods and textile groups generally most prominent.

Baltimore, the third and smallest of the Middle Atlantic region's port-cities, lies at the head of one of the branches of

Chesapeake Bay, where the mouth of the Patapsco River provides a fine natural harbour. Although founded only in 1729,
Baltimore had by 1800 become the third port of the United
States. As 'the most southern of northern ports and the most
northern of southern ports', it has always drawn upon a wide
hinterland for its traffic, and suffered in consequence when the
Civil War cut off its important southern trade area. Recovering
rapidly after 1865, Baltimore exploited to the full, as we have
seen, its connexions with the interior in the era of railway competition, but its function as a port was nevertheless hampered
until the 1930's by the necessity of routing all but the smallest
ships down Chesapeake Bay and round the Virginia Capes, 170
miles to the south of the city. With the enlargement of the
Chesapeake and Delaware Canal across the Maryland–
Delaware Peninsula, however, a short cut, 27 feet deep, has
been created for northbound traffic out of Baltimore.

With its freight rate advantage, and with good rail connexions to the coal and steel regions, Baltimore's chief port
function has been the bulk handling of goods to and from the
interior, with a particular emphasis on the export of grain, steel,
and coal. Imports are mainly ores and petroleum for local use,
and the coastwise traffic consists largely of receipts of petroleum
either from the Gulf ports or from the Pacific coast by way of the
Panama Canal.

As an industrial centre, Baltimore is usually regarded as the
south-eastern outpost of the Manufacturing Belt. Its industrial
employment structure, which is dominated by the manufacture
of primary metal goods, transport equipment, and clothing, is
characteristic of the Middle Atlantic region, while the southern
cities that lie beyond it reveal different patterns of both employment and layout (see Chapter XIII). Its metal-working industries include both copper refineries and the Sparrows Point
works of Bethlehem Steel Corporation, situated on the shore of
the bay some 10 miles from the city centre. It shares with
Philadelphia the east coast shipbuilding industry, and meat
packing, oil refining, and the production of men's clothing are
among its important manufactures.

Similar in size, but otherwise contrasting sharply with it,
is Baltimore's neighbour to the south, *Washington*. Baltimore is
an industrial city: one person in every ten of the population is

engaged in industry. In Washington the proportion is one in 140, and only reaches this level by the inclusion of employees in the printing and publishing trades, who make up half of the 'industrial' total. The business of Washington is government; the city was founded for this purpose, and its only other significant business is to cater for the thousands of tourists who come each year to gaze at their government in action.

The site of Washington, on the banks of the Potomac, was chosen for reasons of political equilibrium rather than for its geographical advantages. Much of the area now covered by the city was marshland, unhealthy and liable to inundation. On this unpromising base was imposed one of the most grandiose settlement plans of modern history, the fruits of which, after a century and a half of reclamation and construction, are to be seen in the broad vistas and carefully aligned buildings of the capital.

In order to free it from any pressure from the states, the seat of the federal government was established in an area—the District of Columbia—carved out of Maryland, which ceded the territory. For the small affair which was the eighteenth-century federal government, this was lavish provision. Its gigantic modern counterpart finds the District (which has an area of 69 square miles) all too small, and, especially in times of national emergency, overcrowding of both offices and workers is a serious problem. The modern expansion of Washington (its population in 1960 was 767,000 within the federal District) dates from the New Deal of 1933 when, under President Franklin Roosevelt's administration, the federal government enormously increased its field of operations. Events since that time have merely emphasized the trend.

With so great a concentration of city dwellers enduring the summer climate of the Atlantic coast, escape from the city has become a major seasonal operation. The coast is lined with resorts, of which the most famous is Atlantic City (161,000), and a series of east to west routes through the pine barrens link the cities with their summer annexes by the sea. Some of these resorts are also fishing ports. The sheltered waters of Chesapeake and Delaware Bays support extensive fisheries, and the region's shellfish catch is particularly valuable, although pollution from urban sewage is a problem.

This last comment brings us to the concluding point of our survey of the Middle Atlantic Region. The coastal section of the region has become well-known to both geographers and general public in the past ten years under the name given to it by Jean Gottmann—*Megalopolis*. This sprawl of urban areas along the coastal plain certainly deserves some distinctive name, if only because of its enormous length, its total population, and its distinctive problems. Gottmann drew attention to three of these as being outstanding: they are (1) water supply, (2) sewage disposal, and (3) administrative splintering and diversity.[1] In a conurbation of such unique shape and size, it is vital to co-ordinate public services and plans for the future. Megalopolis provides a test case which is probably the most pressing, and certainly the most complex, in the western hemisphere today.

The lesson of Megalopolis is perhaps best summarized in this way: For many centuries, we have thought of the distinction between town and country as consisting mainly of the fact that the space between the towns was used to grow food for the urban populations. We must now recognize that this is not the only, or the most important, function of non-urban space. In Megalopolis, the chief function of space is simply to keep the cities apart—to provide not food, but water, air, elbow-room, and recreation for the huge concentration of people which is to be found in the cities.

FURTHER READING

CONSIDERING the importance of this region, there is an astonishing lack of published geographical work about it. A selection of publications available is: *Pennsylvania, A Regional Geography*, by R. E. and M. Murphy; *Garden State; The Story of Agriculture in New Jersey*, by J. T. Cunningham, and *The Population of New Jersey*, by J. E. Brush. On regional agriculture, see 'The Three R's of Rural Northeastern United States', by J. Fraser Hart, *The Canadian Geographer*, vol. vii, pp. 13–22. See also 'Some Aspects of Population Trends in Pennsylvania', by E. W. Miller, *Journal of Geog.*, vol. liv, pp. 64–73.

For the Seaboard cities, there is J. Gottmann's 'Megalopolis, or The Urbanization of the Northern Seaboard', *Econ. Geog.*, vol. xxxiii, pp. 189–201, followed by his book of the same title published in 1961, and W. von Eckardt's *The Challenge of Megalopolis*. For New York, there are the nine

[1] Volume 8 of the *New York Metropolitan Region Study*, by R. C. Wood, is entitled *1400 Governments*.

volumes of the *New York Metropolitan Region Study*, directed by Raymond Vernon, which contain much interesting material on social geography: by geographers, there is almost nothing, but see 'The Diversity of New York City', by J. K. Wright, *Geog. Review*, vol. xxvi, pp. 620–39, and 'Distribution of Puerto Ricans on Manhattan Island', by R. T. Novak, ibid., vol. xlvi, pp. 182–6. For the other cities, there are 'Factors in the Economic Development of Baltimore', by P. Blood, *Econ. Geog.*, vol. xiii, pp. 187–208; 'Washington, D.C., Entwicklung und Gegenwartsbild', by F. Ahnert, *Erdkunde*, Bd. xii, pp. 1–26, and 'General Cargo Hinterlands of New York, Philadelphia, Baltimore and New Orleans', by D. J. Patton, *A.A.A.G.*, vol. xlviii, pp. 436–55. References to the industries of the Appalachian coalfields, Pittsburgh, &c., are listed in Chapters V and XII, but see 'The Southern Anthracite Region', by E. W. Miller, *Econ. Geog.*, vol. xxxi, pp. 331–50.

For the Appalachian hinterland, an unusual photographic commentary is provided by 'A Bird's Eye Cross Section of the Central Appalachian Mountains and Plateau', by J. L. Rich, in *Geog. Review*, vol. xxix, pp. 561–86.

IX

NEW ENGLAND

1. *Introduction*

THE north-eastern corner of the U.S.A., lying between the Canadian border, the sea, and the Hudson–Mohawk line, is occupied for the most part by a rolling upland, forested, lake-strewn, and agriculturally uninviting. The gentler relief and greater fertility of the south-eastern section of the region are offset by the barren emptiness of much of the north. The indices of population density and industrial concentration in eastern Massachusetts and Rhode Island are among the nation's highest, but decline, northward across the region, almost to the opposite extreme in central Maine and upper New York State.

The Adirondack Mountains that lie between the Mohawk and the Champlain lowlands do not, properly speaking, belong to the New England region. But there is more than sufficient resemblance for the two areas to be treated together here. Both are underlain by old, hard rocks, the Adirondacks by a southward extension of the Laurentian Shield, and the New England Upland by the northward continuation of the Old Appalachians. Both are similar in present form; as a result of intensive glaciation, mountain summits are generally rounded and lakes and swamps abound. In both areas the soil cover that has survived the ice action is thin and patchy, and offers little assistance to the farmer.

The main mass of the New England Upland proper is divided into two by a north–south line of lowland which is occupied today by the Connecticut River. This is the same Triassic lowland that we have already encountered in the Pennsylvania Piedmont and shall meet again in the Annapolis Valley of Nova Scotia, and nowhere is its significance for agriculture and industry greater than here in southern New England. West of the valley lie the Taconic Mountains, the Berkshires, and the Green Mountains of Vermont; east of it are the White Mountains, which stretch away north-eastward through Maine, to where the Upland is broken along the Canadian border by an area of softer rocks that underlie the valleys of the Aroostook and the Saint John.

If glacial erosion has been the decisive natural influence in northern New England, smoothing relief and diverting drainage, glacial deposition has played a role of equal significance in

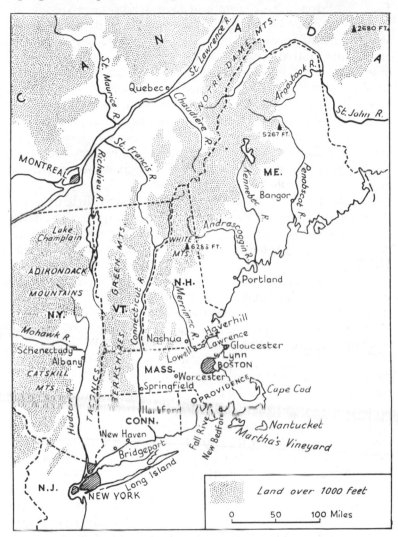

Fig. 39. The New England States: Location Map

the south. This is a region of outwash plains and moraines. At its seaward edge, the frontal moraine of the ice sheet, deposited on the barely submerged northern extremity of the Atlantic Coastal Plain, has given rise to a chain of islands—Long Island, Nantucket, Martha's Vineyard—and to the peninsula of Cape Cod. The presence of abundant loose ice-borne material has made this a coast of sand bars and spits under the action of the waves. Inland spreads the drift cover, here sandy and there stony, and dotted with drumlins or marked by the lines of eskers. In the valleys terraced clays and gravels remain as a product of the action of either ice or melt-water; much of the lower Connecticut Valley was filled by an ice-front lake, whose legacy takes the form of a clay bed into which the present river has cut a series of terraces. It is in these southern valleys, together with the lowlands round Lake Champlain and along the Maine–New Brunswick border, that there are found the region's most fertile farmlands.

New England has no coal or petroleum, and little iron ore. To offset this meagre natural endowment of minerals, however, the region does possess three types of resources that, over the years, have brought it prosperity—forests, fisheries, and building stones.

The splendid stands of New England timber early caught the attention of the British Admiralty, and throughout the colonial period the region's forests were one of the prime assets of England's transatlantic possession. Today, after three centuries of settlement and commercial use, while much of the forest cover remains (some 75 per cent. or 31 million acres of New England are classified as forest land, and forests cover the greater part of the Adirondacks), its value has greatly diminished. It is almost entirely second growth that has developed after the cutting and clearing of earlier years, and today, although the region possesses 5 per cent. of the nation's forest area, it has only 2½ per cent. of the nation's saw timber. The best of the timber has long since gone; New England contributes much less than 2½ per cent. of the United States' annual lumber production, and the only forest products the region supplies in quantity are wood pulp from Maine and maple sugar. For all its 31 million acres of forest, New England imports lumber from distant Oregon and Georgia.

The region's fisheries have fared somewhat better over the years. In 1961 New England's 21,000 fishermen were respon-

PLATE IX

The Shenandoah Valley in Virginia looking east towards the Blue Ridge. The valley is noted for its apple orchards and its dairy cattle

PLATE X

(*a*) Mills beside the Blackstone River at Woonsocket, Rhode Island. In some cases, old New England factories like these have been converted from their original use as textile mills to serve the needs of newer industries in the region

(*b*) Fishing vessels in the harbour of Gloucester, Massachusetts, which, although it has a population of only 25,000, lands the largest quantity of fish of all New England's ports

NEW ENGLAND

sible for about 15 per cent. by weight of the total United States catch. The principal species landed in New England are haddock and ocean perch, while in some years the haul of herring rivals these. The shellfish catch, although small in weight, brings in nearly half the returns by value. Among the fishing ports that are scattered along the coast, Gloucester, Boston and New Bedford receive by far the greatest share of the landings.

The upland interior of New England yields a variety of valuable building materials. Vermont's granite and marble are famous, and the state is the leading United States producer of both these stones and of asbestos. Elsewhere in the region, granites, marble, slate, and limestone are quarried, together with a variety of lesser-used materials such as mica and quartz.

2. *The New England Economy*

No part of the North American economy has been so frequently and critically analysed over the past twenty-five years as the regional economy of New England. Most of the statistical temperature-taking has resulted in gloomy diagnosis, and indeed, to some observers outside the region, the patient's case has seemed hopeless. While the New Englanders themselves are far from accepting this verdict, they are none the less conscious of the serious problems that confront them.

The explanation of this flurry of interest is not far to seek. There was a time when, in terms of population, industry, or wealth, New England possessed a high proportion of the national totals. Its history went back to 1620; its people were industrious and turned early to commercial pursuits; it was here that factory industry in North America began. But the thirteen colonies on the Atlantic coast gave place to a nation stretching across the continent, and inevitably the relative position of the east within the nation declined.

But this was not all. The *relative* decline applied to all parts of the east alike. What has marked New England out for special attention is that it has also suffered, in some respects, an *absolute* economic decline. The well-publicized fact that textile firms have left New England for the Southern states is taken as a symbol of failure. For in the climate of United States opinion, and in the light of the nation's long history of successful expansion, failure to go on expanding is in itself bad enough; actually to lose ground is to incur a sort of social stigma.

Yet this absolute decline by no means applies to all aspects of the economy, and even if it did it would still only represent a logical and, for the most part, beneficial redistribution of the nation's population, when better endowed and more productive lands lie farther west. The present size of New England's population and the character of its economy are not primarily the outcome of the region's natural attractions, but of historical chance—that it was from Europe that the great immigrant stream into the New World flowed. It is one of the main strengths of the American economy that, within a great free-trade area, covering 3 million square miles of variegated resources, the effects of such an historical coincidence can be adjusted with the passage of time. It is this process of adjustment which we are witnessing in New England today.

Furthermore, as an analysis of the situation made in 1954 was at pains to point out, textile mills are not the be-all and end-all of economic development. Beyond the primary level of economic activity—agriculture or forestry—and the secondary—manufacturing—there lies a third level, at which it is the service 'industries', legal, financial, or administrative, that form the main source of income. In a region like New England, it is argued, a decline in manufacturing may merely denote a welcome maturing of the region's economy at the tertiary level. Among the regions of so large a country as the U.S.A., New England may—indeed, already does—find its place in providing services for the economically less mature regions farther west.

What this means in geographical terms is that the landscape alone will not give an accurate indication of the region's wealth. This is perhaps best illustrated by the New England city of Hartford, Conn. The city has a population of 525,000, and important industries producing machinery and instruments. Yet its most famous 'industry' is one whose presence here affords the geographer little evidence and less explanation: it is a great insurance centre.

In short, success or failure for New England in the future is not to be judged solely by the size of its industries or the dilapidation of its farms, but by its ability to adapt to the

changing economic circumstances of the times. For the past,
like the present, has called for changes, and New England has
responded, over the years, to write a story of economic development that leads logically to the present situation. This
development must now be briefly sketched.

3. *Rural New England*

European settlement in New England began with the establishment of the Massachusetts Bay colony in 1620. From the
early centres in the coastal lowland the new-comers spread
westward; but here, even more than in the middle and southern
groups of colonies, the westward movement was hampered by
obstacles, both physical and human. On the one hand, the
forested slopes and rock-strewn surface of the interior made progress painfully slow, and, on the other, there was the recurrent
menace of hostile Indians who, with the sponsorship of the
French in Canada, ravaged the borders of the settled area.

Behind this double barrier, cut off for the first 150 years of its
history from the great 'safety-valve' of the empty west, New
England experienced serious pressure of population. The result
was an expansion of settlement, within the pale, into remote
and forested upland margins where the means of livelihood
were meagre. With the great new immigrant waves of the early
nineteenth century, expansion continued, and indeed was
hastened, because of the rise of New England's industrial cities
and the resultant demand for food supplies—supplies which, in
this period before the coming of the railways, had of necessity
to be provided from local sources.

The amount of cleared farmland in southern New England
reached a peak in the 1850's, and somewhat later in the north.
Agricultural production was varied and, although the growing
of grain had already declined (in consequence of the opening of
the Erie Canal in 1825), sheep and beef cattle were plentiful in
the north-west, while the south-east concentrated on the
supply of vegetables and dairy produce to the towns.

In the second half of the century, however, a general agricultural decline set in. It manifested itself in the first place by the
fact that after 1850 there was little increase in the rural population. On the contrary, as the century wore on, a reverse flow

P

developed—from poor farms to expanding industries, from the isolation of the uplands to the fuller life of the towns. Highwater mark had been reached by the tide of settlement. Far to the westward, in any case, the Homestead Act was making available to would-be farmers, at nominal cost, 160 acres of land that made New England's rocky margins look like a wilderness by contrast. Meanwhile, the westward-spreading railway network brought ever closer to the eastern cities the produce of this new Agricultural West.

These changes had two effects. Firstly, they brought about a gradual retreat of the farmers from the margins of settlement. Farms were abandoned, and scrub crept back to cover the cleared pastures. Essentially, it was an abandonment of the remoter and higher regions, to concentrate upon the better soils of the valley terraces and drumlin slopes, and upon the more accessible farmlands. It was a retreat from the lands that would never have been farmed at all if the west had been opened earlier, and it was a move to lands that offered the New England farmers at least the advantages of fertility and accessibility with which to meet western competition. The process of abandonment was not continuous; there were fluctuations of the frontiers of settlement, but in general it began earliest and has gone furthest in the vicinity of the cities, while in the north of the region the story of advance and retreat has unrolled with a time lag of 20 to 30 years behind the south.

Secondly, New England's changed circumstances meant a change from the diversified farming of the 1850's to a concentration, under the pressure of western competition, on a few staples like dairy products and poultry. In statistical form these changes are indicated by the table on page 213. In spite of a decrease in agricultural land from 13·5 million to 5·5 million acres throughout the period, the area of cropland harvested declined, proportionately, rather less—from 5·0 to 2·5 million acres.

New England seems to have reached its agricultural nadir after the First World War. Since then, its farmers have been actively seeking a solution of the problems that are created by position and by poverty of natural resources. In this search for a new role the New England farmers have had to reckon with three main physical limitations:

1. Over much of the upland interior, the growing season has a length of only 90 to 100 days, as against 160 to 200 days on the coast, and 130 to 150 in the Champlain area. One particular aspect of this handicap is that the season in the interior is too short for corn to be grown.

2. Snowfall is heavy—well over 100 inches per annum in the mountains. This represents a factor in accessibility which, as always in the eastern U.S.A., is a matter of the utmost importance to the farmer.

3. The soils are often thin and stony, and are generally heavily leached. Where the hazard of glacial action has left the poorest soil cover, there the process of farm abandonment has usually begun; the influence of the soil is generally decisive.

Circumstances, as we have seen, have long been forcing upon the farmers the 'solution' of abandonment. There is, however, still need for further withdrawal, and especially for planned withdrawal, in the sense that the abandoned fields should be planted back to forest, rather than be allowed to revert to scrub. This would mean that the farmers were not merely cutting their losses, for such a withdrawal should enhance rather than reduce the value of the uplands. Forestry and recreation create new values, and the 'yield per acre' from timber and tourist hotels should exceed that from marginal agriculture. But the scrub that spreads over farmland which is simply abandoned is neither scenic nor useful, and yet it is this scrub that, at least from the air, is the most prominent feature of the rural landscape today in the north-eastern U.S.A.

New England Land Use, 1880–1954[1]

	1880	1910	1930	1945	1954
Land in farms (as % of total area of New England)	52·3	51·8	38·2	34·5	27·6
Land in farms ('000 acres)	20,725	20,566	15,142	13,948	11,121
But % of this farmland which is woodland	34·5	42·6	52·9	51·2	50·6
Thus, agricultural land in farms ('000 acres)	13,570	11,800	7,129	6,800	5,500
Cropland harvested ('000 acres)	5,053	4,790	3,890	3,800	2,493

[1] Figures for 1880–1945 based on J. D. Black, *Rural Economy of New England*, Harvard, 1950, p. 149. Figures for 1954 from the *Statistical Abstract of the United States, 1957*, pp. 617–19.

A variant of the solution provided by abandonment is seen
in the widespread development of part-time farming. This

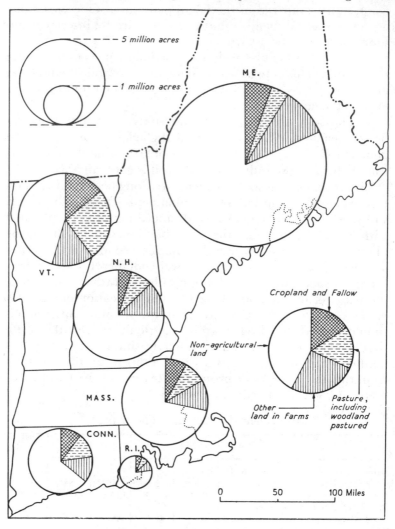

FIG. 40. The New England States: Land Use. The circle in each state is
drawn in proportion to the total area of the state; its segments represents
the percentage of land devoted to each of the uses specified in 1954.

means either that the farmer recognizes that his farm alone
cannot support him, and that he therefore supplements his

farm income by other work during his slack season, or else that city dwellers have taken up vacant farms, as yearlong or as holiday homes. Many a farmstead has become a 'summer home', and often these part-timers from the city have brought a welcome infusion of capital into the countryside. By 1959, more than one-third of New England's farms were classified as part-time.

But the abandonment of the margins has been accompanied by a greater concentration of effort upon the better lands. Here the farmer's solution involves picking the right lands, and then picking the right products to take advantage of the one circumstance squarely in his favour—the existence of a large urban market almost on his doorstep.

In the event, there is a strong resemblance to the agricultural pattern of the Middle Atlantic region, with production geared to the needs of the cities and the marketing of perishable produce, but with differences resulting from the less favourable natural environment of New England. Over most of the region, the importance of dairying is unchallenged: in Vermont, 90 per cent. of the commercial farmers are classed as dairymen. Only in the urbanized south-east is this situation modified. Here, land values are for the most part too high to support a relatively extensive form of farming like field dairying; more intensive land use is necessary, and poultry production dominates the output, with local specializations in vegetables and fruits resembling those of Pennsylvania and New Jersey. Where dairying does penetrate the 'inner ring', it is with the aid of concentrated feeds brought in from the Midwest.

Dairying developed in New England as the earlier forms of farm production declined, in the second half of the nineteenth century, before the competition of the west. It further increased with the improvement of communications that made it possible to supply eastern Massachusetts with milk from farms 200 to 250 miles away across the mountains. Today Vermont is the leading dairy state of the region, with a dense concentration of dairy farms all through the lowlands east of the Richelieu–Champlain line, and there is a second concentration in eastern Connecticut. Because of the limitations imposed by soil and climate, the New England farmer relies, to an extent probably greater than anywhere else in the U.S.A., on simple grass feeds for his cattle.[1] Some corn is fed in the southern parts of the region, and oats are important in Vermont, but there is nothing here to compare with the Pennsylvania Rotation. Yields are likely, therefore, to be low, unless the farmer supplements with expensive concentrates, and although there has been a steady rise in milk yields, a further programme of pasture improvement would seem to be one of the region's pressing needs.

Like the Middle Atlantic region, New England is essentially a fluid milk producer. In this role it holds its own in interregional competition, and supplies its internal markets almost unchallenged except in times of seasonal shortage. But in butter, and even in cream, production, where the advantages of proximity are less, it feels the force of Midwestern competition.

The other main group of farm products in New England come from poultry keeping. This type of activity has shown a considerable development since the First World War, especially around the cities of south-eastern New England, for it is well suited to the suburban fringe areas, and can often be carried on in farm buildings no longer needed for other types of agriculture. From being a widespread secondary source of income on dairy and general farms, it has gradually become a specialized type of production, and the chief areas in which it is now concentrated are in eastern Connecticut and around Bangor in Maine.

Besides these two principal farm activities, New England has a number of crops of local importance to which reference must be made. The chief of these is potatoes. A century ago potato-growing was widespread throughout the region. But, as in other parts of the continent, recent years have seen a concentration of potato production in a few areas which specialize in this one crop. What has happened is that the force of competition, the cost of labour and the appearance of new crop diseases have turned potatoes from a general to a specialist farm crop, which can only be produced commercially where yields are at a maximum and where production can be profitably mechanized.

---

[1] Except in the Aroostook Valley and on Cape Cod, hay represents more than half the cropland harvested all through New England. In Vermont and New Hampshire, it represents more than three-quarters.

As a result of this change, the potato acreage has shrunk everywhere in New England (in Vermont to only 15 per cent. of the 1840 figure) except in the extreme north. Here, by contrast, production has intensified until four-fifths of New England's commercial crop is grown in Maine, and the bulk of it in a single area—the lowlands of Aroostook County, on the Maine–New Brunswick border. Glacial action has provided soils well suited to the crop, production is extensively mechanized, yields are high, and the farmers of Aroostook grow potatoes with a single-minded zeal that amounts to dangerous monoculture. For not only are output and price notoriously variable in the potato market, but the remoteness of Aroostook forces the farmers to market at full stretch. A large part of the crop travels by rail to the coast, and thence by boat to Boston, to New York, or to markets as far away as Philadelphia. In spite, however, of transport difficulties and periodic slumps, Maine late potatoes continue to supply a wide range of markets throughout the whole of the north-eastern U.S.A.

Other local specialities are the blueberries of the Maine coast and the cranberries of Cape Cod. Both of these crops, although occupying only a small area of the coastal sands and marshes, supply a national market and profitably utilize land that would otherwise have little value. Elsewhere in southern New England a wide variety of tree fruits and berries is grown, especially apples, pears, and peaches, but the orchards have declined in number in recent years; the number of apple trees, for example, in only one-third what it was in 1900. Tobacco is grown in the Connecticut Valley.

New England's agricultural situation might be summarized as follows: in a region of meagre natural endowment there is concentrated a dense population, whose presence is related not to food supply but—as in Old England—to position, history, and industrial development. As long as the keynote of agricultural production was regional self-sufficiency (that is, until the coming of the railways and canals made movement of goods in bulk possible), New England necessarily expanded its farmlands as its population increased, and the farm frontier was forced far into the uplands. But once the compulsion to self-sufficiency was gone, and the region became merely part of a larger, competitive complex, such marginal agriculture

was unnecessary; nor could it hope, economically, to survive. It
has therefore been necessary, largely by a painful process of trial
and error, to contract the region's agriculture to more modest
proportions, to accept and concentrate upon limited objectives,
and to discover how New England's farmers can survive and
prosper in a nation that includes so many better-endowed
regions. In all these difficult tasks, the evidence suggests, a real
measure of success has been achieved.

4. *Industrial New England*

The American Revolution opened an era of great industrial
opportunity for the United States. The old restrictions on native
manufacturers which had been a feature of the colonial period
(and, indeed, a contributing cause of the revolution) were gone;
and the U.S.A. was estranged from Great Britain, its principal
source of manufactured goods. The revolution, too, was
followed by the beginnings of large-scale movement into the
west, a movement upon which the Louisiana Purchase of 1803
set the seal; and as the nation's territory expanded, so too did
the demand for the means of conquering the wilderness.

In this era of opportunity New England emerged as
America's first industrial region. This resulted partly from the
fact that New England's interests had long been commercial
rather than agricultural, which in turn can be attributed to the
lack of opportunity offered by the region's farming. Partly it
was the product of New England's labour situation; not only
was there a surplus to be tapped in the poor farm areas, but
there was also an immigrant stream that brought to the ports
of the north-east a supply of skilled craftsmen from Europe. And
when the age of factory industry created a need for power, New
England's rivers provided an abundant supply, and their falls
became the sites of the earliest mills and factories.

From these early beginnings, the industrial history of New
England has run remarkably parallel to that of Old England.
Both set out to be 'workshops' supplying non-industrial areas;
both lost their early lead through the competition of newer
rivals and through changes in the source of industrial power;
both find themselves today with a wealth of experience in
manufacturing, but with out-of-date industrial equipment that

places them at a disadvantage in relation to their rivals. Both, too, have made strenuous efforts to remedy the situation.

Today southern New England (Massachusetts, Rhode Island, Connecticut, and southern New Hampshire) remains, as it was a century ago, the most highly industrialized area of the continent. Out of every 100 people employed, Rhode Island had 44 and Connecticut 42 engaged in manufacturing in 1950, the highest proportions for any state; New Hampshire ranked fourth on the list and Massachusetts sixth. But with the passage of time this great dependence on manufacturing has ceased to be a measure of strength; it has become a liability in a nation where New England's relative advantages have markedly declined.

There are three main factors responsible for the change in the region's position.

1. The change in the sources of industrial power. Great Britain's supremacy in manufacturing was made possible by her coal, and her industrial advantages have dwindled with the coming of newer fuels. But New England's asset—water power—belonged to a yet earlier phase of industrialization; the phase passed and the advantage to a region which has neither coal nor petroleum was short-lived (although with the coming of hydro-electricity it has, of course, in some measure returned). The outcome is that fuel costs in New England are generally high, and consequently the region is handicapped in the establishment of heavy industry.[1]

2. The westward shift of the nation's 'centre of gravity'—both in production and in markets—has left New England on the periphery. This is particularly damaging to a region that must, like New England, import not only its food but also its fuel and raw materials, as well as export its manufactures; almost the only local resource that the region possesses today is its labour force.

3. The change in industrial materials. New England's industries developed in a period when a large proportion of all manufactured goods were made of cloth, wood, or leather, all of which were available in quantity. But industry has become

[1] For a fuller statement of the position, however, see W. Isard and J. H. Cumberland, 'New England as a Possible Location for an Integrated Iron and Steel Works', *Econ. Geog.*, vol. xxvi, pp. 245–59.

increasingly based on metals, and more recently on a whole range of synthetic materials, and this, too, has reduced the advantages of the older industrial region.

Apart from these three main factors, a number of local causes are blamed for New England's industrial decline: the weakness of the railway system; the restrictive influence of the strong trade unions; the conservatism of manufacturers and their failure to keep their plant up-to-date; the less pleasant working conditions in the old industrial towns than in the newer areas of the nation.

In a region whose industry is diverse, the decline of one or two branches may be accepted as a necessary, nation-wide adjustment. The particular problem of southern New England, however, has been that it depended very heavily on only two types of manufacture—textiles and leather goods. In 1939, 45 per cent. of all the region's industrial workers were employed in the textile, apparel, and leather-goods groups—in spite of the previous loss to the southern states of a large part of the cotton goods industry, as we saw in Chapter V. Moreover, these old industries were rather heavily concentrated in eastern Massachusetts and Rhode Island. What then complicates New England's problem still further is that demand for these particular goods has risen much more slowly than demand for other manufactures: in other words, New England's basic industries have been obtaining an ever smaller share of the market for goods representing an ever smaller proportion of total industrial demand.

The result has been a steep drop in industrial employment since the war. Between 1947 and 1960, employment in textiles fell from 280,000 to 120,000, and it is expected that another 40,000 workers may be lost by the industry in the fairly near future. The region as a whole lost 200,000 production workers between 1947 and 1958, a decline of 16 per cent. Most of this loss was concentrated in Massachusetts and Rhode Island.

What could New England do, in the post-war years, to re-form its economy and recruit its industrial strength? Clearly, two tasks lay before it. One was to develop other industries which could replace the older and faltering groups. Given the circumstances of the region, the most suitable type of new industry would be those that require large amounts of skilled,

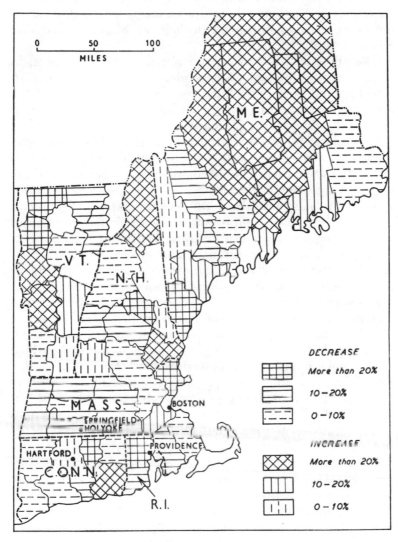

Fig. 41. The New England States: Percentage changes in the number of industrial production workers, 1947–54

or at least semi-skilled, labour, but little fuel or bulky raw
material. This kind of industry already flourished in south-
western New England: the problem was to establish it in the
hard-core area of industrial decline, in Massachusetts and
Rhode Island.

The other task was to expand alternative employment, in
order to reduce the region's dependence on manufacturing. In
New England, with its declining agriculture, this could only be
done by concentrating on such activities as commerce and
research to serve a national market.

How successful has this adaptation of the regional economy
been? In 1939, the three old industrial groups—textiles,
apparel, and leather—had accounted for 45 per cent. of the
region's employment in industry. In 1958, they accounted for
23 per cent. In Rhode Island, the decline was from 58 per cent.
to 30 per cent. More important, however, is the question of
what has replaced these industries. The main replacements
have been transport equipment and electrical engineering.
New England has plunged into the space age with all the vigour
at its command, backed by its long industrial experience and
the resources of its unrivalled collection of universities and
technical institutes. In place of the old textile mills have sprung
up plants manufacturing the most sophisticated gadgets for
rockets and planes. The transport equipment industry (which
in this case is mainly concerned with things that fly) has added
over 50,000 new jobs in the past fifteen years. This is certainly
the right industrial direction for a region to follow which is
situated, like New England, far from fuel and raw materials.

Undoubtedly, the change-over will go further: the textile
industry will contract still more, and electrical engineering will
increase as each new research frontier is opened. However,
there is a danger here, in that already the region is becoming
sensitive to a new pressure: at least half of the output of electronic equipment is for the government's defence programme,
and so is susceptible to changes in budgetary policy. Southern
California (p. 419) has already experienced the economic sea-
sickness that this may lead to. Having successfully thrown off
one form of industrial over-dependence, it would be unfortu-
nate if New England were to succumb to another, however
sophisticated.

The task of expanding alternative employment has also been carried out successfully since the war, as the following figures for the decade 1950–60 show:

New England—Percentage Changes in Occupational Structure

Professional and technical	+41
Clerical workers	+26
Skilled workers	+ 7
Machine operators	− 6
Unskilled workers	−17
Farm labourers	−36
Total employment	+ 7

On both counts, therefore, New England can feel that it has been successful in adjusting to the changed industrial conditions of the present day.

Within the region, however, there are local variations in the character and prosperity of manufacturing. The industrial cities of south-western New England, among which the largest are Springfield–Holyoke (478,000), Hartford (525,000), New Haven (312,000), and Bridgeport (334,000), contain a very wide range of light industries, mostly metal goods of various kinds.[1] North-eastward across New England the relative importance of the older industries increases. In centres like Providence (816,000) and Worcester (323,000) there is a rough balance between older and newer industries. For example, in Providence, the capital of Rhode Island and second only to Boston among New England's cities, textiles account for some 25 per cent. of the industrial employment, but there are also a famous jewellery industry and important manufactures of hardware and machine tools. Beyond this intermediate zone lie the old one-industry cities: the textile centres like Fall River–New Bedford (281,000), Lawrence, and Lowell, or the shoe towns of Lynn and Haverhill.

The heart of this industrial area is to be found in metropolitan Boston (2,589,000) which contains a sixth of the region's industrial workers and half the manufacturing plants

[1] Observation during a brief train journey through this area yielded the following selection: typewriters, aeroplanes, hats, rubber goods, pianos, automatic signals, locks and keys, nuts and bolts, machine tools, steel windows, vacuum cleaners, and refrigerators.

of Massachusetts. In terms of employment the most important industry in 1958 was the great new electrical engineering group. It was followed by machinery, apparel, and leather, so that the Boston area reproduces in miniature the industrial dilemma of transition from old to new and the hopes of the region as a whole.

Today Boston is the regional capital of New England. Considering, however, its long history and the role of the city in colonial days, it is perhaps interesting that it has so largely failed to become anything more than that. In the rivalry between the Middle Atlantic cities for national pre-eminence Boston took little part; many of its interests were maritime; its railway building was less vigorous than that of its neighbours, and although the Taconics are a much narrower obstacle than the Appalachians, in an economic sense they have effectively shut Boston off from the interior. Furthermore, the equalization of freight rates from all the Atlantic ports to Europe robbed Boston of the advantage it might have enjoyed through its position in relation to the great circle route to western Europe. As a result, its magnificent and well-equipped harbour handles only 18–19 million tons of traffic annually, of which no more than a third is foreign trade, while nearly two-thirds consists of coastwise receipts. Thus Boston has failed to count significantly in the country's foreign trade, and at the same time suffers, as a port, the disadvantage of a one-way flow of goods; effectively, it merely ships in coal and petroleum to meet New England's needs.

It seems clear that the city's basic problem is that it has become overshadowed, economically, by New York. One may argue that this is inevitable, in that there is room for only one primate city on the coast, just as all the other ports of the European North Sea coast are subordinate to Rotterdam: that as Rotterdam holds its primacy because there is only one Rhine, so New York holds its primacy because there is only one Hudson River. At any rate, while Boston is the undisputed capital of New England, its territory is suffering constant erosion in the south-west, where an increasing section of Connecticut is tributary to New York. It is New York which dominates the routes to the interior and the foreign trade of the country; New York which plays the national, and Boston

PLATE **XI**

(*a*) Steel mills at Sydney, Nova Scotia. The mills use local coal supplies and iron ore from Newfoundland

(*b*) Paper mills at Trois Rivières, Quebec, looking west. The town and mills are located at the junction of the St. Lawrence (flowing from the left of the picture towards the lower edge) and its tributary the St. Maurice (entering from the right)

CANADIAN INDUSTRIES

PLATE XII

The Maritime Provinces: On the frontier of farming in New Brunswick. The natural features of this granite country remind the British reader of comparable farm areas in northern Scotland, but the fences and buildings are as distinctively American

the regional, role. One important consequence of this is that New York, and not Boston, is the main outlet for New England's goods—a sample survey in 1948 revealed that 81 per cent. of the region's shipments were being sent by this route. Symbolically enough, Boston's main link with the interior, the Boston and Albany Railroad, is owned by the New York Central.

The New England region possesses a marked individuality, which is the product not so much of geography as of history. It dates from the time when the New England colonies formed the most wealthy block on the Atlantic coast, and when the Atlantic coast was America. If other Americans feel that New Englanders should awaken to the fact that times have changed, none would deny the vast contribution made to the economic and cultural life of the U.S.A. by New England's men of business and letters. Less and less does the New England tradition represent the American norm, yet the region occupies in the United States today a position not unlike that of the senior member of some club, overtaken in accomplishments, and sometimes outvoted, by the younger members, but still wielding the influence that his prestige warrants over the conduct of business.

FURTHER READING

AMONG the many analyses of the New England economy, the following may be mentioned, and are arranged in order of publication: *New England's Prospect, 1933*, ed. J. K. Wright; 'New England's Economic Prospects', by C. D. Hyson and A. Neal, *Harvard Business Review*, vol. xxvi, pp. 156 80; *The Rural Economy of New England*, by J. D. Black (1950); *The New England Economy*, by the Council of Economic Advisers (1951); *The Economics of New England*, by S. E. Harris (1952) and *The Economic State of New England*, ed. A. A. Bright Jr. and G. H. Ellis (1954). On the decline of the textile industry see either Harris's study mentioned above, or the *Report of the New England Textile Industry* which he edited for the Conference of New England Governors.

New England agriculture is further dealt with by H. F. Wilson, *The Hill Country of New England . . . 1790–1930*; L. E. Klimm, 'The Empty Areas of the North-Eastern United States', *Geog. Review*, vol. xliv, pp. 315–45; E. C. Higbee, 'The Three Earths of New England', ibid., vol. xlii, pp. 425–38, and J. W. Goldthwait, 'A Town That Has Gone Downhill' (Lyme, N. H.), ibid., vol. xvii, pp. 527–52.

On the New England fisheries, see *New England's Fishing Industry* by E. A. Ackerman. On the role of Boston, see 'Hinterland Boundaries of New York City and Boston in Southern New England', by H. L. Green, *Econ. Geog.*, vol. xxxi, pp. 283–300. For a study of the conversion of an old industrial area, see W. H. Wallace, 'Merrimack Valley Manufacturing: Past and Present', *Econ. Geog.*, vol. xxxvii, pp. 283–308.

X

THE MARITIME PROVINCES
AND NEWFOUNDLAND

1. *General Situation*

ALTHOUGH the history of European settlement in the Maritime Provinces of Canada and in Newfoundland is as long and as distinguished as that in Massachusetts or Virginia, in economic development this region has lagged far behind the newer lands to the west and south. The physical handicaps of the area—which in any case are shared by much of New England—cannot by themselves explain this economic difference. Such an explanation must also take into account the position of the region, in relation both to the rest of Canada and to the continent as a whole.

The Virginians and New Englanders of the colonial period found their progress westward from the Atlantic coast obstructed by the mountain and forest barriers of the Appalachians and the New England ranges. Against these barriers, as we have seen, the flow of migrants was dammed for long enough to produce a relatively dense population, and to promote the early growth of cities and industries. Further north, however, the barriers were outflanked by the St. Lawrence route, which led directly to the continental interior. The Maritime Provinces lay not astride the main line of westward movement but to one side of it; and their forested and often infertile lands offered little incentive to costly clearance and settlement, when contrasted with the vastly superior areas of Lower Canada that lay within easy reach to the west. There was, in other words, not the same geographical compulsion about the occupance of the Maritimes—and still less of interior Newfoundland—as there was about that of the coastlands farther south. The early settlements in many cases looked seawards to the fishing grounds rather than landwards, and, significantly enough, the earliest agricultural areas were not forest clearings but coastal marshes reclaimed by dyking.

The position occupied by the Maritime Provinces has further drawbacks. Projecting far to the eastward as they do, it might be expected that the provinces would be particularly well

Q

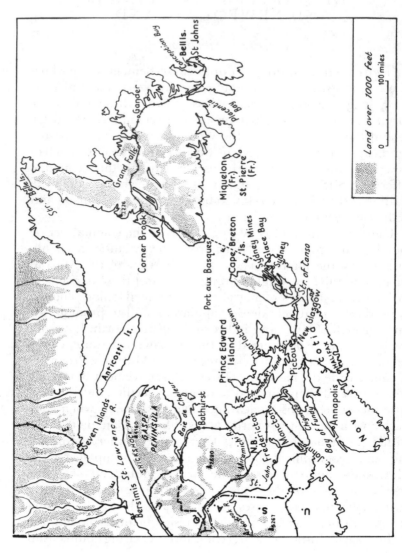

Fig. 42. The Maritime Provinces and Newfoundland: Location Map.
Since this map was drawn, a new iron ore port, Port Cartier, has been developed just west of
Seven Islands (Sept Iles) on the St. Lawrence.

placed to participate in foreign trade, especially in winter, when the St. Lawrence is frozen. In reality, however, although the winter transit trade is considerable, it forms an insufficient basis on which to develop regional industries. Furthermore, it has become apparent (and not only here, but in other continents also) that in foreign trade, as distinct from passenger traffic, the greatest advantage lies usually not with the area which projects farthest oceanwards, but with that which surrounds the deepest penetration of the sea inland. It is at the head of deep water navigation that both manufacturing and foreign trade concentrate. This head of navigation on the St. Lawrence was at one time at Quebec, then later at Montreal; now, with the Seaway giving access to the Great Lakes, it is at Fort William and Port Arthur.

But perhaps the most influential factor in moulding the outlook and the economy of the Maritimes is the international boundary. The provinces are connected to the rest of Canada only by a narrow corridor, 30 miles wide, where the state of Maine reaches almost to the St. Lawrence. Through this sparsely populated corridor run a road and two railways, forming a slender and somewhat roundabout link between east and west. But the shortest route from Montreal to the Maritimes (that of the Canadian Pacific) passes through the U.S.A. Indeed, the 'natural' connexion of this region, in so far as it has any, is with the north-eastern United States rather than with Canada, and here the border intervenes. This is a fact whose significance we must later consider.

In physical character the Maritime Provinces form a continuation of the New England system, which is related in turn to the older, eastern half of the Appalachians. The grain of the country still runs from north-east to south-west, with two upland areas separated by a lowland which, structurally, is a geosyncline. The coastline is deeply indented, with numerous drowned valleys. Inland the relief is nowhere impressive; the mountains of Gaspé rise above 4,000 feet but in the Maritimes proper there are few areas of the ice-smoothed surface above 1,000 feet. The main relief features are determined by a number of granite batholiths and other igneous intrusions. One of these underlies the mountains of north central New Brunswick, and others are found in the 'arms' of southern Nova Scotia and Cape

Breton Island, and along the north shore of the Bay of Fundy. For the rest, the upland areas in the north are based upon formations of Silurian age or earlier, while the lower-lying south-eastern part of New Brunswick, much of central Nova Scotia, and the whole of Prince Edward Island are underlain by Carboniferous limestones and sandstones. Coal measures occur in Cape Breton Island, in the vicinity of Pictou in western Nova Scotia, and around the head of Chignecto Bay. Finally, in south-western Nova Scotia appear formations of Triassic age; the curious form of the southern shore of the Bay of Fundy is produced by parallel bands of Triassic trap rock and sandstone flanking the Nova Scotia granites.

The effect of this pattern on the economic balance sheet is that, in general, the areas of younger, sedimentary rocks are farmed, while the areas of older crystallines are not. The value of these non-agricultural lands lies in their forests and, to a lesser extent, in the building materials they yield—granite, marble and slate.

The Maritimes, as their name would imply, have a climate much modified by proximity to the Atlantic. Summers are cool; winters in the hills and along the St. Lawrence are cold. Precipitation is ample and well distributed throughout the year. The chief climatic handicap of the region, however, is its lack of sunshine in summer. The southern coasts are often fog-bound (for some 70 days in the year), and consequently the moderating influences of the sea on this long, indented coastline are offset by the fog. Inland the governing factor becomes the danger of frost: the growing season shortens by as much as 100 days between the coast and the interior, and indeed in some upland areas of New Brunswick no month of the year is frost-free. From this combination of climatic circumstances derive the region's two main natural resources—its forest cover and its abundant supplies of water power.

2. Land and Livelihood

In its origins the population of the Maritime Provinces is thoroughly mixed. The earliest mainland settlements were made in the seventeenth century by the French, in order to provide shore bases for the Grand Banks fishing fleets, and the region was known as Acadia. The main period of British immigration began with the founding of Halifax in 1749, and in 1775 several thousands of French Acadians were deported for security reasons. There followed influxes of Germans, of British

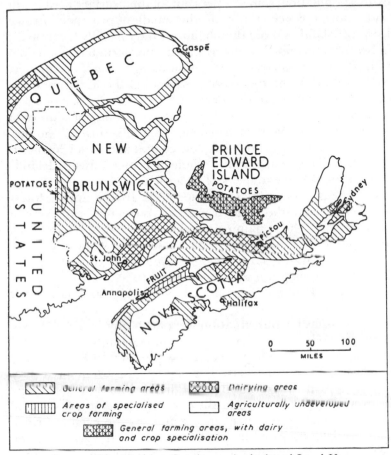

FIG. 43. The Maritime Provinces: Agricultural Land Use.

loyalists who chose to move north rather than remain in the new American republic after 1783, and of Scots and Irish who, entering in their thousands in the nineteenth century, accepted the hardships of the pioneer life in preference to the famine and evictions of their homelands. Today, about one-third of the population of the three provinces is of English origin; the

French and Scots each account for about a quarter, and the Irish for perhaps one-tenth.

Perhaps the most enlightening statistic about the Maritime Provinces, however, is that after three centuries of occupance by this population, some 70 per cent. of their surface area is still under forest cover. Only in the smallest province, Prince Edward Island, is more than half the land officially 'occupied'; in Nova Scotia and New Brunswick the proportion is about one-fifth. If we then focus our attention on *agricultural* occupance, we find that, in the two large provinces of the Maritimes, the ratio of 'improved' land to 'occupied' land is only 1 : 4 or 1 : 5.

Agriculture, in fact, stands well down the list of sources of income in the Maritimes—below manufacturing, mining, forestry, and fishing. Only in a few coastal and valley lowlands (but these include almost the whole of Prince Edward Island) would it be realistic to speak of an agricultural region; over the rest of the provinces the farmlands are scattered among forest and scrub, and the farm frontier is retreating rather than advancing. Of the remaining farming, a good deal is part-time, in the sense that the farmer relies on seasonal work in forestry to supplement the farm income. And gradually the small farmers are giving up, and turning full-time to other employment. Their land is either merged with larger holdings, or left to nature.

The reasons for this situation are partly physical and partly economic: physical, in that soils and climate limit the range and output of farm products; economic, in that the overriding problem is that of markets. Throughout the whole area, hay and oats easily outrank all other field crops—in both New Brunswick and Nova Scotia they occupy some 90 per cent. of the cropland, and they account for 70 per cent. even in Prince Edward Island, with its greater agricultural variety. They form the basis, as we might expect, for dairying and stock raising, for which natural conditions are quite favourable. But where are the markets for these products? With only three centres of any size within the region—Halifax (184,000), Saint John (95,000) and the steel town of Sydney (33,000)—the Maritimes' market for fluid milk and meat is small, so that the dairy farmers must enter the competitive business of butter and cheese manufacture, and sell outside the region. The only real alternative to dairying is one that New Scotland has copied from Old Scotland, and that is to concentrate on stock breeding —the sale of animals rather than their products. This has been developed, but it is interesting that it is based largely on imported processed feeds rather than improved pasture within the region.

Besides this basic hay-oats combination, the Maritimes have two cash crops: potatoes and fruit. Potatoes are grown on Prince Edward Island and in the upper Saint John Valley, across the border from the Aroostook potatolands of Maine (p. 217). Fruit growing is widespread, but the chief producing area is the Annapolis Valley of Nova Scotia with its apple orchards. These two crops, once again, are well suited to physical conditions in the Maritimes—and wholly unsuited to the conditions under which they have to be marketed. Both must be sold outside the region, yet both are bulky and perishable. Prince Edward Island potatoes, for example, must begin their journey to market on the mainland by travelling in heated vans on a train ferry. Maritimes' apples compete directly, inside Canada, with Quebec apples grown nearer to the centres of population; their other main market is in Great Britain.

Just as the cattle farmers have tried to overcome their disadvantages of position by specializing in a quality product —pedigree stock—so, too, have the potato and fruit farmers. The potato growers (and here there is an interesting parallel with the situation in Northern Ireland, whose positional problem is rather the same) specialize in seed potatoes, and they supply half the Canadian market and export a considerable amount. But quality increases costs, of course, and the market for potatoes in North America is a contracting one: consumption per person is steadily falling. The apple growers have tried various forms of processing and canning as a solution to their own problem, but this can never be more than a partial answer: most of the demand for apples is for the fresh fruit.

Since agriculture is limited by the conditions we have been considering, and there are few large towns, the Maritimes depend heavily on non-agricultural and non-industrial employment—mining, fishing, and forestry. Of the three, mining or quarrying is limited to a few areas, the chief of which are the coalfields of Cape Breton Island—in the Sydney and Glace Bay area, where the seams run out under the sea—and the shores of Northumberland Strait, around Pictou. Nova Scotia produces about one-half of Canada's coal; it is of good coking quality. Nevertheless, output is declining. Elsewhere, there are gypsum, salt, and some valuable copper-lead-zinc ores in the Bathurst, N.B., area.

Fishing is everywhere important on the coast. Traditionally, the fishermen of the Maritimes have fished the inshore waters in small boats operating from small ports. A modern fleet using large boats, and fishing the offshore banks, is only slowly coming into being. Nevertheless, the fisheries yield good returns from cod and lobsters, and processing and canning employ several thousand workers. But here again arises the persistent problem of the Maritimes, the absence of a local market. The obvious market for either the fresh or frozen product is the north-eastern U.S.A.—but it has its own fisheries. Some 20 per cent. of the catch has to be disposed of by drying it, and selling it in distant South America and the Caribbean.

Forestry plays a vital part in the regional economy, especially in New Brunswick. Seasonal work in logging gives winter employment to many farmers, and the rivers provide power and transport. The forest products' industry accounts for some 40 per cent. of the industrial employment of New Brunswick. The manufacture of pulp and paper, dependent as it is on huge quantities of both water and power, is concentrated at a few big plants close to the principal rivers and to tidewater. The sawmills, on the other hand, vary greatly in size: small ones are to be found wherever logging is carried on, but the bigger mills are again near the coast.

Most of the industries of the Maritimes are based on the activities already mentioned—food and fish processing, paper, and lumber. The other main industry of the region is the manufacture of steel at Sydney and New Glasgow. These towns lie on the Cape Breton coalfield, and iron ore is brought 400 miles by sea from Newfoundland: it could presumably also be obtained from Labrador, but the industry has survived until now in its remote location largely because it is concentrated in one large corporation, whose ownership covers the Newfoundland mines. The level of costs is inevitably high, and markets for as much of the output as possible must be found within the region. In the future, this is likely to be even more true than in the past, since the Montreal area, to which Sydney has sold steel in the past, now has steel mills of its own. Prospects are not encouraging at the moment for this remotest of all North America's steel producers.

3. The Prospect Before the Maritime Provinces

The North American Century, the hundred years of amazing development which have fashioned the present geography of the continent, has been a discouraging era for the Maritimes. The indices of population increase and industrial expansion lagged far behind those of the rest of Canada. The region gave an impression of becoming economically stunted after its early start. The opinion was sometimes voiced that federation was a mistake; that the Maritimes exported more, in brains and energy, to the rest of Canada than they received in federal help; that perhaps a political connexion with the U.S.A. would have served them better.

Since the war, the Maritime Provinces have clearly shown that they do not intend to resign themselves without a struggle to second-class status within the nation. Led by such regional bodies as the Atlantic Provinces Economic Council (A.P.E.C.), they have taken stock of their resources and laid plans for their use.

What can be done to improve the region's economic position? As we have surveyed the various sources of income available, it should have become clear that the key to the position in each case is the supply or availability of capital: that, given investment, farming, fishing, or forestry can be made to yield better returns. The raising of pedigree stock can have this effect: the problem is to find the capital for improvement of pasture and purchase of the first stock. The fishing industry can prosper: the problem is to modernize the fleet, finance larger boats for off-shore work, and extend the facilities for freezing and canning. Forestry confronts an ever-growing market for newsprint and pulp in the U.S.A.: the problem is to create the huge mills which form the basic units of the industry. In every sphere of the economy, the critical factor is the size of investment necessary.

It is therefore the first task of the A.P.E.C. and the provinces to obtain this capital. Various federal schemes already provide a groundwork—payments to farmers for land improvement, and loans towards the building of fishing vessels. Beyond these, however, the region must find its own sources, by attracting to itself more transit trade and more industries; using the capital these generate to develop by its own research fresh uses for its products, and exerting itself to sell them in new markets. After so long a period of frustration, there is plenty of welcome evidence that the worst is over, and that the regional effort of the Maritime Provinces is bearing fruit.

4. *Newfoundland*

As a political unit, the province of Newfoundland consists not only of the island of that name, with an area of some 43,000 square miles, but also of 110,000 square miles of Labrador, the great eastward projection of the Canadian mainland, whose administration the province shares with Quebec.

The island, with which we are here concerned, was Great Britain's earliest colony. It was for long, however, no more than a base for fishing fleets. Underlain in large part by old igneous and metamorphic rocks, its surface—part forested, part swamp and barrens—has never offered encouragement to the farmer, except in a few sheltered valley locations.[1] Summers are cool and precipitation is high, so that the physical handicaps of the Maritimes are here reproduced in severer form. Ice closes all but the southern coasts in winter, and fog replaces it, as a sailor's hazard, in summer.

In an island, so much of whose life is bound up with the sea, it is not surprising that the population (some 458,000 in 1961) is mostly found in coastal settlements. Since the coasts are closed in winter by ice, and overland communications are poor outside the St. John's–Conception Bay area of the south-east, the population lives in isolation for much of the year.

Today, as throughout the island's history, fishing remains the principal occupation of its people. Because of its remoteness from both the American and the European consumer, the

---

[1] Among the 43,000 sq. mls. of the island, only 38 are classified as improved agricultural land.

staple product of Newfoundland has long been dried cod. With the development of fish processing, however, whether by canning or freezing, it has been possible to place on the market other types of catch.

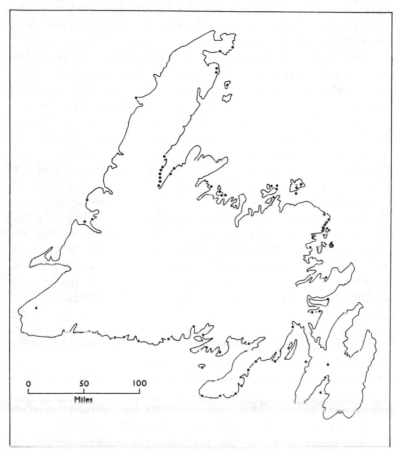

Fig. 44. Newfoundland: The Centralization Programme. Each of the dots on the map represents a small settlement (usually a fishing community) which has been closed and transplanted under this programme to a more favourable location.

The old style of fishing, however, in small boats based on tiny, scattered settlements, is hardly suited to twentieth-century conditions. The government of the province, recognizing this fact, has set on foot a process of 'centralization'. The inhabitants of the coastal settlements are encouraged to ask to be removed to larger communities, where they can enjoy better services, and incidentally form part of larger fishery units. The government, which subsidizes the move, profits by reducing the great cost of servicing the former scattered communities. Under this programme, about 100 small fishing villages have been abandoned, (see Fig. 44).

Since the days of the early fishing settlements, only two other forms of employment for the population have arisen as serious rivals to the original occupation. One of these is mining, for the island possesses a variety of minerals. Among them is the iron ore that supplies the blast furnaces of Nova Scotia. This is mined on Bell Island, in Conception Bay, and as with the Sydney coal to which it is partner, the workings extend under the sea. The other main occupation of the island is forestry. The forest cover on the island's bleak surface is less extensive than that of the Maritimes, but it nevertheless constitutes a major resource and is largely in the hands of two big pulp and paper companies which ensure efficient exploitation. It is the paper industry which is largely responsible for the interior settlements of Newfoundland; Grand Falls and Corner Brook, for example, are company towns which, with the mining settlement on Bell Island, form the only centres of any size outside the capital, port, and processing centre of St. John's (91,000).

In the course of a varied political past, Newfoundland has possessed, at different periods, the status of both colony and dominion within the British Commonwealth. In 1948, however, the islanders voted, by a slender majority, for confederation with Canada. The majority vote was almost certainly swelled by appreciation of the services made available by the Ottawa government to the provinces, in federal grants for social security and welfare schemes. This recognition that Newfoundland would get from the federal government more than it could give probably touches the heart of the island's problem—its perennial poverty.

To past generations of islanders, Newfoundland offered a rough, lonely life between the sea and their small farm plots which was, nevertheless, adequate in the sense that it was better than the life they had left in Scotland or Ireland. But today's standard of comparison is not the Old World environment their ancestors left, but that of the New World they might have reached by going on a little farther. The limitations of the environment make it as difficult for Newfoundland to support its population at a 'modern' American standard of living as it would be for the Outer Hebrides or Connemara to become as prosperous as the English Midlands.

If the concentration of resources within an area is—as in all the cases mentioned—too thin to support a high standard of living, the only alternative solution to emigration lies in introducing into the area sources of wealth from outside that are independent of the natural poverty within. One such source, either in Scotland or in Canada, is government payments and this is, of course, precisely the effect of confederation on Newfoundland—the wealthier provinces of the Dominion contribute to the support of the less prosperous.

For a time during and after the Second World War it seemed as if Newfoundland had discovered another such source—in its strategic location. Placed as it was on the North Atlantic transit routes, it profited enormously from the presence of military bases, and built after the war a great civil airport at Gander. Here again was income independent of resources. But the prosperity has proved ephemeral. With the coming of the jet plane, Gander has become little more than an emergency stop, an unnecessary stepping stone in waters that are now narrow enough to be crossed at a single bound. Perhaps for a land which had yielded, over the centuries, so grudging a livelihood as Newfoundland it was, after all, too good to last.

FURTHER READING

Much of the earlier work on the Maritimes was done by D. F. Putnam, and embodied in the book *Canadian Regions*, which he edited. On the early settlement, see 'Settlement Patterns in Maritime Canada, 1687–1786', by J. B. Bird, *Geog. Review*, vol. xlv, pp. 385–404; 'Prince Edward Island—The Story of Its Agriculture', by W. R. Shaw, *Can. Geog. Journ.*, vol. lii, pp. 182–203, or A. H. Clark's *Three Centuries and The Island* [P.E.I.], and his articles, 'The Sheep/Swine Ratio as a Guide to a Century's Change in the Livestock Geography of Nova Scotia', *Econ. Geog.*, vol. xxxviii, pp. 38–55, and 'Old World Origins and Religious Adherence in Nova Scotia', *Geog. Review*, vol. l, pp. 317–44. See also 'The Agricultural Background of Settlement in Eastern Nova Scotia', by R. L. Gentilcore, *A.A.A.G.*, vol. xlvi, pp. 378–404, and 'A Land Use Reconnaissance of the Annapolis–Cornwall Valley', by B. Cornwall, *Geog. Bull.*, No. 9 (1956), 23–52.

On other activities, a selection of references, all in *Can. Geog. Journ.*, is: W. A. Dixon, 'Power in New Brunswick', vol. lviii, pp. 137–49; J. A. Paterson, 'Industry Comes Back to New Brunswick', vol. lix, pp. 23–31; B. J. McGuire, 'Maritime Industrial Empire', vol. liii, pp. 124–45; G. G. Campbell, 'Mining in Nova Scotia', vol. lix, pp. 3–13, and M. Van Steen, 'The New Halifax Faces Old Problems', vol. li, pp. 118–27. On Newfoundland, see 'Some Recent Changes in the Economy of Newfoundland', by W. E. Greening, *Can. Geog. Journ.*, vol. lv, pp. 128–48, and 'The Corner Brook Area, Newfoundland', by W. C. Wonders, *Geog. Bull.*, No. 5 (1954), pp. 29–58.

XI

THE LOWER ST. LAWRENCE VALLEY

1. *Introduction*

THE region of North America whose focus is the Lower St. Lawrence Valley is small but very distinct. On the one hand, it possesses a physical separateness which leaves it with few connecting links with the remainder of the continent. On the other hand, and more significantly, it has the cultural distinctiveness proper to an area in which some 80 per cent. of the population speak, by preference, a language different from that of the other 200 million inhabitants of Anglo-America. This is French Canada.

A map of population distribution shows the extent to which this region is isolated by natural barriers from its surroundings. On the north shore of the St. Lawrence, population density thins rapidly up the slope to the plateau surface of the Laurentian Shield, and there are few communities more than 50 miles from the shore; beyond lies the immense emptiness of northern Canada. On the west the Shield encloses the St. Lawrence and Ottawa Valleys, swinging south to cross the former at the Thousand Islands Bridge. Here there is, on the population map, only a slender 'connecting link' of settlement to join Lower Canada to Upper Canada; and the traveller between Montreal and Toronto is conscious that, although the Shield produces no relief obstacle, yet he has crossed an economic and cultural no man's land. On the south settlement spreads across the broad plains of the St. Lawrence and Richelieu Valleys until it ends, rather abruptly, along the edge of the Adirondacks and the mountains of northern New England. There the map reveals the one major link with settlement in other regions, where the Champlain Lowland cuts across the international boundary and Vermont adjoins southern Quebec. Finally, on the east, settlement becomes progressively sparser as the river widens into the Gulf of St. Lawrence, until nothing but a string of fishing and logging villages lines the narrow corridor that joins Laurentian Canada to the Maritime Provinces.

Yet for all its separateness, this region plays a vital part in

Canadian life. It contains some 25 per cent. of the nation's population including Montreal, its largest city, port, and manufacturing centre. Its railway links across the adjacent

FIG. 45. The St. Lawrence Valley: Location Map.

empty areas are good enough to enable it to handle a major share of Canada's foreign trade. And in the 1960's, in the era of the St. Lawrence Seaway, it has acquired a 'back door' which opens through it a new international routeway and does something to reduce its present isolation.

It is some 400 miles from the Thousand Islands Bridge to the end of continuous settlement on the north shore of the St. Lawrence, beyond Quebec; some 650 miles from Ottawa to Gaspé. At their broadest the lowlands stretch for 120 miles from north-west to south-east. Only in the junction area between the Richelieu–Champlain Lowlands and the St. Lawrence Valley are there wide stretches of fertile soils. There, however, much of the land is of excellent quality, as a result of the deposition of marine sediments in post-glacial times, when the lowlands were submerged beneath a gulf known as the Champlain Sea.

Climatic conditions in the valley are also distinctive: winters are severe, snowfalls are heavy, and weather changes are frequent. These conditions reflect, as was noted in Chapter I, the convergence of storm tracks on the Great Lakes–St. Lawrence line. The passage of the depressions is responsible for the variability of conditions, and for the considerable winter precipitation, which brings snowfall of 100 inches per annum or more to many valley stations, even at sea-level.

Over most of the valley precipitation is more than 35 inches, evenly distributed throughout the year. The January mean temperature is 14° F. at Montreal and 10° F. in Quebec City, and it falls rapidly, on the slopes above the river, to 0° F. in the Laurentide Mountains. The St. Lawrence is closed by ice from December to April; and the frost-free period available to farmers in the valley is usually limited to 120 or 130 days. July mean temperatures fall from 70° F. at Montreal to 58° or 60° down-river, opposite Anticosti Island. The Gaspé Peninsula, in spite of its long coastline, has the wide annual temperature range (50° to 55° F.) typical of eastern continental margins in these latitudes (Bangor, in Maine, has a range of 48° F. and Vladivostok, U.S.S.R., one of 63° F).

2. Settlement and Landscape

For geographers, the St. Lawrence Valley has long provided a useful illustration of the maxim that, to interpret the landscape of a region, it is necessary to be familiar with its settlement history. The valley was settled by the French in the seventeenth and eighteenth centuries, and although by the end of French rule in 1763 there were only some 65,000 of them (whereas the British colonies farther south in the continent had more than a million inhabitants), they nevertheless created by their presence a landscape whose distinctiveness remains to the present day. Not only the place names of the Lower St. Lawrence, but also the rural settlement pattern, reflect the legal and social arrangements of the French colony which later became Lower Canada and, upon federation in 1867, the province of Quebec.

R

French settlement in Canada may be dated from 1608, when Quebec City was founded by the man whose leadership dominated the whole enterprise—Samuel Champlain. Although Champlain planned to establish the colony on a firm agricultural basis, it was, from the first, the fur trade which attracted the French, and to which their main efforts were devoted. Since agriculture and the fur trade were generally considered to be bad partners, the permanent settlements on the shore of the St. Lawrence languished, while the French pioneers spread over the interior the peculiarly impermanent form of occupancy and control that fur trading implied. Officials, missionaries, and free-lance fur traders—the *coureurs de bois*—pushed swiftly inland, becoming embroiled in inter-tribal Indian wars; adopting Indian modes of life and travel; constantly seeking new fur supplies as they pushed westward across the northern Great Lakes to the Upper Mississippi. In 1670 French sovereignty was proclaimed at Sault Ste Marie. In 1682 La Salle followed the Mississippi to the sea, and claimed a vast Louisiana for the King of France.

In the meantime the neglected settlements on the St. Lawrence had achieved, by 1660, a population of about 3,000. They had spread along the river, and were later to spread along its tributary, the Richelieu, in a single line of waterfront settlement. This pattern developed partly because movement by river was simpler than ashore; partly because of the importance of fisheries in the early colonial economy; and partly because the river verges offered unforested patches where the initial labour of forest clearance might be avoided. Holdings were laid out in long, narrow strips, at right angles to the river frontage, with the homestead close to the water's edge, so that 'at the end of the French régime, a traveller could have seen almost every house in Canada as he made the canoe trip along the St. Lawrence and Richelieu'.[1]

On the inland side the limit of the holdings was usually only a distant line towards which clearance of the forest slowly progressed. But as the population of French Canada increased, not only were the holdings subdivided into still narrower frontages,

[1] P. Deffontaines, 'Le Rang: Type de Peuplement rural du Canada français'. *Proc. 17th Internat. Cong. of the Internat. Geog. Union, Washington, D.C.*, 1952, p. 723. This article is an excellent brief summary of the social geography developed within the French Canadian settlement pattern.

but a second line (or *rang*) of settlement was laid out, parallel to that along the waterfront. Here the process of parcelling out and clearing the narrow strips was repeated, the rural road replacing the river as the base line. Thus there developed a pattern in marked contrast to that of the areas farther to the west and south, where a survey based on mile-square sections produced the familiar 'gridiron' settlement pattern of the American interior. The French pattern has survived in Quebec to the present day; indeed, in a modified form, it has been used in the most recent expansions of settlement in the province, in the Abitibi and Temiscaming areas. Twenty-eight per cent. of the population of Quebec today live in the *rangs*.[1]

At the end of French rule in Canada, in 1763, the settled areas still extended only a short distance back from the shores of the St. Lawrence and Richelieu. The period of British rule that followed, and especially the early nineteenth century, saw an expansion of the settled areas, first into the broad lowland, south of the St. Lawrence and east of the Richelieu, which is known as the Eastern Townships. Here the original settlement was predominantly British, and the place-names sturdily Anglo-Saxon. But as the population of the older French areas increased rapidly in the nineteenth century (by 1830 it had risen to about 400,000) it overflowed into the Eastern Townships. Today the French-speaking population of the Townships is six times as numerous as the English-speaking, and such place-names as St. Germain de Grantham and Ste Anne de Stukely reflect the changing cultural affiliation of the area.

The French Canadians have continued to increase in numbers, and have been obliged to seek still other outlets for their excess population. These they have found along the edge of the Laurentian Plateau, on the south shore of the St. Lawrence and in Gaspé, but even so, there has of necessity been a heavy emigration from the rural areas to the cities and factories, both of Canada and of New England.

The agriculture of modern Quebec makes this region a part of the Hay and Dairy Belt, with more than 60 per cent. of the crop acreage under hay, and a further 20 per cent. under oats. The cities of the St. Lawrence Valley provide markets for fluid milk, and butter and cheese are manufactured in large quanti-

[1] P. Deffontaines, op. cit., p. 726.

ties; Quebec accounts for more than a third of Canada's butter and cheese output. In addition to this basic farm activity, however, the valley's agriculture includes the production of a number of special crops. The presence of Montreal and its suburbs has encouraged the rise of market gardening in their vicinity. Small fruit crops are numerous in the valley, and Quebec produces more than a quarter of Canada's apples. Finally, the forests of southern Quebec provide a large part of Canada's output of maple products.

As is the case everywhere in the Hay and Dairy Belt—in northern New England, for example, or in northern Michigan and Wisconsin—there is a marked falling-off in the intensity of land use and activity on the remoter fringes of Quebec's farmlands. Even in the long-settled Eastern Townships only about a half of the farmland is improved. Away from the valley markets and the creameries, agriculture slips towards a subsistence level, and the farm income is supplemented to an increasing extent by fishing, or by work in the forests or in industry.

3. Power and Industry

The St. Lawrence Valley possesses no coal and no petroleum. It does, however, have two resources which are important on a world scale: it is the world's leading producer of asbestos, and it possesses almost a half of Canada's installed hydro-electric generating capacity, which is itself the second largest in the world, after the U.S.A. The asbestos is mined in the Eastern Townships, in the neighbourhood of Thetford Mines and Asbestos, and 1960 production was about 1 million tons, the bulk of which was exported to the U.S.A. The hydro-electric power is produced mainly on the southern edge of the Laurentian Shield. There conditions for power development approach the ideal on the rivers that descend, through chains of lakes, from the elevated south-eastern corner of the Shield to the St. Lawrence. Of these rivers, the largest power producers are the Saguenay, flowing out of Lake St. John past the great Shipshaw power stations; the St. Maurice River, on which the development around Shawinigan accounts for half a million horsepower of generating capacity, and other works above and below the falls for a further $1\frac{1}{2}$ million; the Ottawa River, with its tributary the Gatineau; and the St. Lawrence itself. These rivers, affording suitable sites within easy reach of the St. Lawrence Valley power users, have been exploited first, and a large part of their potential has been realized. Since, however, demand has continued to rise, more remote reserves have been tapped, such as those of the Bersimis and Manicougan Rivers,

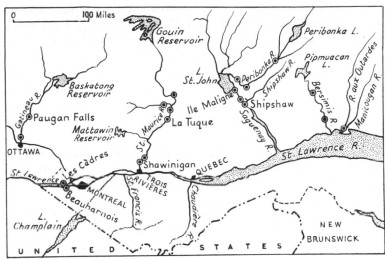

Fig. 46. Quebec: Hydro-electric Development. The stations shown, when all completed to full capacity, will account for more than 90 per cent. of the province's generating capacity. (Based on a map prepared by the Quebec Hydro-Electric Commission, by permission.)

200 miles below Quebec on the empty north shore of the St. Lawrence. But the remoter potential of the Shield is more than adequate for the foreseeable future—the province is at present using less than half its potential at ordinary six month flow,[1] and in any case the construction of the St. Lawrence Seaway presents the valley with a huge hydro-electricity bonus, produced at the very doorstep of Montreal, a bonus which Quebec will share with Ontario and New York State.

As a location for industry, the St. Lawrence Valley thus enjoys the advantage conferred by its power supplies, to add to the advantage of its position as the funnel through which goods leave and enter Canada's eastern side. Although this latter ad-

[1] i.e., the volume of water which can be expected to be available for generating purposes for at least six months in the year.

vantage is limited in winter by the closure of the river, the valley exerts sufficient attraction upon industry to account for almost one-third of Canada's industrial output by value.

Its industries fall into two main categories. One of these is made up of the wide variety of manufactures found in the Montreal area; that is, the group of consumer goods industries which is commonly found in the metropolis of a nation. Among these (and the parallel with New York is evident), the clothing and textile industries are the largest employers, while Montreal is also the leading national producer of such other consumer goods as shoes and tobacco products, and is an important manufacturer of transport equipment for railways and airlines. In all, the industrial labour force of Montreal represents about 13 per cent. of the nation's total, and more than half that of the province of Quebec.

The other category of industries in the valley comprises those attracted by the availability of electric power. Of these, two are outstanding: the manufacture of wood pulp and paper, and the smelting of metals, especially aluminium. Some 80 per cent. of Quebec's power consumption is accounted for by these two industries.

The Laurentian Shield is not merely a rich source of hydroelectricity; it is also a great forest area, and these two resources, in perfect partnership, combine to produce the pulp and paper industry. While this industry represents only a part of the total forest products output of Quebec, the whole of which gives full or part-time employment to many thousands of workers, nevertheless it consumes about two-thirds of the annual cut from the forests, and ranks as the province's largest single industry. The industry is located in close proximity to the power sources, along the Saguenay, the St. Maurice, and the Ottawa Rivers, and large mills are located in Montreal, Trois Rivières, and Quebec City. The province of Quebec accounts for 40 per cent., by value, of Canada's output of pulp and paper. These form, as we have seen in Chapter VII, the nation's principal exports, the item of greatest value being the sale of newsprint to the United States. Since the demand for this is likely to increase rather than to decline, it seems probable that Quebec will experience a gradual northward shift of the lumbering frontier, away from the St. Lawrence and into the vast, and at present largely inaccessible, areas of timber reserves that cover the Shield.[1]

Aluminium smelting, another power-hungry industry, is carried on at three main locations, Arvida on the Saguenay, Shawinigan on the St. Maurice, and at the mouth of the Bersimis. The fact that Canada itself produces no bauxite, so that all the raw materials for the smelters must be imported, and the additional fact that a large part of the smelter output is exported again, is evidence of the attractive force of the power factor to this industry. The same attraction will doubtless continue to draw new industries, such as chemical manufactures, to this area at the edge of the Shield, as fresh power supplies become available.

With the launching of the St. Lawrence Seaway project, already referred to in Chapter VI, it was at once apparent that changes would take place, not only in the geography of the Upper St. Lawrence, once it became accessible from the sea, but equally in that of the lower valley, where these changes were viewed with some apprehension. The last occasion when the effective head of St. Lawrence navigation was moved upstream was in 1870, when the channel was deepened to Montreal. As a result of this, Quebec City, the older settlement and political capital, found itself at a disadvantage; since it possesses little productive hinterland in its own right, and lies more remote than Montreal from the source areas of St. Lawrence trade, its industrial and commercial functions have tended to languish, and although its communications and its harbour are good, and are used in winter, it is as a cultural and political centre that the city (357,000) has developed.

The question naturally arises whether the transfer of the head of navigation to Chicago and Duluth will diminish the importance of the Montreal area in the same way. Up till now the city (2,109,000) has carried on a considerable trans-shipment business, with all the opportunities for local manufacture that trans-shipment brings.

It seems clear that, as use of the Seaway increases, Montreal

---

[1] In 1950, out of some 300,000 square miles of productive forests, only 126,000 square miles were described as 'presently accessible'. (Figures from Putnam, *Canadian Regions*, p. 161.)

must expect to lose some of this business. But the loss sustained in trans-shipment should be more than compensated for by the increase in total traffic volume. In 1963, the cargo tonnage through the St. Lawrence canals was more than twice that of the best pre-Seaway year. The foreign trade tonnage handled by Montreal itself has risen, not declined, since the Seaway was opened (the increase between 1958 and 1961 was almost 40 per cent.) To exchange the role of terminus for that of gateway is proving, and should prove, no hardship. In any case, the city's economic basis is very broad, and its advantages of position are great. It is the largest centre of land communications in Canada, and one of the two financial centres of the nation. Its industries are expanding, and a sign of this expansion is the siting of new steel mills just east of the city to supply local markets. It is a natural focus of routes—which Quebec never was—routes running north-westwards to the federal capital, Ottawa (429,000) and southwards to the Hudson and New York, as well as east and west along the St. Lawrence.

Perhaps a more immediate question is whether construction of the Seaway may not allow Toronto to take over Montreal's historic position as Canada's largest city and manufacturer. At the moment, the statistics show Montreal to have a clear lead in population and industry. At the same time, the Seaway has had a striking effect on Toronto as a port; it, even more than Chicago, has gained in importance through the new foreign trade connexions of the Great Lakes. What is more, Toronto has been the goal of many of the immigrants into Canada since the war: it is estimated that one in every four has settled in the vicinity of the city, and the skills represented by this immigrant labour add to the other considerable attractions of the Toronto area for industry. Thus the Seaway may have tipped the balance for the 1970's in favour of Toronto. But the question is clearly only one of relative size and, as we have seen, the prospects for Montreal remain bright.

Prediction of a prosperous future for the St. Lawrence Valley region accords well with the record of past development. A population of 65,000 Frenchmen in 1763 has grown to a present provincial total of 5¼ millions, in which the French element, far from being swallowed up by alien rule and majority affinities, has not merely held its own but has expanded to over 4 millions, and that without benefit of any large French immigration. Considering that the French population began its settlement with so little official encouragement and help, and that the natural endowment of the valley is meagre, such an expansion says much for the vitality and perseverance of its inhabitants. This is a population which today, as the vast resources of the Laurentian Shield are gradually being brought into service, is showing once again that it is ready to man new frontiers and face new problems in order to support the continuing expansion.

FURTHER READING

THE major regional description of the St. Lawrence Valley is contained in R. Blanchard's three books, *L'Est* . . ., *Le Centre* . . ., and *L'Ouest du Canada Français*, the main points of which are to be found in his single volume study, *Le Canada Français*. B. Brouillette has contributed 'Les Régions géographiques et économiques de la province de Québec', *Cahiers de Géog.*, 3 année, No. 6, pp. 65–84, and 'La Côte nord du Saint-Laurent', *Revue Can. de Géog.*, vol. i, No. 1, pp. 3–20 (continued in later numbers); he is also the author of the three chapters on Quebec in *Canadian Regions*, ed. D. F. Putnam. On the population, see H. H. Lewis, 'Population of Quebec Province', *Econ. Geog.*, vol. xvi, pp. 59–68; see also P. J. Bailey, 'The Geography of Settlement in Stanstead Township' [in the Eastern Townships], *Geography*, vol. lxi, pp. 39–48. Urban studies have been made by R. Blanchard, 'Montréal', *Revue de Géog. alpine*, Tome 35, Fasc. II, pp. 133–328; L. Beauregard, 'Géographie manufacturière de Montréal, *Cahiers de Géog.*, 3 année, No. 6, pp. 275–94, and J-M. Roy 'Québec', *The Canadian Geographer*, No. 2 (1952), pp. 83–98 (all in French).

On agriculture, see Hon. J. A. Godbout, 'Agriculture in Quebec: Past—Present—Future', *Can. Geog. Journal*, vol. xxviii, pp. 157–81. The *Revue Can. de Géographie*, the *Cahiers de Géographie*, and *L'Actualité Économique* all cover numerous topics of geographical interest, see, for example, F. Cormimbœuf, 'Les Ressources agraires de la Province de Québec', *L'Act. Écon.*, 20 année, vol, i, pp. 353–71. On power supplies, see 'Quebec Water Power', by B. J. McGuire, *Can. Geog. Journal*, vol. liv, pp. 219–37, and 'Bersimis: The Development of a River', by W. McNaughton, *Can. Geog. Journal*, vol. lx, pp. 115–35.

XII

THE INTERIOR

1. General

THAT part of the great Central Lowland of North America which lies between the Appalachian foothills, the Ozarks, the Great Plains, and the Laurentian Shield is an area which, for all its size, defies satisfactory subdivision into smaller sub-regions. So closely interdependent are the patterns of its life and economic activity that distance, variety of physical setting, and even the international boundary must not be allowed to hinder the geographer from viewing the region as a whole.

Two basic reasons underlie the decision to treat this area as a single region. The first is found in its agricultural and industrial patterns. Shorn of its details, the agricultural pattern takes the form of a series of concentric circles, focused on the central Corn Belt. The industrial pattern, on the other hand, reveals a distinction between a heavily industrialized eastern half of the region and a less heavily industrialized western half; that is to say, the agricultural pattern grades out from the centre, while the industrial gradient is from east to west. Furthermore, drawn across the region from north-west to south-east is the great diagonal slash of the Great Lakes, whose presence profoundly modifies the other cultural patterns, and upon whose shores are the homes of so large a part of the region's population. To subdivide the region means, inevitably, to destroy one or more of these patterns.

The second reason is that to subdivide the Interior means to break up one of the greatest realities in American life and thought—the Midwest. To delimit this cultural Midwest by means of precise boundaries is, of course, impossible. As Graham Hutton points out,[1] it includes the states of Ohio, Michigan, Indiana, Illinois, Wisconsin, Minnesota, Iowa, and Missouri, but in the cultural sense it can also be said to include much of the area of heavy industry in Pennsylvania and West Virginia. 'In other words, the real Midwest, the Midwest of the midwesterners, is the core composed of most of the area of these eight states; but beyond that core you will still find a Midwest,

[1] G. Hutton, *Midwest at Noon*, Harrap, 1946, p. 4.

thinning out into something else the farther you go from the centre.'[1]

What underlies this Midwestern sectionalism? To explain it, we might refer to such economic factors as the firm Midwestern balance between industry and agriculture; to the farmers' freedom from the marketing problems of East and West that were reviewed in Chapter IV; to the wide range of Midwestern manufactures, all making for a high degree of regional self-sufficiency. We should necessarily take account, too, of the historical factor—the uniformity of the conditions under which, in the first half of the nineteenth century, this vast tract was rapidly occupied. Much of this explanation lies outside the scope of the present volume: suffice it to say that there results from these factors a marked degree of economic and cultural individualism within the region.

On the Canadian side of the border, a different set of factors creates a regional distinctiveness no less definite. The term 'Midwestern' is not in common Canadian use, but the part of Canada over which the geographical patterns of the Interior spread is easily defined. It is that section of Ontario which is cut off from the rest of the country, to the north and east, by the empty barrenness of the Laurentian Shield. It is, in geological terms, Palaeozoic Ontario and, in a historical sense, Upper Canada, the area which consciously balances the Frenchness of Quebec; the area which, it is sometimes remarked, keeps Canada British.

2. *The Agricultural Interior*

The farmers of the Interior are generally favoured by natural conditions. The region possesses vast, smooth plains, which make cultivation easy, and wide areas of remarkably fertile glacial drift. It has an adequate rainfall (30 to 40 inches, of which one-third to one-half falls in the months May to August inclusive) and hot summer weather, to offset the short frost-free period of a continental interior. If the town-dweller finds cause for complaint in the stifling summer heat, the icy winds of winter, and the almost complete absence of 'in-between' spring weather, these things cause little inconvenience to the farmer,

[1] Hutton, loc. cit.

whose methods are adapted to the climate, who will delight to 'hear the corn growing' during the hot summer nights, when the cities are sleepless, and whose chief fear is of an occasional thunder or hailstorm that may spring up suddenly in a hot afternoon and lash down with tropical violence on his crops. This hazard apart, he has little cause for complaint in the natural conditions.

The effect of this favourable combination of circumstances is to produce an agriculture of intensive land use, with high land values, a high percentage of the farm area under crops, and the conversion of much of the output of the fields into livestock products. Because of the historical circumstances under which the area was settled, all this is associated, typically, with family farms, where hired labour is at a minimum and the average size ranges (thanks to the Homestead Act) between 120 acres and 160 acres—the famous 'quarter-section'.

But if these are the general characteristics of Interior farming —high land values; intensive land use; widespread cropping; and a dense livestock population—it must at once be added that, over so vast an area, all of these circumstances do not by any means apply everywhere. Natural conditions limit and modify their application in various parts of the region, creating the local differences that will be described later. The area where, however, they are most fully developed, where most of them apply most of the time, where lies the heart of this great agricultural region, is the Corn Belt.

THE CORN BELT

The Corn Belt is one of the best-known entities in American geography, its fame enhanced by Russel Smith's classic phrase, 'The Corn Belt is a gift of the gods.'[1] Yet to define it is almost as difficult as to set limits to the Midwest itself. There is an area where corn is the first-ranking crop in acreage,[2] and this emphasis on corn gives place to an emphasis on hay or oats or wheat on the outskirts of the area. But such a definition will hardly do justice to the reality. Perhaps the best definition is obtained simply by saying that the Corn Belt is that area of the

[1] J. R. Smith and O. Phillips, *North America*, Harcourt Brace, 1942, p. 360.
[2] For detailed maps of this area, see the articles in Further Reading, p. 293 under the authorship of J. C. Weaver.

Interior where the agricultural characteristics which we have already listed are found in the most marked conjunction. In other words, a definition of the Corn Belt involves a criterion not merely of type, but of intensity of land use.[1]

The existence and character of the Corn Belt are to be explained, in the first instance, by a fact of physical geography: that in the heart of the Interior, south of the Great Lakes, is a belt of the Central Lowland where conditions for farming approach the ideal. Large parts of this area are former lake beds, and are perfectly level. Elsewhere, a mantle of drift, product of the continental glaciation, has smoothed local relief and provided fertile till plains for farming. In other areas, notably in Iowa, a mantle of loess fulfils the same functions. Once the forests that covered the eastern half of these plains were cleared, and once the numerous swamps were drained, there was no major obstacle in the way of the plough for hundreds of miles. Away from this fertile core area, on the other hand, whether north into the lake and drumlin country of Wisconsin, south into the Ohio Valley and beyond, or east into the Appalachian foothills, the terrain becomes more broken and the soils more patchy.

For the second stage of our explanation, we must turn to the facts of agricultural economics. Here, the basic factors are twofold: that in terms of output per acre, the crop that yields the best returns[2] in the Interior is corn, and that, given a market for the product, it is generally more profitable to market this corn 'on the hoof', by turning it into livestock products, than to sell it as grain. The Corn Belt is the area where, thanks to natural advantages and the excellent markets nearby, this sequence can be most profitably followed. The Belt extends as far as conditions of marketing, terrain, and especially climate permit, and beyond that the corn crop is replaced, as pivot of the farming system, by an alternative crop—wheat or alfalfa in much of the west, hay or oats in the north.

For the Agricultural Interior, a particular importance therefore attaches to the climatic limits of successful corn growing within the region. In general terms these are: (1) on the western

[1] D. J. de Laubenfels, 'The Nature and Boundaries of the Corn Belt,' *A.A.A.G.*, vol. xliii, p. 165.

[2] And the crop that produces the meat which the American customer prefers to buy, as is indicated by use of the sales tag 'corn-fed pork' to tempt the consumer.

edge of the Corn Belt, the point beyond which summer rainfall becomes inadequate (less than 8 inches in the three summer months) or where the hot, dry winds off the Great Plains would parch the corn; (2) on the northern edge, the line beyond which summer heat, so necessary for the ripening of the crop, is insufficient (although, as we shall see, corn is grown farther north nevertheless, and is cut green); (3) on the southern edge, the point beyond which growing season temperatures are *too* high, and corn is replaced by cotton.

This pattern did not, of course, immediately form itself by natural logic when the area was settled in the first half of the nineteenth century. Its first export was cattle, and it was traversed, between 1840 and 1860, by the westward-moving Wheat Belt (p. 90). Nor was its fertility at once appreciated; much of it was swampy, and in any case the first settlers, emerging in Illinois from the forests through which they had travelled all the way from the Atlantic coast, were suspicious of land that would grow only grass. The present pattern is an outcome of the growth of Midwestern cities and communications—that is, of the existence within the region of a virtually insatiable market.

Let us now consider some of the features of this pattern. They are:

1. The high percentage of the total area in crops. Over large sections of the Corn Belt, notably in Iowa and Illinois, the figure is in excess of 70 per cent. The forest cover, originally extensive in the east and patchy in the west, has been almost entirely cleared, and in the Corn Belt landscape the presence of trees usually implies planted windbreaks—straight lines on the edges of holdings, or clusters round farmhouses. There is little permanent grass either; pastures are planted as part of the crop rotation. It is not difficult, indeed, to argue that cultivation has been carried too far—an outcome of great fertility, high land values, and the ease of ploughing in long, straight lines.

2. Farms are generally small. One of the most important forces shaping the Corn Belt landscape was the 1862 Homestead Act, which made 160 acres the basic size of holding, and which gave full scope for the American penchant for laying out property lines in squares. The gridiron landscape pattern thus created, with straight roads and farms evenly spaced along

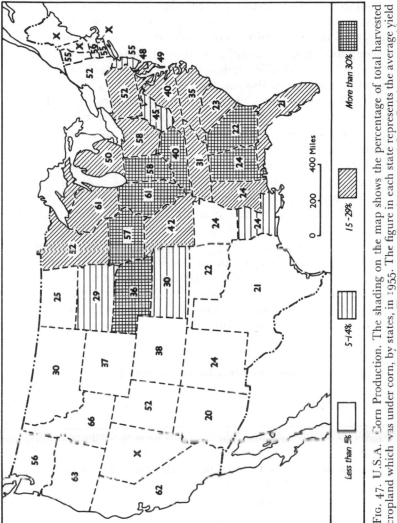

FIG. 47. U.S.A. Corn Production. The shading on the map shows the percentage of total harvested cropland which was under corn, by states, in 1955. The figure in each state represents the average yield of corn in the state over the years 1945–54. The pre-eminence of the central Corn Belt is at once evident.

them, persists to this day over much of the area, especially its western end. As a system of land occupance, however, it is far from ideal under modern conditions. The 160-acre unit, which was a suitable size for a family farm in the 1860's, is in these days of mechanization too small to run economically. The need, and desire, to enlarge their holdings on the part of 'underemployed' Corn Belt farmers is one of the reasons for the high cost of land within the Belt.

3. The actual place of corn in the farm operations. It is important not to be misled by the name Corn Belt into visualizing a sea of standing corn stretching from horizon to horizon. The Belt is in reality an area of genuinely mixed farming, with a notable diversity of crops and stock on most holdings. Of the total farm land within the Belt, corn occupies, in any given year, about one-quarter. In relation to the area under crops, throughout most of the central Corn Belt the proportion exceeds 40 per cent., and rises, in some small areas, above 60 per cent. Corn is usually grown in rotation with at least one other grain and a hay crop, and an increase in the importance of these alternatives in the cropping system marks the fringes of the Belt. Thus wheat, oats, barley, sorghum, and alfalfa all play an important *secondary* role in parts of the central Corn Belt, and assume *primary* importance in various areas along its fringes. This corn-grain-grass rotation not only operates in the interests of soil fertility, but it also serves to spread the farm's labour requirements over a longer summer season, an important consideration in an area where, as we have seen, most farms are operated by their owners, with only family labour.

4. Livestock in the Corn Belt. We shall not understand the agriculture of the Corn Belt without a clear statement of its last and most basic feature: that in terms of farm activity and farm income, it is not a Corn Belt at all but a Meat Belt. Three-quarters of the Belt's farm income is derived from the sale of animal products, and it is to this that the cropping is geared. Even when the farmer does sell his corn in the sack, rather than on the hoof, it is highly probable that the buyer merely requires it to feed to other stock within the region.

This intensive and well-integrated livestock farming takes several forms. Apart from the dairy farming and poultry keeping which, as in other regions, are common here wherever there

is a market to be found, the Corn Belt farmer may both raise his
own stock, and also act as fattener and finisher of stock bought
from farmers farther west. In either case his output is destined
for the meat packers in the Corn Belt cities.

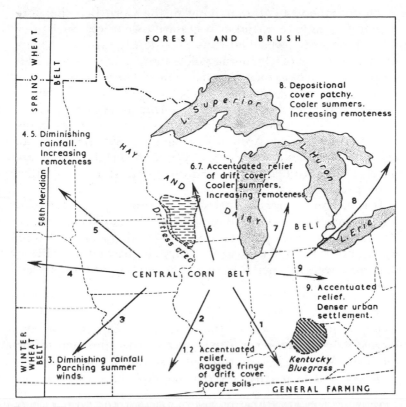

FIG. 48. The Agricultural Interior and Its Subdivisions. The map represents
diagrammatically the transition between the central Corn Belt and adjacent
regions which is described on pp. 260–70.

Thus pigs, which are the principal native product of the Belt,
are raised wholly within it, and the hog pasture is a standard
feature of its farms. But the cattle seen in Illinois or Iowa may
well have been raised on the Great Plains. The ranges of the dry
west can usually neither support cattle all the year round nor
give them the finish required by the packers. The farmers of the
Corn Belt, like those of the famous Meath pastures in Ireland,
act as intermediaries—intermediaries who play a role of special

S

importance when a drought year in the fickle Great Plains climate faces the ranchers with the alternatives of either killing or shipping away east the cattle that their own pastures can no longer support.

The numbers of cattle arriving in the Corn Belt therefore vary from year to year, and so, necessarily, do prices. Such price fluctuations, whatever their cause, constantly raise for the farmer the question of whether it will be more profitable to sell his output as grain or as meat. His decision will be governed partly by the comparative state of prices for the two types of product, (which in turn probably reflects government support policy,) and partly by such local considerations as freight rates to the nearest main market. Around Chicago, for example, there are curious anomalies in the rate pattern, and certainly there are parts of the Corn Belt which, year after year, ship grain rather than meat.[1]

It is, however, precisely because, already enjoying the solid advantages of natural conditions and nearby markets, the Corn Belt farmer has the option of producing grain or meat, that he has been able to build up over the years a high standard of living that may well be envied by his colleagues who farm in less favoured regions.

THE SOUTHERN MARGINS

The southern margin of the Corn Belt is marked by the increasingly broken terrain that heralds the approach to the Ohio and Missouri Rivers. Here, at its southern limit, the cover of glacial drift is patchy; the streams flowing south have cut down into it, and the loss of fertility and of smoothness is clearly reflected in a decline in both prosperity and intensity of cultivation in southern Indiana and Illinois, and in northern Missouri.

Beyond the Ohio, in Kentucky, the same trend continues. Relief is more pronounced; woodland and waste appear more frequently. With the transition from the fertile till plains to the wooded uplands of Kentucky, and with increasing distance from the main markets of the Midwest, agriculture on the Corn

[1] Attention is called to these anomalies by J. W. Alexander in 'Freight Rates as a Geographic Factor in Illinois', *Econ. Geog.*, vol. xx, pp. 25–30. See also J. J. Hidore, 'The Relationship Between Cash-Grain Farming and Landforms', *Econ. Geog.*, vol. xxxix, pp. 84–89.

Belt pattern gives way to mixed farming of a less intensive type, with increasing amounts of pasture, grading off into what is virtually subsistence farming in the most remote areas.

South of the Missouri much the same conditions apply. Where the land rises to the Ozarks the proportion of farmland under cultivation declines, and woodland and pastures replace crops. Once again the remote hill farms support little more than subsistence agriculture and the Ozark hillsmen, like their counterparts in the Appalachians, are by repute 'hillbillies'.

In general, then, this southern edge of the Interior is an area of increasing physical limitation. But it also embraces some agricultural lands of a higher quality. Apart from the superbly fertile alluvia of the Mississippi Valley bottomlands, the most notable of these are associated with the limestone areas of Kentucky and Tennessee—the Bluegrass and the Nashville Basin.

When the first migrants struggled through the Cumberland Gap and along Boone's Wilderness Road in the last years of the eighteenth century, they were spurred on by reports of an area of incredible fertility beyond the hills. This was the Bluegrass country of Kentucky, where the limestone core of an eroded dome has weathered to form soils that support a rich grassland. Today, as a hundred and fifty years ago, this region has a great agricultural reputation—for the racehorses it breeds; for its dairy and beef cattle and its tobacco; for the splendour of its stud farms, with their pillared façades and white fences. Less spectacular, but basically similar in its pasture-corn-livestock farming, is the basin in Tennessee, with its famous dairy herds of Channel Island stock. Focused on Lexington and on Nashville respectively, these two basins form islands of prosperity in the broad zone of 'general farming' that stretches across the U.S.A. south of the Ohio.

The cash crop of much of this general farming area of Kentucky and Tennessee is tobacco, a crop whose cultivation has, over recent years, come to be so closely controlled by a system of government quotas that possession of the right to market it enhances the selling value of the farm; the purchaser must pay for the acreage allotment along with the land.[1] West of the Missis-

[1] M. Prunty, 'Land Occupance in the Southeast', *Geog. Review*, vol. xlii, pp. 439–61. 'The only device open to a newcomer [wishing to grow tobacco] is to

sippi the southern margin of the Corn Belt sees a transition from the intensive livestock production, based on feed grains, that characterizes the Belt north of the Missouri, to a less intensive, pasture-based livestock industry on the Springfield Plateau, the northernmost section of the Ozarks. Pigs and cattle are raised on the Plateau, and there is some dairy farming. The less favourable physical conditions, however, and the use of natural pasture (which accounts for more than half the farmland) reduce the rate of stocking, and make it necessary to send many of the animals to the Corn Belt for fattening before they are ready for the meat packers of Kansas City or St. Louis.

Only about one-quarter of the land in the northern Ozarks is under crops, with corn and wheat of roughly equal importance. The special crops of the area are fruits, especially grapes and apples. Many of the district's farmers, however, rely for their income less on these than upon seasonal employment as lumbermen in the forests which still cover much of the area.

THE WESTERN MARGINS

If the controlling influences on the southern margins of the Corn Belt are those of relief and soils, the western limits are governed by climate. Here there is no topographic obstacle to terminate the Belt: the lowland of the Interior continues with scarcely a break to the foot of the Rockies, and the all-important drift cover extends far out over the Great Plains. But there is a gradual decrease of precipitation which, on the one hand, enforces a less intensive type of farming and, on the other, obliges the farmer to replace corn by a crop better adapted to the drier conditions—in practice, by wheat or sorghum.

The agricultural transition on this edge of the Corn Belt takes place in two stages.

1. On the western borders of Iowa and Missouri, wheat (which is the second crop of most of the western Corn Belt) becomes the dominant grain crop, with sorghum accompanying it in the south, and alfalfa, oats, or corn in the north. This change in crop emphasis is essentially a precautionary one, made as the limits of secure corn growing are reached; it makes

purchase a farm that has traditionally grown the crop under allotment, but he finds that the allotment . . . has value far beyond the customary value of the land. . . . The crop probably serves as the best agricultural example of a new brand of determinism—political determinism' (op. cit., p. 450).

little difference to the form of the farm economy which, although based on less intensive land use, remains dependent on livestock production.

2. With further decrease in precipitation, the intensive livestock raising of the Corn Belt is no longer possible. Here there is a change to cash-grain farming, and wheat growing becomes the dominant agricultural activity. West of this second zone of transition, which runs through the eastern Dakotas and eastern Kansas, lie the Spring and Winter Wheat Belts, separated by the western extremity of the Corn Belt (see Fig. 17).[1]

The Wheat Belts (the distinction between which is simply a question of latitude and, consequently, of the date of sowing the crop) have been described as 'the end product of a sort of destructive evolution which was impressed upon the European farming types as they advanced into the sub-humid and semi-arid lands of the New World'.[2]

It is worthwhile pausing to understand what this comment implies. The farmers who settled the Agricultural Interior were men whose experience had been gained either in eastern North America or in Europe; that is, in areas of mixed farming. This mixed farming they set out to practise in their new homes—say in the humid central Corn Belt. But as they moved westwards into drier areas what happened was that, one by one, the various elements in the mixed farming economy—the alternative crops and the livestock population   proved unsuited to the new conditions, and had to be dropped, until only wheat (with perhaps barley, flax, or sorghum in support) remained of the variety with which the farming had begun. Indeed, on the driest edges of the Wheat Belt, in the west, a point in the process was reached where the only alternative to wheat growing was to leave the ground fallow, but, as we shall see in Chapter XV, there has been some retreat from this ultimate of 'destructive evolution'.

Farming in the Wheat Belts contrasts strongly with that in

[1] The explanation of this curious break in the Wheat Belt seems to be (1) that there is a climatic no man's land between the two halves, where winters are too cold for winter wheat, and summers are too hot for spring wheat, so that neither can be grown, and (2) that in eastern Nebraska, climatic and relief conditions permit the growing of corn farther to the west than elsewhere—as far west, in fact, as the fringe of cultivation, where the grazing areas begin, so that there is no need for a transitional belt of another crop.

[2] S. N. Dicken, *Economic Geography*, D. C. Heath, Boston, 1955, p. 175.

the Corn Belt. With wheat as almost the sole source of income, farms must necessarily be much larger than the Midwestern quarter-section, and the usual modern size is one or two sections. The wheat farms generally occupy the smooth inter-fluves of the plains, while the valleys are given over to irrigated crops, and the rougher lands to grazing. The main contrast with the Corn Belt, however, is a social one: the Wheat Belt farmer has often only a slender attachment to his land. Thanks to the progress of mechanization, labour requirements on an all-wheat farm are restricted to a few days at the beginning and end of the season, and this makes possible a type of non-resident, 'suitcase' farming which leaves the farmer free to spend most of the year elsewhere.[1]

A final point of contrast between the Wheat Belts and the Corn Belt is that, while the agricultural markets of the latter lie within the Belt, those of the former do not. Much of the Spring Wheat Belt is in Canada, and only one-quarter to one-third of the Canadian wheat crop is consumed within the country, let alone within the sparsely-settled wheatlands themselves. The produce of the Wheat Belts travels, in the first instance, to Winnipeg, Kansas City, or Minneapolis, and there-after in part to Montreal, Baltimore, or Houston, and on to foreign markets.

As we complete the traverse from the central Corn Belt to the western Wheat Belt we find, therefore, that every one of the economic factors which gave to the Corn Belt its distinctive character has been lost along the way. Only in a physical sense —in their smooth topography and fertile soils—do the Wheat Belts preserve the characteristics of the Agricultural Interior; in an economic sense they are more akin to the Cotton Belt and the grazing lands that adjoin them on the south and west.

THE NORTHERN MARGINS—THE WESTERN GREAT LAKES AREA

On its northern edge the Corn Belt gives place to the Hay and Dairy Belt, which stretches from Minnesota in the west to Nova Scotia in the east. Increasing remoteness, rougher terrain, poorer soils, and summers too cool to ripen corn all contribute

[1] On this, see W. M. Kollmorgen and G. F. Jenks, 'Suitcase Farming in Sully County, South Dakota', *A.A.A.G.*, vol. xlviii, pp. 27–40 and refs.

to this transition. On the positive side the local markets for milk in the Great Lakes cities, and the national market for butter and cheese, make the Dairy Belt a vital part of the Agricultural Interior and a no less logical adaptation to market conditions than is the 'Meat Belt' farther south. Corn loses importance in comparison with hay and oats, dairy cattle replace beef cattle and pigs, and the ratio of farmland to forest and waste decreases rather rapidly northwards; but the basic relationship between cropping and livestock remains unchanged. Hay, oats, and corn, all grown for fodder, occupy over 90 per cent. of the crop-land area; the corn is cut green and made into silage, and live-stock products form the principal item of farm income.

Yet the prosperity and apparent stability of farming in today's Dairy Belt conceal a checkered story of sequent occu-pance. Wisconsin grew wheat before it became 'America's Dairyland', and some of the region's early farm production catered for long-vanished markets to the northward, rather than for those in the lake shore cities of today. It might, in fact, be argued that stability on the northern edges of the Dairy Belt, in the Northwoods of Minnesota, Wisconsin, and Michigan, has not yet been achieved.

Farm settlement in Wisconsin serves well to illustrate these changes. During the first phase of agricultural land use, be-tween 1835 and 1880, Wisconsin was a wheat state. The centre of North America wheat production, whose movement we have followed from New England (p. 90), passed across Wisconsin between 1850 and 1880. Wheat was a crop well suited to the circumstances of the early settlers, but their farming was en-tirely unscientific, and so a constant need for fresh land drew them north-westward across the state, and on into Minnesota. Peak acreage was reached in 1878; by 1905 it had dropped to a negligible figure. The wheat boom was over, and in the south farmers had already begun to see where their more permanent profit lay—in dairying.

But meanwhile another phase had intervened, to postpone the coming of stability. This was the lumber boom in the North-woods. The opening of the dry, treeless west in the 1870's and 1880's led to a great demand for timber, a demand which the Great Lakes area could meet. Northward the lumbermen led the way, clearing ground for the farmers who would follow to grow their supplies. Disregarding or burning all but the particular timber they sought, they cut their way through the area between 1875 and 1905, and then, as abruptly, left for the mountains of the west. The farmers who had settled the Northwoods (like their neighbours who had followed the copper miners into Upper Michigan a few years earlier) found themselves virtually marooned in the wilderness, without local markets; the state governments found themselves left with the cut-over.

The third phase of occupance has been marked by two processes—the establishment of commercial dairying in the southern Great Lakes area, and the retreat of the farm frontier in the north. The western half of the Dairy Belt has become North America's greatest surplus-producing area for dairy products. The area is divided fairly clearly into those parts which produce fluid milk for urban markets—as south-east Wisconsin, for example, serves Chicago and Milwaukee—and the remoter areas where absence of such markets encourages the manufacture of butter and cheese. Most important of these is the butter region of western Wisconsin and adjacent parts of Iowa and Minnesota, while half of all the cheese produced in the U.S.A. is manufactured in Wisconsin, with the descendants of European cheese makers still producing the cheeses of their homelands. So great, indeed, is the milk surplus of these areas that (as the geographer of the Dairy Belt, Loyal Durand, has shown[1]) apart from shipping so large a share of the nation's butter and cheese, they have produced enough to act as a milk 'reservoir', to supply fluid milk to other regions and cities where a rapid rise in population has created a temporary shortage locally. In this way, Wisconsin had, for a time, a daily 'milk run' by tanker lorry, to Phoenix in Arizona, 1,750 miles away.

Farm organization in the western Dairy Belt does not differ greatly from that of the Corn Belt. Farms are generally family-operated, and less than 150 acres in size. As the delivery point for farm produce, the local crossroads creamery replaces the grain elevator and the stockpens at the railway station. Because of the cooler summers and rougher terrain however, permanent pasture is more widespread than in the Corn Belt (in Wisconsin, for example, it accounts for two-fifths of the farm-

[1] For references to his principal articles, see Further Reading, p. 293.

land) and the area under crops is considerably smaller.

Meanwhile the northern margin of the Dairy Belt has advanced into the Northwoods and retreated again. Once the stimulus of the lumbermen's demand was removed, farming on the Superior Upland or in the devastated cut-over generally proved uneconomical. Rather than provide, at great expense, the services required by these outlying northern farms, local governments have closed whole sections of the Northwoods. Here, then, is one American frontier on which, for reasons of administrative economy, a planned withdrawal has taken place—a withdrawal which, in these days of agricultural surplus and intense competition, can only be regarded as a wise response to economic conditions. It is thus possible to trace, running through the northern parts of Minnesota, Wisconsin, and Michigan, a *northern* limit to the Dairy Belt, product of both physical handicaps and remoteness from markets.

THE NORTHERN MARGINS—SOUTHERN ONTARIO

The peninsula of southern Ontario, between the Great Lakes and the edge of the Laurentian Shield, forms a true part of the Agricultural Interior, although a part which, thanks to the incidence of the international boundary, lies in Canada. Judged by most of the criteria we have already discussed, the southwestern tip of Ontario—the Essex Peninsula—belongs to the Corn Belt. Much of the rest of the area falls within the Dairy Belt; then to the north of the zone of dairying there is a belt of mixed farming; and at the edge of the Shield commercial agriculture ends abruptly.

Peninsular Ontario is, structurally, a continuation of the Central Lowland, with the Palaeozoic formations meeting the Shield along a line from Georgian Bay to the Thousand Islands on the St. Lawrence. Most of the peninsula's surface features, however, are of glacial origin. During the Wisconsin glaciation two lobes of ice occupied the approximate positions of the present Lakes Huron and Ontario–Erie, pressing southward and encircling southern Ontario. When the ice retreated, it left behind a legacy of morainic clays and sands on the flanks of the peninsula, while much of the centre was covered by till plains and morainic hills. Thus the general effect of the glaciation was favourable to an agricultural future, and especially on the south-eastern edge of the area, where settlement was later to concentrate, the morainic slopes and lacustrine plains of the present-day lake shores offered fertile soils for farming.

Climatic conditions also favour agriculture. The presence of the Great Lakes on two sides of the triangle of southern Ontario has a modifying influence on the region's climate which is marked, even in contrast to, for example, the St. Lawrence Valley below the Thousand Islands. The peninsula has a smaller seasonal temperature range than areas to the east and west of it, so that winters are warmer and the growing season is longer. Indeed, the lake shore in the extreme south-west of the peninsula has, for its latitude, the exceptionally long frost-free period of 175 days.

Thus favoured in its soils and climate, southern Ontario has become eastern Canada's largest area of intensive agricultural land use. With little land excluded from farm use for reasons of climate or physique, and with suitable market outlets available to—and, thanks to the international boundary, secured for—the Ontario farmer, a pattern of close settlement has developed that is quite unlike that of French Canada, below the Thousand Islands, but bears a marked similarity to that of the Corn Belt and southern Dairy Belt. As in intensity of settlement, so in layout, the southern Ontario pattern is Midwestern rather than Laurentian, gridiron rather than linear.

But here, as elsewhere on the margins of the Agricultural Interior, there is a steady decline in intensity of land use towards the fringes (in this case, from south-west to north-east across the area) in keeping with a shortening growing season, poorer soils, and increasing distance to market. The Essex Peninsula corresponds to the Corn Belt; it is the only part of the area where corn will regularly ripen, and over 70 per cent. of its farmland is in crops. Besides corn, tobacco, soyabeans, and fruit and vegetable crops are grown. Elsewhere livestock production is general, as a heavy emphasis on hay and oats (together they occupy some 65 per cent. of the cropland) indicates. There is a difference, however, between the livestock farming of the closely-settled areas and that of the remoter parts of the peninsula. The one is given over to dairying, the other largely to the raising of beef cattle. For this distinction two factors are mainly responsible: (1) the market for dairy products, not only in Ontario but also in the Montreal district, can be fully supplied by farmers close to the markets, so that farmers in the hinterland must necessarily turn to other forms of production, and (2) in the north, the type of pasture available suits beef cattle better than dairy stock. Over the greater part of the peninsula, therefore, it is more accurate to speak of hay-and-livestock agriculture than of a Hay and Dairy Belt. The true dairying areas are to be found in the Toronto district, in the south centre of the peninsula (the upper Thames River Valley), and in its eastern angle, where it meets the Shield and forms part of the milkshed of Montreal.

Besides the Essex Peninsula, one other small area of southern Ontario stands out as exceptional in its agriculture—the fruit-growing region of the Niagara Peninsula. The southern shores of the Great Lakes are favoured, thanks to the presence of these great bodies of water, with a long growing season and with markedly reduced frost risks, even as compared with areas only a few miles inland. As a result, these shores are the location of several important fruit-growing areas, such as those in south-western Michigan and on the southern side of Lakes Ontario and Erie; but none shows a more detailed, or more complete, adaptation to local conditions than that which lies beneath the scarp of the Niagara Cuesta. Here orchards occupy almost all the available farmland, and peaches, grapes, cherries, and other fruits are grown. Since there is a noticeable tendency in American fruit and vegetable production towards specializa-tion, the importance of such specialist areas as those of the lake shores seems likely in the future to be fully maintained. The Niagara region, however, faces competition of quite a different kind—competition for space. Lying, as it does, between Hamil-ton and Niagara at a point where rail and road routes converge and circle the end of the lake, this orchard region is too close to the encroaching suburbs and highways, and has been seriously cut into by them.

Southern Ontario forms an agricultural region which, like the Corn Belt, is to a considerable degree self-contained, in that its farmers' markets lie largely within it. Some 70 per cent. of the farm output is sold either in the peninsula, or in the many thriving towns which its relatively intensive agriculture supports, or in the Montreal district. Compared with those parts of Canada whose agriculture is geared to the export trade, peninsular Ontario possesses an enviable freedom from marketing problems and a useful degree of economic balance in its activities.

THE EASTERN MARGINS

The eastern limit of the Corn Belt is generally taken to lie in western Ohio. Eastwards from here the land rises gradually to the plateaux of the Appalachians, with the rivers deeply incised and with increasing local relief. To the eastward, too, there lies the heavy industry region of Ohio and western Pennsylvania, whose urban markets exercise a powerful influence on farm production. This eastern margin of the Interior is therefore characterized, on the one hand, by a decrease in the amount of land in crops but, on the other, by a close adaptation to local market conditions.

The resulting pattern shows a marked similarity to that which has developed, under comparable conditions, on the Middle Atlantic coast, with dairying widespread over the uplands, and intensive concentrations of truck farming at strategic supply points near the cities. As in southern Ontario, the only significant variation of this pattern occurs along the shores of Lakes Ontario and Erie, where a fruit and vegetable farming area extends the full length of the lake side, famous alike for the orchards of the Finger Lakes in upper New York State and for the acres of glasshouses around Cleveland.

3. The Industrial Interior

The continental Interior contains a large proportion of all North America's industry. It is, in fact, precisely the combination of intensive agriculture and widespread industrialization that gives the region its character and that underlies its prosperity. The eastern half of the Interior is also the western half of what has become known as the Manufacturing Belt. Even beyond the limits of this Belt, although the industrial centres are more widely dispersed, the manufactures they support form no less vital a part of the Midwestern economy.

So diverse and so numerous are the industries of the Interior that it will perhaps be useful to attempt a rough classification into three groups. The first group consists of industries associated directly with agriculture—milling, meat packing, and the supply of farm equipment. The second group consists of various heavy industries, whose locations are related to mineral deposits. Pre-eminent among these is, of course, the iron and steel

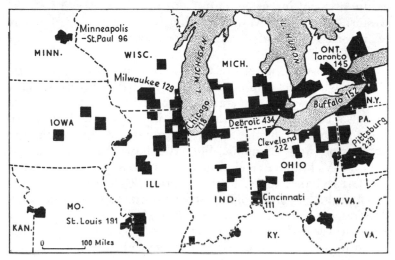

FIG. 49. The Industrial Interior, showing counties which possessed more than 10,000 industrial production workers in 1954. Figures (in thousands of workers) are given for the major cities.

industry, but the group also includes manufactures of glass, brickware, and chemicals. The third, and largest, group is made up of an assortment of medium and light industries, whose presence may be explained in several ways. (1) Some of them are steel-using industries (such as the automobile industry) located within reach of their materials. (2) Others represent an overspill from more crowded industrial areas farther east—industries which have resettled in the less densely occupied western end of the Manufacturing Belt. (3) Almost all are industries for which the Belt is a highly important market, in the sense either that they are supply industries (the manufacture of machine tools is an example), or that they are consumer goods industries attracted by the dense concentration of population in the industrial areas.

In various parts of the region, one or other of these groups tends to predominate—the heavy industry group in eastern

Ohio and western Pennsylvania, for example, and the agricultural industries group in the western half of the Interior. Thanks to their special advantages of position, the Great Lakes ports, and particularly Chicago, characteristically possess industries representing all three groups. In the years since 1940, however, as the areas of intensive manufacturing have spread into the western parts of the Manufacturing Belt, it is the third group, of 'assorted' industries, which has contributed most to the expansion.

The industrial pattern of the Interior, like the agricultural pattern whose development we have traced, is far from being permanent. Its apparent stability is belied by its history, which reveals a continuous westward shift, in keeping with the westward movement of the centre of gravity of the continent's population and economic life. We have already seen, in Chapter V, how the steel industry has spread westward, along the Great Lakes route, from its former concentration round Pittsburgh. The group of industries associated with agriculture illustrates this trend even more clearly. When the Agricultural Interior was first opened up, the farmer's base, both for equipment supply and for processing of farm produce, was in the east. The long west-to-east haul for grain or livestock and the return flow of farm supplies were basic—and costly—elements in the North American economy. Over the years, however, this group of industries has followed the farmers westward, more than keeping pace with the agricultural frontier, and so meeting the flow of farm produce ever closer to its source. In the 1850's the meat-packing industry, for example, was centred in Cincinnati —prominently enough for the city to earn the name of 'Porkopolis'. By 1870, however, Chicago had replaced Cincinnati in importance. Then in the 1880's, and more definitely since the First World War, Chicago in its turn began to lose ground relative to cities still further west, such as Omaha and Kansas City.[1]

----

[1] It is perhaps possible to date the completion of this move westwards by the fact that, on 22 June 1959, *Time* reported that the last of the 'Big Three' meat packers was closing down its Chicago operations and leaving 'the World's Ex-Hog Butcher'. The explanation of the move is to be found partly in improved transport and refrigeration, partly in changes in procedure by the packers, whose buyers now buy on the farm and not at the stockyard, and partly in improved western land use which enables farmers to fatten and finish stock farther west than formerly.

PLATE XIII

The Agricultural Interior: A farm landscape in Wisconsin; rolling hill country with a considerable proportion of woodland, family-sized farms, and cropping along the contours

PLATE XIV

The Industrial Interior: The Monongahela River at Pittsburgh, looking down-stream towards the city centre and the junction with the Allegheny River. Steel works and railway tracks line the river banks, and coal barges lie along the quays

These changes can be stated in another way. Over the Interior have spread two waves of industrialization. The first was that of the agricultural processing and supply industries which, following in the wake of the farm frontier, settled in the country towns of the Interior. The second wave spread from the old industrial areas farther east, and it represented an extension into new areas of the nation's main Manufacturing Belt. Thus the Belt has spread across Ohio, southern Michigan, and northern Indiana, to link up with the Chicago industrial concentration, and it has outliers farther west, along the Mississippi, and in the Rock River Valley of Wisconsin and Illinois.

During the Second World War, and up to 1947, the position of the Interior in North American manufacturing was fully maintained, in spite of the continuing expansion of the economy in the western states and provinces. The province of Ontario retained its all-but-50 per cent. share of Canada's industrial employment, while in the U.S.A. all the states of the Interior experienced between 1939 and 1947 an increase in the numbers of their production workers which was above the national average. Since 1947, however, the principal industrial states of the American Midwest, although still containing over one-quarter of the nation's production workers, have lost some ground (as we saw in Chapter V) in terms of employment. It would seem that, while Ontario's industries continue to expand, the United States Midwest is approaching its industrial saturation point under present conditions. It remains to be seen what new impulse to industrialization may be provided by the general increase which is continuing in the Midwest's population, and by the specific stimulus of the St. Lawrence Seaway.

THE HEAVY INDUSTRY AREA OF PENNSYLVANIA
AND OHIO

North America's Black Country, whose location owes much to the position of the Appalachian coalfield, but something also to the personal influence of past generations of industrialists, is to be found in an area that is ill-suited to the purposes of heavy industry—in the narrow, winding valleys of the upper Ohio and its tributaries, where they cut into the northern part of the Appalachian Plateaux. While the combination of horizontal coal seam and steep valley wall aids the miner, and the river system serves both for transport and for industrial water supply, these advantages are seriously offset by industrial congestion in the smoke-filled valleys, where there is neither room for expansion nor attraction, in an area of 'clean' industry, for the notoriously mobile American worker to settle.

So great, however, was the initial advantage of proximity to the great Appalachian coalfield that this area is not only the most important steel-producing region in the world, but also the centre of North America's manufacture of glass and clay products. Within the area are localities specializing in one or other of these types of industry: more than half the industrial workers of Youngstown are engaged in primary metal production, and a half of those in Akron produce rubber goods, while the valley of the Kanawha in West Virginia has been described as 'the Ruhr of the United States chemical industry'.

At the heart of this great industrial concentration stands the city of *Pittsburgh* (2,405,000). Almost one-half of Pittsburgh's industrial workers are engaged in primary metal production, while a further one-third produce machinery and steel goods of various kinds. As a steel city its main natural advantage is that of location at the junction of the Allegheny and Monongahela Rivers, at the hub of the upper Ohio routeways and close to the Appalachian coaking coals. Yet it was not situation alone that made Pittsburgh what it is. To explain its ascendancy we must recall a historical coincidence: that in the years after the Civil War of 1861–5 three things were happening simultaneously. The first was that the demand for steel, especially steel for railways, was rising as the west was opened to settlement. The second was that the Bessemer process for making steel was introduced, as a result of which steel could be produced both more cheaply and more quickly than ever before. The third element in the situation was the appearance in Pittsburgh of Andrew Carnegie, an industrial wizard who, by his bold application of the Bessemer process, and by his ability to appreciate the economic realities of steel making, came rapidly to dominate the industry. Securing an alliance with Henry Frick, whose comparable talents had given him control of the coke-making phase of the industry (then centred at Connellsville, 50 miles to the south-east of Pittsburgh), Carnegie made

Pittsburgh and steel into synonyms, before selling out, in 1901, to the newly formed United States Steel Corporation. Thus by the conjunction of location, timing, and personal initiative, Pittsburgh became the centre of the steel industry; and its steelmen imposed on the industry, as a mark of their hegemony, the 'Pittsburgh Plus' arrangement that lasted until 1924, and itself assured the continuance of the régime (see p. 139).

From Pittsburgh the ribbons of industrial development stretch along the valley floors of the Ohio system, south and east into the coalfield, and north and west towards other manufacturing centres. Youngstown (509,000) and Wheeling-Steubenville (358,000) are the principal steel cities, while a number of smaller centres, such as East Liverpool, produce clayware or glassware, much of it for use in the industries of the area. Farther south, in West Virginia, the output of the Kanawha Valley ranges from heavy chemicals, such as ammonia and caustic soda, to synthetics for the plastics and textile industries, and includes also steel alloys, glass, and synthetic rubber. To the north-west, between Pittsburgh and Lake Erie, are Akron and Canton with their satellites, the latter a steel goods city and the former holding, with little fear of challenge, the title of 'rubber capital of the world'. This remarkable concentration of rubber goods production in Akron seems to be due, in the first instance, to individual initiative on the part of early manufacturers, and in the second place to the fact that the industry is a relatively young one which, in a sense, has not yet had time to adjust and spread to its most suitable distribution throughout the continent.

Like New England, and like Old England, the Pittsburgh and Ohio Black Country is suffering today the disadvantages of its early pre-eminence. Inevitably its relative importance has waned, with the change to newer sources of power; with the lack of space for expansion; with the competition of new and more efficient producers farther west who have profited by its experience; with the abolition of 'Pittsburgh Plus'. Changes in industrial techniques have killed some of its activities, such as the coke-making at Connellsville, and structural unemployment is a recurrent problem. But in spite of these difficulties, it remains the greatest industrial concentration of the continent. The attachment of its industries to coal and clay, the wealth of

T

labour skill at its command, and the enormous investment that has gone into its heavy industries are all factors which are resistant to change and which should assure the area of a continuing importance.

THE CITIES OF THE GREAT LAKES

The six great cities that lie on the shores of the Great Lakes— Chicago, Milwaukee, Detroit, Cleveland, Buffalo, and Toronto —are the home of some 8 per cent. of the population of Anglo-America. They are both ports and route centres, both industrial cities and commercial headquarters. Their size and activities derive in part from their position along the route by which Appalachian coal and Lake Superior ore move to meet each other, and in part from their relationship to their hinterlands, which stretch far into the Agricultural Interior. With the opening of the St. Lawrence Seaway, they have added to their other functions that of being ocean ports, and can now capture, for part of the year at least, some of the foreign trade formerly funnelled through Montreal, New York, or Baltimore.

To these six metropolitan centres must be added a number of smaller cities—Erie and Toledo, Hamilton and Windsor— whose functions are more limited; they are port and manufacturing cities along the coal and iron route. Their existence and their growth underline the fundamental importance in the economy of the Great Lakes Region of this movement of ore and coal, totalling over 100 million tons annually, that makes up so large a proportion of the lakes' cargoes.

From Duluth and Superior the flow of iron ore divides roughly into three—to the Chicago area, to the ports of Lake Erie, and through these ports to the Pittsburgh area. On the Lake Erie shore, the principal receiving ports are Cleveland, Conneaut, Erie, and Ashtabula. The return flow of coal, however, shows a different pattern; the total quantity handled is much smaller, and the greater part of it passes through Toledo and Sandusky. What has happened is that as the centre of Appalachian coal production has shifted south-westward into West Virginia and Kentucky, so the shipping route has increasingly favoured the western Lake Erie ports over those farther east in the Cleveland area. The result is that this whole line of ports suffers from a one-way traffic system, with receipts

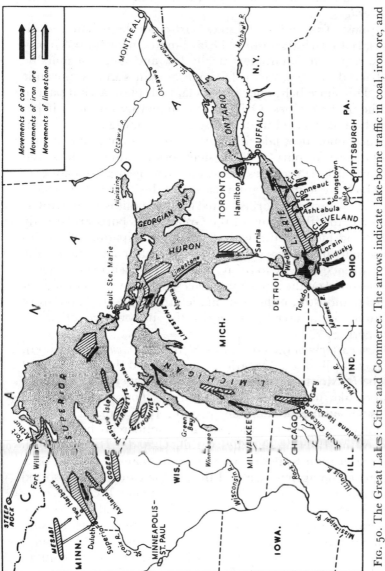

Fig. 50. The Great Lakes: Cities and Commerce. The arrows indicate lake-borne traffic in coal, iron ore, and limestone, and the thickness of the arrow is roughly proportional to the weight of each movement. In recent years, the total amount of ore moving down the lakes has been about twice as large as the reverse movement of coal. With the development of the Labrador ores iron ore now moves up from Montreal as well as down from Duluth (see p.137).

exceeding shipments by thirty to one at Cleveland, and an opposite unbalance in the ratio of five to one at Toledo (1960–61 averages).

In most of these Great Lakes port-cities the urban and industrial pattern is the same. The lake shores in the southern part of the region are characteristically low and sandy or marshy, but backed by the terraces of former shorelines and by morainic hills. This shore belt, once it is reclaimed, plays a vital part in the life of these cities. Originally shunned by builders, it has often been converted into an asset, as at Chicago, by the construction upon it of lakeside parks. More to the point, it provides the site for port facilities, steelworks, grain elevators, and railway yards. It provides space, also, for the great stockpiles of ore which are so important a feature of this seasonal ore route, on which water transport is halted for five months every winter. It is here, too, that many of the Great Lakes ports are already reclaiming more of the waterfront in anticipation of the increase in their business which they expect the completion of the St. Lawrence Seaway to bring. The business centre of the cities is to be found on the adjacent terraces, but the waterside cluster of heavy industry, either on 'made ground' on the lake front or lining local creeks, bespeaks the importance of water transport.

Most easterly of the Great Lakes cities is *Toronto* (1,824,000), the metropolis of the Ontario Peninsula, and the great rival of Quebec's Montreal. Lacking the advantages of a strategic location like that of Montreal or Chicago, Toronto nevertheless fulfils something of the role of both. It is Canada's second manufacturing centre, and it is the commercial hub of that part of the Interior that lies within Canada. In spite of an absence of industrial raw materials, its manufacturing, both that based on agriculture and that in the category of assorted light industries, is highly diverse; if we include the towns of its immediate hinterland such as Oshawa and Oakville, where General Motors and Ford have plants, the range is wider still. Commercially, the importance of its banks and insurance companies is felt not only in Ontario, of which it is the capital, but throughout the nation. In particular, it is the financial base of the northern mining industry, the prime force in the present economic development of the Canadian Northlands. And as a port it has experienced a rapid expansion since the Seaway was opened: in terms of foreign trade tonnage, it now ranks with Quebec.

Forty miles west of Toronto is *Hamilton* (395,000), Canadian counterpart of the United States steel cities on the Lake Erie and Lake Michigan shores. It is a matter for conjecture whether Hamilton, which draws both ore and fuel from United States sources, would ever have developed as it has were it not for the presence of the international boundary. But this question becomes almost monotonous when we are considering Canadian industrial development; Hamilton exists and flourishes, and the new conjunction of circumstances that brings ore from Labrador through the St. Lawrence Seaway should increase Hamilton's advantages, without disturbing its strong position in the large, protected Ontario market.

Between Lakes Ontario and Erie lie the Niagara River and its 'by-pass', the Welland Canal. The isthmus which they cross is one of North America's most favoured locations for industrial development, for here is to be found, within easy reach of power, fuel, and raw materials, one of the great crossroads of the continent. The Great Lakes waterway provides transport to the north and west. Eastward runs the route to the Mohawk and the Hudson, with the entrance to the New York State Barge Canal at Tonawanda, and five railway routes linking Buffalo with New York. The northern end of the Appalachian coalfield lies 100 miles to the south; and in the heart of the region is to be found its prime resource, the power of the Niagara Falls, exploited jointly by Canada and the U.S.A.

This strategically located industrial area is dominated by *Buffalo* (1,307,000). Goods which have been brought east by the water route through the lakes are transferred there to the land routes which lead to the Atlantic coast, and at the point of transfer there have sprung up a wide variety of industries. Lying as it does on the iron ore route, Buffalo is a steel and machinery city, but its outstanding industrial feature is that it is the continent's largest flour-milling centre. An arrangement which equalizes the railway freight rates on grain and on flour makes it equally suitable to mill the grain anywhere between the farmer and the baker, and thanks to its location Buffalo established a dominant position in the industry. However, the opening of the Seaway has been a threat to Buffalo more, perhaps, than to any other city, for the grain it milled formerly left the water route at this point and travelled by rail to the Atlantic coast. Now it must be reloaded into ships which are going on past Montreal to the sea, and the unique advantage of its position has been lost.

The power potential of the Niagara Falls has given Buffalo's manufacturing another facet. It has attracted to the banks of the Niagara River many industries that require access to large supplies of power—such as chemical manufactures and aluminium. Like the Kanawha in West Virginia and the St. Clair between Lake Huron and Windsor, the short Niagara River flows through a veritable 'Chemical Valley'.

The principal business of the ports that are situated along the southern shore of Lake Erie is, as we have already seen, the handling of iron ore and coal moving to and from Pittsburgh and West Virginia, and their manufactures are related to this advantageous position astride the industrial artery. In detail the sites of these ports have been decided by harbour possibilities and by the existence of valley routes connecting with the interior. It was this route factor—the linking of the Cuyahoga River to the Muskingum, and thus to the Ohio, by a canal in 1834—that gave *Cleveland* the initial advantage which has enabled it to become the great city of the Erie shore.

The natural advantage, however, was short-lived, for the mouth of the Cuyahoga is narrow and winding, the harbour works were for long neglected, and as the Great Lakes freighters grew larger, the problem of entering the port became more serious (and more expensive), so that business was lost to neighbouring ports. To some extent, therefore, the development of Lorain and of Conneaut may be regarded as an overflow from Cleveland made necessary by the limitations of the latter's site. In the meantime, however, Cleveland, now a city of 1,796,000 inhabitants, has developed a list of industries which is long even by the standards of a Great Lakes city; it ranges from steel to paints and from motor vehicle assembly to men's wear, and does credit to the home base of the late John D. Rockefeller, who set out from Cleveland to capture North America's oil industry in the 1860's, and who made Cleveland, for a short period, the refining centre of the continent.

No city on the Erie shore, however, can compare in location with *Detroit* and *Windsor*, at the western entrance to the lake. Here, where the Detroit River forms a passage, half a mile wide, between Lake St. Clair and Lake Erie, is an unrivalled position from which to tap the flow of lake traffic. Yet Detroit took only a small share in the traffic of the lakes, and made little attempt to develop its port (perhaps because of the narrowness of the passage at this point on the Detroit River), and it required other influences to set it on its way to becoming the great city of 3·7 million inhabitants which it is today—the genius of Henry Ford and the growth of a nation-wide road network.

Detroit is the fifth largest industrial city in the U.S.A., after New York, Chicago, Los Angeles, and Philadelphia. Like other southern Michigan cities within its orbit—Flint (374,000), Lansing, and Pontiac—it depends very heavily on the motor vehicle industry, which is spread all over this region and which gives direct employment to 35 per cent. of Detroit's industrial workers. This is a high percentage for so large a city (although it does not compare with the situation in the smaller cities, like Flint, where the proportion is 80 per cent.) and it is a very serious problem to Detroit: it limits the number of different kinds of work available, and so the types of workers who are needed. The city itself has been carrying out a huge, and very necessary, programme of urban clearance and re-newal, but in spite of this it is a place which other manufacturers have tended to avoid. With its fortunes so dependent on the sale of motor cars, it is essential that Detroit and its satellites should create, and be able to show, clear locational attractions to other types of industry in the future.

There remains for consideration the greatest of all the urban areas of the Great Lakes Region: that which sprawls round the southern shores of Lake Michigan and contains the cities of Chicago and Milwaukee. From Gary in Indiana to the northern edge of Milwaukee is over 130 miles, and although the built-up area is not continuous for the whole of this distance, the traveller along the lake front might certainly be forgiven, by anyone but a local patriot, for thinking that Milwaukee was merely one more northern suburb of Chicago, instead of a city of 1,194,000 inhabitants, lying 88 miles from the centre of Chicago.

Milwaukee possesses that mixture of heavy and light industry which we have seen to be characteristic of the Great Lakes port-cities, and in addition is one of North America's leading brewing centres, a fact not unconnected with the presence of a large German element in its population. It manufactures a range of vehicles and engines, while nearby Kenosha is the headquarters of one of the few automobile firms that are not located in Michigan. With a first-class harbour and a hinterland that includes the most prosperous sections of the central Dairy Belt, Milwaukee has a soundly-based economy and loses nothing by comparison with, even if in its functions it is overshadowed by, its great neighbour Chicago.

CHICAGO

Simply to list Chicago among the cities of the Great Lakes would be as misleading as to treat it among the cities of the Interior, for it belongs to both and yet transcends both. It lies on the Great Lakes waterway, but is also the focus of the rail routes of the continent. It functions not only as the 'big city' of the Corn Belt, but also as the capital of the Midwest and the headquarters of Interior agriculture, while for many enterprises whose business is nation-wide it provides a more central location for a base than does New York.

It is easy now, with the wisdom of hindsight, to point out how the southward projection of Lake Michigan, and the low watershed between the Great Lakes and the Mississippi system, gave an inevitable importance to the settlement at the lakehead. But early visitors to Chicago were unanimous in condemning the site as unfit for habitation, and few cities have had to overcome more natural handicaps in their expansion— as anyone who has tasted Chicago's drinking water quickly realizes. The city's importance grew, in fact, by stages. First it was the head of navigation for the lakes emigration route to the west. In 1848 the Illinois and Michigan Canal was cut, to link Lake Michigan with the Mississippi. Then in 1852 Chicago was linked by railway with New York. The coming of the railway marked its real beginnings, and when, during the Civil War, the choice of an eastern terminus for the new transcontinental line went, by default of its southern competitors, to Chicago, its future was assured. In the 1870's it was the development of the stockyards and of the clothing and furniture industries that marked its growth; in the first decade of the twentieth century it was the rise of the steel industry on the southern lake shore. Today the metropolitan area has 6·8 million inhabitants, and is the second largest manufacturing centre in North America. In terms of area, it is one of the largest urban concentrations in the world, with miles of suburbs spreading unchecked over the featureless Illinois plains. By contrast, its central business district is now far too small for it, jammed between the Chicago River, the lake, and the tracks of half the railway systems of the U.S.A. (see Fig. 51).

Chicago's heavy industry and oil refineries are concentrated close to the lake shore on the south side of the city, where the steel town of Gary was created by United States Steel Corporation and named after its first president. The Union Stockyards are also on the south side, 5 miles from the city centre, and formerly the meat-packing plants were grouped about them. For the rest, industries tend to cluster along the railways radiating from the city, and especially along the 'belt' (or ring) lines, which play a part of particular importance in a city where so many separate railway companies operate. This pat tern calls attention to a general tendency for industry to move out from the overcrowded central districts (where the older industries, such as clothing manufacture, were situated) to the suburbs, leaving the central area—Chicago's famous 'Loop'—to be cleared for much-needed road improvements or occupied by commerce. Several planned and fully equipped industrial estates have been created, such as the Clearing and Central Districts, and northern and western suburbs 10 to 12 miles from the city centre have become industrialized.

In terms of employment, Chicago's largest industries are primary steel production and the manufacture of machinery, particularly electrical communications equipment. The city's older industries—the manufacture of clothing and of furniture —nevertheless remain important, and in the railway centre of the continent the production of railway equipment naturally also finds a prominent place. Altogether, some 912,000 (or 35 per cent.) of the city's gainfully employed workers are engaged in industry. That the absolute figure is so large is a reminder of the prominence of Chicago as a manufacturing centre. That the percentage figure is no larger is equally a reminder of the importance of the city's other functions, in the fields of commerce and of transport.

Chicago, like New York, suffers from an unusual number of

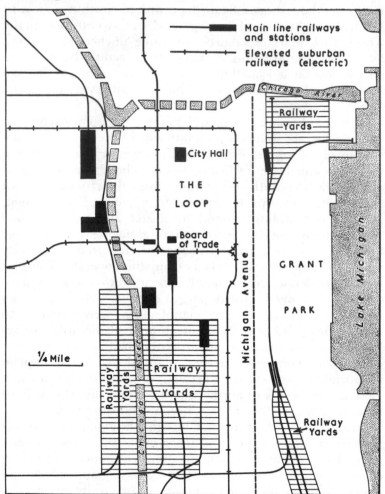

FIG. 51. Traffic Problems in Chicago. The map shows how access to the central business district ('The Loop') is barred by railways and by the Chicago River, with its swing bridges. The line of Michigan Avenue represents the city's original lake front; as in most of the Great Lakes cities, the shore area lying on the lakeward side of this line has been reclaimed for railway yards and for parks.

obstacles to movement of traffic, and this, ironically enough, precisely because of its importance as a traffic centre. On the flat lake shore almost all the railways run at ground level, and cross each other, and the city streets, by means of level crossings. Of the few railways which do not, the main one is the loop of elevated electric railway which gives the central business district its name (see Fig. 51). This, by contrast, runs above the street, level with the first-floor windows, and the roadways beneath are dark, obstructed and clangourous. Even worse, through the heart of the city runs the canalized Chicago River, traversed by a series of swing bridges. Each time these are opened—and fortunately for the motorists this is not often, since a canal cut-off has been built to enter Lake Michigan south of the city—the traffic of the business district comes to a stop. Immense sums have been spent to solve these problems by bridging and tunnelling, for Chicago is above all a vigorous city. Nor is there any reason to suppose that its expansion is at an end. For Chicago, as for all the lake shore cities which we have been considering, the completion of the St. Lawrence Seaway offered new opportunities in the form of a direct link with foreign markets, which should be cheaper and more convenient than the old rail-and-water route through New York or Montreal. Furthermore, Chicago is the only Great Lakes port with direct water connexion to the Mississippi System, so that it is the natural transfer point between the ocean traffic using the Seaway and the water-borne commerce of the whole western Interior. To serve this purpose, it has enlarged its port, south of the city.

While this development is occurring in the sphere of water transport, Chicago has, with no apparent difficulty except that of accommodating the aircraft, become the busiest air traffic centre in North America. As in the heyday of railway construction, its central position within the continent and its densely populated hinterland have attracted routes to it, swamping the facilities of one airport and making necessary the construction of a second, much larger, field to handle the ever-increasing traffic.

THE CITIES OF THE INTERIOR

The cities that remain to be considered under this last head-

ing are both numerous and varied in size. Their common
feature is a certain characteristic 'Midwestern' quality, which
is the product partly of economic function and partly of social
atmosphere. It results in a general similarity, both of appearance and of layout, among cities in the same size group, a
similarity which tends to weary the visitor but to give to the
Midwesterner a reassuring sense of sectional solidarity.

Fig. 52. The Urban Hierarchy of the Interior: The upper ranks. A suggested
classification of the most important centres of the Midwest, with examples
of centres of the fourth rank.

The cities of the Interior are best considered as forming a
hierarchy with five or six ranks. In solitary eminence in the
highest rank are Chicago in the U.S.A. and Toronto in Canada,
regional capitals in the fullest sense. The cities of the second
rank are more numerous; their populations range from half a
million upwards, and they are the region's major supply centres
and commercial headquarters. Most of them have achieved

greater growth than their neighbours by virtue of a longer history, or of a river port function, or both. In this category fall St. Louis (2,060,000), Cincinnati (1,071,000), Kansas City (1,039,000), Minneapolis–St. Paul (1,482,000), and Louisville (725,000).

It was the importance of the Ohio–Mississippi route, as the main road to the near west, which led to the settlement and early growth of Cincinnati, Louisville, and St. Louis. The falls in the Ohio River at Louisville interrupted river transport; the position of St. Louis at the junction of the Mississippi and Missouri made it the natural fitting-out point for movement westward along the Missouri; and subsequently Kansas City and Independence derived a similar advantage from their situation at the places where the overland trails left the hazardous water route and struck west for Santa Fé and Oregon. Farther north the Falls of St. Anthony marked the head of Mississippi navigation, and provided a focus for the growth of Minneapolis. Later came the railways, to lend momentum to the rise of these cities as the natural foci of the routes of the Interior.

Cincinnati has greatly altered since its 'Porkopolis' days, when it was a meat-packing, flour-milling town, and one of North America's principal ports. The agricultural industries, as we have seen, moved west, but the city's proximity to the heavy industry areas of the Appalachian coalfield provided the basis for a new industrial career; and today Cincinnati has a well-balanced industrial structure and a world-wide reputation for its machine tools, which find a wide market in the adjacent Manufacturing Belt. *Louisville*, on the other hand, has retained the two industries for which it has long been known tobacco processing and furniture making—as well as adding more recent, metal-based industries.

The modern city of *St. Louis* is Chicago's only real rival for the position of economic focus of the United States Interior. It ranks not far behind Chicago as a railway city, and claims additionally to be the nation's second most important trucking centre for road transport. It is the market headquarters for much of the produce of the southern Interior, and stands ninth on the list of the manufacturing cities of the U.S.A. Its industries are as diverse as those of any city in the nation, with a special emphasis on shoes, women's clothing, hardware, and the assembly of motor vehicles. This combination of excellent transport facilities and numerous local manufactures has given the city·an important trade area that stretches not only across the southern Interior, but well into the middle South.

It is interesting to notice that this group of 'second-rank' cities all lie near the periphery of the Interior, adding to their functions *within* the region important connexions with areas outside it. Of none of them is this more true than of the two western Interior metropolitan areas of Minneapolis—St. Paul and Kansas City. On any showing—newspaper coverage, agricultural marketing, or mail-order business—the hinterlands of these cities stretch far out into the Great Plains. They serve, in fact, both the Agricultural Interior and the Great Plains, both the intensive-farming areas of the region we are considering and the drier lands of less intensive use that lie farther west. If, for purposes of regional subdivision, we distinguish between the Interior and the Great Plains, then these cities should, strictly speaking, be treated under both headings, for while they are located in one region, they play a part in the life of both.

Kansas City, whose beginnings date from its days as an outfitting point for the overland trails, grew up as a receiving and processing centre for grain and livestock from the Corn Belt and Wheat Belt and for cattle from the ranges. This share of the nation's agricultural processing industries it has steadily increased, but it has also achieved in recent years a broader industrial base, that has changed it from a specialized to a general manufacturing city. This has been partly the result of proximity to the south-western oil and gas fields, which have provided industrial power, and partly a product of the general westward-moving tide of industrialization, which has brought to it numerous concerns seeking a central location within the United States, and attracted by Kansas City's exceptional advantages as a distribution centre.

Today, therefore, Kansas City is an outlier of the Manufacturing Belt and not merely a convenient processing point for farm produce. To use again the terms which were mentioned earlier (p. 273), the second wave of industrialization has crossed the Interior and reached as far west as Kansas City, bringing to it sophisticated modern industries to reinforce the older Midwestern 'regulars'. Yet with Kansas City, as with Chicago and St. Louis, much of the city's importance derives from its roles of market and transport centre. This is particularly true of the cities at the margin of the Great Plains, where the next major market centres lie hundreds of miles to the west, and where, in consequence, the cost of distribution or collection over the sparsely settled rangelands is exceptionally high. Thus Kansas City's wholesalers operate over an area that includes much of the Winter Wheat Belt and the southern Great Plains, and the role of its warehouses and wheat market is no less vital to the region's economy than that of its factories. As a trade centre, it has the advantage of excellent rail and road services, and local opinion in Missouri is divided on the question of whether it or St. Louis can claim to rank second to Chicago among the route centres of the Interior.

Minneapolis and *St. Paul*, the 'Twin Cities' whose centres lie some 8 miles apart and on opposite banks of the Mississippi, fulfil a similar role for the Spring Wheat Belt and the northern Great Plains. With three transcontinental railways running west from Minneapolis, the Cities' tributary area stretches well into Montana, and is only limited northward by the international boundary. Between the sections of the metropolitan area there is a marked 'division of labour'. St. Paul is a combination of state capital and railway junction, whose shopkeepers deplore a general St. Paul habit of going to Minneapolis to shop. Minneapolis, in turn, having the water power of the Falls of St. Anthony at its disposal, developed the early industrial core, participated as a mill town in the Great Lakes lumber boom (see p. 265), and then settled down to a more stable career as one of the continent's flour-milling centres (its grain elevator capacity of 115 million bushels is the largest in North America), with important manufacture of machinery in addition.

The cities of the third rank are, for the most part, cities whose functions tie them closely to their surrounding farmlands; their industries supply rural needs, and their commerce covers a trade area similar to that of the major centres, but overshadowed by it and smaller in scale. These cities vary greatly in

size; the largest of them is probably Indianapolis, whose
population of 697,000 would warrant it a place among the
major centres, but whose functions are essentially those of a
local supply city. In the eastern half of the Interior, also, the
urban pattern is complicated by the westward spread of the
areas of intensive manufacturing. Thus there are, in Ohio, the
cities of Columbus and Dayton which, while they belong basically to this group, have been swollen by the coming of overspill
industries from farther east, and so have expanded their populations rapidly to the half-million mark. Much the same process
has underlain the growth of other manufacturing cities in
southern Michigan and northern Indiana. At the other end of
the population scale, however, these same urban functions are
performed, in the western Corn Belt, by centres whose population does not greatly exceed 100,000, and in south-western
Ontario by the city of London, with a population of 181,000.

While many of these cities are nationally known for the
manufacture of a particular product—especially those like
Peoria and Moline, which make tractors and farm equipment
—their industries are, on the whole, related to local needs.
Characteristically, their employment structure is broadly
based. In Indianapolis, for example, industry accounts for
some 30 per cent. of the employed workers, and marketing for
rather more than 20 per cent. No single industry predominates.
Machinery, including farm equipment, accounts for 20 per
cent. of the industrial labour; food products and metal goods
for 10 per cent. each; and electrical machinery, chemicals, and
clothing for between 5 per cent. and 10 per cent. each. Although
in the smaller cities farther west, the proportion of the population engaged in industry is not so high, the diversity is generally
preserved.

Below these cities of the third rank, the hierarchy continues
down to include various grades of country towns, whose spacing
throughout the Interior depends on the intensity of farming,
and whose importance is to be gauged by the range of services
which they offer. About these towns two general remarks can be
made. The first is that in the wide, fertile Agricultural Interior
every hamlet has had roughly the same chance, geographically,
as the next to become a metropolis, and development has followed strict Darwinian principles: the fittest have survived and

expanded at the expense of the rest. What has given particular
significance to this competitive growth is the fact, already men-

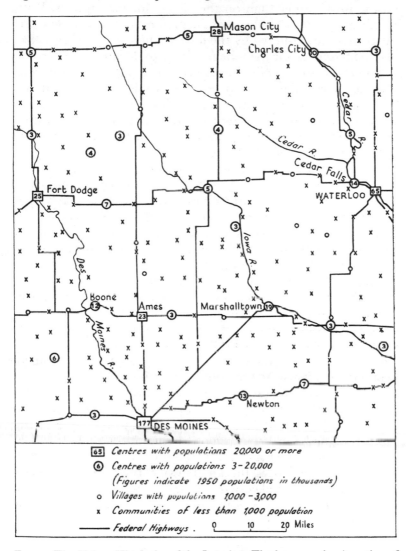

FIG. 53. The Urban Hierarchy of the Interior: The lower ranks. A section of
central Iowa, showing major and minor centres and rural communities.
Notice the straight Midwestern highways, with their occasional right-angle
bends, corresponding to the 'gridiron' pattern of land sections laid out by
the original government surveyors.

U

tioned in Chapter IV, that as the range of the farmer's daily
needs has been widening, so he has tended to rely increasingly
on the town rather than on the village for his supplies. With
motor transport at his disposal, he prefers the fuller, if remoter,
range of services offered by the towns. There is therefore a continuing tendency for the villages either to decline or to become
purely residential, while the service and supply industries congregate in ever larger centres. The whole development has
taken place recently enough and rapidly enough for the competitive spirit to remain; there is in Illinois a community with a
census population of 1,621, which greeted the traveller of the
1950's with the proud, if belated, boast that it was 'the capital
of the Corn Belt'. In fact, no sooner were the small towns in
being than they began to lose ground to the larger ones, and
they in turn to the greater cities along the waterways. It is
interesting, therefore, to trace the influences, personal or
communal, which have given one town in Iowa or Ontario a
present population of 40,000 and its neighbour only 5,000—
interesting, too, to speculate on how far this process of 'up-
grading' of service centres may continue.

The second general point about these towns is that, as a result
of the process already discussed, they support a range of industries which is surprisingly large for towns of their size. Indeed,
in the view of Smith and Phillips[1] it is often *too* large, and is a
product of the competitive community spirit rather than of
economic necessity. Yet to supply, as many of these towns do,
the farmers within a radius of 20 to 30 miles with their day-to-
day requirements, when these farmers operate some of the most
highly mechanized farms in the world and have one of the
world's highest rural standards of living, has clearly involved
the growth of a rather specialized type of industrial centre. With
its numerous industries, the small town of the Interior is, nevertheless, intimately linked with the land, and upon this association is based the social structure of the greater part of the
Midwest.

The Interior possesses most of the geographical advantages,
and almost none of the disadvantages, of the other major
regions of North America. If it is charged with isolationism,

[1] *North America*, pp. 393–4.

then it is the isolationism of economic self-sufficiency; if it is charged with monotonous uniformity, then at least it is the uniformity of a well-distributed prosperity. To leave the Interior and travel in almost any direction means to travel down the economic gradient, and to enter regions whose problems are manifest in the landscape—soil erosion by wind and water, rural overcrowding or abandoned farmsteads on rugged, infertile lands. The Interior has its problems too, but they are almost all the problems of prosperity—how to dispose of its huge agricultural output; how to control the prices that farmers and industrialists are willing to pay for its land; and how to transact, within the confines of its crowded cities, the volume of business which its richness creates.

FURTHER READING

THE basic reference on this region is the recent *The North American Midwest*, ed. J. H. Garland. The agricultural patterns of the Midwest have been considerably clarified by four articles on land use and crop combinations (each containing numerous maps) by J. C. Weaver, appearing in *Econ. Geog.* vol. xxx, pp. 1–47; *Geog. Review*, vol. xliv, pp. 175–200 and 560–72, and vol. xlvi, pp. 536–65. 'Corn Yield and Climate in the Corn Belt' is dealt with by J. K. Rose, ibid., vol. xxvi, pp. 88–102. Good pictures of life on Corn Belt farmsteads are given in relevant chapters of *Rural Life in the United States*, ed. C. C. Taylor, or J. R. Smith and O. Phillips' *North America*, and other details are added by W. E. McIntyre's 'Land Utilisation of Three Typical Upland Prairie Townships' (of Illinois), *Econ. Geog.*, vol. xxv, pp. 260–74, and H. L. Smith's 'Agricultural Land Use in Iowa', *Econ. Geog.*, vol. xxv, pp. 190–200.

The agricultural geography of the southern borders of the Interior is dealt with in 'Geographic Regions of Missouri', by J. E. Collier, *A.A.A.G.*, vol. xlv, pp. 368–92; 'Changing Economy and Landscape in a Missouri Ozarks Area', by E. W. Kersten, *A. A. A. G.*, vol. xlviii, pp. 398–418, and 'Land Use in the Bluegrass Basins', by R. W. Johnson, *Econ. Geog.*, vol. xvi, pp. 315–35. For the Dairy Belt, the series of articles by Loyal Durand form basic references; see his 'The American Dairy Region', *Journal of Geog.*, vol. xlviii, pp. 1–20, and other articles in *Econ. Geog.*, vol. xvi, pp. 416–28, vol. xxiii, pp. 32–40, vol. xxvii, pp. 163–83, vol. xxxi, pp. 301–20, and vol. xl, pp. 9–33. Occupance of the Northwoods is covered in M. E. McGaugh's 'The Settlement of the Saginaw Basin', *Univ. of Chicago Research Papers, No. 16*, and in L. Durand's 'The West Shawano Upland of Wisconsin', *A.A.A.G.*, vol. xxxiv, pp. 135–63, a case study of the cut-over lands.

Agriculture in south-western Ontario can be studied in *Canadian Regions* and in L. G. Reeds' 'Agricultural Regions of Southern Ontario, 1880 and 1951', *Econ. Geog.*, vol. xxxv, pp. 219–27. The Niagara fruit belt is well covered by J. W. Watson in 'Mapping a Hundred Years of Change in the Niagara Peninsula', *Can. Geog. Journ.*, vol. xxxii, pp. 266–83, and 'Changing Land Uses in the Niagara Fruit Belt', by R. Krueger, *Geog. Bull.*, No. 14 (1960), pp. 5–24.

On the industrial sections of the region, many of the published studies are unfortunately now out of date. However, some of the more recent articles are 'Connellsville Beehive Coke Region', by E. W. Miller, *Econ. Geog.*, vol. xxix, pp. 144–58, 'The Mesabi Range', by G. Langdon, *Journal of Geog.*, vol. lvii, pp. 119–29, 'The Iron and Steel Industry of the Mahoning and Shenango Valleys', by A. Rodgers, ibid., vol. xxviii, pp. 331–42, 'The Industrial Development of the Allegheny Valley', by E. W. Miller, ibid., vol. xix, pp. 388–404, 'Economic Development of the Great Kanawha Valley', by L. M. Davis, ibid., vol. xxii, pp. 255–67, 'Industrial Development in the Ohio Valley', by J. F. Lounsbury, *Journal of Geog.*, vol. lx, pp. 253–62, 'Changing Patterns of Coal Production in the Eastern Interior Field', by H. G. Roepke, ibid., vol. xxxi, pp. 234–47, and 'Manufacturing in the Rock River Valley' (of Wisconsin and Illinois), by J. W. Alexander, *A.A.A.G.*, vol. xl, pp. 237–53.

An interesting case study of the lower ranks of the Midwestern communities is J. E. Brush's 'The Hierarchy of Central Places in Southwestern Wisconsin', *Geog. Review*, vol. xliii, pp. 380–402. For the larger centres, see 'The Twin City District', by R. Hartshorne, ibid., vol. xxii, pp. 431–42; 'Evolution of Metropolitan Detroit', by B. Hudgins, *Econ. Geog.*, vol. xxi, pp. 206–20, and 'Detroit, A Case Study in Industrial Problems of a Central City', by H. Black, *Land Economics*, vol. xxxiv, pp. 219–26; 'Windsor, Ontario', by J. L. Robinson, *Can. Geog. Journ.*, vol. xxvii, pp. 106–20; 'The Port of Milwaukee', by E. Hamming, *Univ. of Chicago Research Papers, No. 26*; the description of Hamilton which is included in Griffith Taylor's *Geography in the Twentieth Century*, pp. 484–98, or his article 'Hamilton and Its Environs', *Can. Geog. Journ.*, vol. xxx, pp. 240–52, by J. W. Watson. For Toronto, see N. A. H. Deacon, 'Geographical Factors and Land Use in Toronto', ibid., vol. xxix, pp. 80–99.

For Chicago, besides a number of general and lively accounts such as E. Dedmon's *Fabulous Chicago*, there are H. M. Mayer's *Chicago: City of Decisions*, and his 'Prospects and Problems of the Port of Chicago', *Econ. Geog.*, vol. xxxi, pp. 95–125, and 'The Railway Terminal Problem of Chicago', ibid., vol. xxi, pp. 62–76, and a number of interesting studies of the industries of particular sections of the Chicago region, included in the series of *Univ. of Chicago Research Papers in Geography*. Among them are those by M. J. De Meirleir (No. 11), R. I. Cramer (No. 27), J. B. Kenyon (No. 33), R. N. Gold (No. 36), G. M. Ahmed (No. 46), and H. M. Mayer (No. 49). There are two other recent articles on the same subject, by M. W. Reinemann and E. N. Thomas respectively, in *Econ. Geog.*, vol. xxxvi, pp. 139–44 and 158—70.

Manufacturing, in Ontario in general and in Toronto in particular, is dealt with by D. Kerr and J. Spelt in three articles to be found in *The*

Canadian Geographer, No. 15 (1960), pp. 12–25; ibid., No. 12 (1958), pp. 11–19, and *Geog. Bulletin*, No. 10 (1957), pp. 5–22.

Traffic on the Great Lakes routeway is described in 'A Turn-Around on a Great Lakes Freighter', by A. G. Ballert, *Econ. Geog.*, vol. xxv, pp. 146–55, and the same author's two articles on the coal trade and coal ports, which are in ibid., vol. xxix, pp. 48–59, and *Geog. Review*, vol. xxxviii, pp. 194–205.

As a general account, covering every aspect of life in the United States Midwest, Graham Hutton's *Midwest at Noon* can be highly recommended to students of the region's geography.

XIII

THE SOUTH

1. *The Old South*

BETWEEN the Potomac and the Gulf coast (the latter of which, for a variety of reasons, is best considered separately) there lies an area whose regional distinctiveness cannot be denied. It may be variously defined, and its western limit in particular is open to question, but no regional analysis could possibly overlook the Old South. This region developed a distinctive plantation economy, maintained a large Negro population to operate it, fought a war to preserve it, suffered the bitterness of defeat and the chaos of the aftermath, and has since been struggling to regain both its regional self-esteem and its place in the nation.

It is, perhaps, the extent of the plantation system of the period before 1860 which gives the clearest single indication of the extent of the Old South, for it embodied both the economic and the social elements that made up the region's character. In the Civil War of 1861–5 the Confederacy drew little support from the upland areas in the Appalachians to which the plantation system could not, for geographical reasons, spread. While the state of Virginia fought on the side of the South, the independent upland farmers' sympathies remained with the North, and they seceded to form the state of West Virginia. Kentucky, southern in so many other respects, was not a plantation state and, after wavering for a time, joined the North. But define the area how we may—in terms of its former economy, its war memorials, or its Negro population—the South remains a reality in American life. And embedded almost equally deeply in the consciousness of the twentieth-century American is a second impression: the Old South is a depressed area.

During the difficult years of the 1920's that culminated in the depression of 1929–32, there crystallized what became the familiar concept of the South in the American mind. The chief features of this picture may be summarized as follows:

Southern agriculture was based almost exclusively on cotton, corn, and tobacco. These crops, grown year after year on the same fields, had eaten the heart out of the land, and left the soil

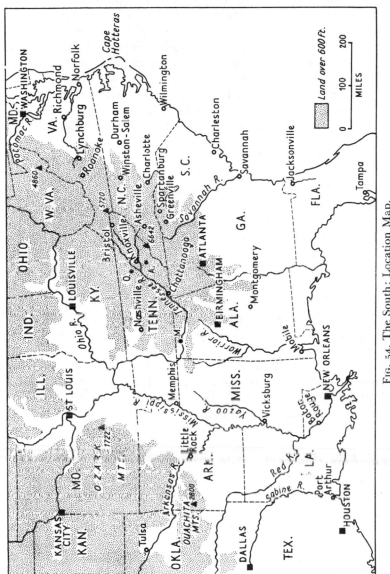

Fig. 54. The South: Location Map.
(A = Alcoa; M = Muscle Shoals; O = Oak Ridge.)

particularly liable to erosion. Southern farmers, mostly small tenants, farmed hopelessly on in an era of low world agricultural prices, and knew the despair of declining yields and gully erosion, without having the means or the will to arrest the process. Farm buildings fell into disrepair, and mules did the work for which more fortunate farmers used tractors. The poverty of the white farmers was only exceeded by that of many of the Negroes, most of whom held land as 'sharecroppers', paying their rent by a fixed proportion of their crop—a crop which might disastrously glut the market one year, and be stricken with blight the next.

Southern industry offered little palliative for the region's distress. The industries traditional to the South—tobacco manfacturing and textiles, for example—happened to be those in which the returns per worker are always low. With an exceptionally high regional birth-rate, there was an abundance of cheap labour, and wage levels were far below the national average. New industries were slow in appearing; rather, the region's raw products were shipped north to be processed elsewhere, and the population remained overwhelmingly rural.

Yet in the early nineteenth century this region could bear comparison with any part of the nation in respect of its wealth and of the leaders it produced in cultural and political fields. Even if we make allowance for the fact that our concept of the ante-bellum South owes something to the author of *Gone with the Wind* and her colleagues, the contrast with the South of the 1920's is remarkable. This is much more so when we take into account the rich resources of this region, whose natural endowment ranks it high among the regions of North America: freedom from climatic hazards, areas of fertile soils, vast timber supplies, and a variety of minerals, which included the world's most strategically combined coal and iron supplies for steel making.

If we attempt to account for the great contrast between the 1850's and the 1920's in the Old South, we should begin by recalling that the prosperity of the earlier years was in some ways only illusory. There was soil erosion in the 1850's, and earlier too, but its importance was concealed by the fact that there was always new land available in the west, and abandonment of the old in favour of the new masked the seriousness of the problem. The plantation owner and his mobile labour force, the slaves, could, if necessary, move west—into Alabama, into Mississippi, finally into Texas—and there begin again. Further, the South depended on the sale of cotton to a dangerous degree. Such was its concentration on this one crop that, although it was an agricultural region with little industry, the South at the beginning of the war in 1861 was having to *import* basic foodstuffs for both men and animals. Again, we must recall that the early Southern prosperity was concentrated in one narrow section of the population, so that, to a large part of its people, the South's varying fortunes made no difference: they simply remained poor.

But despite all these reservations about the earlier Southern prosperity, the fact remains that the Civil War was a great underlying cause of the later Southern ills. The South was invaded and occupied, and physical destruction was immense. The Southern ports were blockaded, and cotton exports that should have paid for industrial imports never left the quays of New Orleans. Then, in the midst of the war, came Lincoln's emancipation of the slaves. For the South it was, apart from anything else, a staggering economic blow. For generations, Southern landowners had been buying slaves as a form of capital investment. To abolish slavery meant the elimination of more than $2,000 million of Southern capital. When the time for rebuilding came, the loss was acutely felt.

The end of the war in 1865 brought little relief. Military occupation, enforced liberal reforms, and Southern reaction followed each other over the succeeding fifteen years. This was a period, too, when the 3 to 4 million emancipated slaves were trying to adjust to their new positions as citizens and farmers, hindered on the one hand by white prejudice (typified by the Ku-Klux-Klan) and on the other by ignorance of farm methods. In practice, they were often forced to turn to their old masters for instruction, and many became sharecroppers.

Beyond the immediate, impoverishing effects of the war and the peace, there were other factors which foreshadowed the future weakness of the Southern economy. About 1879 there began an economic revival in the South. Up to that date much of the war damage remained unrepaired; factories and port installations lay derelict. But after 1879 the North, encouraged by Southern propaganda, 'discovered' the South as a field of investment. Capital flowed in, to repair railways and factories, or to create new industries. An industrial boom resulted, but when it was over the South was almost as firmly in Northern hands financially as it had been politically in 1865. This financial hold (of which the South had by no means ceased to complain even in the 1950's) allowed the North to exploit Southern lands and timber resources, and has probably had other lasting effects, such as that of maintaining high freight rates between Southern factories and the great market areas of the North. Since the railways were controlled by Northern interests, it was possible to exclude Southern goods, and to enjoy undisturbed occupation of the markets.[1]

Then poverty and lack of education made themselves felt in the all-important sphere of agriculture, where the old mistake of over-specialization was repeated, this time over a wider area that included newly settled lands in the western South. Small-holders wore out their plots by persistent cultivation of the same three row-crops—cotton, corn, and tobacco—either because these were the only crops they knew how to grow or, in the case of the sharecroppers, because they were necessary to pay the rent. Equipment was as scarce as experience, and only labour was abundant—labour without the capital to make it productive.

These, then, are some of the reasons why by 1930 the annual income per person in fifteen Southern states was only 45 per cent. of that in the other thirty-three. The depression years after 1929 widened the differentials between the South and the rest of the nation. The depression hit the farmers with particular severity, and the South, with its dense farm population and its marked dependence on cash crops, suffered greatly. Migration to the towns, which had provided some relief in the 1920's, was halted and in some cases reversed. The passing of the depression left the South with gigantic problems for solution; both the material problem of increasing the wealth of its people and the psychological one of throwing off the stigma of backwardness under which it had laboured so long.

---

[1] The tone of these statements is intentionally vague, since the validity of the Southern charges on this score has been much disputed. For a thorough examination of the problem's background, see W. Joubert's *Southern Freight Rates in Transition*, Univ. of Florida Press, 1949.

To solve these problems, certain objectives would have to be realized. In agriculture, these objectives were: (1) to consolidate and enlarge farm units for more efficient handling, which would mean fewer, but better farmers; (2) to reduce the proportion of tenant farmers (which was 20 per cent. above the national average) and to deal with sharecropping which, although actually preferred by some Southern tenants to a cash tenancy, was such a stimulus to the persistent production of cash crops; (3) to encourage scientific farming. Only so could the South overcome its basic handicap—low productivity. Dependence on the cotton-corn-tobacco cycle must be reduced; new techniques and information about alternative crops must be circulated, and not only circulated but applied.

If Southern agriculture was to reach these goals, it was clear that not only would many farmers have to revise their methods, but also that much of the rural population would have to cease farming and find employment elsewhere. Improvements in farming would therefore depend upon the availability of other sources of employment. Only, in fact, by matching agricultural improvement with industrial development could the Southern standard of living be raised.

In industry there were, once again, certain clear objectives. (1) Fuller use must be made of local materials, agricultural and mineral. (2) Instead of shipping raw materials out of the region, the South should play a far larger part in processing its own products. It would thereby retain within its borders the additional values created by turning trees into furniture and cotton into high quality cloth, instead of seeing those values pass to Northern workers. (3) The South must strive to develop its own capital resources and finance its own industry, so that it might cease to be a 'colony' of the North, and bargain on equal terms with other regions over such matters as freight rates and factory locations. (4) New employment must be provided within the region for an unskilled rural population surplus, as the only alternative to mass emigration from the area.

2. The New South

Today the South presents a different picture. In almost every detail the account given in the preceding section must be modified in the light of developments since 1933. For the changes that have taken place some of the credit must go to the Roosevelt administration which, taking office at the low point of the depression in 1933, enacted the New Deal measures that opened the way to recovery. In a more local sphere much of the credit goes to the Tennessee Valley Authority, established as a part of the Roosevelt programme. But no one can deny that, apart from these outside forces for good, there has been a remarkable revival within the South itself. It has not yet caught up with the rest of the nation, but the gap has narrowed. In 1961, average income per person in sixteen Southern states was 77 per cent. of the average for the nation, as gainst 59 per cent. thirty years earlier. A description of the South as it is today will reveal the progress made towards the objectives set out in the previous section.

THE PHYSICAL SETTING

Physically the region which we are considering is not well-defined, but it lies mainly within two physiographic divisions—the Atlantic–Gulf Coast Plains and the Appalachian System—and extends beyond them into the Ouachita Mountains and the Eastern Transition Belt. For historical and economic reasons, its northern limit should be set across northern Virginia into central Kentucky; thence across the southern tip of Missouri (an important cotton area) into central Arkansas; and south-west to Dallas. If the present extent of cotton cultivation is taken as a guide, the region ends on the west at the boundary of the Great Plains, but definition of this western edge is difficult and not particularly profitable.

Within this region, relief and soils vary considerably. The Atlantic Coastal Plain remains, today, to a large extent what it has always been, sandy and swampy in turn, infertile and widely forest-covered. Inland across the plain, altitude and fertility generally increase together, up to the Appalachian Piedmont. The southern end of the Appalachians protrudes into the heart of the region, and the main areas of both agricultural and industrial production are grouped around it in the shape of a wide U. Within the mountains themselves much of the terrain is rough and the soil poor, but in the Ridge and Valley section, at least, fertile valleys invite settlement. West of the Appala-

chian Plateaux, the soils of central Tennessee and Kentucky
are famous, and relief beyond the plateau edge is, on the whole,
gentle. Farther west again lie the bottomlands of the Mississippi, where the lime-rich alluvia, once drained, have a high
agricultural potential.

West of the Mississippi the Ouachitas somewhat resemble the
southern Appalachians in terrain and soils, with a small number of fertile valley areas. Finally, at the western edge of the
region, the land rises gently to the level of the Great Plains, and
the yellow pedalfers of the wetter south-east give way to the
pedocals of the grasslands. The black earths of the Texas Black
Prairie roughly mark the limit of the region.

Climatically the region is well favoured from most points of
view. Only on its western fringe is it liable to drought; everywhere else the rainfall is over 40 inches per annum, and in the
Great Smokies it rises to 80 inches. Snow seldom falls, and only
in the Appalachians does the frost-free period last less than 200
days. On the other hand, much of the rain falls in heavy
thunder-showers, which increase the danger of erosion, while
high humidity over most of the area makes for summer
lassitude, and cloudiness reduces evaporation and increases
leaching of the soil.

The region is well endowed by nature. Forests stretch across
the Appalachians, the Ouachitas, and much of the coastal
plain. These forests represent only a remainder of a far greater
former cover, but even after the cutting and burning of the past
decades the South remains possessed of a tremendous asset—40
per cent. of the nation's commercial forest, including the bulk
of its hardwood reserves. Fuel supplies are also available within
the region. The Appalachian coalfield extends through
Kentucky and Tennessee into Alabama, and the western end of
the region lies athwart the great Mid-Continental and Gulf
oil and gas fields. Other mineral resources are numerous.
Bauxite is minded in the neighbourhood of Little Rock, Ark.,
and these deposits account for over 90 per cent. of the United
States' domestic production. Round Birmingham, Ala., lie the
haematite iron ore deposits that serve its steel industry. Phosphate rock is worked south of Nashville, Tenn., while man-
ganese, copper, and chromite are found in the mountains of
eastern Tennessee and of the Carolinas. Finally, any account of

the region's resources must include mention of the great amount of electric power, potential and developed, which is available from the rivers of this area, of which the development on the Tennessee is the best publicized, but by no means the only, example.

SOUTHERN AGRICULTURE

We have seen how a century of misuse left its mark on the region, in the form of eroded hill slopes, low crop yields, and dilapidated farms. Today the picture is altogether different; the scarred hillsides are covered with vegetation once more, and if many of the farms still have a tumbledown appearance, it is often only because the owners gave priority to the purchase of a car and a refrigerator, rather than to house painting.

The principal features of this change may be briefly summarized. Cotton is no longer the principal crop throughout the south-east. The cotton and corn areas have contracted, and much of their former extent is given over to a series of new, localized special crops. Meanwhile, the total area under crops has declined, and pasture has come in as a replacement. This in turn has been accompanied by a rise in the number of beef and dairy cattle. New crops have been brought in to arrest erosion and revitalize the soil, so that the old staples can be grown on proper rotations and with less risk. Farm mechanization is increasing, while farm size has grown larger. Finally, and in view of what has been written about the historical background of Southern problems, very significantly, the number of tenant farmers and the total number of agricultural workers have shown a sharp decline since 1940.

Throughout the history of Southern agriculture, cotton has been the mainstay of the region's farm income. Although the 'Cotton Belt' was probably never as compact or as continuous as the map of agricultural regions implies, yet it is true that, at some time or other, cotton has been grown on most of the lands in the South where there is a frost-free season of 200 days or more, and where the rainfall is suitable—not less than 25 inches annually, or more than 10 inches in the autumn harvest season. However, over the years, the 'belt' has shifted its position. Throughout the nineteenth century it spread westward, as areas in the south-east became infested with the boll weevil or worn out by the years of monoculture. After spreading into central Texas, however, it contracted again, and the eastern end of the belt found a new vitality. Today it seems clear that a Cotton Belt, as such, no longer exists. The most recent change has been a contraction into certain limited areas, where cotton is the special crop of the locality, and where it is raised even more intensively, but more scientifically, than before.

The underlying cause of this latest trend has evidently been

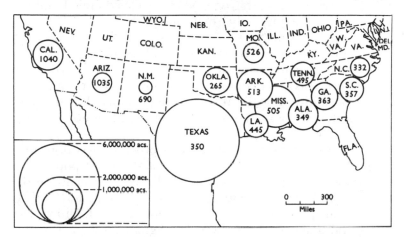

Fig. 55. U.S.A.: Cotton Production, by states, 1961. The size of the circle in each state is proportional to the area under cotton in that state in 1961, while the figure in the circle gives the state's average yield (in pounds per acre) over the harvest years 1961 and 1962. The high yields obtained under irrigation in the west are evident from the map.

a move for efficiency in production. Cotton growing is now concentrated on those lands which are best suited to it and which permit of the mechanisation of work on the crop. As this increased efficiency has been made possible by the move to lands suitable for mechanized farming, so it has been made necessary by the fact that the United States' capacity to produce cotton is far in excess of its ability to consume, or dispose of, the product. Since the early part of the century, schemes have been discussed for limiting the cotton crop, and in 1933 came the government's acreage reduction programme (see p. 118) and a system of production quotas for the farmers. Since 1933, however, the situation has been further aggravated by the amazingly rapid expansion of cotton production under irrigation in states farther west, especially California and Arizona, so that the quotas must now be shared among more producers than before, and in practice the marginal producers drop out. However, when the government simultaneously restricts acreage and supports the price of the harvested product, the way to wealth clearly lies in raising yield per acre. It is therefore no surprise to find that, while the cotton acreage in the South dropped from an average of 40 million acres in 1928–32 to 14 million acres in the years 1959–60, the yields doubled and the total crop declined by only about one-sixth.

The South is still North America's great cotton-producing region, but within the region the crop's status has changed. From holding region-wide pre-eminence, it has declined to the rank of one speciality among half a dozen which flourish in specific localities. Locally it retains importance, but the days when cotton accounted for over half of all Southern farm income are long since gone.

As the cotton areas contract, and the processes of cotton cultivation become mechanized, the life of the rural population throughout the region is profoundly affected. As recently as the 1930's there prevailed a widespread feeling that cotton cultivation was one process that *could not* be mechanized. Differences in cultural practices throughout the region, consequent variations in the size and nature of the plant, and the fact that the crop did not all fruit at once—all these factors seemed to form barriers to mechanization. It was therefore assumed that the South would continue to need its enormous, mobile hand-labour force as long as it continued to grow cotton. Indeed, it seemed clear that, if complete mechanization became a fact, the South would be saddled with a mass of unemployed workers, most of them Negroes, with no means of livelihood.

The reality has proved very different. In the 1940's it proved possible to complete the chain of mechanized operations and replace the labourer at every stage. (Mechanization of weeding, for example, has been as important a labour-saver as mechanization of the harvest operation.) Total mechanization has proved to cut labour requirements even more strikingly than the pessimists feared; in the Mississippi Delta, where the cultivation of a bale of cotton by mule-power and hand labour had required 155 hours, complete mechanization has cut the time to 12 hours.[1] But such has been the pace of change in the South that the unemployment problem has scarcely arisen. Indeed, in a few localities, farmers have been urged on to mechanization by an incipient labour shortage. It is true that, statistically, the transition is only just beginning. In the south-east in 1960, only 5 per cent. was mechanically harvested. In Arkansas and Texas the figure was 25 per cent., but neither of these could compare with the 70 per cent. of California's crop. Certainly, however, the swift and peaceful transfer of this huge unskilled labour force from its traditional occupation to a variety of new functions promises to be one of the outstanding social develop-ments of twentieth-century America.

The areas where cotton has retained its importance are: (1) The coastal plain of Georgia and the Carolinas, inland from the coastal sands and swamps. This is the oldest cotton area, and it has suffered greatly from the boll weevil and from soil exhaus-tion. It continues in production, thanks to heavy—and costly—applications of fertilizers. (2) The Piedmont in Georgia and South Carolina. The history of this area is similar. (3) Northern Alabama. In the 1920's cotton production in Alabama was focused upon the 'Black Belt' that ran from east to west across the centre of the state. Today this belt is relatively unimportant, and production is concentrated in a small area adjoining the valley of the Tennessee River.[2] (4) The alluvial lands of the Mississippi and its tributaries, such as the Yazoo and Red River, areas of great fertility and high yields. (5) The Black Prairie ('Black Waxies') of Texas. Production in this area has declined somewhat from its peak, but it remains a great cotton area. (6) Southern Texas. In the coastal strip and the lower valley of the Rio Grande, there are a number of recent develop-ments, which are mainly based on irrigation. (7) The High Plains of Texas and Oklahoma. This dry area lies outside the South, as we have defined it. It is, however, an important cotton district, since its dryness renders it safe from the menace of the boll weevil.

In order to trace the changes which have accompanied this

[1] J. II. Street, *New Revolution in the Cotton Economy*, U. of N. Carolina Press, 1957, p. 170.

[2] J. A. Tower, 'Cotton Change in Alabama, 1879–1946', *Econ. Geog.*, vol. xxvi, pp. 6–27.

x

decline in the region-wide importance of cotton, let us now return to the events of 1933. Cotton prices were poor, and the government was paying the farmers not to plant. Throughout the South, thousands of acres were lying derelict, ruined by erosion and ravaged by the weevil. Farther north the tobacco lands were in little better heart. The dual problem of the farmers was: what should replace the cotton crop, and could the derelict land be brought back into production? The changes in land use since that time represent, on the one hand, a search for profitable alternatives to cotton and, on the other, government-sponsored and private efforts to bring Southern agriculture back into balance with its environment.

Like cotton, both corn and tobacco have, from the first, been grown in the South—corn on every farm and plot, tobacco especially in the Atlantic seaboard states, Tennessee, and Kentucky. Like cotton, these crops remain important, but the acreage of corn has declined considerably, and that of tobacco is rigidly controlled by the government. Alongside them have come to prominence a series of new and profitable specializations, replacing cotton locally as a cash crop. Among the most important of these are peaches in Georgia and Southern Carolina, peanuts in south-eastern Alabama and southwestern Georgia, soyabeans in the Mississippi Valley, and rice in Arkansas. Perhaps the biggest of these new developments has been that of poultry farming, which yields a 'cash crop' of broiler fowls. Poultry farming is well suited to the worn-out lands of the south-east, since it makes little demand on the soil. The Piedmont of northern Alabama and Georgia has become the largest producing region in the nation for a food product whose popularity has greatly increased in recent years.

So much for the profitable alternatives to cotton. The other Southern need is for an agriculture so balanced as to maintain the land in good heart. A number of new crops, such as soyabeans and peanuts, not only bring profit to the farmer, but nourish the soil as well. Conservationists have encouraged the planting of these crops either in replacement of, or in rotation with, the old staples. The adoption of such rotations has brought the cultivation of cotton and tobacco on to a scientifically safe level. Cotton today is typically grown on a three-year rotation with hay and legumes or grain.

But the problem of the derelict lands remained, and to these had to be added the many Southern hillsides that were too steep for cultivation but were cultivated nevertheless. It was only a matter of time until they, too, were derelict. For these lands the only solution was to take them out of cultivation altogether. By 1949 there were in the South 7½ million acres less under crops than in 1930; by 1959 20 million less than in 1949.

Much of the land taken out of crops was closed to agriculture altogether; the rest was put down to pasture. To aid the process, a number of pasture crops were imported into the South. From as far away as Asia have come kudzu and lespedeza, crops which combine high fodder value with the ability to cover bare, eroded ground quickly. These changes mean, in their turn, better pasturage for cattle, and make possible higher yields of beef and milk. The south-east is not, at present, an important raiser of either type of cattle, and there is room here for a good deal of expansion within the region's agriculture— an expansion which may well take place as the region's standard of living gradually rises.

WORKERS AND INDUSTRY IN THE SOUTH

Such basic changes in the land use of the South have naturally had their effect on labour needs and population distribution. All along, as we have seen, one of the main needs of the region has been to improve the man:land ratio in its agriculture, which has been far too high for efficiency. In part, this high ratio was due to the small size of Southern farms, on which labour was badly underemployed. Partly, it was due also to the presence of hired farm-labourers, who made up a poorly-paid labour force which worked for daily or hourly wages, and which the region had to carry throughout the year. Even in 1959, almost a half of all the United States' farm labourers were still to be found in the South. Elsewhere, such labourers were a vanishing breed.

Between 1940 and 1959, the number of workers on the farms of sixteen Southern states dropped by over 40 per cent. The number of farms in the same area was reduced by 45 per cent. and the average size of farm greatly increased—in Georgia from 109 to 185 acres, and in Mississippi from 65 to 135 acres. By 1960, out of an employed population of 18½ million, the

South had only 1½ million dependent on farming for their livelihood. The South, in statistical terms at least, had ceased to be a rural slum. In particular, large numbers of share-croppers had abandoned their usually meagre livelihoods.

How had these changes come about? They had obviously been necessary in the interests of agricultural efficiency and conservation, but they could only take place if some way could be found of draining off the surplus rural population. This could be done by two means—provision of other jobs within the region, or emigration out of it.

In fact, these are the two means by which the change *has* been made: two remedies for the regional dilemma which have applied in roughly equal proportions. Since 1939, the South has gained a million and a half jobs in industry, and many more than that in the service industries and administration. And between 1940 and 1960 there was a net migration out of the South of 6¼ million persons, almost exactly equal numbers of Negroes and white people.

Migration out of the South did not begin in 1940—it has been going on for decades—but it was the attraction of the northern war industries which gave it fresh momentum. It has continued since the war; in fact, the out-migration of the 1950's was slightly larger than that of the 1940's. For the white migrants, the attraction has been strongest for those at the top and bottom of the economic scale—for the go-ahead, educated men who realized that professional facilities were better elsewhere, and for the whites in the labourer class who were reacting against Negro competition for their type of job. For the Negroes, the attraction was obvious, although all too often illusory: to get away from the region where their ancestors had been slaves.

Had this safety-valve of inter-regional migration not existed, the Southern situation today would be serious indeed. It is perhaps interesting to consider what the present state of the South would have been if secession had become permanent, and the transfer of Southern labour to Northern markets had been blocked by political barriers while the rural population went on increasing. It is under circumstances similar to these that the rural slums of the Caribbean and the Orient have come into being.

So much for those who have left the region. For those who have remained, the changes in employment have meant a change from rural to urban work. During the decade 1950–60, increases in the numbers of those in professional, technical, and clerical work in the South were even more striking than of those in industry; there was an increase of almost 50 per cent. in these categories during the decade. As a result, there has been a general movement to town. While this has been happening all through North America, the movement within the South has had one interesting characteristic: it has not contributed so much to the expansion of the large urban centres—there are, in any case, few of them in the South—as to the growth of the small industrial towns. It is not primarily to Atlanta or Birmingham that the workers have moved, but to the towns of the Carolina Piedmont and the Tennessee Valley. It is true that the population of Dallas increased phenomenally between 1940 and 1960, but the circumstances creating this situation had their origins (see p. 340) largely outside this region.

This type of urban development is to be explained in part by the character of Southern industrialization. In a region where one of the main attractions to industry is the availability of labour, there is a genuine incentive to locate plants in the rural communities where the labour surplus is to be found. Furthermore, the power resources of the South are mainly electricity and oil (or gas), which allow considerable flexibility in locating plants. It has therefore been unnecessary, and certainly Southern opinion has judged it undesirable, to crowd workers into manufacturing cities; instead, the factories are located in small centres. While there is, of course, an element of risk in thus linking a town's employment exclusively to one or two plants, it is more than outweighed in most cases by the advantages of a garden city atmosphere and a freedom from the ills of industrial life on the nineteenth-century pattern. For this satisfactory state of affairs much of the credit must go to the Planning Commissions of the various states which have encouraged the policy of rural industrialization to provide work for the rural population. Local authorities also offer a variety of inducements to suitable industries, and business groups have been active in creating local enterprises.

The net result is that, apart from the Birmingham iron and

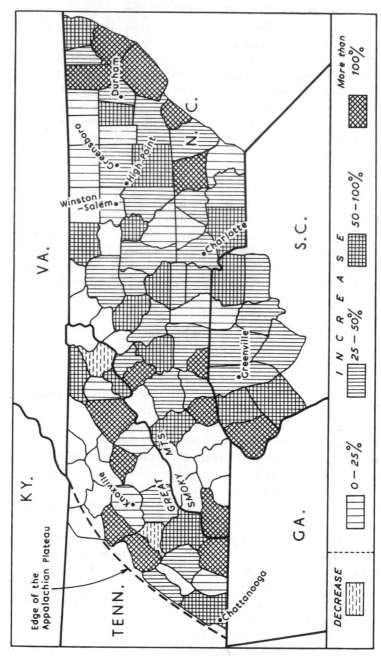

Fig. 56. The South-East: Percentage increase in the numbers of industrial production workers, by selected counties, 1939–54. The map emphasizes the diffused character of Southern industrialization. (Data from the U.S. Census of Manufactures, 1947 and 1954, vol. iii.) Counties with less than 1,000 such workers in 1954 excluded from consideration. Centres marked are those with more than 10,000 industrial workers in 1954.

steel area and the Piedmont around Charlotte, N.C., there is
no prominent industrial area within the Southern region.
Industry is dispersed throughout the whole South, and only on
the map (p. 130) which shows intensity of employment are the
small centres, with their heavy dependence on industry,
emphasized.

Considering that industrial employment has now passed its
peak in the United States, as we saw in a previous chapter, the
South has done well to secure 1½ million new jobs in manufacturing since 1940, and it is worthwhile examining this
phenomenon more closely, to discover what industries are
involved and why, in some cases, firms have moved from other
parts of the country to resettle in the South. Such an explanation in respect of the textile industry has already been
attempted in Chapter V; a wider solution must now be sought.

Since before the Civil War, the South has been noted for its
manufactures of textiles and tobacco. But these traditional
Southern industries, though they remain important, are not
primarily responsible for the expansion since 1940. This has
been produced by the emergence of three other classes of
industry. The first consists of branch plants of concerns producing for nation-wide markets. As the Southern standard of
living has risen, so the consumer-goods market in the south-
east has become increasingly attractive to producers, who have
created local supply points to meet the growing demand. In
this category fall such manufactures as those of agricultural
machinery and household equipment. The second class consists
of a few firms which have migrated from elsewhere into the
South to secure a more favourable business location. They are
not numerous, but a good deal has been heard of them, for
political reasons. The third class consists of industries which
have only recently come into existence—the plastic and petro-
chemical industries are good examples—and which, in seeking
a national headquarters, chose to settle in the South.

What advantages can the South offer, to attract these new
industries? A study of a number of Southern firms[1] has shown

[1] G. E. McLaughlin and S. H. Robock, *Why Industry Moves South*, National Planning Assocn., 1949. It is safe to assume that, in almost every case, the market factor
was the *second* reason for moving, even if not the first. In a survey of firms which had
moved to Florida up to 1960, 724 out of 752 gave the market as an 'important' reason
for their move.

that their reasons for establishing plants in the South could be generally grouped under three heads: 45 per cent. gave proximity to markets as their main reason, 30 per cent. proximity to raw materials or power, and 25 per cent. cited labour supply. The first of these has already been mentioned: at last the South has become a worthwhile market for the American business-man. The second heading, 'power', needs little comment in the land of the T.V.A. and Southern oilfields. The industries attracted by raw materials have been mainly those exploiting forest resources, or else members of the bewilderingly expanding family known as petro-chemical.

The third, apparently innocuous, heading of 'labour supply' has been the source of much debate. What makes Southern labour attractive? Since wages in the South have always been low, it has been argued that Southern labour is wanted because it is cheap. Whereas this was formerly true, it seems certain that the differential is getting smaller; firms with plants in several regions pay the same wages in all, and in 1953, under pressure from the national trade union, the differential in wages between Southern steelworkers and their colleagues elsewhere was abolished. It is sometimes argued, also, that Southern labour, after training, is more efficient than that elsewhere. But statistical studies permit of no generalization on this score. It is suggested, again, that in the South labour law and trade unionism are less restrictive upon production than in other regions. This seems to be true, but not to have exerted any great influence upon plant location.

The real factor making Southern labour popular with manu-facturers seems rather to be its attitude to industrial work. In this formerly backward, rural region, industrial employment means both social advancement and material benefit; average income from agriculture in the South in 1949 was $1,735 as against $2,900 in industry. When this differential is coupled with the social amenities offered by many Southern industria-lists to their workers, the attraction of the factory is clear.

The industrial development of the South has been very varied. Forest products, cotton, tobacco, and oil have been the native raw materials: motor-vehicle assembly, aluminium smelting, and fertilizers have been brought into the region,

along with a score of other industries, by the changing standards
and circumstances of its life. As we have already seen, the new
industries have been located typically in small towns, and it is
significant that the only areas of the South which resemble the
industrial regions of the North antedate this period of recent
expansion.

One of these is the steel area round *Birmingham* (635,000),
developed in the 1880's, originally on the initiative of the Louisville and Nashville Railroad. Here, where coal and iron ore are
found within a few miles of each other, and where much of the
ore, lying in formations of dolomitic limestone, is self-fluxing,
is the 'Pittsburgh of the South', its night skies lit by the characteristic glare of the blast furnaces. There is a well-developed
railway network, and water transport has been made possible
by a canal joining Birmingham to the Warrior River, which
gives access to the Gulf by way of the Tombigbee.

Unusually favoured in its raw material supply, and strategically placed to supply steel to the Far West as well as to the
south-eastern states, Birmingham's prospects at the turn of the
century were indeed bright. Their very promise, however,
worked to the city's disadvantage, for the steelmen of the North-
East could hardly tolerate such a challenge to their hegemony.
In 1907 the bulk of the Birmingham industry passed under the
control of the great interests centred in the U.S. Steel Corporation; that is, it became simply a unit in a nation-wide industrial
complex, whose headquarters and basing-point were in Pittsburgh, and consequently many of its local advantages were lost.

The other, though very different, industrial region of the
South is the Piedmont of Virginia and the Carolinas. Even here
there are no large cities (Charlotte, the largest, has a population of only 272,000), although we might perhaps regard Richmond (408,000) as an outlier of this region. Instead there are a
number of smaller centres, such as Spartanburg and Greenville
in South Carolina, Asheville and Winston-Salem in North
Carolina, and Roanoke and Lynchburg in Virginia. The three
principal interests of the region are: (1) tobacco processing, for
which Richmond, Durham, and Winston-Salem are particularly noted; (2) industries based on the Appalachian forests,
such as furniture making and the manufacture of paper and
boarding; and (3) textiles. Besides being the centre of the

nation's cotton textile manufacture, the district is also noted for its rayon mills: those at Asheville and Roanoke are among the largest in the world. On the strength of its past record, it might also be considered the centre, or at least one of the 'poles of growth', of the whole Southern revival, for the North Carolina Piedmont, possessing a number of universities and research institutes, and having the advantage of local capital supplied by the tobacco industry, has taken the lead in planning and redevelopment for the South.

Across the Blue Ridge, in the valley of the Tennessee, a somewhat similar, diffuse industrial area is growing up, with Knoxville, Bristol, and Chattanooga as its urban foci. Hydro-electricity accounts for the presence here of one of the United State's first atomic plants, at Oak Ridge near Knoxville, and of the great Alcoa aluminium works, as well as the smaller plants of the valley towns. So successful have been the joint efforts of the T.V.A. and the valley communities to attract industry that one of the most serious obstacles to further industrial development in the world's most famous 'Electricity Valley' has been—shortage of power.

Finally, mention must be made of the two large, isolated industrial centres of the South. One of these is *Memphis* (627,000), strategically placed at a Mississippi crossing, and a great inland port. Since 1940 Memphis has been one of the nation's most swiftly expanding manufacturing centres, and today it is the regional headquarters of many national concerns, with every type of industry represented. It is also the world's largest cotton market, handling over 4 million bales annually.

The other city is *Atlanta* (1,017,000), metropolis of the southeast. It has a wide variety of industries (counting among its distinctions the headquarters of Coca-Cola), but its chief importance is that it is the regional capital. It is the focus of the railway system, and is used as a distributing centre by many firms, so that its warehouses are as important as its factories. (It may be compared, in this respect, to the cities at the eastern edge of the Great Plains.) It is also used as administrative centre by a number of agencies of the federal government, and has today recaptured much of the region-wide significance which it possessed before it fell to Sherman in the tragic days of 1864.

3. *The Tennessee Valley Authority*

Initiated at the nadir of Southern fortunes in 1933, and working in one of its most depressed areas, the T.V.A. has become a symbol of Southern progress. Great as its material achievement has been, it could be argued that its psychological effect has been even greater. At a time of deep depression it showed that, with a little 'pump priming', the Southern economy could achieve a new vitality and sense of purpose.

Much has already been written about the T.V.A., and not all of it is complimentary. Before we discuss the subject, one point must be made quite clear, a point which, if overlooked, makes an understanding of the literature on the T.V.A. impossible. It is that, although control of the Tennessee had been discussed by engineers for over a hundred years, the decision to create the T.V.A. was a *political* decision. It was taken by Roosevelt's Democratic administration in 1933, and for millions of Americans it was a decision prompted by party politics. It was therefore just as important for the Democrats to be able to show that the scheme was a success as it was for the Republicans to be able to demonstrate that it was expensive, unnecessary, or plainly unconstitutional.

The Tennessee Valley early in 1933 epitomized the South's most pressing problems. Low prices and uninstructed farming had undermined the valley's agriculture, and soil erosion had reached frightening proportions. Erosion affected run-off and drainage, so that the river constituted a real menace. On the one hand, its irregular flow and vast soil load made it wellnigh useless for navigation. On the other, it presented an acute flood danger to the low-lying farms and cities not only along its own course, but also on the lower Mississippi, to whose flood crests it made its contribution.

This was the background to Roosevelt's decision to create the T.V.A. Clearly the menace of the river was only a symptom of the human problems of the valley. But the approach to these problems had to be indirect. Under the Constitution, as we have seen in Chapter III, the powers of the federal government are restricted. The President could create an Authority to control the Tennessee, on the ground that it would be removing barriers to interstate commerce; all else that he hoped for must grow out of that basic activity. Just how much might grow out of its one legitimate activity has been the great point of debate in the story of the T.V.A.

Thus it came about that the Authority was created with the dual mandate of flood control and navigation improvement. From the works constructed for these two purposes it was to produce and sell electric power. It was in this somewhat backhanded way that the great Tennessee power development was initiated. The T.V.A. was also given charge of a nitrate plant at Muscle Shoals, relic of an earlier project, so entering the fertilizer business and, therewith, the sphere of agricultural improvement, to which it has made such an outstanding contribution in the succeeding years.

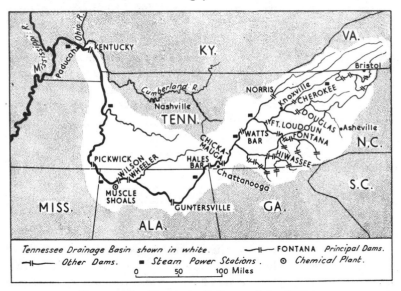

FIG. 57. The Tennessee Valley and the T.V.A.

The area within which the T.V.A. operates is some 40,000 square miles in extent. The Tennessee is formed by a number of rivers which rise in the Blue Ridge, and which flow into the 'corrugations' of the Ridge and Valley country, where they merge to form the Tennessee proper. The main river follows the trend of the valley system to Chattanooga, where it turns west, cuts through the southern end of the Appalachian Plateau, and flows west and north to join the Ohio, just before the latter joins the Mississippi. The area comprises parts of seven states.

By 1963 the T.V.A. had been in existence for over a quarter of a century. In pursuit of its primary objectives it had built 20 dams (11 other, non-T.V.A. dams are owned or operated by it); it has created a 9-foot channel for shipping from Knoxville to the Ohio, 625 miles away; and it operated 12 million kilowatts of electric generating capacity, with schemes in hand to create another $2\frac{1}{2}$ millions. So great, however, had been the increase in demand that thermal power stations have had to be built by the T.V.A. to supplement the capacity of the dams. In fact, three-quarters of the electricity the T.V.A. supplies is now thermal generated. Lastly, flood damage along the river has been much reduced, and on a number of occasions control of the Tennessee reduced the flood volume by a few vital inches that saved the levees farther south.

It was, however, obvious from the beginning that if the Tennessee was to be controlled, it would be necessary not only to build dams, but also to penetrate to the headwaters of the river and there to rectify the conditions responsible for the floods. So the sphere of the T.V.A's activities widened. As a complement to the programme of dam construction and nitrate production, there was initiated, with the help of the Soil Conservation Service, an anti-erosion campaign on the valley farms. Gullying was checked and trees were planted on eroded hillsides, for otherwise the newly built dams would rapidly have become silted up. This has led in turn to the T.V.A.'s participating in a detailed soil survey of its area. As a further by-product of the original construction, the Authority has joined with the U.S. Geological Survey in the topographic mapping of the valley. Finally, where dams have been built and reservoirs created, the shores have been landscaped to create parks and to encourage a growing tourist trade to the 'Great Lakes of the South'. At the same time, it has been possible to campaign against the malaria which has for so long undermined the vitality of Southerners. Newly formed shorelines have been engineered to avoid the creation of breeding places for mosquitoes, and swamps and standing water have been sprayed.

The construction of the Tennessee navigation channel also led to an enlargement of the T.V.A.'s activities, for, once it had achieved the 9-foot channel, the Authority set out to build up traffic over the route. Its economists have tried hard to attract to the river a curious assortment of cargoes, and in the process have fought a number of battles over freight rates which have benefited the South as a whole.

It is in the sale of electric power that the T.V.A.'s interests have found their widest extension, for it has embarked upon a campaign to fulfil its creators' hopes by raising the whole standard of living in the valley. In this campaign the sale of cheap electricity and fertilizers, the Authority's two commercial products, is clearly of basic importance. In its widest context, therefore, the T.V.A. can be portrayed as a kind of regional fairy godmother, helping the farmers with advice and fertilizers, and providing the cheap power which attracts industries to the area. Alternatively, of course, it can be portrayed as a ruthlessly undemocratic agency, whose economic dictatorship hangs over the valley like a thundercloud. It is perhaps noteworthy that, *within* the valley, the thundercloud viewpoint has steadily lost ground with the passage of time.

This may suitably lead us to a brief discussion of the controversy aroused by the T.V.A. There are two main grounds on which it is attacked. The first is purely political, and assails as unconstitutional the whole idea of the federal government's engaging in what President Hoover (who vetoed an earlier proposal for a T.V.A.) called 'barter in the markets', by the sale of fertilizers or electricity.

The second point of attack, however, is not a matter of doctrine but of cost. It is argued, on the one hand, that the scheme was unnecessarily expensive and, on the other, that the Authority, by taking advantage of the distribution of costs between the different parts of a multi-purpose scheme (see p. 114), is claiming to produce electricity more cheaply than its real cost, and so is able to undersell the private power producers with whom it competes. To all this the T.V.A. replies that the work needed doing, and that there is no evidence that costs could have been lowered by placing the task in other hands; that, furthermore, the electricity rates are economically just and are actually not as low as those of private producers in some other parts of the country.

It seems fair to conclude that, commissioned to control the

river and to produce power, the T.V.A. has done both, and done them efficiently. That it may sometimes have been over-enthusiastic in its claims is understandable, if we remember the political background. In a wider context the T.V.A. may be said to have raised Southern morale. It has brought prosperity to the area, but throughout the South the indices of prosperity are rising everywhere, and not markedly more so within the valley than outside it. Rather, it seems as if this injection of federal capital and initiative into the South resulted, through the whole region, in a new appreciation of what could be made of the rich resources that lay ready to hand.

In the widest context of all—the national significance of the T.V.A.—the lessons of this great experiment are not so easy to read. That its objectives were desirable has never been in question, but endless debate has surrounded its methods of reaching them. Specifically, the problem has been how to fit into the framework of the Constitution a federal agency that could carry out true *regional planning*. Although the T.V.A.'s charter gave it authority to do so, what has emerged has been not so much planning as intelligent co-operation between a number of federal and state agencies. Indeed, the former general manager of the T.V.A. has said that 'it is without authority to prescribe and enforce a plan';[1] and it is difficult to conceive of true regional planning that would not immediately bring into conflict, for example, the T.V.A. and the states' Planning Commissions. It seems reasonable to assume that the creation of a real regional plan would require a reinterpretation of the constitutional position, and this, in turn, would necessitate a change in the emotional atmosphere that surrounds the topic. Whether or not this is in itself desirable is a point of debate among students of the subject. Meanwhile, uncertainty and argument surround the projects for new authorities in the great Missouri and Columbia Valleys of the west. There is much yet to be learned in the expensive school on the Tennessee.

4. Conclusion

After half a century of backwardness, the South has at last

[1] *An Approach to the Development of a Region*, Lecture by Gordon Clapp at the University of Chicago, 15 Feb. 1954.

begun to achieve reinstatement among the regions of the United States. Most of this improvement has occurred since 1940, and much of it since 1948. The struggle is by no means over; a vast deficit remains. All we can say is that, after lagging for years ever farther behind the rest of the nation, the South's rate of progress has now caught up with, and may even be a little greater than, that of the country as a whole. Somewhere ahead should lie a time when economic differentials are gone, and only a cultural difference remains to mark the South, in J. H. Franklin's delightful phrase, as 'a tattoo upon the arm of the nation'.

For the improvement that has taken place, much of the credit must go to the people of the South themselves. There is, however, another factor that must not be overlooked. Since 1933, and especially since 1941, the contribution of the government to economic development has enormously increased. Agricultural subsidies, federal loans, and the financing of war industries have all meant a spending of the nation's money which is independent of regional poverty or wealth. At the same time, minimum-wage legislation has come into force, and, as an additional factor within the South, the social status of the Negro has been improving, so that he has been better placed to profit by, and contribute to, the economic growth of the region. It is surely no coincidence that, precisely during this period, the South (which in a political sense wields an influence in the federal sphere out of all proportion to its contributions to the federal revenue) should have made such spectacular progress.[1] The greater the contribution of the central government to local finances, the smaller should become the differences in regional prosperity within the nation.

By one means or another, at least, the South has rid itself of the stigma of being the poor relative of the rest of the nation. Today, when poverty is discussed, it is Appalachia and Kentucky coal miners, rather than the South and Mississippi sharecroppers, which are the subjects of discussion. The South has its permanent, and apparently intractable, problem—that

[1] A Northerner calls attention to the following facts, which seem to bear on the above: while New England and the Central states obtain some 4 per cent. of their major income from the federal government, and the Middle Atlantic states 5·5 per cent., the South-East obtains in this way 8·3 per cent. (S. E. Harris in 'Interregional Competition', *Amer. Econ. Review*, vol. xliv, p. 379).

of race—still to confront. But at least it can be tackled against a background of rising prosperity for all its inhabitants.

FURTHER READING

THE pre-war character of the South was analysed in H. W. Odum's *Southern Regions of the United States,* and W. J. Cash's *The Mind of The South* discusses Southern sectionalism. For the changes that are taking place, see *This Changing South,* by J. M. Maclachlan and J. S. Floyd; *The Emerging South,* by T. D. Clark, or *Economic Resources and Policies of the South,* by C. B. Hoover and B. U. Ratchford. The agricultural aspects are dealt with by J. L. Fulmer in *Agricultural Progress in the Cotton Belt Since 1920,* and by J. H. Street in *The New Revolution in the Cotton Economy.* The articles of M. Prunty are all valuable, especially the first of the following series: 'Land Occupance in the Southeast', *Geog. Review,* vol. xlii, pp. 439–61, 'The Renaissance of the Southern Plantation', ibid., vol. xlv, pp. 459–91, 'The Woodland Plantation as a Contemporary Occupance Type in the South', ibid., vol. liii, pp. 1–21, 'Recent Expansions in the Southern Pulp-Paper Industries', *Econ. Geog.,* vol. xxxii, pp. 51–57.

On the industrial and urban aspects, see also 'Functional and Occupational Structure of Cities of the American South', by J. F. Hart, *A.A.A.G.,* vol. xlv, pp. 269–86, and 'Population Distribution and Trends in North Carolina', by C. T. Phillips, *Journal of Geog.,* vol. lv, pp. 182–93.

On the T.V.A. see D. Lilienthal, *T.V.A.; Democracy on the March,* 20th Anniversary Edition which, apart from giving a 'founder-member's' views on the T.V.A., contains a full bibliography. A most useful source on all matters affecting the regional economy is the *Southern Economic Journal.*

Y

XIV

THE SOUTHERN COASTS AND TEXAS

THE southern coasts of the U.S.A. and the peninsula of
Florida are sub-tropical in climate and vegetation. Brownsville, on the Texas–Mexico border, and New Orleans are
in 26° and 30° N. latitude respectively, while the southern tip
of Florida—Key West—is only one degree from the Tropic of
Cancer. East of the Texas–Louisiana border, no part of these
coastlands has less than 45 inches of rain per annum, a January
mean temperature of less than 50° F., or a July mean of less
than 80° F. The Florida Keys are frostless, the tip of the
Mississippi Delta almost so, and the frost-free season on most
of the coast is more than 270 days (although the very rarity of
frost increases its economic impact when it does occur.) West
of the Texas border the rainfall diminishes rapidly to a coastal
minimum of 24 inches in the extreme south-west, but the temperature conditions remain the same, and the Texas coastlands
have a frost-free season of 300 days or more.

1. *The Humid Sub-Tropical Coastlands*

Under the climatic conditions of the humid sub-tropical
coastlands east of the Texas–Louisiana border a luxuriant
natural vegetation has developed. To these climatic conditions,
however, can be added another factor, which combines with
the climate to give these coasts, and with them much of peninsular Florida and south-eastern Georgia, their distinctive
landscape. It is the low-lying and swampy character of the
terrain on this gently sloping, lagoon-fringed coast. The combination of these circumstances creates the well-known,
idealized Gulf Coast landscape: tree-filled swamps, with
Spanish moss festooned on the branches of oak and cypress,
and winding creeks that form a maze penetrated by no one but
the local fishermen and moss gatherers.

Yet this tangle of trees and water is without doubt one of the
fastest-developing regions of the U.S.A. Repeatedly, over recent years, it has provided materials for headlines, in a country

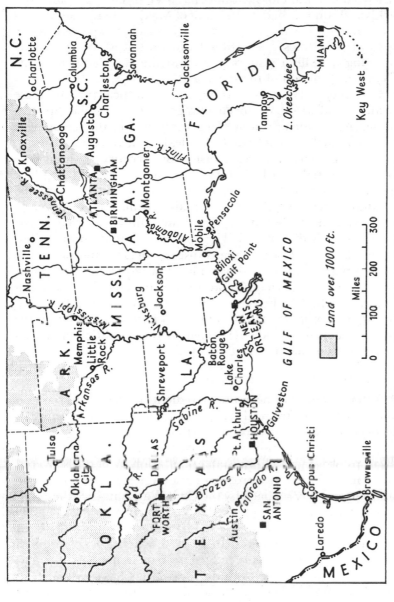

Fig. 58. Southern Coasts of the U.S.A.: Location Map.

where competition for headlines has been intense: off-shore oil-fields and sulphur beds in the Gulf of Mexico; magnesium from sea-water in Texas; in Florida an industrial expansion since 1946 at five times the national rate, a tourist boom that is bringing 5 million visitors a year to the state, and now the Clapham Junction of the space age.

Certainly there was nothing in the appearance of these swamps and sandbars to encourage in the original Spanish settlers in Florida any hope of a great future for the region. Nor did the French, who founded Mobile, Biloxi, and New Orleans, and occupied the Lower Mississippi territory of Louisiana early in the eighteenth century, show much interest in exploiting the resources of their new colony. Sugar and rice were the commodities for which the coastlands became known, developing a system of plantation agriculture similar to that of the Cotton Belt farther inland. The Spaniards imported cattle, but the herds suffered from so many diseases that the mortality rate made progress in livestock farming slow. After the Civil War, with plantation agriculture at a standstill and the coastlands sharing the fate of the rest of the South, there was a brief and tragic lumber boom in the forests of southern pine. As late as the 1920's much of Florida remained in the condition in which Ponce de Leon had found it in 1513.

INGREDIENTS OF PROSPERITY

What, then, have been the ingredients in the rise to power of the humid sub-tropical coastlands? Out of a number of associated factors, it is possible to isolate five.

(a) *Soils*. Once drained, the black muck soils of the coastal swamps prove, as the Louisiana plantation owners discovered, immensely fertile. The process of drainage has been a long one, and was severely set back by the Civil War, but since the 1930's it has made rapid progress; between 1940 and 1950, in the Mississippi Delta alone, the land in drainage enterprises increased by 8 million acres. In Florida, where nearly a million acres of the Everglades are judged to be reclaimable for agriculture, the efforts made to drain these lands have met with repeated setbacks. With little local relief to carry off surface water, and hurricane weather to breach the dykes, it was not until 1949 that a comprehensive drainage plan, in the $250 million price range, was finally agreed by the federal and local agencies concerned.

Where these soils have been drained, however, they have proved ideal, not merely for the production of the sugar and rice crops, but also for truck farming. With the advantage of its southerly position, the Gulf Coast has been able to establish itself as a principal United States producer of fresh winter vegetables and early new-season fruits, with a harvest season from January to April. (In terms of latitude, it does for the cities of the northern U.S.A. what the Canary Islands do for North-West Europe.) Meanwhile the production of sugar cane has steadily increased,[1] and is becoming mechanized; that of rice has trebled since 1930. While rice of the Louisiana coastlands grows under much the same physical conditions as in the paddies of Asia, there could hardly be a greater contrast than that between the production techniques of the Orient, where labour requirements are in the neighbourhood of one man per acre, and those of the Gulf, where the ratio is one man to 100 acres and the crop is harvested by combines.

It may seem curious to add, after describing the part played by drainage in the Gulf's new prosperity, that irrigation is of equal importance. But it is true, nevertheless, that in the drained areas supplemental irrigation is responsible for important increases in crop yields, as well as for overcoming occasional seasonal drought. Irrigation water is applied, often by sprinklers, to citrus trees, vegetable fields, and orchards. In experiments carried out in Georgia with irrigated and non-irrigated sweet potatoes, irrigation which cost $41 per acre gave an astonishing increase of $441 in the value of the yield, with smaller gains for other crops.[2]

(b) *The citrus fruit industry.* Included within the general topic of agriculture, but deserving a special place in this list of the forces that have built today's Gulf Coast economy, is the development of the citrus fruit industry. Oranges and grape-

[1] It must, however, be explained that, under the terms of the United States Sugar Act, the market for sugar in the U.S.A. is apportioned by quota between several groups of producers—the Puerto Rican, Hawaiian, Philippine, and Gulf cane sugar producers, and the beet sugar producers of the northern and western states. The fact that United States production of sugar-cane rose from some 3 million tons in 1930 to about 7 million tons in the 1950's does not, therefore, give a true index of productive capacity.

[2] *Water*, The Yearbook of Agriculture, 1955, U.S. Dept. of Agriculture, p. 526.

fruit are grown over much of central Florida and in parts of Louisiana, as well as farther west in Texas, and to Florida alone they represent an annual income of some $200 million, which makes them the state's most valuable crop. As with most forms of fruit growing, however, the industry's fortunes have fluctuated markedly over recent years; indeed, almost the only element of permanence in the situation has been the long-standing duel between Californian and Floridan growers to capture the markets in the northern states.

The development of citrus growing has been marked by two trends. One is the steady rise in the amount of citrus fruit consumed in the U.S.A. Between 1919 and 1945 the total consumption of all fruit doubled, but almost the whole of this increase was represented by a growth in the consumption of citrus fruit. While the trend has weakened since 1945, the growers have clearly been catering for an expanding market, and have planted new trees accordingly. Indeed, there has been a tendency to overestimate expansion, and to produce unsaleable surpluses.

The second trend, which is to some extent the result of these surpluses, has been towards new methods of marketing the fruit. In this development, aimed at increasing total consumption, the Floridans have played a full part, if only because their fruit lacks something in appearance by contrast with that of the Californians. Profiting by the fact that people would eat more citrus fruit if only they could do so without getting sticky in the process, and faced with unsaleable fresh fruit after the Second World War, the Floridans turned to the process which has revolutionized the industry—freezing. By this means the producers not only increased total sales, but they obtained a product that could be marketed all the year round, instead of only seasonally (the Gulf citrus harvest time is from November to March.) Since the Second World War the balance of the interstate rivalry between the southern and western producers has swung in favour of the south.

(c) *Beef cattle production.* A third feature of the Gulf Coast development is, in a somewhat curious way, an outcome of the second. This is the rise of the eastern Gulf region as a beef cattle producer, a development which has depended on two contributing causes—the production of a breed of cattle adapted to the region's natural conditions, and the discovery of a cheap and nutritious feedstuff. In the first of these the largest part has been played by the Brahman cattle, first imported from India in the middle of the nineteenth century, which have proved themselves, in various crosses, to be hardy animals and good beef producers in both the humid and arid sections of the southern states. The second contributing factor has been the discovery that waste products from the citrus processing industry can be used as cattle feed, to the mutual advantage of both the fruit processers, who have a market for their by-products, and the cattlemen, who have responded by increasing the size of their herds.   •

(d) *Sunshine and tourism*. Basic to all these developments, how-ever, is the one great natural advantage from which they all derive—the Gulf Coast's sunshine, that makes the region not only a leading producer of sub-tropical produce for a continent lying mainly in the temperate zone, but also a great resort area for the growing number of Americans who can afford to go south to dodge the winter.

The rise of the tourist industry has indeed been spectacular, particularly on the east coast of Florida, and especially around the metropolitan area of Miami, whose population of 42,000 in 1920 had risen by 1960 to almost a million. To turn these sandy beaches and coastal swamps into a string of thriving resort cities has involved a vast investment; vast, too, have been the rewards within the reach of those who have participated in this astonishing boom, in which worthless sandbars, suddenly appreciated as 'palm-fringed', have become valuable pro-perties almost overnight. Further west, such cities as Biloxi, Miss., and Pensacola, Fla., have participated in the growth of the resort industry, and the Gulf Coast, like California, has become an area to which northern businessmen like to retire.

As has already been suggested, the boom in the southern resort industry must be seen as an expression of a rising stan-dard of living, in that a growing number of Americans possess the economic freedom to move with the sun—farmers who fly their private planes south from the Wheat Belt; New York businessmen who conduct their affairs in winter by long-distance telephone. But while the tourist industry on the Gulf is primarily a winter one, the resorts are by no means idle in the summer. They do, however, suffer from one undeniable draw-back in the summer months, and that is the hurricane. While an essential part of the hurricane's unpleasantness is that its habits are unpredictable, it can be said that there is tendency for these violent storms to be generated east of the Antilles, and for them to move west and strike the American coast once or twice each year, in the later part of the summer. Southern builders have learned to prepare for these emergencies, but the hurricanes inevitably take a heavy toll of crops, orchards, and communication lines, while the high seas usually associated with their passage batter the coastal settlements and endanger shipping on this treacherous shore.

A number of the resorts along this coast are also port-cities whose trade, in keeping with their situation, is mainly with the Caribbean area and South America. United States trade with Latin America forms, as we saw in Chapter VII, an important proportion of the country's whole foreign commerce, and imports range from Guiana bauxite (bound for the aluminium plants at Alcoa, Tenn., or at St. Louis) to bananas from the United Fruit Company's plantations in Central America. In this trade the more important participants are New Orleans, Mobile, Tampa, Jacksonville, Savannah, and Charleston.

(e) *Missile Development.* The effect of the four factors which we have so far considered has been to broaden greatly the base of the regional economy. The 1·6 million people who arrived in Florida alone between 1950 and 1960 have drawn after them industries to supply this new market, and at the same time have provided a pool of labour for other new industries which have followed. As if this were not enough, however, the effect of the first four factors is compounded by the fifth—the establishment of defence installations in the area, and especially the missile range on Cape Kennedy (*née* Canaveral.)

With Cuba only 90 miles from Florida, it is to be expected that there would be conventional military activity in this corner of the U.S.A., but the choice of location for the missile range is a pure bonus for Florida. Around the range area are gathered the plants and the housing needed to operate it. The federal government's space programme has brought an immense additional revenue to the state, and it arises out of an area which had, previously, almost no value at all.

NEW ORLEANS

But not everything in the south-east is so new as the missile range. Dominating the central Gulf Coast, today as for more than a century past, is the great port of New Orleans (868,000). The port statistics of recent years show New Orleans to be losing ground to its rival, Houston, and to other ports farther west. But the rise in tonnage of cargo handled at the Texas ports is almost entirely accounted for by the growth of the coastwise traffic in petroleum and agricultural produce; only Houston has a significant amount of foreign trade, and in this trade pride of place is still held by New Orleans, with a considerable share going to Mobile and the older ports of the eastern Gulf. Thanks to its unrivalled position at the mouth of the Mississippi, New Orleans carries on a volume of foreign trade twice as great as that of Houston, and construction of its new ship canal (see p. 166) will further increase its advantages. In addition, ocean-going vessels can penetrate up the Mississippi a further 100 miles inland to Baton Rouge, whence the 9-foot navigable channel of the Mississippi extends north to Minneapolis and (via the Illinois Waterway) to the Great Lakes, as well as giving access to the 1,000 miles of the Ohio channel and the 600 miles of the navigable Tennessee.

New Orleans' greatest days admittedly lie in the past. In the riverboat era between 1820 and the Civil War, before the west-ward-spreading railways established a new, safe overland link between the Midwest and the Atlantic coast, the Mississippi served as the great routeway for goods to and especially from the Interior. For all its length down the Mississippi, through the process of trans-shipment at New Orleans, and round the Florida peninsula to the Atlantic ports—this route was, in an economic sense, a cut-off. Its importance grew as the Interior was opened up. 'In the [1840's] the West had more marine tonnage than the entire Atlantic Seaboard, New Orleans alone in 1843 having twice that of New York, our greatest Atlantic port of the time.' As early as 1843 the steamship tonnage on the Mississippi 'was nearly half that of the whole British Empire, and it multiplied sixfold in sixteen years'.[1]

[1] J. T. Adams, *The Epic of America*, 1945, pp. 220–1. Mark Twain's comment on the subject was very much in character: 'Mississippi steamboating was born about 1812; at the end of thirty years it had grown to mighty proportions; and in less than thirty more it was dead. A strangely short life for so majestic a creature.'

But already, in the 1850's, the railways were bringing the steamboat era to an end, even before the Civil War closed the Mississippi, and the Union blockade left the cotton bales lying, and the grass growing, on the quays of New Orleans. The revival of the port's commerce waited upon the development of trade with Latin America, and upon the improvement of inland navigation. Today its trade depends on a more harmonious balance between river and ocean traffic, and between water, road, and rail transport, then during the picturesque, but hazardous, Mark Twain phase of Mississippi navigation. Meanwhile, out of its colourful past—its background of French culture and its riverboat days—New Orleans has built up a carefully preserved reputation for Old Worldliness which, in a continent where one city is much like another, is an asset worth millions of dollars annually to it in tourist traffic.

2. *The Western Gulf Coast*

West of the Sabine River, which marks the Texas–Louisiana border, rainfall rapidly diminishes, and the dense forests of the humid sub-tropical coast give way, first to coastal prairies with scattered woods, and then to the dry rangelands that stretch to the Mexican border. Under Spanish and Mexican rule, before 1836, there was little agricultural development, and the area was used only for ranching. In modern times, however, while ranching remains important, the introduction of techniques of dry farming and of irrigation, together with the increase in the region's population, have brought agriculture to these drier coastlands. The type of crop grown varies with the availability of rain or irrigation water. In the better-watered parts of eastern Texas there has developed a characteristic combination of rice culture and cattle raising. In the central section of the state's coastlands, where rainfall is between 30 and 35 inches annually, and in the irrigated areas farther west, it is the cultivation of cotton and vegetables that accompanies cattle raising. In the valley of the Lower Rio Grande the irrigated sections which are scattered among the brush-covered ranges form an oasis area, where a very wide range of fruits and vegetables are raised. At the inland edge of this irrigated belt lie the counties that form the 'Winter Garden' of Texas, noted for its onions and spinach, and acting, like Florida, as a supplier of fresh winter vegetables. Nearer the coast in western Texas, citrus production has become widespread, and Texas, as a comparative new-comer in the competition, has made considerable headway against the older-established producers of Florida and California. Other fruits, including dates, have been introduced, and over much of the area it is possible to achieve double cropping by following winter vegetables with cotton or feed crops.

These dry Texas coastlands, like the area of southern California which they resemble and rival, suffer a major handicap to further progress in their shortage of irrigation water. With an annual rainfall of 20 to 25 inches, an annual evaporation rate of 60 to 70 inches, and a June-August mean temperature of 85° F. or more, the area is dependent on the few major rivers flowing south from better-watered regions. Like southern California, too, western Texas has to divide even this available supply between its farms and its rapidly growing industrial cities. And like southern California with the Colorado River, Texas has to share the flow of its main river, the Rio Grande, with its neighbour Mexico—and that after the farmers farther upstream, in the irrigated areas of the state of New Mexico, have taken their share of its waters.

While shortage of water places a definite upper limit upon the expansion of the cultivated area, the agricultural prosperity of the southern coastlands is firmly based, none the less, on their special climatic character within the U.S.A. But position is by no means the only natural advantage which the region enjoys. It both contains, and is surrounded by, a rich variety of natural resources, whose exploitation has brought employment and, often, sudden wealth to its inhabitants, and a huge volume of transit business to its ports and cities It is, in fact, to economic expansion in the Cotton Belt and the southern Great Plains as much as to the development of its own potential that the coast owes its new commerce and industries; as much to the mineral wealth that lies beneath the shallow waters of the Gulf of Mexico as to the mineral wealth that geological circumstances have, for the present, left beneath dry land.

The discovery of oil at Spindletop, near Beaumont, Texas, in 1901 presaged the opening of North America's greatest oil and gas fields. Today Texas, Louisiana, and Oklahoma rank with California as the four major oil and gas producing states of the U.S.A.; Texas alone produces more than one-third of the nation's oil, and the south-western district contains some three-quarters of the known natural gas reserves of the nation. The fields form an almost continuous coastal belt from the west bank of the Mississippi to beyond the Mexican border. Inland they stretch into Kansas and Arkansas; seaward the deposits extend beneath the Gulf, and their working has provided not only technical problems on a formidable scale, but also a first-class political issue—the question of federal or state control of the tidelands oil. Drilling has been carried farther and farther out to sea; the limit reached in 1955 was in over 100 feet of water, 18 miles offshore, where the well was 10,000 feet deep, and the rig alone cost $1½ million.

As with oil, so with sulphur; the Gulf coastline has been merely an incidental barrier to mineral prospecting. The coast-land sulphur deposits, already the largest known in the world, are being supplemented by further finds offshore from western Louisiana and eastern Texas, and this region supplies virtually the whole of North America's sulphur production.

Associated with the same subterranean domes that contain the sulphur and petroleum deposits is a third mineral, rock salt, and this, too, is mined in quantity in Louisiana. The fourth major mineral resource of the southern coast is phosphate rock, the importance of which to the nation has steadily increased with the development of the fertilizer habit among American farmers. North-western Florida is the continent's leading producer of this mineral.

Yet this rich natural endowment has in turn created problems for the region, particularly in relation to oil and gas production. As the continent's principal source of these minerals, the central Gulf Coast has become the focus of a huge network of pipelines which carry its products, overland to the northern states, and southward to the Gulf ports, for shipment to even remoter destinations. The Gulf states are primarily exporters, and only a small proportion of their output is used within the states. But this situation is bound to cause them grave concern, for the drain is so great that the life expectation of their oil and gas reserves is a matter for recurrent anxiety. Lacking alternative sources of power, they confront the situation that their primary resource is being exploited at a rate which may force them, in two generations' time, to import fuel once again from outside—and that it is being exploited on behalf not of the Gulf states themselves, but of other regions whose coal or water power reserves will last for centuries.

Thus a clear division of interest separates the nation from the state; the state from the individual producer; the conservationist from the oil or gas consumer, who is only conscious of the present cost advantage of these fuels over coal. In the best interests of the Gulf states themselves, it is clearly desirable that the rate of use of petroleum reserves should be reduced, and that some restraint should be placed upon short-sighted overproduction. In the oil-producing states this restraint is achieved be means of a commission which, operating within the framework of the national quota system mentioned in Chapter V, controls the level of oil and gas production within each state. Meanwhile the problem is growing greater, because the market for natural gas is still enlarging, as increasing numbers of manufacturers and householders are converting to this fuel.

But in a region where present achievements are so spectacular, and where so much wealth has been created so rapidly, the general atmosphere is anything but gloomy. On the contrary, an impression of breathless progress pervades the cities of the Gulf Coast and the adjacent interior. They are an expression of the region's wealth, a wealth that might prove ephemeral but is, for the present, as spectacular as anything that North America can show.

Oilfields have seldom become the location of large industrial or urban centres, for their life period is too uncertain to attract the more costly forms of settlement. Where, however, within the vicinity of the fields, some other factor creates a particularly favourable location, there it is probable that the *combination* of circumstances will stimulate the growth of industries connected with the oilfields, and create centres of importance. This is the background to the growth of the western Gulf Coast ports. They are the logical, nearby location for the refineries and chemical industries which accompany oil production. At the same time they would never have achieved such importance as ports (they are almost all man-made to some extent) had it not been for their proximity to the oilfields. It is this combination of oilfield and coastline (that is, of producing point and shipping point) which has brought into being the 'Golden Crescent', the Gulf coast between Brownsville in Texas and Pensacola in Florida which is the location of 75 per cent. of the nation's petroleum processing industry.

Other influences, too, lie behind the rapid development of these cities. One of these is that, since the oilfields were opened, the western Gulf Coast has become, in E. A. Ackerman's phrase, 'one of the foremost areas of recent capital accumulation in the nation'.[1] So great has been the wealth created by the oilfields that it far exceeds any possibility of merely ploughing back the profits into the industry, and the oilmen have had to seek other investment outlets. These they have found in part by entering the wider sphere of national finance, and in part by investing in real estate, and embellishing the cities of the region.

The other important influence in the growth of these cities has been the westward spread of farming into dry Texas, which has given the western Gulf ports an agricultural hinterland. In the days of the riverboat the produce of the western Cotton Belt was funnelled through New Orleans to the outside world, and the capture and closure of the port was thus a primary objective of the Union forces. But since then, cotton production has spread west and has been supplemented, as we have seen, by other forms of farming made possibly by irrigation. It was as a result both of this westward trend of agriculture and of the development of the oilfields that by 1950 Houston had replaced New Orleans as the Gulf's principal port (in terms of total tonnage handled). And it is in view of these developments that both New Orleans and the Texas ports are sponsoring rival projects to improve water transport in the south-west and thus to draw off its commerce, in the one case to the Mississippi and in the other to the western Gulf Coast.

While the ports of the Texas coast possess undoubted advantages of position, they could hardly have been less suitable, half a century ago, for purposes of navigation. The alternation of sand-bars and shallow lagoons along this coast has meant that almost all the ports west of New Orleans have been created only

[1] E. A. Ackerman, in *The Changing World*, ed. W. G. East and A. E. Moodie, Harrap, 1956, p. 297. (See the reference in Further Reading for Chapter III.)

PLATE XV

The Gulf Coast: Activity in this rapidly developing region is symbolized alike by (*above*) its oil refineries, such as the one illustrated which is near Houston, Texas, and (*below*) the orange groves of the citrus fruit belt in central Florida

PLATE XVI

Houston, Texas: Docks and turning basin, with oil refineries in the background. Houston is linked with the Gulf of Mexico by a canal 58 miles long. Since some 10% of the United States' crude oil is produced in the vicinity of the city, petroleum products form a large part of the cargoes handled by the port, while it also exports cotton from the western end of the Cotton Belt

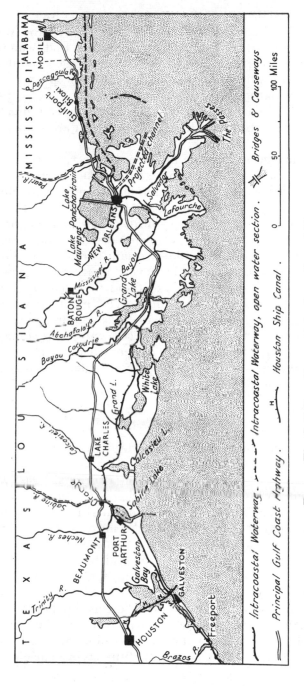

Fig. 59. The Gulf Coast Ports and the Intra-Coastal Waterway.

by means of costly dredging and cutting. Indeed, the two ports which handle the largest tonnage—Houston and Beaumont—both lie on the inland side of the lagoon fringe, 50 miles from the sea, with which they are connected by deep-water canals. The ports, in turn, are connected with each other by the shallower Intra-Coastal Waterways which, throughout much of its length, makes use of the line of lagoons that are impassable to ocean shipping.

Such has been the scale of these engineering works that in 1960 the United States Gulf ports from Lake Charles to Brownsville handled over 125 million tons of commerce, with Houston, Beaumont, Port Arthur, and Lake Charles playing the largest part in this traffic. Some two-thirds of this tonnage, however, is made up of shipments of petroleum products coastwise to the north-eastern states, and a large quantity of cotton follows the same route. It seem probable, nevertheless, that in view of the growth of south-western markets and the excellence of these ports' facilities, they will, in time, develop much more extensive foreign connexions. Around their docks and dredged channels are to be found the new industrial concentrations of the south-west—petroleum refineries and chemical plants; smelters for imported ores; and processing plants for deriving magnesium from the waters of the sea.

3. Texas

The concluding section of this chapter must take account of one problem that confronts every writer who attempts to treat the geography of North America on a regional basis: what to do about Texas. If he adheres rigidly to his regional subdivisions, then this vast state, which contains one-twelfth of the land area of the continental U.S.A., must be divided between at least three major regions—the Great Plains, the South-East, and the Gulf Coast. But while he will have satisfied his geographical conscience in thus dissecting it, he will have destroyed one of the most famous—and self-conscious—realities of American society, the Texas of the Texans. That its inhabitants are Texans first, and only secondarily Americans, has become a commonplace in the nation's reckoning and the nation's humour. That the state's individualism has been heightened by national recognition of it is an equally observable fact. Expected to be separatists, the Texans set out with gusto to live up to expectations.

Beneath this phenomenon, however, there lies a certain basis of historical fact and economic reality. Texas is the only part of the U.S.A. that had a separate existence, as an independent republic, before it joined the American Union. It was in 1835 that the 20,000 or so settlers who had entered Texas from the eastern U.S.A. revolted against the province's Mexican government, and in the next year a republic was established and obtained recognition. Only after this young republic had, by a plebiscite in 1845, accepted annexation, did Texas become part of the U.S.A. The conditions of its entry into the Union were such that it retained somewhat more of its state sovereignty (for example, the ownership of its public lands) than did those other western parts of the nation which began as sparsely populated territories, and which only 'graduated' to the rank of states after an intermediate period.

Here, then, is the historical background to Texan self-consciousness. As a contributing factor on the geographical side, we may note that the huge dimensions of the state (it is roughly 800 miles from north to south and from east to west, and there are 20 Texan acres for each inhabitant) give its people both a wide range of resources and a sense of space and self-sufficiency. Perhaps most important of all, the great south-western oil boom of the last half century has created wealth and made available capital, with an ease and speed in relation to effort expended that can seldom have been equalled in the world's history. In these circumstances, a belief that the dry soil of Texas possesses magical properties is, perhaps, understandable.

Much of the wealth created by the oilfields has found expression, as we have already seen, in the growth of the metropolitan areas of the south-west. Of these, the largest is Houston, whose 1950 population of 806,000 had by 1960 risen well above the million mark. We have already noted its leading position among the nation's ports; its industrial development has been no less spectacular. Between 1939 and 1954 its industrial labour force more than doubled. Within some 50 miles of the city is produced almost one-tenth of the nation's crude oil; it has more

z

than a dozen refineries, as well as numerous plants producing chemicals and synthetic rubber; and it is the main steel-milling centre of the south-west. The availability of cheap oil and gas fuel has attracted to the area numerous other industries, among which the manufacture of mining equipment is the largest employer of labour. As port and as industrial centre, there seems no immediate reason why the meteoric rise of Houston should not continue.

By contrast with Houston, the western metropolis of San Antonio, with a population of half a million, derives its importance principally from the agriculture of its hinterland. East of it lie the cotton lands of central Texas; not far to the west, cultivation gives place to ranching. In a country where the general movement of agricultural produce is from west to east, however, San Antonio, like most of the cities on the margin of the dry plains, looks west rather than east. Thus it was here, in 1874, that there was given the first demonstration in the south-west of a new device to solve the ranchers' fencing problem—barbed wire—and the interests of San Antonio have been bound up with the rangelands, with cattle and sheep, ever since. With the westward shift of agriculture and the coming of irrigation, however, the city has also become a collecting point for the produce of an area that raises cotton, corn, and vegetables.

There remain for consideration Dallas (1,083,000) and Fort Worth (573,000). The disparity in size between them does nothing to mitigate the intensity of the famous rivalry between these two cities, whose centres are 33 miles apart; proximity is a stimulant to the contest. From the geographical point of view, however, it is not their competitive similarities, but their differences of function, that are of real interest. For these two cities, standing as they do close to the frontier between humid east and arid west (the long-term record gives Dallas a mean annual precipitation of 33·6 inches and Fort Worth one of 31·6 inches) divide between them those relationships with both regions that Kansas City, for example, combines with a single metropolitan area.

Dallas belongs primarily to the western Cotton Belt; after Memphis it is the largest cotton market in the U.S.A., and it is linked with cultivation and the more humid east. Fort Worth is a cattle town, grown prosperous and industrialized; it looks

westward to the ranges, and its stockyards are the largest anywhere south of Kansas City. Thus the descriptions of these cities
belong, properly speaking, to the separate chapters of this book

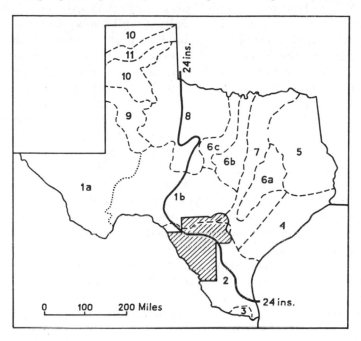

FIG. 60. Texas: Agricultural Regions. In Texas the agriculture of the Cotton
Belt, the Sub-Tropical Gulf Coast, and the Dry West meet and merge. The
regions arc: 1. Grazing areas of (a) The High Plains and Western Texas,
and (b) Edwards Plateau. 2. Rio Grande Plains area: grazing, irrigated
vegetables and cotton. 3. Lower Rio Grande Valley area: irrigated vegetables and cotton. 4. Coastal Prairie area: western end—grazing dominant,
eastern end—rice, centre—cotton. 5. East Texas Woods area: small-scale
mixed farming. 6. East Central mixed farming area. diversified cropping
and grazing; (a) Post-Oak area, (b) Grand Prairie, (c) Western Cross
Timbers. 7. Black Prairie area: cotton and corn. 8. Low Plains area:
cotton, feed crops and grazing. 9. High Plains cotton area, with some
grazing. 10. Panhandle wheat area. 11. Canadian River grazing area. The
shaded portion represents the counties which contain the 'Winter Garden'
(see p. 332). The continuous line marks the 24-inch annual isohyet. (Data
from *A Description of the Agriculture and Type-of-Farming Areas in Texas*, Texas
Ag. Exp. Station Bull. No. 544, 1937.)

on the South and the Great Plains, with the regional boundary
cutting across the narrow gap that lies between them. But in
reality they form one urban concentration whose functions, like

those of the cities in the western interior, link it with both east and west, and whose common possession is the quality of being Texan.

As with Houston, so with Dallas and Fort Worth, it is oil that has made these market-cities wealthy, while cheap fuel, and the sunshine and space of Texas, have brought industry to them. Dallas has developed a well-balanced structure of consumer industries, and become a clothing fashion centre and regional commercial capital in the process. Fort Worth's post-war employment has been dominated by the aircraft industry, which moved to Texas, as it did to California, to profit by the availability of space, by low heating costs, and by the possibility of carrying out in the open air some of the industry's space-consuming operations.

Texan boasts have been loud, but the impressiveness of Texan progress over recent years cannot be denied. Although its dry western half must seem uninviting to anyone but a local enthusiast, the state has maintained a rate of population increase since 1945 that is among the most rapid in the nation. Such rapid development has been made possible by the realization of the state's greatest asset—its petroleum resources. Income has accumulated more swiftly than it could be usefully invested. Inevitably, some of the investment has been unwise, some even frivolous. But an increasing and welcome sense of maturity in the Texan attitude to the state's rich resources should ensure for the South-West an ever-growing influence among the regions of the nation.

FURTHER READING

DEVELOPMENT has been so rapid in this region that the geographical literature has failed to keep up. However, a general selection of articles on the Humid Gulf area is: S. Diettrich, 'Florida's Climatic Extremes', *Econ. Geog.*, vol. xxv, pp. 68–74; R. F. Carson, 'The Florida Tropics', *Econ. Geog.*, vol. xxvii, pp. 321–39; L. L. Stephan, 'Vegetable Production in the Northern Everglades', *Econ. Geog.*, vol. xx, pp. 79–101; G. A. Stokes, 'Lumbering and Western Louisiana Landscapes', *A.A.A.G.*, vol. xlvii, pp. 250–66; S. H. Bederman, 'The Citrus Fruit Industry in Louisiana', *Southeastern Geographer*, vol. i, pp. 1–8; H. R. Padgett, 'The Sea Fisheries of the Southern United States', *Geog. Review*, vol. liii, pp. 22–39.

On Texas, there is W. T. Chambers' *Geography of Texas*, or F. Goodwyn's *Lone-Star Land*. Other useful articles are: R. J. Russell, 'Climates of Texas',

A.A.A.G., vol. xxxv, pp. 37–52; J. J. Parsons, 'Recent Industrial Development in the Gulf South', *Geog. Review*, vol. xl, pp. 67–83; T. L. McKnight, 'The Distribution of Manufacturing in Texas', *A.A.A.G.*, vol. xlvii, pp. 370–8, and E. J. Foscue, 'The Ports of Texas and Their Hinterlands', *Tijds. voor econ. en soc. geog.*, Jaarg. 47, pp. 1–14.

XV

THE GREAT PLAINS AND THE PRAIRIES

IT is one of the splendid paradoxes with which North America abounds that the region of the continent which possesses least physical distinction has been the scene of some of the most dramatic episodes in the story of its human occupance. On the smooth surface of the Great Plains, which stretch from southern Texas north to the Arctic Ocean, have occurred the continent's sharpest clashes of group interest. And while these deceptively innocent-looking grasslands have attracted successive generations of settlers, nature has provided, both above and beneath their surface, hazards which, time and again, have forced the settlers to recoil before an environment they have failed to tame.

For in terms of human geography the Great Plains form a problem region—one of the diminishing number of areas which force, even upon twentieth-century Americans, a respect for natural conditions. As we leave the humid, fertile Midwest, whose problems are essentially those of prosperity, and move westward across the central lowlands of North America, we are moving into a region where the natural controls of man's activities—climate and soil—assert themselves with increasing vehemence; a vehemence, moreover, which the smoothness of the relief masks but does nothing to mitigate. This is an area whose problems are dramatically apparent to the most casual passer-by; they are seen in blizzards and in dustorms, in eroded fields and abandoned farms. They serve notice that to adapt themselves to Great Plains conditions, to accept the limitations of this fierce but fascinating environment, and to develop a system of land use which is truly compatible with it, is the unfinished task of government and settlers alike. Indeed, they raise the question whether, where nature is so unpredictable, a sedentary population can be ever be stable and secure.

This 'problem area' does not exactly correspond in extent with the physical province of the Great Plains as we have defined it in Chapter I. For the eastern edge of that province is an area of settled and generally prosperous farming which comprises the western parts of the Wheat, Corn, and Cotton Belts. The regional problem is one of security against climatic hazard, for as we move west across the plains the threat of climatic accident, negligible in the Midwest, grows steadily greater, and becomes acute after we pass the 98th or 100th meridian of longitude. Thus defined, the 'problem area' covers much of western Texas, the western parts of Oklahoma, Kansas, Nebraska, and the Dakotas, and the south-western part of the Prairie Provinces. On the west it terminates at the foothills of the Rockies, where not only is rainfall more plentiful, but also the increasingly broken terrain removes the temptation to unwise agricultural activity. On the east and north the boundary between the problem area and the rest of the Great Plains province fluctuates year by year; it is a boundary not of relief but of risk; it differentiates between the relatively secure farming of the Agricultural Interior and the relatively hazardous business of occupying the dry plains.

1. *The Physical Circumstances*

The factors which govern the character of Great Plains settlement are primarily climatic. The plains lie in a continental interior, intermediate between the humid east and the definitely arid west, and this location governs the climatic régime.

PRECIPITATION

With the high wall of the Rockies blocking their western margin, the Great Plains depend for most of their precipitation on the northward intrusion of moist air from the Gulf of Mexico There is thus a general decrease in the amount of precipitation from south-east to north-west across the plains; Abilene, Texas (32° N., 99° W.), averages 25 inches per annum, and Oklahoma City (35° N., 97° W.) 32 inches, while Miles City in Montana (47° N., 106° W.) has 13 inches, and Medicine Hat, Alberta (50° N., 111° W.), has slightly less than this amount. In the winter season, both rainfall and snowfall are light—a fact to which we must shortly return—and over the plains generally, some 70 to 80 per cent. of the precipitation occurs between May and September; that is, in the vital months of summer plant growth.

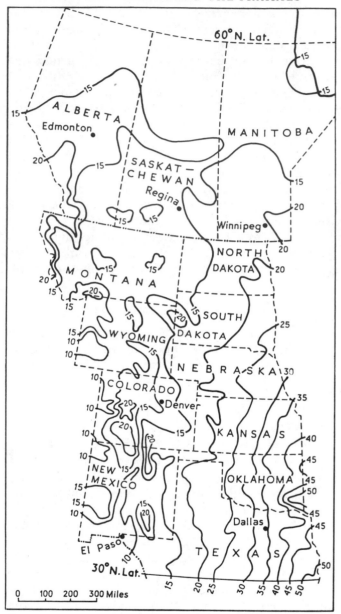

FIG. 61. The Great Plains and Prairies: Annual Precipitation.

While this rainfall régime discourages tree growth, and while the rains fall at the time when evaporation rates are highest, the small quantity of moisture received by the plains does, nevertheless, arrive at the season of maximum demand for the farmer or rancher.

However, the rain-bearing Gulf air, upon whose intrusions the Great Plains depend, is not altogether reliable in its habits. As it moves northwards over the continent this tropical maritime air generally trends north-east rather than north-west, with the result that the amount of rain reaching the plains, and in particular the quantity of the vital summer rains, varies greatly from year to year. Over much of the plains the mean annual variation is as much as 25 per cent. of the annual precipitation. This variability is greatest in the southern plains, where the rainfall is somewhat more plentiful; the dry northern plains have less precipitation, but their supply is slightly more reliable, for they lie closer to the source areas of the polar continental air, whose interaction with the humid Gulf air forces the latter to deposit its moisture.

TEMPERATURE

The Great Plains experience the extremes of temperature which are characteristic of a continental interior. The northern plains, on both sides of the international boundary, have recorded the lowest winter temperatures experienced in any populated part of the continent—between 50° and 60° F. below zero. On the other hand, summer temperatures in all parts of the Great Plains soar to maxima of over 100° F. In rather general terms winter temperatures tend to vary with latitude: the southern edge of the plains has a January mean of 50° F., while at the Canadian boundary the figure is 0° to 5° F. Summer temperatures, on the other hand, are governed partly by latitude and partly by altitude, the higher, western edge being in general cooler than the eastern edge, which is some 3,000 feet lower. However, this general pattern is disturbed by the fact that, at least statistically, the western edge of the plains is a little warmer than the eastern edge in winter, in spite of its elevation, because of the effects of the Chinook. Dry air from the Pacific coast, which is warmer than the prevailing winter air over the plains, crosses the Rocky Mountain barrier and, descending the eastern slope of the mountains, brings a sudden and spectacular increase of temperature to the foothills and western plains, and a welcome, if brief, break in the intense winter cold of the area.[1]

CLIMATIC HAZARDS

But the statistics which we have so far considered tell only a part of the story of the struggle with the Great Plains environment. It is not the basic climatic conditions, unpleasant as they are, which are the menace of the region, but the climatic hazards that accompany them. These are of four kinds.

(a) *Frost.* Since temperatures are affected by two wholly different air masses, whose influences tend to alternate over the area, the length of the frost-free season varies greatly from year to year. On the average, its length is about 100 days in the southern Prairie Provinces, and 240 days in central Texas, but over a forty-year period it has varied from 129 to 181 days at stations on the Nebraska–Colorado border, and from 89 to 172 days in western North Dakota, near the international boundary.

(b) *Hail.* The central and southern Great Plains are the area of the continent most subject to hailstorms, and, infrequent though they may be, a single storm is sufficient to do immense damage to crops.

(c) The *winds* that sweep this smooth, treeless area unchecked. There are several types of wind peculiar to the plains, and all of them are deadly in their effects. On the southern plains the summer wind danger is provided by the hot winds that blow from the interior and parch the crops, while in winter this same area suffers from the visitations of the Norther, a cold wind causing sudden drops in temperature and so representing a serious frost hazard.

But the 'grizzly of the Plains', in W. P. Webb's phrase, is the blizzard. In winter the principal storm tracks cross the continent from west to east, approximately in the latitude of the international boundary, but occasionally there occurs an overspill of cold air out of the north, which breaks across the

---

[1] For an appreciation of the impact of these temperature conditions on the early white settlers, see R. A. Billington, *Westward Expansion*, Macmillan, 1949, chapter xxxiv.

storm tracks, moves south-east along the front of the Rockies, and swings out into the central Great Plains. There the storm may last for several days, while its centre shifts and circles unpredictably.[1] Apart from the immediate danger created by the wild weather, the particular menace of the blizzard is that it usually brings with it a heavy snowfall, which the wind builds up into deep drifts. On the Great Plains which, as we have already seen, generally experience little snowfall, ranchers usually leave their stock to winter outdoors. But the snowdrifts deny the stock access to food supplies, so that the animals are the chief victims of the blizzards, and serious economic loss may well follow the passage of these vicious winter storms.

Quite apart from the effects of these particular winds upon temperature and humidity, however, there is the ever-present threat of wind erosion on the Great Plains. With little in the way of an obstacle above the surface, and with parent materials below it which are at best seldom consolidated, and at worst simply loose sand, the soil of the Great Plains, if once bared to the wind's action, falls an easy victim. In few other regions of the world does unwise cultivation receive such prompt and embarrassing publicity as when the dust-storms rise to darken the skies above the Great Plains.

(d) *Drought*. We have already seen that the principal source of precipitation for the plains is the unpredictable intrusion of moist air north-westward from the Gulf of Mexico, and that this produces wide variations in rainfall from year to year. But what complicates the problem of the settler in this area is that the years of sub-normal rainfall have a tendency to occur in groups, so that it is by no means safe to assume that a year of meagre rainfall will be followed by a year of compensating excess. On the contrary, the records of the past half-century show that rainfall may be above or below average for a decade at a time. In Montana, for example, during the years 1906–16 inclusive, the rainfall was above average in every single year (and was 125 (or more) per cent. of normal in six of them). Then between 1928 and 1937 inclusive, it was below the fifty-year average for eight of the ten years, and for the three years 1934–6 never exceeded 75 per cent. of normal.

[1] The conduct of one of the worst blizzards in recent experience is described in 'The Winter of 1948–49 in the Great Plains', by W. Calef, *A.A.A.G.*, vol. xl, pp. 267–92.

Such a rainfall régime as this clearly increases the difficulties
presented by the environment, for the wetter-than-normal

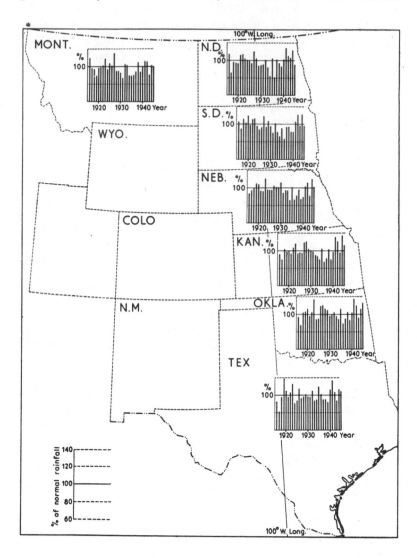

Fig. 62. The Great Plains: Rainfall Variability. The map shows the rainfall
each year, from 1916 to 1945, in each of seven Great Plains states, expressed
as a percentage of the forty-year average. (Data from *Climate and Man*,
U.S. Dept. of Agriculture Yearbook, 1941, with later additions.)

decade gives a false impression of humidity and fertility, and so lures the settler to the margins of possible farming, and then the drier decade that follows robs him of any possibility of tiding over from one season to the next. In other words, on the Great Plains the average rainfall figure is doubly deceptive: it conceals year-to-year fluctuations, which a resolute farmer can survive, and it also conceals decade-to-decade fluctuations, which he cannot.

In very general terms, the decade of the 1930's on the Great Plains was a bad one. Even without the general depression, which was causing acute distress throughout the nation, the drought years of 1934 and 1936 (when most of the plains had less than 75 per cent. of average rainfall) would have been serious; the coincidence of the events was catastrophic. The 1940's, on the other hand, were years when, happily for war-torn nations elsewhere, rainfall was somewhat above normal, and farm yields on the Great Plains were high. The 1950's, however, proved to be another decade of general rainfall deficiency; on the southern plains, farmers and ranchers suffered a succession of drought years, and many gave up hope of holding out and abandoned their holdings.

SOILS AND VEGETATION

The general decline in the amount of precipitation from east to west across the Great Plains produces a fairly regular progression in the types of soil and vegetation found there. The soils grade from black earths in the more humid east, through dark brown, to brown on the dry western margins of the plains. As a result of glacial deposition over the northern part of the region, these soils are developed from a wide variety of materials, almost all recent, but they all support a grassland vegetation whose character likewise varies with the amount of rainfall. The black soils support—or rather, supported, for most of them are now under cultivation—a tall-grass, sod vegetation, while in the semi-arid west, the vegetation consists of shorter grasses, which form a mat cover in the moister parts and a cover of scattered bunch grasses in the driest sections.

The soil factor which governs this progression is a layer of salts accumulated in the subsoil, beneath which is a permanently dry zone. The depth of this layer beneath the surface varies with the amount of rainfall and with the length of the 'wet' season. In the black earth belt it lies between 30 and 40 inches below the surface, so that long-rooted grasses and cereals can flourish. Westwards, the salt layer rises nearer the soil surface with the increasing aridity, until at the western margin of the plains it is only 8 to 12 inches down, and root development is only possible for short grasses. At the point where the depth of the layer beneath the surface is 25 to 30 inches is an important dividing line: it is the line of change from black earth to brown, from tall, prairie grass to short, plains grass; and, in terms of human occupance, it is the line that divides the eastern Great Plains from the 'problem area' to the west. Lying as it does between the 98th and 100th meridans of west longitude, it is this line that accounts for the prominence of those meridians in every discussion of the settlement of the Great Plains.

But if this is the general pattern established by nature, it has been modified by man. For reasons which we must shortly consider, the 'natural' vegetation of much of the Great Plains, especially in their south-western section, is quite different today from that of a century ago. The character of the range vegetation has changed with use. In particular, changes have occurred in the balance between grasses and shrubs, and a tough, woody shrub vegetation of sagebrush or mesquite has spread over millions of acres of former grasslands, to change the appearance of the south-western plains and increase the severity of soil erosion.

Because the character of the plains vegetation is an index of the amount, reliability, and seasonal duration of rainfall, it serves also as a guide to the areas which may safely be cultivated, and to those which are better left under the native grass cover. Most of the tall-grass prairie has been under cultivation for several decades without serious mishap. The area covered by shorter, grama-wheatgrass associations, on the other hand, represents an agricultural margin where cultivation is risky, while the sections of the plains which are covered by a grama-buffalograss combination, or even more, by a mesquite-sage-thorn association, carry in their vegetation a warning which the cultivator ignores to his cost.

2. Land Use in the Great Plains

In the years between the end of the War of Independence
(1783) and the 1830's the frontier of settlement in the U.S.A.
spread rapidly westwards, across the Mississippi Valley, to the
eastern edge of the Great Plains. From there it jumped across
1,500 miles of intervening plain, mountain, and desert to the
Pacific coast, and not for almost half a century was progress
made in filling the gap with permanent settlements. In Canada
the sequence of events was comparable. Beyond the wilderness
barrier of the Laurentian Shield small, farm-based colonies
were planted at the eastern edge of the Great Plains (in what is
is now the Winnipeg area) in the decade 1810–20. But for over
fifty years these struggling colonies knew little expansion; the
population of Manitoba at the census of 1871 was 25,000 and
the west continued to be of interest as a source not of agricultural products, but of furs and gold.

The reasons for this abrupt halt to the westward spread of
settlement have become familiar to a later generation as a
classic example of environmental control upon man's activities.
For this was an area with an annual rainfall of 20 to 30 inches
and a smooth surface, which could, in statistical theory, have
been cultivated, but which, in terms of the techniques available
in the 1830's, might as well have been a desert. Indeed, so hopeless did the task of settling it seem to early travellers, that the
firm conviction took root that it *was* a desert, and it was treated
as such, in the 1840's and 1850's, by American geography
teachers and policy makers alike. As early as 1843 some scores
of pioneer farmers had decided that agricultural prospects in
Oregon were better than those in the Great Plains, and had
made the hazardous transcontinental journey by the Oregon
Trail; and their reports, backed by the discovery of gold in
California in 1848, encouraged others to follow. In the south
the Spanish-Mexican population had been equally unsuccessful
in establishing permanent settlements on the plains. If the area
possessed any virtue at all, in mid-nineteenth-century eyes, it
was that at least it was possible to cross it swiftly, on the way to
pleasanter places.

The environmental problems were threefold.

1. The area was treeless. It was not merely that, to eastern

minds, land that would not grow trees was poor land, but also that, in the 1840's, there was in the west neither coal nor cheap iron, and consequently no substitute for wood as a domestic necessity. There was no means of fencing land, and no means of building homes; the earliest dwellings were 'sod houses', which were merely pits, roofed with turf and with a few precious timbers. The only substitute for wood as a fuel was buffalo dung.

2. The sheer dryness of the plains found the eastern farmer ill-prepared, his crops unsuited to the short wet season, and his farming techniques adapted to a more humid climate.

3. The limited supply of water that was available raised its own problems; rivers often flowed only seasonally, and water holes were few and far between. Under the cheap land policies prevailing at the time, and even more under the Homestead Act of 1862 (1872 in Canada), the earliest arrivals took up the lands adjacent to the water-supply, and so made valueless the waterless lands on the interfluves and away from the water holes. Only slowly were legal measures adopted to control the use of western water, and indeed, in spite of progress made in both legislation and provision of water, the problem of waterless lands remains acute up to the present day.

The farmer who had migrated from the humid east was, therefore, simply not equipped to deal with the plains environment; in this technical sense the Great American Desert was a reality. But the pioneers in the U.S.A. (for here the story of settlement on the Canadian prairies tends to diverge from that of the United States plains, and will be treated separately in a later section) had also to face another obstacle to westward progress of a different kind—the Plains Indians. We have seen, in Chapter II, how, between the arrival of the Spaniards in Mexico and that of the United States pioneers on the Great Plains, the horse had become available to the tribes of the interior. Because this gave the Indians a new mobility, and in particular because the horse made it possible to hunt the buffalo which roamed the grasslands, there took place a migration of tribes from the surrounding forests to the plains, to exploit the new situation.

Thus there occurred in the Great Plains an encounter between the two groups of new-comers, the red and the white, which has become the most publicized culture clash in history.

Indian resistance was ferocious, and on the western trails travel was safe only in convoy. Nowhere else, on a continent which had known a long and tragic series of Indian wars, was the struggle so bitter, or the Indian strength so great, as on the Great Plains.

If peace came at length, it was due partly to the development of superior fighting skills on the side of the white man, with his famous Colt revolver, and partly to the virtual extinction of the buffalo, rather than to the triumph of sedentary agriculture. The time for that had not yet come. Throughout the history of white settlement of the plains there have been two principal claimants to the grasslands—the rancher and the wheat farmer —and of the two, the rancher was there first. While the farm frontier was halted, without means to settle the plains, from the 1840's until the 1880's, the cattlemen lived through their heyday.

'The physical basis of the cattle kingdom was grass,' says W. P. Webb, 'and it extended itself over all the grassland not occupied by farms.'[1] Ranching represented the most profitable means of occupying a grassland area which was, for the moment, useless to the agriculturalist. Its origin was in Texas, where the early settlers had already developed a type of stock raising that was suited to the Great Plains environment, for 'in the final analysis, the cattle kingdom arose at that place where men began to manage cattle on horseback. It was the use of the horse that primarily distinguished ranching in the West from stock farming in the East.'[2]

The 'cattle kingdom' was built up by two processes. Firstly, there was the process of delivering Texan cattle to eastern markets. After some groping by the Texan drovers for the best method of doing this, a pattern emerged. Cattle were driven north along trails, from the source region in Texas, until the trail met the westward-thrusting railways that led to Kansas City, St. Louis, or Chicago. There the drovers sold the cattle and the buyers shipped them north and east by rail. As the railways built west across the plains in the 1870's, so the shipping points moved west also. Under these conditions the grasslands simply served as a great transit camp, providing forage along the way for the north-bound stock.

[1] W. P. Webb, *The Great Plains*, Ginn & Co., N.Y., 1931, p. 207.   [2] Idem.

Aa

The second feature of the cattle era, however, was the spread of ranching from its original location in the southern plains, until it covered the whole of the unfarmed grassland. Texan cattle supplied not only meat for eastern markets, but stock for other western ranches. By the mid-1880's ranching had taken hold of an area which only fifteen years earlier had been empty of productive activity.

Of this early, romanticized cattle era it is necessary at once to say that, economically, it was an unimproved and unimproving activity. Its basis was the natural range, open and unfenced; the stock was almost wild, and breeding to improve the strain was out of the question. It is, therefore, not surprising that, once the plains began to fill up, the cattlemen had to change their ways. In the 1880's the farm frontier began, at last, to advance once more. Equipped with the new barbed wire, the plainsmen began to fence the range, the farmers to protect their crops, and the go-ahead ranchers to improve their stock. The old-style, open-range cattlemen cut all the wire they could find, but gradually they were forced either to retreat farther still to the west, or to accept a more sedentary life. Ranchers and farmers came to divide the ranges between them, the ranchers taking the rougher, drier western plains and the farmers the smoother and more humid east. The days of the cattle kingdom ended abruptly, as they had begun abruptly, only twenty years before.

The advance of the farm frontier across the eastern part of this debatable land occurred in the 1880's, while the more westerly farmlands have been occupied in a series of advances and retreats lasting from the 1890's to the present day. The advance was made possible by a series of developments in technique and equipment, which opened the plains to the cultivation of cereals. These were (1) the development of drought-resistant and frost-resistant grains, suited to conditions on the plains; (2) the evolution of dry-farming techniques, upon which such great hopes were pinned in the 1880's; (3) the mechanization of grain farming, the effect of which was to increase the area one man could cultivate, and so to make it possible for him to live by extensive farming, even when yields were low; (4) the invention of barbed wire, as a cheap fencing material in place of timber, to enable the plainsmen to keep the ranchers' cattle out of the crops and away from each other; and (5) the development of a cheap, easily-erected windmill. This made it possible, on the one hand, to raise water from greater depths, and in more constant supply, than by hand pump; and, on the other, to provide a water-supply at isolated and waterless places on the grasslands, so that cattle could be fenced into separate pastures, instead of crowding round the few natural water sources and overworking the waterside areas.

In the years between 1880 and 1890, therefore, while the population of the U.S.A. rose by 25 per cent., that of the Great Plains states increased by 78 per cent. (If Texas, which already had over 1,500,000 inhabitants in 1880, is excluded, the increase was 110 per cent.) But the 1890's were years of drought, and the advance of settlement faltered. Hundreds of those who had arrived only a few years previously to plough up the western plains left, defeated. The population of Nebraska increased by only 4,000, as against an increase of more than half a million in the previous decade. Only after 1896, when there began a series of wetter years that lasted until 1910, did the westward movement again gather momentum. The early 1890's had provided a fair sample of the experiences that lay ahead of the farmers on the plains.

The new-comers planted grain; between 1900 and 1910 the wheat acreage on the southern plains increased by 600 per cent. They did this in face of the difficulty of securing from the all-powerful railways satisfactory rates for transport to the flour mills, and under constant threat of catastrophe by drought, blight, and insect pest. In an area where yields of wheat might vary from 15 or 20 bushels per acre in a good year to 5 bushels, or nothing, in a dry one, they came to depend to a dangerous degree on this single, wholly hazardous form of livelihood, each series of wetter years tending to obliterate the memory of the preceding drought, and to deceive a fresh group of newcomers.[1]

The effects of both ranching and wheat farming on the Great Plains soon became apparent; the ranching areas began to

[1] For a fuller discussion of the effect of climatic variations on Great Plains wheat yields, see either 'Risk in the Central Great Plains', by L. Hewes and A. C. Schmiedling, *Geog. Review*, vol. xlvi, pp. 375–87, or 'Weather-Crop Relationships', by E. M. Frisby, *I.B.G. Trans. & Papers*, 1951, pp. 79–96, with additional references. In Miss Frisby's study, the most important correlations established were between the yield and (1) precipitation in the pre-yield year, (2) May-plus-June precipitation in the yield year, and (3) mean July temperature in the yield year.

suffer from overgrazing and the wheat areas from unwise cultivation. Because the rainfall of the plains varies from year to year, the amount of range forage available also varies, and this in turn requires that the numbers of stock that are grazed be adjusted to the condition of the range. But the adjustment has seldom been made in time; the temptation to graze the ranges to their peak capacity is always strong, and the grasslands have deteriorated in consequence. The grasses which the stock graze most heavily have declined, and have been replaced by shrubs and plants that are either less sought-after or entirely worthless. As the carrying capacity of the ranges diminishes, sheep and goats replace cattle,[1] brush replaces grass, and the forces of erosion meet less and less resistance to their attack. In 1936, when the famous government report, *The Future of the Great Plains*, was issued, it was estimated that the western ranges as a whole were 70 per cent. overstocked, and that their carrying capacity had been reduced by more than a half in eighty years.

For this deterioration, as Chapter III suggested, the individual rancher is not wholly to blame. If he has overgrazed the ranges, it is partly because his government, failing to appreciate in time that the institutions of the humid east would not suit the dry west, prevented him from securing legally a holding adequate to provide him with a living. Marion Clawson has written of an 'institutional fault line' at 98° W.—that is, a line to the west of which new policies and laws were needed, adapted to the thinner scatter of resources and the possibility of using land in large blocks or in common. Before such a policy had been formulated, much of the plains had been homesteaded in 160- or 320-acre blocks, as if they were tall-grass prairies in Iowa or Illinois.

The results of wheat cultivation have been equally serious and far more spectacular. Removal of the natural grass cover on the dry plains, especially during the days of the 'dust mulch' régime described in Chapter IV, has exposed the soil to powerful erosive action. That the frontier of grain farming was too far to the west has needed no demonstration in dustbowl years, or when low prices have made production, at 5 bushels to the acre,

---

[1] This trend has been especially marked in southern Texas, which is now the main sheep-raising area of the U.S.A. The number of sheep in Texas rose from 2·5 million in 1920 to 6·0 million in 1959, although for the U.S.A. as a whole numbers fell from 40 million to 34 million during the same period.

hopelessly uneconomical. The real problem has arisen in better years—especially in the humid 1940's, when the stimulants of wartime demand and support prices made grain farming of almost any standard profitable. It is in such years as these that the challenge of conservation farming has been hardest to face, and the temptation to plant more wheat has been strongest. To quote Marion Clawson again, 'The real problem is not to put poor wheat land into grass—the real problem is to keep it there, when unusually favourable weather and/or price years come again.'[1]

3. A Middle Way

The account so far given of the Great Plains serves to show that in the manner of their settlement there have been two weaknesses. One of these lies largely outside the scope of the present work, but is, nonetheless, of great importance; it is the application, to an environment whose chief feature is variability, of administrative and financial concepts that have been transferred from humid regions farther east. As Kraenzel expresses the problem, 'It is not the fact of semiaridity that causes the difficulties in the Plains, but the fact of an unadapted culture that does so.'[2] If it be true that, in Starch's colourful phrase, 'Management principles for the Great Plains farmer must be such that he can shift quickly and roll with the punch,'[3] then the farmer must have legal and financial freedom to do so.

The other weakness has been the dominance of wheat farming and ranching in an 'either-or' relationship which raises the question whether, in land use, there is not a middle way, a way that will bring security and stability. In recent years there have been numerous and welcome signs of just such a swing from the extremes of a single-product farming to a more varied, yet harmonious activity. On the one hand, the rancher has come to rely more on improved pastures and feed crops, rather than be dependent on the natural range. On the other hand, the

---

[1] M. Clawson, 'An Institutional Innovation to Facilitate Land Use Changes in the Great Plains', *Land Economics*, vol. xxxiv, p. 75.

[2] C. F. Kraenzel, *The Great Plains in Transition*, Univ. of Oklahoma Press, 1955, p. 287.

[3] E. Starch, 'The Future of the Great Plains Reappraised', *Journ. Farm Econ.*, vol. xxxi, p. 919.

wheat farmer has diversified his cultivation, by introducing sorghum and grasses into a regular rotation of crops, and by using the grass to raise cattle.

Progress on the ranches of the western plains has depended on overcoming two handicaps—the seasonal quality of the range grazing (which limits the numbers of stock that can be kept throughout the year) and the constant threat of drought. To overcome these obstacles, the solution which has gained favour is to establish—in most cases, with the aid of irrigation— a firm base of cultivated pasture or fodder crops, which will act both as a safety reserve for the surrounding ranches in case of drought, and as a source of stock feed during the off-season of the natural range grasses. With the aid of such small-scale irri- gation, and the construction of additional stock reservoirs (some 300,000 have been built in the past twenty-five years), the ranchers can not merely increase, with safety, their rate of stock- ing, but can also give the natural range a chance to recuperate. At the same time, they can develop on the 'infield' more intensive farm activities, such as fattening stock or dairying.

Over much of the Great Plains, however, the range grasses have deteriorated beyond the point where respite from grazing alone will bring them back into condition. In these areas the solution of ploughing and reseeding the grasslands has some- times been adopted. By reseeding it has proved possible either to increase the carrying capacity of the range, or to lengthen the grazing season, or, in some cases, to do both. The process is, however, an expensive one; the financial benefits may not appear for seven to nine years, and unless previous experiment has clearly shown what *type* of grass will suit the area, there is a serious risk of failure.

For the cultivator, also, methods have changed. In its simp- lest terms the error of the wheat growers in the dry plains has been to imitate west of the 98th meridian the pattern of farming which has produced the Wheat Belts to the east of it. The error has been twofold: (1) in the Wheat Belts, as we have seen in Chapter XII, wheat is not grown to the exclusion of other crops, but in conjunction with them, while in the drier west, the num- ber of crops that can alternate with wheat is smaller; (2) the more arid western conditions increase the dangers of mono- culture, both to the soil and to the farmer.

In the wheat areas improvement has taken two main forms. (1) Conservationists and scientists have come to the farmer's aid with new techniques, such as contour-ploughing, and with new strains of crops, to give production a greater degree of physical and economic stability. (2) Farmers have been encouraged to set up regular crop rotations, replacing the older pattern of alternate years of wheat and fallow by longer cycles, in which wheat is associated with other crops and with grass. In this respect an interesting feature of Great Plains agriculture has been the expansion of the acreage under sorghums. Sorghums combine good drought-resistant quality with high feed value, and have been introduced on former wheat lands, especially in areas where the wheat acreage quota system obliged farmers to find some other use for their land.

In the new rotations wheat is grown in one-third or one-half of the years of a fifteen- or sixteen-year cycle. Experiment has shown that, in such a rotation, the same amount of wheat can be produced, but from a smaller acreage than before, while the area in profitless fallows is reduced. Meanwhile, the acreage under grass yields livestock products, so that the farmer derives income from each field for ten or eleven years in the fifteen-year cycle, rather than for only seven or eight years under the old wheat-fallow alternation. At the same time, the presence of livestock improves the pasture fields in preparation for the next plough-up.

These changes may, perhaps, best be summarized as follows: just as there has developed a belt of hay and livestock farming in the area round the western Great Lakes—the area known as the Hay and Dairy Belt—so there is developing on the drier Great Plains a wheat and livestock region which in some ways resembles it. The livestock farming, which is becoming steadily more prominent in the plains wheat country, consists of both dairying and fattening stock imported from the drier ranges farther west.

But welcome as these changes are, there is still room for great improvements in Great Plains agriculture. If all the conservation methods at present being recommended were also being applied by all the plains farmers—and they are not—the wheat acreage would still be too great for safety, and the average size of farm, rapidly though it is increasing, would still be too small to suit the environment. Three factors militate against the introduction of the changes necessary to stabilize plains agriculture: (1) the high support price for wheat continues to encourage farmers to plant it, and the response to the Soil Bank scheme (see p. 119) was not as great as had been hoped; (2) the mechanization of grain farming involves the plains farmer in a huge outlay on machinery, and to obtain a return on his investment he needs to increase, rather than decrease, his cultivated acreage; farms are only just large enough, as it is, to make profitable use of the latest machinery; (3) as a result of their past development, most of the Great Plains are overvalued for tax assessment purposes, and many farmers feel that, with the shadow of tax delinquency falling close to them, they cannot afford the initial cost of switching to conservation farming. Here, once more, is an evident need for adaptation of the present administrative arrangements, in order to remove such obstacles from the farmer's path to self-improvement.

This, in fact, is the point to which any discussion of Great Plains land use must lead—the need for the farmer to have the widest possible freedom of choice in planning his operations. Most of the Great Plains are in private hands, unlike the remoter west where the federal government is the majority owner. The western farmer will not welcome government interference, and the object of all planning must, in any case, be to make the region as nearly as possible self-supporting: if conditions are such that it needs federal help every few years, or that soil erosion continues, then a proper solution for its problems has still to be found. There is a tendency to think of these problems too narrowly in terms of the 'either-or' of public-private ownership. But is there not, perhaps, a 'middle way' in ownership and administration, as well as in land use?

Marion Clawson, drawing upon a long experience of the problems of the dry west, has suggested that there is. Since the individual farmer's difficulty is that, in this region where natural conditions vary so much, he is tied for better or worse to an acreage which does *not* vary, it might be possible to establish in each district a finance corporation on which the federal government, the state, and the individual would all be represented. This would buy up the poorest plains lands, especially those which are badly eroded, rehabilitate them, and let them as grazing to the local participants. These lands would then serve as some kind of reserve, but a reserve fully under local control, in mixed ownership.[1]

These, then, are the manifold problems that confront the Great Plains farmer. For most of them some solution exists, and individual farmers will apply the solutions in so far as their means and their skill allow. In the heart of the Great Plains problem area, however, there lies a region which invites a far more comprehensive solution; a region where every known measure of conservation and agricultural adaptation could be applied as part of a unified regional plan—the Missouri River Basin. Any account of the future of the plains must necessarily include a consideration of developments in the Missouri Valley.

The basin of the Missouri embraces the whole of the northern Great Plains of the U.S.A., south to, and including, northern Kansas and north-eastern Colorado. Since the 1930's it has been repeatedly urged that the Missouri Valley presents a close parallel to the Tennessee Valley; that since both have suffered from natural hazards and economic distress, the problems of the Missouri Valley might yield to the same kind of bold, large-scale rescue work that has been carried out by the T.V.A. These proposals have called for the establishment of an M.V.A. on similar lines, and for the development of a comprehensive plan for the Missouri Valley, such as the T.V.A., for all its success, never formulated.

As the outcome of these proposals, there exist today both a plan—known as the Pick Sloan Plan—and a Missouri Basin Inter-Agency Committee, on which are represented departments of both the federal government and the governments of the interested states. Among the features of the plan are the construction of 150 reservoirs and some 5 million acres of new irrigation projects; the improvement of river navigation and field drainage; and the putting into force of a land management programme which would convert several million acres of cropland to grass, and bring benefit to 100 million acres remaining in cultivation. Since its inception in 1944, this plan has been

[1] Clawson, op. cit.

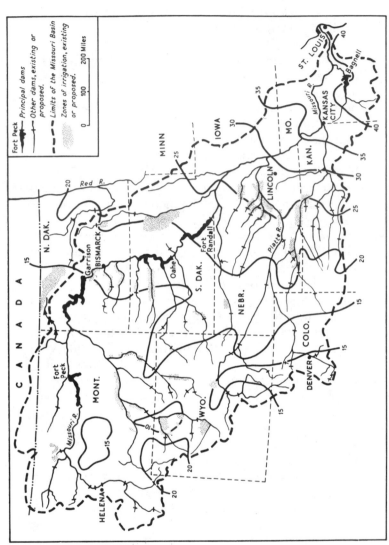

Fig. 63. The Missouri Valley, United States section, to illustrate the Missouri Valley Project. Solid lines represent the annual precipitation (in inches). Notice how the Missouri Basin narrows to a 'funnel' at its southeastern end, thus increasing the problem of flood control.

put into effect, step by step, as Congress voted instalments towards an estimated total cost of between 8,000 and 9,000
million dollars.

In theory such a plan should provide the best possible
solution for the problems of the Great Plains. It should make
available central irrigated areas, strategically located to act as
a firm base for farming and ranching; it should ensure the best
disposal of the available water-supply, and bring additional
benefits, in the form of cheap electric power or agricultural
education, to isolated plainsmen. In the event, however, it is
difficult to be enthusiastic about Missouri Valley development
to date. This is because, while the Tennessee Valley formed an
intelligible and satisfactory unit for development, the Missouri
Valley does not. It falls, in reality, into two parts, whose natural
characteristics are different and whose interests, in consequence, are opposed to each other.

The south-eastern tip of the Missouri Basin receives over 40
inches of precipitation per annum. Through it flows the silt-
laden river, often in flood and always difficult to navigate. The
eastern end of the basin is interested, therefore, in flood control,
in navigation improvement, and in hydro-electricity. Much of
the western part of the basin, however, receives less than 15
inches of rain per annum, and the interests of its population are
in water for irrigation and stock reservoirs. In short, the
upstream section of the river has too little water, and the
downstream section, periodically at least, has too much.

As a result, two separate plans for the valley were drawn up,
one—the Sloan Plan—by the Bureau of Reclamation, representing the interests of the dry, western section, and the other
—the Pick Plan— by the U.S. Corps of Engineers, whose
responsibility for flood control and navigation focused its
attention on the eastern section. To resolve the dilemma of
choosing between two plans which were far from being obviously compatible, the government adopted the peculiar
expedient of combining the two plans, and in 1944 Congress
approved a Pick–Sloan Plan, which was simply the Pick Plan
united to the Sloan Plan, in what Rufus Terral has succinctly
described as 'a shameless, loveless, shotgun wedding'.

The wedding occurred in 1944, and it was not until five years
later, when the Pick–Sloan Plan had already advanced through

its early stages, that the Department of Agriculture produced its parallel programme of agricultural improvements. Since that time development has gone on, project by project, as funds have been made available by Congress. There is no question that each of these projects has, in itself, been of value; nor can there be any doubt that the expenditure of $8,000 million on the Missouri Valley will enormously improve both the quality of the valley's lands and the stability of its economy. But it seems regretable that, amid the interplay of political forces and the complications of a federal system, a truly regional solution seems likely to elude those who most desire it, for lack of a sufficient authority to impose it upon the region as a whole.

4. The Prairies of Canada

The Canadian part of the Great Plains region, although separated from the American part by no natural divide, must be treated individually, for in several important respects it differs from the area south of the border. These differences are best grouped under four headings.

PHYSICAL DIFFERENCES

In many respects the natural conditions of the Canadian Prairies are indistinguishable from those of the plains in the U.S.A.; there is the same generally smooth relief; the same gradual rise towards the west, interrupted by a number of low scarps; the widespread cover of glacial deposits; and a climate which resembles that of the plains to the south in its continental characteristics and its summer rainfall. But the most clear-cut feature of the American plains environment—the regular east-to-west progression, from humid to arid conditions, and from tall grass to desert shrub vegetation—is missing from the Canadian pattern of natural features.

On the Canadian plains, the distinctive zones of climate, soils, and vegetation, which run from north to south in the southern plains, curve to run almost at right angles to this direction through the southern part of the Prairie Provinces. Thus the better-watered plains, or sub-humid prairies, form a loop round the northern end of the more arid zone (the area with 12 inches or less of precipitation per annum), and the east-to-west progression which exists farther south is replaced by a north-east-to-south-west progression of similar character. The dry heart of the prairies, statistically defined, is an elliptical area, some 300 miles from east to west, and 200 miles from north to south, that runs across the Saskatchewan–Alberta boundary, somewhat north of the Canadian border. But the better-known, if cruder, definition of the dry area is under the name of Palliser's Triangle, after the surveyor who, in 1857–60, presented a series of reports on the prairies, in which he described as unfit for agricultural settlement most of Saskatchewan and Alberta between the 49th and 51st parallels.[1] Surrounding this dry area on the north-east and north are zones of somewhat higher rainfall, which correspond to the short-grass plains, and beyond these again, between them and the northern forest, is the zone that corresponds to the tall-grass prairie—the Park Belt, a zone that receives up to 20 inches of rainfall and that supports the densest rural population on the Prairies.

DIFFERENCES IN THE SEQUENCE OF SETTLEMENT

The settlement of the American Great Plains was a logical outcome of the occupation of the Mississippi Valley; the frontier of settlement moved west without a geographical break, with the ranchers in front and the farmers following behind as their means permitted. In Canada there was no such regular sequence. The first settlers on the Prairies—the Selkirk colonists of 1812–13—arrived via Hudson Bay, and many of the later arrivals had trekked north from the U.S.A., following the Red River Valley. Between 1812 and 1870 there was virtually no westward advance; the whole of the empty west was the preserve of the Hudson's Bay Company, which discouraged agricultural colonization, and not until the Prairies were sold to the Canadian Government after federation did a movement westward begin, a movement which can truly be said to have got into its stride only after the construction of the Canadian Pacific Railway in 1885.

When Prairie Settlement did finally become a reality, its pattern was somewhat different from that across the border. For

[1] See I. M. Spry, 'Captain John Palliser and the Exploration of Western Canada', *Geog. Journal*, vol. cxxv, pp. 149–84.

one thing, by the 1880's some of the technical problems of plains agriculture had been overcome, and their lessons learned. For another, the Canadian government assumed, from the start, a greater degree of control over the western lands than did that of the U.S.A. Its policy may have been rather hit-and-miss to begin with, and it was certainly nationalistic, but at least it was positive: it wanted the Prairies occupied.

The first phase of settlement saw two divergent lines of advance. In this phase, which lasted from 1872, soon after confederation, to about 1900, the Canadian government granted grazing leases on big areas of the dry Prairies. These leases, however, were subject to cancellation if the land was needed for agriculture; in other words, the cultivator had official priority, and the ranchers obtained security of tenure only when and where areas were declared unsuited to agriculture.

Meanwhile, the cultivators were advancing the farm frontier, and the railways were extending, north-westwards along the Park Belt. They were feeling their way along what was effectively a corridor walled in by climatic boundaries—aridity to the south and frost to the north. Before they could penetrate these barriers, new varieties of wheat had to be developed (and a major breakthrough occurred when the Marquis variety became available in 1911). But even with these new varieties the climatic hazards were such that the government encouraged Park Belt farmers to practise mixed farming, and not to rely too heavily on wheat. Today's agriculture in the Park Belt is the lineal descendant of this early, government-sponsored mixed farming.

When, therefore, the great boom in Prairie settlement took place, in the first years of the twentieth century, it was a more restrained affair, in land-use terms, than that on the Great Plains. The distinction between ranchlands and wheatlands was clearer, and there were natural restraints on wheat growing. This did not, however, prevent some of the same mistakes being made on the Prairies. As the population of Saskatchewan and Alberta increased by 500 per cent. in the first decade of the century, settlers pushed out into the Triangle during a series of wetter-than-average years, displacing the ranchers. Then came the inevitable reaction: dry years followed, and the farmers retreated. Around Lethbridge, as an example, the average wheat yields for the years 1911–21 were: 20, 16, 18, 6, 43, 34, 7, 5, 13, 9 bushels per acre. It was the familiar story of advance and withdrawal: of all the lands 'entered for' in this region under the Homestead Act, only about a half ever became the settlers' property. The rest were abandoned before the four-year occupance period was up.

There was one other factor in the early days which made life on the Prairies somewhat more secure than on the United States plains. The Canadian government took a more realistic view than the United States government of the size of farm needed in the dry west, and while it only offered the same 160-acre homesteads, it encouraged settlers to acquire extra land. This could usually be obtained from the railways, whose land grants gave them alternate sections over most of the best prairieland. The companies were generally glad to sell the homesteader the part of their land which adjoined his own. By the end of the Prairie boom, 70 per cent. of the farms were over 200 acres in size, and some settlers who would otherwise have been defeated by drought or frost were enabled to hold on because of their extra acreage.

For all these reasons, the pattern of land use that developed in the Prairie Provinces had more harmony, and less of the 'either-or' contrast, than that of the plains farther south. In the years since then, the difficulty of marketing the wheat crop (and the need to have, in consequence, other sources of farm income) has had the same effect of discouraging over-dependence on wheat. Thus, while there are areas which, owing to their roughness or their aridity, are primarily ranching areas, the wheat areas are by no means without livestock. In the heart of the Wheat Belt pasture generally occupies some 30 per cent. of the farmland, and oats—grown principally for stock feed— occupy about 20 per cent. of the cropland of the three provinces.

These trends are illustrated by the figures on the next page for Alberta in the period 1931–56.

In the black and grey-wooded soil zones the percentage of cropland under wheat actually dropped from 55 in 1931 to 16 in 1956. For as settlement has consolidated in the sub-humid prairie, and in the Park Belt in particular, there has grown up here, as there is growing up in the U.S.A., a Wheat and Live-

Province of Alberta; Area Seeded to Various Crops as a Percentage of the Area in Field Crops

	1931	1941	1951	1956
Wheat .	66	53	44	36
Oats .	20	23	20	20
Barley .	6	13	21	24
Tame Hay .	1	5	8	11
Other .	7	6	7	9
	100	100	100	100

Source: R. E. English, 'Agriculture in Alberta', *Can. Geog. Journ.*, vol. lvi, p. 110.

stock Belt, in which both elements of farm income are import-ant. As the cities of the Prairies have increased in size, dairying has developed around them, and with irrigated crops on the increase too, Prairie farming is becoming more diversified than ever before. Today, the Prairie Provinces produce a quarter of Canada's milk and butter, and a half of all the cattle and pigs marketed.

In spite of the somewhat greater degree of harmony that characterizes farming in the Canadian section of the Great Plains, however, the area suffered much the same fate as did the American section in the hard years between 1930 and 1935. The conjunction of low, depression-hit prices and drought seasons during these years brought the Prairie farmers to de-spair and bankruptcy, and obliged the federal government to intervene on their behalf. The Prairie Farms Rehabilitation Act of 1935 made available funds for restoring the ravages of drought and erosion. With the passage of time the scope of P.F.R.A. work has been extended, in parallel with the work of government agencies in the U.S.A., to cover a programme of instruction in conservation, a programme of irrigation works, and a system of controlled grazing on common lands. Small irrigation projects abound on the Prairies, while the larger schemes are, for the most part, to be found along the South Saskatchewan River in southern Alberta and Saskatchewan. There is no lack of irrigable lands in this area, but the estimated costs of developing them are very high.

DIFFERENCES IN SPACE RELATIONSHIPS

If the sequence of land settlement has been different on the Canadian Prairies from that on the plains of the United States, the simplest explanation of that fact lies in the difference in location of the two areas in relation to the more settled, eastern parts of the two countries concerned. In the U.S.A., as we have seen, settlement spread westward without a break from the Mississippi to the plains, because there was no geographical obstacle to such a logical extension. In Canada, on the other hand, there existed a most formidable obstacle—the southward extension of the Laurentian Shield, which interposed a barrier, in the form of 1,300 miles of forested wilderness, between the settlements of Ontario and the site of the future city of Winnipeg. When the westward spread of settlement was resumed on the Prairies, in the years after 1870, it was, from the Canadian viewpoint, settlement in a world apart. A new natural environment was encountered not, as in the U.S.A., after a period of adaptation in the sub-humid eastern plains, but abruptly, and the connexions of the new settlements with Canada proper were tenuous in the extreme. Many of the early settlers, in fact, were not from Canada at all, but arrived either direct from Europe, by way of Hudson Bay, or from the U.S.A. (where movement northwards down the fertile Red River Valley offered a less hazardous prospect than movement westwards into the dry plains). Only in 1855, with the opening of the Soo Canal, was a practicable route established to link the Prairie settlements to the east. The earliest railway line into Winnipeg reached the city from the south in 1878, and only in 1885 was the transcontinental rail link with Ontario completed. Not until the Trans-Canada Highway was completed did there exist a road link of modern standards; before that time, it was easier to 'cross' this part of Canada by making a southward detour into the U.S.A. Connexion across the Shield was virtually connexion with a foreign country.

The break in the sequence of settlement has its effect also upon the present distribution of population and the urban pattern. We have already seen, in Chapter XII, that the Great Plains of the U.S.A. lie within the hinterland of a line of cities which are located to the east of the region itself—Minneapolis, Kansas City, and Dallas–Fort Worth in particular. On the plains themselves there are no large cities between the 98th meridian and the Rockies except Denver, which owes more to the fertile Piedmont zone than it does to the plains, and whose economic domain stretches west rather than east. Just as the surface of the Great Plains slopes east to the Missouri and the Mississippi, so the economic 'gradient' runs the same way; the density of settlement increases from west to east; the products of the plains flow eastwards; cattle from the ranges are fattened and finished in the Midwest; and, in turn, manufactured goods needed on the plains are distributed from Midwestern factories and warehouses.

The commercial situation of the Canadian Prairies is different. While there is the same contrast in density of settlement and communications network between the Dry Belt and the Park Belt as there is between the western and eastern plains in the United States, the economic 'slope' ends abruptly at the edge of the Shield. The Canadian section of the Midwest, with its markets and its industries, is separated from the eastern edge of the plains by a vast area which is virtually uninhabited, and so neither provides markets nor generates traffic for the railways that cross it. Across this empty area all goods leaving or entering the Prairies must be ferried, either literally, by lake steamer, or economically, in the sense that they are carried by railways whose whole maintenance cost must be borne by consumers at either end.

To reduce the obstacle presented by this 'ferry service', the Prairies have developed their own industries, while the United States plains remain largely non-industrial.[1] In particular, the industries which process the agricultural produce of the plains have been established farther west than in the U.S.A., in order to reduce the bulk of raw materials making the long journey east. Thus it comes about that, in all three of the Prairie Provinces, flour milling, meat packing, and butter and cheese making are three of the four leading industries, and that processing is carried on in cities as far west as Edmonton (337,000) and Calgary (279,000), as well as in Regina (112,000), Saskatoon (95,000), and smaller centres. None of these manufacturing

---

[1] Except, of course, in their most southerly parts, where the presence of the oilfields (as in the Prairies) and proximity to the Gulf coast combine to give the Texas plains some industry. It should, in fact, be explained that while what has been written about the 'economic gradient' from west to east across the Great Plains holds true for most of the region, proximity of the Gulf coast to the southern end of the plains gives to that part of the region a north-to-south 'gradient', of a similar kind, towards the coastal cities and factories.

cities is large by North American standards, but their significance lies in their very existence, which in turn calls attention to the isolation of this great Canadian food-producing area.

By virtue of its position, both at the foot of the Prairie slope and at the western end of the route-bridge over the Shield, it is the city of Winnipeg (476,000) which dominates Prairie manufacturing. It is the funnel through which must pass all east-bound produce from the plains; it is the focus of the railway network; and the lake cities of Fort William and Port Arthur serve, in a sense, as its outports. It is the distributing point for goods received from the east, and corresponds to the supply and market cities along the Missouri and Mississippi farther south. Besides its basic food-processing industries, it possesses important railway workshops and a large number of light manufactures which have grown up in the wake of Prairie development in the post-war years. Today it ranks as the Dominion's sixth industrial centre, both by employment and by value of product.

The industrial development of these provinces has served the valuable purpose of providing alternative local employment for agricultural workers whom mechanization on the farms has rendered redundant, and who, in the U.S.A., must leave the Great Plains altogether to find employment. This industrial development has served another purpose also (indeed, the development may be partly attributed to it)—the supply role in relation to the northern frontier of Canadian settlement. The nature of this frontier will be examined in Chapter XIX; for the moment, we need only note that the Prairies' industries must supply both the west and the north, and that on this Northlands frontier there is a continuing expansion in progress, expansion which must be equipped and maintained from the nearest available supply bases—the cities of the Prairies.

THE EXPLOITATION OF PRAIRIE OIL

The fourth factor which gives to the Canadian section of the Great Plains a distinctive character is the development of the Prairie oilfields. This is a phenomenon of the post-war years, and production is by no means yet at the foreseeable peak level. But already exploitation has wrought changes in the economic geography of the western prairies.

Although Alberta possesses large reserves of coal, and Saskatchewan of lignite, these have never been worked on a scale much larger than local markets warranted. It was in 1947 that the first major Prairie oilfield came in, with strikes in the Edmonton area which drew continent-wide attention. In a development notable for its restraint, southern Alberta became the scene of numerous other strikes; later Saskatchewan and, to a lesser extent, Manitoba have come to share in the stimulating economic effects of oil discovery. Production of petroleum rose to 29 million barrels in 1950 and 192 million barrels in 1960, of which 130 million were produced in Alberta. It could have risen higher, but the Prairie Provinces have been careful to control production and avoid the waste that characterized the early days of the United States oil era. Supply industries for drilling operations and for the oilfield population have rapidly increased, and the cities of southern Alberta have expanded under the impact. Edmonton, at the heart of the oilfield area, almost tripled its population between 1941 and 1956, and that of Calgary more than doubled.

It is necessary, however, to be precise about the importance of this oilfield development. Revolutionary as the effects of an oil strike may be upon the local communities, on a continental scale the present oil production of the Prairies (and even total proved reserves, at 5,000 million barrels) are trivial in contrast with a total North American output which would drain these reserves in two years.

The particular importance of Prairie oil lies not so much in its quantity as in its location (see p. 142).

1. It is Canadian oil. Before the opening of the Prairie fields, Canada was almost entirely dependent on imports, most of which came from the United States. In its twentieth-century advance into the ranks of world powers, as well as in resolving its balance of trade problems, Canada's oil discoveries have come in time to play a strategic part.

2. It is northern oil. The centres of North American oil production are located in the southern and south-western parts of the continent. This geographical discrepancy between supply and demand was strikingly brought out in the Second World War, when North American bases in the northern Pacific coast region, and especially in Alaska, had to be supplied with fuel

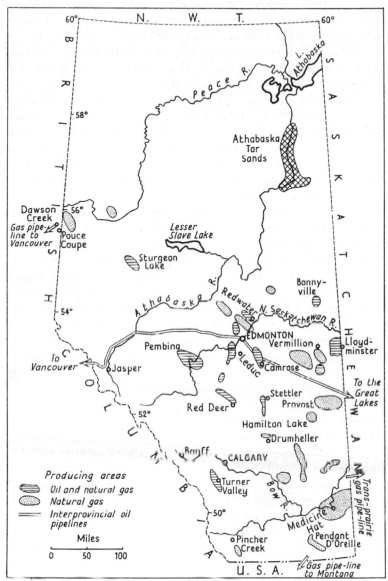

FIG. 64. Alberta: Oilfield developments, 1947–58. (Based on a map prepared by the Provincial Government of Alberta, by permission.) Another, rather more detailed map is to be found in M. Parrott's 'Turner Valley', *Can. Geog. Journ.*, vol. lxix, 1964, p. 140.

oils from these southern fields. It was a measure of the difficulty of the situation that, during the war years, it was found necessary to develop the oilfield at Norman Wells, on the Mackenzie at 65° N., and, further, to pipe the oil from there over the wild Mackenzie Mountains for more than 400 miles to a refinery at Whitehorse on the Alaska Highway.

In the years since the war this same discrepancy has become more evident, both because of the rapid increase of population and industry in the Pacific North-West, and because strategic considerations have given to the far north of the continent an altogether new importance. The Prairie fields were, in fact, brought in at a time of critical importance, from both an industrial and a military point of view.

The first task in Prairie oil development, however, was to distribute oil and gas as widely as possible throughout Canada. Two major pipelines have been constructed. One of them runs east across the Prairies to the Superior lakehead, and then across the U.S.A. to Sarnia and Toronto, with a branch serving markets in the U.S. lakes' states. The other set of pipes carries oil and gas to Vancouver, and links across the border with the state of Washington. With the passage of time it is certainly to be hoped that two nations so closely linked as Canada and the U.S.A. will co-ordinate oil production and distribution, irrespective of the nationality of the market, and thus will form what will in effect be an oil and gas 'grid'.

The Great Plains and Prairies afford an interest to the geographer, and a challenge to the North American, out of all proportion to their limited variety of scenery or land use. On their eastern margin they constitute a region of the world's most highly mechanized grain farming, with all that such advanced mechanization means in terms of production costs and rural unemployment. In their western section is carried on a livestock industry which, while it may have changed in organization, is only now shaking itself free from the hazards that beset its nineteenth-century counterpart. In between these two regions of relatively consistent land use is the debatable land, with its fluctuating frontiers of settlement and cultivation; its problems of depopulation and isolation; its false hopes in the present and its possibilities for the future.

FURTHING READING

ANY reading list on this region must begin with W. P. Webb's classic, *The Great Plains*, which deals with every aspect of the region's development. Among more recent works, there are C. F. Kraenzel's *The Great Plains in Transition*, and J. E. Weaver's vegetational studies *North American Prairie* and *Grasslands of the Great Plains*, but for a geographical description of the environment and its economic aspect it is difficult to improve on the series of articles in *A.A.A.G.*, vol. xiii, pp. 41–167, by C. F. Marbut, O. E. Baker and others. On the plains climate, see 'Annual-Variability Rainfall Maps of the Great Plains', by E. E. Lackey, *Geog. Review*, vol. xxvii, pp. 665–70, and the relevant sections in *Climate and Man*, U.S. Dept. of Agriculture Yearbook, 1941. The chinook and its effects are dealt with by R. L. Ives, in *A.A.A.G.*, vol. xl, pp. 293–327.

Land use in the Spring Wheat Belt of the U.S.A. is mapped by J. C. Weaver in 'The County as a Spatial Average in Agricultural Geography', *Geog. Review*, vol. xlvi, pp. 536–65, while on the grazing areas a voluminous literature includes useful sections of *Grass*, U.S. Dept. of Agriculture Yearbook, 1948, and the references in Further Reading for Chapter XVI, as well as numerous articles in the *Journal of Farm Economics*, some of which are referred to in the footnotes to this chapter and the next. Three recent localized studies of Great Plains land use are L. Hewes' 'A Traverse across Kit Carson County, Colorado', *Econ. Geog.*, vol. xxxix, pp. 332–40; W. M. Kollmorgen and G. F. Jenks' 'Sidewalk Farming in Toole County, Montana, and Traill County, North Dakota', *A.A.A.G.*, vol. xlviii, pp. 209–31, and 'The Oklahoma Panhandle—A Cross Section of the Southern High Plains', by A. H. Doerr and J. W. Morris, *Econ. Geog.*, vol. xxxvi, pp. 70–88.

On the Missouri Valley, and its proposed development, two lively accounts are *The Missouri Valley*, by R. Terral, and *The Dammed Missouri Valley*, by R. G. Baumhoff, while a new approach to the problem is suggested in H. C. Hart's *The Dark Missouri*.

For the Canadian Prairies, the physical setting and the story of their settlement are both covered by the relevant volumes of the great series *Canadian Frontiers of Settlement* (9 vols.), ed. W. A. Mackintosh and W. L. G. Joerg; see also F. B. Watts' 'The Natural Vegetation of the Southern Great Plains of Canada', *Geog. Bull.*, No. 14 (1960), pp. 25–43. The three provinces are dealt with recurrently in articles in the *Canadian Geographical Journal*, while much of the recent work on Prairie settlement has come from B. G. Vanderhill; see his articles in *Econ. Geog.*, vol. xxxv, pp. 259–68, *Journal of Geog.*, vol. lviii, pp. 325–33, and *Econ. Geog.*, vol. xxxviii, pp. 270–77. Urban studies are 'Land Use and Population Characteristics of Central Winnipeg', by T. R. Weir, *Geog. Bull.*, No. 9 (1956), pp. 5–22, and 'Calgary: A Study in Urban Pattern', by P. J. Smith, *Econ. Geog.*, vol. xxxviii, pp. 315–29. On Prairie irrigation see 'The South Saskatchewan River', by W. Eggleston, *Can. Geog. Journ.*, vol. xlvi, pp. 232–43, or 'They are Changing the Face of Saskatchewan', by Phyllis MacNeill, *Can. Geog. Journ.*, vol. lx, pp. 154–71. On Prairie oil, see the references to Chapter V, and also 'Natural Gas

Industries in Western Canada', by J. R. Peet, *The Canadian Geographer*, vol. vii, pp. 23–32, and 'Saskatchewan's Oil and Gas', by R. Tyre, *Can. Geog. Journ.*, vol. lvi, pp. 120–33.

XVI

MOUNTAIN AND DESERT

1. *The Region and Its Character*

Where the foothills of the Rockies rise, to break the monotony of a thousand miles of plains, the west-bound traveller enters a region of remarkable natural splendour. From the Front Ranges of the Rockies to the crest of the mountains of the Pacific coastlands is some 900 miles, or 15° of longitude, along a line frome Denver to San Francisco; some 400 miles on the line from Calgary to Vancouver. Spread across this great area is a magnificent variety of scenery, a wide range of environmental conditions, and a thin scatter of natural resources, available to a population whose average density is less than 5 per square mile.

Both the variety and the splendour of the region are, in the first instance, products of the relief. It is a region where the mountain ranges—the Rockies themselves, the Uintas, the Sawtooths—occupy only a small part of the area; it is a region of plateaux also, some of which lie at altitudes—7,000 feet or more—above the tops of the highest hills east of the Mississippi. Some of its most interesting sections are the down-faulted valleys in the south-western tip of the region—Death Valley and Salton Sea—where the earth's surface sinks to more than 200 feet below sea-level. In terms of area, this is primarily a plateau region, but one in which the plateaux often rise, step-like, above one another, to give the observer the impression that he is surrounded by mountain ranges.

The physical variety in turn affects the climate. While certain generalizations are possible (the frost-free season, for example, is seldom more than 120 days, and is often less than 100), relief exerts the main control upon temperature and precipitation, and overall description becomes impossible. The north-western parts of the region are under the influence of Pacific Coast air, and have a winter–spring rainfall maximum, while the south-eastern part has a summer maximum, and receives much of its rain from violent thunder showers; but everywhere there are local conditions of rain and rain shadow, produced by the

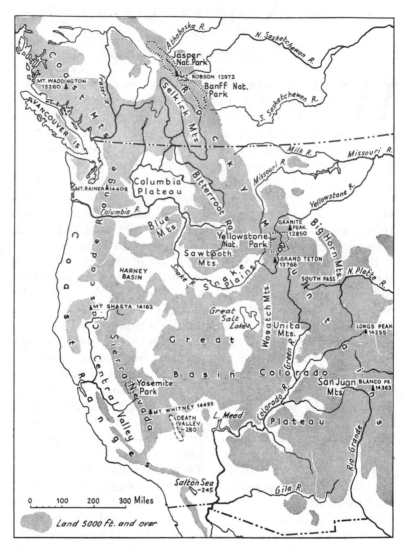

FIG. 65. The Mountain and Desert Region: Physical Features.

relief. The main rain-bearing winds west of the Continental Divide blow from the Pacific, bringing 80 or 100 inches of precipitation, including very heavy falls of snow, to the mountains along the coast. Immediately east of these mountains there occurs a change of dramatic suddenness: the rain shadow falls across the adjoining plateaux and basins, and the dense forests of the mountain slopes are separated by only a narrow transition belt from the desert scrub of areas where annual precipitation averages 8 to 10 inches. Eastward again, the surface rises, and the rainfall gradually increases, towards the Rockies; at their summits a precipitation of 30 to 40 inches is again to be found. In a manner which is even more marked, because the west-to-east distance is shorter, the rainfall of southern British Columbia varies from 150 inches in the coastal mountains, down to less than 10 inches in the Okanagan Valley, and up again to 30 inches or more in the eastern Cordilleras. In both Canada and the U.S.A. the Rockies cast their own rain shadow over the plains that lie to the east of them, beyond their forested slopes.

Climate in turn affects vegetation, which tends to vary with both the amount of rainfall and the time and duration of the wetter season. A regular sequence of vegetation zones can be distinguished, both horizontally and vertically; that is, there is a sequence of zonal changes which generally holds good, both between low elevations and high, and between the heart of the desert and the better-watered lands surrounding it.

The zonal changes are, in general terms, from scrub, through grass and transitional woodland, to forest. At one end of the scale, in the lowest and driest areas, is found the desert shrub vegetation, which covers the floor of much of the Great Basin. Those parts of the area that are beds of former lakes form salt deserts, where saltgrass and sage are found; for the rest, creosote bush dominates the sparse cover. From this vegetational nadir, an increase in rainfall produces a sagebrush-grass combination. In the south-western states there is sufficient *late summer* rain to produce in that area semi-desert grasslands, which provide valuable yearlong grazing. Elsewhere in the intermontane region, however, lack of summer rain restricts the growth of grasses, and the value of the vegetation for grazing purposes varies inversely with the amount of sagebrush.

Beyond the sagebrush-grass zone there is generally a belt of transitional woodland—an area where increasing rainfall encourages the growth of small, scattered trees. In the Rockies and the High Plateaux this zone is represented by the pinyon-juniper combination, and is encountered generally between 4,000 and 6,000 feet; the trees themselves are valueless, but the grasses that accompany them provide some spring forage for stock. In California, on the slopes of the Sierras, a similar belt of transitional woodland exists, of slightly different character, and at a lower elevation, and is known as chaparral. Above the transitional woodlands are the forests, open at their lower limits, and so used for grazing purposes, but becoming denser at higher elevations, until they thin out into the alpine meadows above the tree line.

2. *Land and Livelihood in the Region*

In any account of the settlement and use of the Mountain and Desert Region, pride of place must be given to the Spanish pioneers from Mexico. While they never penetrated farther than the southern edge of the region, the mark they left on that area was so clear and definite that it remains to this day. Many of the place names are Spanish: the Spaniards introduced ranching and opened the first mines; and the style of architecture they brought with them is to be found today in parts of North America that never saw a Spaniard, so pervasive has its influence become.

The Spaniards spread northwards from Mexico during the seventeenth and eighteenth centuries in three main directions. One of these was north-eastwards through what is now Texas, roughly to the line of the Mississippi, where they encountered the French. The second was due north to Santa Fé, which became their northern capital, and the third was north-westwards into California. Each of these thrusts was spearheaded by priests who established missions, around which they gathered Indians and cultivated gardens and fields. They were accompanied or followed, in turn, by military detachments and by ranchers, who were granted huge land concessions and who herded stock over the barren areas between the islands of cultivation represented by the missions. In this way the frontier advanced rapidly northwards behind the chain of missions and forts, and there was established from the earliest years the same combination of land uses which still, over two centuries later, dominate the life of the region.

In such an area as this, where much of the land is either too dry or too rugged for settlement, the ways in which a livelihood can be secured are strictly limited. Indeed, our study of the human geography of the area can be confined to a small number of occupations. They are (1) mining, (2) ranching and lumbering, (3) irrigation farming, and (4) travel and tourism. To these should be added a fifth heading: what is sarcastically called in the west 'non-use'—that is, the reservation of areas for nature and game preserves.

MINING

Many of the explorers and earliest settlers of the Mountain and Desert region were miners. Apart from the agricultural communities on the Pacific coast and at Salt Lake, miners made up the bulk of the population west of the 98th meridian in 1855. Before permanent agriculture spread farther, many a mining town had reached its gaudy heyday and was already on the decline—such mining camps as Virginia City, on the famous Comstock Lode in Nevada, which was discovered in 1859; a town of 10,000 or 20,000 inhabitants at various times up to its peak in the 1880's; declining since to become a ghost town, with a 1950 population of 950, and remaining on the map by grace of the tourist trade alone. Few, indeed, of these early mining camps have had a continuous career from their establishment until the present day; even fewer have, like Butte, Montana, remained to become towns in their own right. The history of the western mineral industry has been one of precipitate change.

Apart from the obviously temporary character of any extractive activity, these changes have been due to several factors. One of these has been the progressive discovery of new mineral ores. The earliest miners were, almost without exception, seeking gold, and so flocked to California after 1848, or British Columbia and Colorado after 1858. After the first rush the miners came to realize that, even if a fortune was not to be made in gold, there was an expanding market for silver and lead, copper and zinc; and this led to new beginnings in many mineralized areas which the gold-seekers had too hastily abandoned.

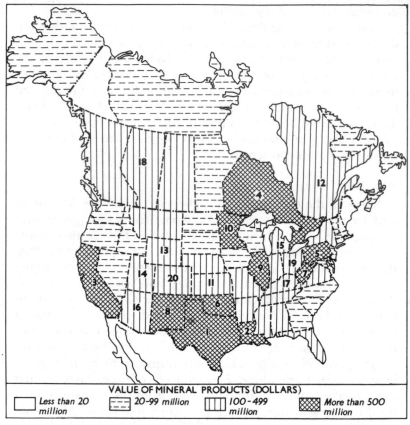

VALUE OF MINERAL PRODUCTS (DOLLARS)

☐ Less than 20 million   ⊟ 20-99 million   ▥ 100-499 million   ▨ More than 500 million

Fig. 66. North America: Value of mineral production, by states and provinces, 1960. This is one distribution map of the continent on which the inclusion of the great empty northern territories of Alaska and Canada is both proper and necessary. But the map shows that their present development is relatively slight: much of their mineral wealth is as yet untapped. The Mountain and Desert Region plays an important role in mineral production, but it is the oil regions which contribute the greatest share of the total value. The numbers rank the leading 20 producers.

Another, and continuing, factor of change has been the discovery of new uses for the rarer minerals. The exploitation of tungsten and molybdenum, for example, waited on the demand for electrical goods and tougher steels; and the use of

PLATE XVII

The Mountain and Desert Region: Copper mining at Bingham, Utah

PLATE XVIII

The Mountain and Desert Region: Vegetation types. *Above*: trees and grassland at the lower margin of the mountain forest in western Texas; scrub oak, pinyon, and uniper. *Below*: open forest with small, seasonal grazing value, on the southern rim of the Grand Canyon, Arizona, about 6,500 feet molybdenum has brought into prominence a valley high in the Colorado Rockies where, at the town of Climax, some three-quarters of the world's supply of the mineral is produced. Even more recently the continent-wide search for uranium has set off a fresh burst of prospecting and brought to light, besides supplies of the mineral itself (notably in the region we are considering), many deposits of other minerals which were previously overlooked.

A third factor of change is the impact of changing techniques of mineral production, and especially the effect of enlarging the scale of production. The copper mines of Upper Michigan were put out of business by the opening of mines in Montana and Utah in the 1880's, where the larger scale of working and the opportunities for open-pit mining created a decisive advantage. Much more recently there have been foreshadowed far-reaching changes in the petroleum industry; research has made commercially possible the exploitation of low-yielding oil shales in Colorado (and thereafter elsewhere), which may add, at a single stroke, several decades to the life of North America's oil reserves.

The conjunction of these factors ensures that the one permanent feature of the western mineral industry is change. The most important features of the pattern in the 1960's can, however, be summarized briefly in relation to value of output and employment figures.

Copper is the region's most valuable single mineral; Arizona, Utah, and Montana are the leading United States producers, and in each of these states copper is the most important product mined. In Arizona the mines are scattered throughout the south-eastern section of the state, chiefly at Bisbee, Morenci, and Miami. In Utah the great open-cut mine at Bingham dominates production, and the smelters are located in the outskirts of nearby Salt Lake City. In Montana, on the other hand, the principal source is underground—at Butte, whose mines have been in production since 1880. For these mines the smelter is at Anaconda, some 20 miles to the west. Copper is also mined in southern British Columbia, both on the coast and in the Interior Plateau.

Zinc and *Lead* follow copper in value of output within the United States section of the region, while in British Columbia they are the leading minerals produced. Idaho, Arizona, and Montana are the main western producers of zinc, and rank high in lead output also; the mining area lies in south-western Montana and in the Cœur d'Alene Mountains of northern Idaho. British Columbia produces 50 per cent. of the zinc and almost 90 per cent. of the lead produced in Canada. Much of this output comes from a single mine near Kimberley, and almost all of it from areas near the United States border. The ores are transported from the various mines to the great smelter at Trail, on the Columbia River, where, thanks to the centralization of smelting operations, both refined metals and a number of valuable by-products, including chemicals, are produced.

Silver, the source of many a fortune on the Comstock Lode in the 1860's and 1870's (it is estimated to have yielded minerals worth $500 million), was almost as great an early attraction as gold in the west. Today, as then, the mountain states of the U.S.A. dominate the output, with Idaho as the chief producer. Ranking above silver, in value of output, is *molybdenum*, although production is very largely concentrated, as we have already seen, at Climax, in Colorado.

Among the region's numerous non-metallic minerals, the most significant is probably *phosphate rock*, which is found over a wide area west of the Rockies, and is worked extensively in Idaho, to supply an ever-increasing demand for fertilizers. The region is also well supplied with *coal measures*, although exploitation of these, originally of interest mainly to the railways, has always lagged for want of wider markets.

A few of the mining settlements have become, or given rise to, genuine industrial towns in this largely non-industrialized region. Butte has become a centre for agricultural processing and assorted industries, and Pueblo, Colo., produces steel. Furthermore, war-time needs in the west provided Utah with a splendid industrial exotic, in the form of the Geneva Steel Works, 35 miles south of Salt Lake City. Although these mills were originally planned to supply rather distant markets on the Pacific coast, the development of the Mountain West as a whole, in the post-war years, has justified their siting and maintained demand upon their 1·3 million tons capacity.

The Second World War disclosed to Americans both the

strategic importance of many minerals whose names were scarcely known to them, and also the possibility of producing almost all these minerals, at a price, in the Mountain West. In consequence of war-time need, many low-grade deposits were worked in the west, in operations which, with the re-entry of economic considerations, proved impossible to maintain. We must, therefore, think of part of the western mining industry as being in suspension; the deposits, and in many cases the plant are available in case of stragetic need or of a rise in price, but for the present it is simpler and cheaper to import from higher-grade sources abroad.

Not only the distribution, but also the character, of mining operations in the west has changed with the passage of time. Large corporations have replaced the highly individualistic operator of earlier years, and this has had the effect of increasing the stability, both geographically and economically, of the modern operations. Where the early miner worked, and perhaps looked for, only one mineral, the application of science to mining has made possible the working of mixed ores found in association; and so, with a wider range of resources to draw upon, the life of the mining community is prolonged and made more secure. The coming of the larger mining unit has also made possible new and more costly prospecting methods. It is only with the entry of the geiger-counter, and the search for radio-active minerals, that the western mining industry has reverted to the free-for-all of its earlier years; that once again, a century after its opening, the Mountain and Desert region has become an El Dorado for the individual treasure-seeker.

RANCHING AND LUMBERING

It may not, at first sight, be apparent why two occupations so different—and, in some senses, so opposed in interest—as ranching and lumbering should be listed beside each other. The explanation lies in the character of the region's vegetation. In area, the greatest part of the Mountain and Desert region is covered with either dry grassland or open forest, and because these grade into one another without a natural break, the use of the one affects the use of the other. In particular, since all but the densest forests are in some measure grazed by stock,

CC

the open woodland must be regarded, economically, as an extension of the grasslands.

Whatever use is made of these areas, certain considerations force themselves upon the users. (1) In the dry west the scatter of resources (and, in particular, of the prime resource, water) is extremely thin. In the driest of the grazing lands, 100 acres or more may be required to feed one head of cattle. (2) Not only are the natural resources meagre, but their value is often only seasonal. Grazing in the open forest, or on the alpine pastures above the tree line, is possible only in summer, while the desert margins offer pasturage of a kind for a few weeks during the winter rains. This second fact, coupled with the first, means that the rancher must not only have sufficient land for a herd of worthwhile size to graze, at a carrying rate of 100 acres per head, but must also have access to other grazing lands, to which he can move his stock when the seasonal forage is exhausted. Ranching in the west has always had about it an element of the Bedouin. (3) Because the value per acre of the region is so low, it is generally true that its exploitation must be multi-purpose; only by combining all the values, both social and commercial, of the region can its development be made worthwhile. O. E. Baker calculated[1] that in 1924–5 the annual regional return from grazing alone was no more than 35 cents per acre. Considering the risks that must attach to all development in this region, it was, and is, essential to raise this low level of return.

All these considerations point to one conclusion: that in the land use of this region, the decisive factor is that of land ownership. Either land must be common, and priorities in its exploitation must be left to the discretion of interested users; or it must be held in very large units, within which a system of priorities can be enforced. The first of these 'solutions' was adopted in the early days of the west, by simple default of any constructive alternative policy. Its effects were devastating. The second solution is the one that concerns the geographer of the 1960's. While some of the largest ranches in the western U.S.A. and the Plateau of British Columbia might qualify as 'very large units', and are admirably managed, the factor here which is of overwhelming importance is the single ownership

[1] See O. E. Baker, 'The Grazing and Irrigated Crops Region', *Econ. Geog.*, vol. vii, pp. 325–64 and vol. viii, pp. 325–77.

of a very large unit indeed—the 400 million-acre public domain of the United States Government. In all that concerns

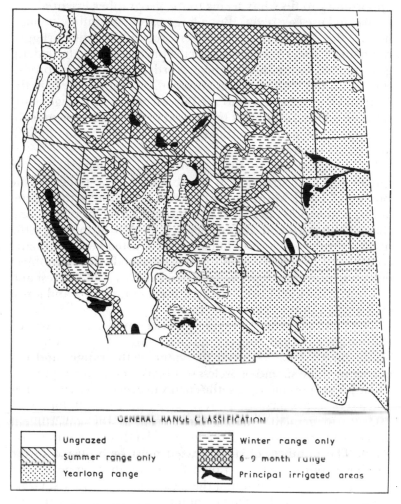

GENERAL RANGE CLASSIFICATION

Ungrazed

Summer range only

Yearlong range

Winter range only

6–9 month range

Principal irrigated areas

FIG. 67. The Western U.S.A.: Seasonal Land Use.

the exploitation of the Mountain West, the policies of this great landlord are of paramount importance.

Many of the problems of the Mountain and Desert region

are similar to those of the Great Plains, which were discussed in the last chapter. The Great Plains, however, are largely an area of private ownership and do not, therefore, present an adequate opportunity to do what seems to the geographer essential—to *control* land use (see p. 83). But a large part of the public domain lies in the Mountain and Desert region, the dry, rugged remnant of the 1,400 million acres once held by the federal government. As landlord of these, North America's least promising acres, the United States Government (represented by the National Forest Service and the Bureau of Land Management) is free to adopt the policies best suited to the environment, subject only to recurrent political pressure to release the domain for private exploitation.

Such private use in the past resulted in overgrazing the ranges and in destruction of forest timber. The policy of the Bureau of Land Management (which administers the rangelands) is, therefore, designed to improve grazing practices, and that of the National Forest Service (which administers the higher, shrub- and forest-clad areas) is devoted both to grazing control and to conservation on the watersheds. It is the object of both to prevent *competitive* land use. It is this joint interest and joint control which justify our treatment of ranching and forest exploitation in the region together.

The improvement of grazing practice implies (1) restricted use and (2) enlarged reserves. As on the Great Plains, overgrazing in the past has reduced the value of the ranges and has encouraged the spread of useless scrub, like mesquite or pinyon, or the low-value cheatgrass, the enemy of every western rancher and a serious fire hazard. To reverse this process calls for better range management—management such as the government agencies try to enforce on the grazing lands of the public domain. The numbers of stock grazed must be adjusted to the varying condition of the range from month to month, and especially to the condition of the most 'popular' grasses. Grazing must be deferred at the beginning of the season long enough for the range vegetation to become established, and must be terminated at the end of the season in time to ensure that reserves can be built up for the next year. These principles are recognized by the progressive rancher, and are enforced by the Bureau of Land Management and the National Forest Service by means of grazing permits, which specify when, and in what numbers, stock may be placed on the public ranges.[1]

The second task, that of enlarging reserves, is desirable not only to give greater security to the rancher, but also to reduce in amount the transhumance which is found to be necessary everywhere in the region, from Texas to British Columbia. While transhumance plays a vital role in a region where so much of the grazing is available only for a single season, there are obvious advantages in having as large a part as possible of the year's forage within a single area. This is particularly the case because, while the spring, autumn, and year-long grazing are to a large extent in private hands, the federal government, by its ownership of the highest and driest rangelands, controls much of the summer and the winter grazing.

Enlargement of reserves means the elimination of valueless vegetation on the ranges by mechanical or chemical means; the improved distribution of water for stock and, above all, the extension of irrigated pasture and fodder crops, especially for winter feed. Thus there is a need, as on the Great Plains, for planning reserves on an area basis, with the difference that, in the Mountain West, the problem presented by individual ownership of land is considerably reduced.

This problem of building up adequate reserves of grazing in the west has been eased by the spread of irrigation, but made more acute by afforestation of some federal and state lands which were formerly available for grazing. On balance, however, the west in general is much better placed today to meet the hazard of one, or even two, drought years than it was twenty years ago.

The problem of watershed control overlaps that of grazing control and is equally important, for M. H. Saunderson has suggested that, in the realistic view, the national forests of the west should be considered primarily as *water-producing* lands,

---

[1] This is the theory. W. Calef, in his study of the system of grazing permits in operation, *Private Grazing and Public Lands*, Chicago, 1960, found that in practice the system works less well: specifically, that it is difficult to make the necessary range forecasts accurately, and very difficult to get the local ranchers' committees (who advise the B.L.M. officials) to agree to reductions in numbers of stock permitted on the public lands. Actually, public lands are overgrazed and erode as well as private lands, while in some areas the ranchers do not actually use their grazing entitlement, but hold on to their right to do so, as a means of establishing bank credit, or as a reserve 'just in case'.

and the treeless ranges as *silt-producing* lands.[1] The problem is twofold. On the one hand, it is necessary to check erosion, by preventing over-grazing and unwise tree felling, in order to control run-off. On the other hand, it is necessary, in a dry region such as this, to reconcile conflicting claims on such water as is available. These claims may be made on behalf of irrigation; of industrial or domestic users; of power production or navigation; of sanitation or wild life protection, and all may be countered by the demands of the engineers charged with flood control. In recent years, therefore, the National Forest Service has been more concerned to conserve than to exploit its forests, to use them to regulate water-supply rather than to produce revenue; and while this policy has inevitably provoked criticism, it represents a valuable and indeed essential service to the region as a whole.

In British Columbia, some 50 per cent. of whose population depends, directly or indirectly, on the exploitation of the forests, the problem is necessarily complicated by the need to maintain timber production as well as to practise conservation measures. Here again, however, the fact that the provincial government owns over 90 per cent. of the forests gives, at least, a unified control over the bulk of the forest lands, and the difficulties encountered by conservationists in British Columbia are more financial than administrative. The principal question is the extent to which the province can afford the present costs of conservation in its main industry, while still supporting a population which is increasing by leaps and bounds.

Against this background, then, ranching and lumbering are carried on. Ranching has spread from its original location, in the Spanish South-West, to become the principal form of land use over all but the highest and most rugged sections of the region. Both sheep and cattle are raised, and although, with the passage of time, the average size of ranch units has increased, transhumance—even if it is now motorized—is still general. Fattening is carried out in a variety of locations. In the earlier days of the industry most of the stock, like that of the Great Plains, was shipped east for finishing and slaughter. More recently, however, two other developments have occurred: (1)

---

[1] See M. H. Saunderson, 'Western Range Land Use and Conservation Problems', *Journ. Farm Econ.*, vol. xxxi, pp. 985–97.

With the increase of population on the Pacific coast, more stock has been moving west for slaughter, and the 'divide' between eastward and westward shipments has shifted across the region towards the east. (2) With the development of cultivated and irrigated feed lots, fattening is now possible within the region itself, and such communication centres as Salt Lake City, Ogden, and Phoenix have come to take a share in the processing of livestock products.

Lumbering and the forest products industry are carried on in many parts of the mountains. In general, the forests become denser, and commercially more valuable, towards the cooler north, so that lumbering increases in relative importance through western Montana and northern Idaho, until in British Columbia it overrides all other occupations in its share of employment. The forests of the Rockies are composed for the most part of pine, spruce, fir, and larch, and in the U.S.A. about one-third of the forest area represents virgin growth. The lumber industry south of the border is most fully developed around such centres as Cœur d'Alene and Lewiston, Ida., and Missoula, Mont., where the adjacent mining areas provide an immediate market for timber, but there are important outliers of the industry in the upper Colorado Basin and in the highlands of central Arizona.

In British Columbia, the lumber industry grew up on the coast, where the forests are accessible and the timber is often moved by sea. The forests of the interior, however, contain huge reserves, and the industry is gradually spreading inland to tap the estimated 65 million acres of commercial forest there. The interior now produces more than 40 per cent of British Columbia's timber, and the province has a pulp and paper industry of growing importance. The problems of British Columbia's forest products industry are discussed more fully in Chapter XVIII.

IRRIGATION FARMING

Farming in the intermontane areas is generally oasis farming, and the oases are for the most part man-made. There is, it is true, some dry farming carried on, but the mainstay of the region's agriculture is the irrigated lands, some 11 to 12 million acres in extent.

Irrigation was carried on in the south of the region by the Spanish settlers, and by the Indians before them. The first major development, however, was that of the Mormon community which founded Salt Lake City in 1847, and turned its arid surroundings into some of the greenest farmlands of the west. Today it is the Snake River Plains of southern Idaho which, with the Salt Lake area, the Gila Basin of Arizona, and the Columbia Basin Project, form the main blocks of irrigated land in the Mountain West.

Irrigation, as we saw in Chapter IV, may be used in two different contexts: either to cultivate the desert, or to give security to existing operations on the agricultural margins. The Mountain and Desert region contains examples of both uses. It contains hundreds of small patches of irrigated land, many of them under pasture, that provide winter feed for stock, and represent a wise insurance policy for the region's farmers. It contains, too, several of the major irrigation projects of the Bureau of Reclamation and will, in the foreseeable future, contain more. On these projects a wide variety of crops have been introduced, including fruits and vegetables, sugar beet, and, in the south-western U.S.A., cotton. Thus there has arisen a broad distinction between the use of irrigation for livestock feeding and for growing cash crops. In either case, there is created what may be regarded as the 'typical' agricultural landscape of the region—the green oasis with its irrigated cropland and pastures, surrounded by a belt of dry-farmed grain fields, and encircled in turn by the brown ranges that stretch out to the horizon or up to the forest.

Although, as we also saw earlier, there are differences of opinion about the financing of irrigation in the dry west, there is unanimous agreement about its importance to the region. 'Through irrigation', declared the Commission on Organization of the Executive Branch[1] of the U.S. government in 1955, 'man has been able to build a stable civilization in an area that might otherwise have been open only to intermittent exploitation.' For western land use to advance at all, economically,

---

[1] It is interesting that this same commission came to the conclusion that the financial burden of the newest irrigation schemes *could not* be borne by the farmers concerned, and suggested as a solution that around each scheme financed by public money an irrigation district should be formed, all of whose inhabitants, as direct or indirect beneficiaries of the scheme, should be taxed to pay for it.

irrigation was essential. The questions at issue are simply: who should pay for it, and how large an irrigated area is needed to build a 'stable civilization'?

Among the many irrigated areas in the region, three of the largest may be briefly described, to illustrate the character and problems of these developments. These are the Gila-Salt Valley area in Arizona, the Upper Colorado Project, and the Colorado Piedmont. Large-scale irrigation in central Arizona was made possible by the construction of the Roosevelt and Coolidge Dams (built in 1911 and 1928 respectively) and other works, so that by the early 1930's the flow of the Gila and Salt were fully utilized for irrigation purposes.[1] Since that time, however, the demand for irrigation water has continued to increase; both because of the rapid rise in Arizona's population, and because of the phenomenal expansion within the state of the area devoted to irrigated cotton, which has increased four-fold since 1946. Today cotton accounts for half the agricultural income of the state, and almost half the total area (1·2 million acres) in crops.

With the conversion of Arizona from a ranch state to a cotton state, the increased demand for irrigation water has been met from the only alternative source available besides the rivers— ground water reservoirs. Today more than half the water needed for irrigation is supplied by wells, and the number of these is still increasing. Withdrawals from underground supplies in 1950 were already two and a half times as great as the combined average run-off of the Gila and its two main tri-butaries, the Verde and the Salt. Since then, Arizona's population has doubled.

In these circumstances, the natural reservoirs are failing to recharge, the water table is falling, and further expansion of the irrigated area can only hasten the day when water will become either unavailable or too expensive for the deep-well farmer to afford. A possible remedy would be to substitute for cotton some other crop, or preferably pasture, whose water requirements would be lower, but this suggestion comes inopportunely at a time when mechanization has taken a firm hold on the cotton growing of the south-west, and when the farmer looks for a

[1] The paragraphs on Arizona that follow are based largely on W. G. V. Balchin and N. Pye, 'Recent Economic Trends in Arizona', *Geog. Journ.*, vol. cxx, pp. 156–73.

return on his costly investment. The position remains one for grave concern.

The Upper Colorado presents a very different picture. Here the situation is reversed: the area has water and to spare, but at present this water is utilized not by the population of the upper basin, but by Arizonans, Californians, and Mexicans some hundreds of miles downstream. Some of it is even reversed in its flow, as we shall see, and is passed through tunnels beneath the main watershed of the Rockies, to supplement the meagre flow of the rivers that irrigate the Colorado Piedmont and run east across the dry plains. Only half the Colorado's water is used for any purpose within the whole basin, and of that part which is used the 40 million acres of the upper basin take only 40 per cent. Each basin state is given an allotment of Colorado water, but the state of Wyoming, for example, with an allotment of 14 per cent. of the total, uses only about 30 per cent. of its share. It is not long since the Colorado River was called 'the last great unharnessed river system in the United States'.

The Upper Colorado Project is aimed at remedying this situation on behalf of the farmers, ranchers, and miners who inhabit this vast basin. To the numerous small dams which already stand on several of its tributaries, the scheme would add several major dams on the principal branches of the Colorado itself. Since the rivers cutting through the Colorado Plateaux are for the most part deeply entrenched in canyons, and since this area is at present in a relatively backward state of development, it seems clear that this is a case for action on the scale that almost inevitably involves the resources of the Bureau of Reclamation. There are, however, no lack of objectors to the scheme —notably the downstream users of Colorado water—and there is little doubt that the $1,000 million estimated as needed to carry out the scheme will make this project a continuing source of political friction for some years to come.

The third area whose irrigation we are considering is the Colorado Piedmont. It may seem out of order to consider this example, because the Piedmont is admittedly a part of the Great Plains physiographic region. But if the irrigated farmlands belong to the Great Plains, the irrigation water is certainly supplied by the Mountain and Desert Region—not only in the sense that rivers flow down to the Piedmont from the Colorado Rockies, but also in that some of the water used is Colorado River (that is, *west*-flowing) water, which has been diverted and passed by tunnel under the Rockies to the east.

The Colorado Piedmont is one of the oldest irrigation districts in the west. The early schemes were small, but the area has become thickly settled, and an important producer of irrigated sugar beet, together with alfalfa, beans, and vegetables. Consequently, as Denver and its satellites have grown in size, water has been in increasingly short supply. Eventually, all available streams on the eastern slopes of the Rockies had been tapped, and it was necessary to look farther afield. Since, as we have just seen, the upper Colorado River has water and to spare, the idea was conceived of breaching the watershed and meeting the ever-growing demand of the Piedmont towns and farms in this way. The latest and most ambitious of these diversions will, it is hoped, benefit not only the Piedmont itself, but also the dry upper valley of the Arkansas.

COMMUNICATIONS AND TOURISM

There can be few regions of the world where so large a proportion of the population is involved in the transport business as in the Mountain and Desert region. If to the running of regular communications we add the service of the millions of tourists who annually invade the region, then we account for the livelihood of almost the entire population of some areas, so that if we take as our index the income derived from such services, then we find that this fourth group of occupations in the Mountain and Desert region fully qualifies for its place alongside the other three.

There are two main reasons for the importance of the transport industry in this region.

1. It was transport, in the form of the western railways, that dominated the settlement period in the region, as we saw in Chapter VI. It was the railways that led the way, for all but the hardiest pioneers, into the west; the railways that had land to sell and the means of reaching it; that located the towns; that were, in short, the agents of civilization in the west. Their primacy was incontestable, until the 1930's brought the establishment of a comprehensive road network over the region.

2. As a region of sparse population and scattered resources

the Mountain West has always been, geographically, a barrier between areas of denser population and more intensive activity; a barrier zone in which few Americans had business to transact, and which they were only anxious to cross as speedily as possible. But to maintain communications across an empty region requires almost as large a staff and administration as to do so across populous areas, so that although the regional population in the early years was very small, a large part of it consisted of the railwaymen who manned the division points and the lonely section posts along the tracks. The towns were located primarily for the convenience of the railways and only gradually did they develop functions that linked them with their surroundings. They were simply the piers of the transport bridges that spanned the empty west, strung out in east-west lines along the routes of the Canadian Pacific, the Union Pacific, or the Santa Fé line.

When the era of road travel came in, the same pattern was repeated. The roads, built to cross the area rather than to serve local settlements—which were in any case few—ran for scores of miles through uninhabited wastes. Along them therefore, there sprang up service points for motor traffic that duplicated those of the railways. What the towns were to the early railways, the cross-roads filling station and snack bar have become to the roads; with this distinction, that with the increase in size of the railway locomotive, and especially with the coming of diesel haulage, there is less and less for the railway towns to do, while the business of the road service points, and the number of such points, is still on the increase.

The most important influence, then, on the location of settlements in this region is the requirements of the transport services. Many of the larger towns are railway towns, like Ogden, Ut., or Pocatello, Ida.; most of the smaller ones are. A few, by virtue of strategic location or nearness to irrigated lands, have grown to have a wider significance. The chief of these are Spokane (278,000), where three transcontinental lines meet after crossing the Rockies; Albuquerque (262,000), which has outdone Santa Fé as the centre for the Spanish South-West (partly because the railway that bears Santa Fé's name runs through Albuquerque and not through Santa Fé); and Phoenix (663,000) in the heart of Arizona's irrigated farmlands.

There are two cities, however, whose influence dominates the whole of the Mountain and Desert region, from the Canadian border to northern New Mexico, except where Spokane

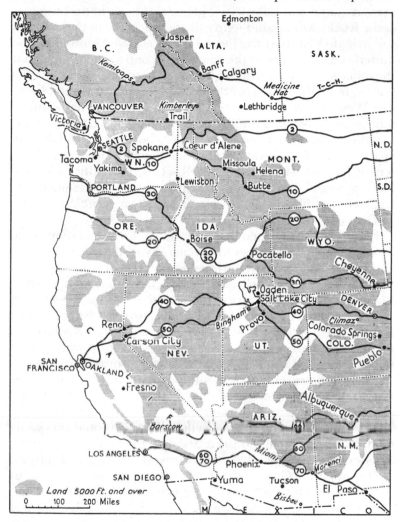

FIG. 68. The Mountain and Desert Region: Settlement and Communications. The map shows the principal transcontinental road routes—the Trans-Canada Highway, and U.S. Highways 2, 10, 20, 30, 40, 50, 60, 66, and 70. The numbering, and in some cases the alignment, of the U.S. highways is now being altered, however, with the introduction of the new, and still incomplete, Interstate network. For rail routes, see Fig. 32.

exerts a lesser, distracting influence in the north-west of the region, and Phoenix has grown with Arizona's settlement boom to dominate the south-west. These cities are Denver (929,000) and Salt Lake City (383,000). One is in the oasis belt of the Rocky Mountain Piedmont and the other in the centre of the irrigated lands at the foot of the Wasatch Mountains; the hinterland of one lies to the east of the continental divide, and the other to the west. Although Denver actually lies outside the region, in all that concerns the economic activity of the Mountain West the two cities are rivals—as railway and road centres, miners' and stockmen's markets, manufacturing cities, and distribution points. Denver is the larger, but Salt Lake City, by virtue of its religious significance for the Mormons, who have settled far and wide west of the Rockies, probably exerts the more powerful influence over its hinterland.[1] In Canada, it is Calgary that fills the same role, from a comparable position, as Denver.

Except on the irrigated lands, therefore, the population of the Mountain and Desert region is generally dispersed, strung out along the transcontinental routes. For all this, it is a population that probably feels itself less isolated than that of the Great Plains or the northern Great Lakes region. Its business brings it in daily contact with people who have just left Chicago or Los Angeles, Toronto or Vancouver. High in the Rockies, or servicing the cars of nocturnal desert-crossers in Nevada, it is in touch, even if vicariously, with the outside world.

There is, however, another antidote to isolation in the Mountain and Desert region, and that is the tourist traffic. While commercial tourism in the west may be said to have begun in 1872, with the opening of Yellowstone National Park, its modern development has been based on the motor-car and the extension of the region's road network. Banff and Jasper, Yellowstone and Grand Canyon have become places familiar to millions who visit each year these products of glacial erosion, volcanic activity, or desert weathering. The distinctive cultures of the Spanish South-West and the Indian Reservations attract other thousands. Tourism has been responsible for the opening of large sections of the region which previously were

---

[1] This influence has been examined in detail by C. D. Harris, in *Salt Lake City: A Regional Capital*, Univ. of Chicago Libraries, 1940.

PLATE XIX

Los Angeles: The city centre from the north-east. The tower at the left is the City Hall; that in the right foreground is the railway station, designed in California's characteristic 'Spanish mission' style of architecture. The earthquake hazard has restricted the height of most of the city's buildings, and rapid development (compare Fig. 33) has prevented the city centre from achieving, on a widespread scale, the urban elegance suggested by this picture

PLATE XX

The Central Valley of California: Irrigated vineyards near Fresno, one of the state's main wine-producing centres. The contrast with European vineyard landscapes needs no stressing

both valueless and inaccessible. Lacking the profitable resource base of the lowlands, the mountain states have made capital out of their scenery. Settlements have sprung up to serve and house the tourists, and many of those who came as visitors have returned later, especially to the southern part of the region, as residents.

There are, in a sense, two separate tourist industries in the west—the summer and the winter trade. In summer, with roads open at the highest elevations, the tourist traffic flows into the remotest parts of the region, by car and on horseback; only the hottest desert areas in the south-west are closed to it. In September, however, the mountain roads begin to close, and with this closure—only the major routes are kept open—the service population withdraws, leaving whole sections of the mountains empty of inhabitants until the following spring. The winter tourist traffic then begins, making either for the winter sports centres, such as Banff, Sun Valley, Ida., or Aspen, Colo., or for the state of Arizona which, like Florida and southern California, attracts visitors by offering them a January mean temperature of 45 to 50° F. and clear, dry weather. Then, too, is the season to explore Death Valley and the deserts of the south-west.

Tourist facilities are constantly being improved; new settlements spring up, and new roads are cut farther into the wilderness. Such roads as the Banff–Jasper Highway, the 'Going to the Sun' mountain road in Glacier National Park, and the roads above the 10,000-foot contour in the Colorado Rockies are, besides being a testimony to engineering skill, a token of the force of modern tourism in opening the remoter west.

So far, we have been considering the *use* of this region. Before concluding this chapter, however, we should briefly consider what has been called its 'non-use'.

In modern North America, with a population which is overwhelmingly urban in character, there is a need, which is both physical and emotional, for open space and the life of the wild. So much of nature—animal and plant life—is threatened by the growth of the cities that there are very strong pressure groups which urge that the preservation of the west as a nature reserve should be undertaken as a matter of policy.

This is not a new idea: the United States already has 31 million acres of national and state parks, and Canada has 55 million. And to press for extension of these areas is extremely aggravating to the westerners who are or would be denied the use of the lands insulated by reservation. On these nature reserves, wild life increases, and the surrounding ranch and farmlands may suffer its depredations. What is more, such non-use, or 'single-use' as it is perhaps fairer to call it, contravenes the basic principle with which we began, that in the west the important economic point is that only by multiple use, the combination of all possible forms of resource value, can these lands pay for themselves. The old 'single-use' problem of the west arose from such activities as wheat monoculture and overgrazing. Today's problem is different in detail, and moreover it is willed upon the region from outside (for the pressure comes from city-based groups.) But it is the same problem in essence: how to make the Mountain and Desert Region a valued and valuable part of the nation.

FURTHER READING

O v e r this large region, descriptive coverage is inevitably patchy. A general work on the whole area is M. E. Garnsey's *America's New Frontier: The Mountain West*; on the specific aspects indicated by their titles, there are S. T. Dana's *Forest and Range Policy* and M. H. Saunderson's *Western Land and Water Use* or, as a short reference, his 'Western Range Land Use and Conservation Problems', *Journ. Farm Econ.*, vol. xxxi, pp. 985–97. M. Clawson's *Uncle Sam's Acres* covers the public domain in the U.S.A. and its problems, as does his article 'Economic Possibilities of the Public Domain', *Land Economics*, vol. xxix, pp. 187–99. See also the references to Chapters III and IV, *The North American Deserts*, by E. C. Jaeger, and *Land Use Policy and Problems in the United States*, ed. H. W. Ottoson.

Ranching is dealt with by E. E. Dale in *The Range Cattle Industry*, M. Clawson in *The Western Range Livestock Industry* and by M. H. Saunderson in *Western Stock Ranching*, and on a local scale by J. I. Colbert in 'Cattle Industry of New Mexico', *Econ. Geog.*, vol. xvii, pp. 155–68; E. Mather in in 'The Production and Marketing of Wyoming Beef Cattle', ibid., vol. xxvi, pp. 81–93, and T. R. Weir in 'The Physical Basis of Ranching in the Interior Plateau of British Columbia', *Geog. Bull.*, No. 3 (1953), pp. 1–22. On the grazing permit system, see 'Administration of Grazing Districts', by J. R. Penny and M. Clawson, *Land Economics*, vol. xxix, pp. 23–34. On all matters affecting western vegetation and its use, the relevant sections of *Grass*, the U.S. Dept. of Agriculture Yearbook, 1948, and *Trees*, the 1949 Yearbook, are valuable references. On the specific effects of overgrazing, see

'Influence of Grazing on Plant Succession of Rangelands', by L. Ellison, *Botanical Review*, vol. xxvi, pp. 1–78.

On irrigation farming, apart from the general works mentioned in Chapter IV, see P. Meigs, 'Water Problems in the United States', *Geog. Review*, vol. xlii, pp. 346–66; C. W. Olmstead's 'American Orchard and Vineyard Regions', *Econ. Geog.*, vol. xxxii, pp. 189–236, and the article on Arizona, by W. G. V. Balchin and N. Pye mentioned above.

On other aspects of the region's economy, see 'Mining Development in British Columbia', by J. F. Walker, *Can. Geog. Journ.*, vol. xlv, pp. 114–32; 'An Analysis of Postwar Industrial Migration to Utah and Colorado', by J. D. Garwood, *Econ. Geog.*, vol. xxix, pp. 79–88, and 'Manufacturing in Arizona', by T. McKnight, *Univ. of Calif. Pubs. in Geog.*, vol. viii, pp. 289–344, and the following urban studies: *Salt Lake City: A Regional Capital*, by C. D. Harris, or his briefer 'Location of Salt Lake City', *Econ. Geog.*, vol. xvii, pp. 204–12; 'Tucson: City of Sunshine', by M. T. Parker, ibid., vol. xxiv, pp. 79–113; 'A Typology of Arizona Communities', by W. C. Bailey, ibid., vol. xxvi, pp. 94–104; 'Pocatello, Idaho, as a Railroad Centre', by R. Wrigley, ibid., vol. xix, pp. 325–36, and 'Barstow, California: A Transportation Focus in a Desert Environment', by J. Garrison, ibid., vol. xxix, pp. 159–67. Useful studies covering parts of the region are 'Das Mormonenland' (the areas of Mormon settlement in Utah, Idaho, &c.), by H. Lautensach, *Bonner Geog. Abhandlungen*, Heft 11, and 'The Indian Country of Southern Arizona', by J. W. Hoover, *Geog. Review*, vol. xix, pp. 38–60; see also his 'The Hopi Indian Country of Arizona', ibid., vol. xx, pp. 425–44, and 'Conservation and Stock Reduction on the Navajo Tribal Range', by L. S. Fonaroff, *Geog. Review*, vol. liii, pp. 200–23. The southern parts of the region are covered in *California and The Southwest*, ed. C. M. Zierer, and *The American Southwest*, by N. N. Dodge and H. S. Zim.

On tourism, see 'Tourism and Recreation in the West', by C. M. Zierer, *Geog. Review*, vol. xliii, pp. 462–81, or the longer *In Search of the Golden West; The Tourist in Western America*, by E. Pomeroy.

XVII

CALIFORNIA

1. *Introduction*

CALIFORNIA has been a name to conjure with for more than a century. Since the gold discoveries of 1848 brought in the 'Forty-Niners', the state has seldom been out of the news for long. Yet it is probable that nothing would surprise the old-timers more, with their memories of dry grasslands and scanty food supplies, than the information that the California they knew had become the home of some 13 million Americans, the site of great cities, and one of the world's richest agricultural areas, and that the value of the gold they so laboriously won had long since been eclipsed by that of the crops and the manufactures produced within the state.

Their surprise would probably increase on learning that the intensive development of today has spread even to those areas which to them must have seemed most forbidding. The deserts of the southern Central Valley have become an area of cotton and fruit farms, while the dry scrubland south of the Tehachapi Mountains is now the site of a conurbation whose population is more than 6 millions; even the Mohave Desert is now dotted with ranches and railway repair shops.[1] Only Death Valley remains largely untamed.

For modern California is, to a considerable extent, the creation of the Americans who have chosen to make their homes there. In particular, it is the water engineer who has made the present measure of settlement possible, by transferring water from rugged mountains to dry plains and from rivers to irrigated fields.

The physical obstacles that confronted the pioneers were formidable indeed. To reach their new homes, intending Californians had first to cross the 7,000-foot passes of the Sierra Nevada and find their way down through snowdrifts, forests, and canyons to the Central Valley. Once they were west of the Sierras, they entered a region where the characteristic landscape consisted of grass-covered hills, dry and brown under the

[1] See J. Garrison, 'Barstow, California: A Transportation Focus in a Desert Environment', *Econ. Geog.*, vol. xxix, pp. 159–67.

summer sun, with shrub-sized trees on their higher slopes and
desert scrub on the valley floors. The Mexicans who were the
first white settlers in California were ranchers, and when the
territory was ceded to the U.S.A. in 1848 the only agriculture
was in the immediate neighbourhood of the Spanish religious
missions, which had been founded in the eighteenth century.

The climate of California, as we have seen in Chapter I, is
generally classified as 'Mediterranean', but this is a serious
over-simplification, which conceals important differences between, for example, the northern and southern ends of the
Central Valley, or between the coastal hills and similar
elevations at the foot of the Sierras. Along the coast, mean
temperatures increase, and rainfall decreases, with fair
regularity from north to south. However, over the coastal
waters of the Pacific, which are cooled by the south-flowing
California Current, fog is frequent, especially in summer, in
the immediate vicinity of the coast. Thus San Franciscans
spend many summer hours in unseasonable gloom, and the July
mean temperature is held down to 59° F., giving the city an
annual temperature range of less than 10°.

In the Central Valley conditions of both temperature and
rainfall show much wider extremes; indeed, the climate is more
accurately classified as continental. We may illustrate this by
comparing the climatic data for three valley stations (identified
on Fig. 70) with those for stations in the same latitude on the
coast. In each of the three pairs listed in the table overleaf, the
valley station is given first, and the coastal station corresponding with it in parenthesis after it.

Rainfall diminishes from north to south through the Central
Valley, and at the southern end true desert is encountered. At
the same time, the eastern side, nearer the Sierras, is generally
wetter than the western. Both on the coast and in the valley
the summer months are almost rainless: Bakersfield receives
only 0·6 inches between May and September. Summer temperatures are high, and winter frosts limit the growing season
in the valley. In all this the effect of the coastal hills in shutting
off marine influences is marked, for the figures given below
reveal that at Stockton, inland from the only break in the hills
(at San Francisco Bay), the July temperature is moderated, and
the growing season is lengthened, by the entry of maritime air.

Climatic Data for Selected Central Valley Stations and Coastal Stations in California

	Growing season (days)	Av. annual precipitation (in.)	July mean temperature
Northern End			
Redding . . .	278	37	82° F.
(Eureka . . .	328	37	56° F.)
Centre			
Stockton . . .	287	14	74° F.
(San Francisco . .	356	20	59° F.)
Southern End			
Bakersfield . .	277	6	83° F.
(San Luis Obispo .	320	22	64° F.)

The coastal hills and the Sierra Nevada turn inwards at their southern end to enclose the Central Valley, and south of their junction lie the plains on which Los Angeles has grown up. Such a southerly position within the state means higher temperatures and lower rainfall than on the coast farther north, but the low elevation of the plains permits air from the Pacific to flow inland without hindrance. This carries the moderating influence of the ocean into southern California, but it also brings Los Angeles its now-famous smog. Maritime air spreads inland until blocked by the mountains farther back, and being very stable it lies over the metropolitan area, where the exhaust fumes of a million vehicles create below it a dense and irritating fog, with a dangerously high ozone content. It is a singular climatic irony that denies to the inhabitants of the two great Californian cities a sight of the sun that drenches the rest of their state.

The great barrier of the Sierra Nevada lies across the path of moisture-bearing winds off the Pacific, its crestline rising from 4,000 or 5,000 feet above sea-level opposite the northern end of the Central Valley to 9,000 feet in the south, with individual peaks thrusting above this level to 13,000 or 14,000 feet. Consequently it receives a very heavy precipitation which, since it falls mainly in winter, produces an annual snowfall of up to 400 inches. This snow cover forms an invaluable reservoir for central and southern California during the rainless lowland summer.

East of the mountains there is an abrupt decline in precipitation, reflected in a swift transition from alpine pasture, through forest, to scrub and desert. From the mountains, only a few ribbons of vegetation run out into the basins of eastern California and Nevada, where east-flowing streams penetrate only a short distance before losing themselves in the desert sinks.

2. *The Settlement of California*

Such is the region to which hundreds of thousands of Americans have migrated since 1848. The original incentive is plain: it was California's gold. The sparse population of Indians and Mexican ranchers was soon engulfed in a wave of miners and camp followers, pouring in either overland, or by sea to San Francisco, which rapidly became the commercial focus of the region. There followed a lull after this before the next wave of settlers came in with the newly constructed railways, the first of which reached California in 1869. Out of the competition between them was born the Southern Californian boom. Heads of families were encouraged to prospect for a Californian home by the offer of a return ticket from Midwestern cities to Los Angeles for $1. The railways brought a host of settlers to the dry southern plains, where commercial orange growing was established before the end of the century. By the First World War, therefore, there were two population nuclei in California, with the newer southern one rapidly overtaking the older-established region round San Fransico Bay.

Since the First World War, California has experienced a continuously high rate of immigration from states farther east. Over the years, however, the character of the immigrants has varied. In the 1920's, when roughly $1\frac{1}{4}$ million people moved into the state, the majority were Midwesterners of adequate means, looking for new opportunities in pleasant surroundings. These new-comers tended to settle in the cities. Then came the depression of 1929–33. The 1930's again brought over a million immigrants to California, but they were of very different character from those of the previous decade. Many of them were destitute farmers from the depression-ridden, drought-hit

Agricultural Interior—the 'Okies' (from Oklahoma, one of the
worst dustbowl areas) immortalized by John Steinbeck in *The
Grapes of Wrath.* Unlike their predecessors, they sought work
on the land. There was little enough work to be had, but somehow California absorbed them too.

The 1940's brought new circumstances—war and the growth
of industry. To man the war industries, some 1½ million people
entered the state; they in turn created a market which attracted
other industries. Between 1940 and 1950 the population of
California increased from 6·9 to 10·6 millions.

The 1950's were like the 1940's, but on a larger scale. Three
million people arrived in California from other states. Most of
these post-war immigrants have fallen into two categories. They
were either elderly people moving to a warm climate where
they could spend their retirement, or they were young and
active people who were impressed by the possibilities and the
wealth of California. Almost all of them made for the cities, for
by this time the state which had attracted first miners and then
farmers was well launched on its industrial and commercial
career.

As the population of California increased, so its agriculture
developed and changed. In 1848 California was cattle country;
huge Mexican ranches occupied most of the lowlands. The
gold rush created a local demand for food supplies, and, while
cattle were raised in increasing numbers, there was a growing
diversification to supply this market. Then in the 1870's
drought undermined the cattle industry, and for the next decade the state's farmers turned to sheep raising. The 1880's
saw another change, this time to wheat growing; the ranges
were ploughed up, and by 1890 California had achieved the
position of second wheat state in the Union.

It was in the last two decades of the nineteenth century that
there began to develop the fruit growing which has brought
California more permanent wealth and fame. The construction
of railways in southern California made possible the shipment
of fresh fruit to worthwhile markets, and the new enterprise,
sedulously publicized by the railways, provoked a tremendous
land boom, as we have seen, in the arid and formerly worthless
surroundings of Los Angeles, while other areas of the state
developed their own fruit and vegetable specialities.

3. Modern Californian Agriculture

California today has the largest aggregate farm income of any state in the U.S.A., and, as in the states of the central Corn Belt and New England, average land values are very high.

It is as a fruit producer that California is now renowned, but its very fame in this connexion may make it necessary to counter at once an impression that fruit trees grow everywhere in the state, or that there is some simple reason why they do so. In reality, about one-third of the state's farm income is derived from sales of fruit and vegetables; livestock products and cotton provide most of the remainder. The fruit areas are of limited extent and well-defined, each specializing in a particular crop. Localizing factors of production vary, not only for each crop, but for each intended crop use, so that peaches for canning, for example, are produced in different areas from those destined for sale as dried fruit.

What are the features of this vast agricultural enterprise? They can be briefly summarized under four headings.

1. Owing to its north–south extent and its climatic range, California produces a wide variety of crops. By guarding against the danger of frost its farmers can produce tropical crops, and by ensuring the water-supply they can produce temperate-zone crops.

2. Although farm production for the state as a whole is very varied, production of individual crops is highly localized. Thus, for example, a farmer in the Watsonville area of the Pajaro Valley is likely to be highly dependent on the apple crop, his colleague at Paso Robles in the upper Salinas Valley on almonds, and at Fresno in the Central Valley on grapes. While these local concentrations illustrate a continent-wide trend towards specialization in fruit and vegetable growing which we have already encountered farther east, they inevitably increase the farmer's risks, and in California they create the extra complication that they make the demand for labour highly seasonal. As a result, California makes use of a large migrant labour force (a considerable part of which is Mexican and Filipino) to harvest the fruit crops, and these workers move from area to area with the harvest seasons. In the Central Valley, for

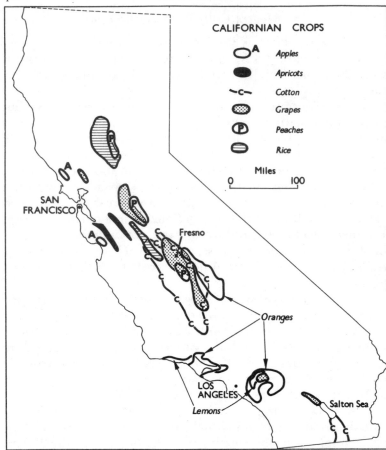

FIG. 69. California: Specialized crop areas. The map gives an indication of the fact that, although the range of products of California's agriculture is immense, the cultivation of these crops is generally highly localized (see p. 409). The areas shown contain over 90 per cent. of the acreage within the state devoted to each crop.

example, the demand for seasonal labour varies from a March low of some 23,000 to a September peak of almost 120,000.[1] While the localization of production is a convenience to these workers, the existence of such a group raises serious social problems.

[1] U.S. Dept. of the Interior, Bureau of Reclamation, *Central Valley Project Studies, Problem 24,* Washington, D.C., 1949, p. 121. For later details, reflecting the impact of cotton growing on the labour situation, see D. C. Large's 1957 article in Further Reading, p. 421.

3. Development of California's special fruit and vegetable crops has resulted in a relative neglect of basic agricultural items, such as stock feeds and livestock products. With a rapidly increasing population, the rising local demand for food supplies has run counter to the Californian habit of producing for sale outside the state. Thus while it possesses some 40 per cent. of the United States' orchard and vineyard area,[1] is the sole United States producer of several exotic crops, and is the major producer of at least ten, the state imports livestock products for local consumption.

This concentration on special crops brings us to what is, perhaps, the most important consideration for the Californian farmer—his dependence on out-of-state markets. His fruit, vegetables, and wine must be sold in highly competitive, distant markets, and against the hazard of fluctuating consumer tastes. He must rely on good transport and attractive packaging, if he is to out-sell rivals situated nearer the markets in the east.

4. From this last consideration we pass, logically enough, to the final feature of Californian agriculture—large-scale operations in production, processing, and marketing. For the success of California's speciality crops has been secured by organization, an organization taking two forms. Firstly, market agencies have been set up to provide quality controls, selling arrangements, and bargaining power over against the railways, from which they have obtained favourable freight rates on Californian produce moving east (see p. 76). Secondly, specialized crop production has given rise to a situation in which each line of production is dominated by two or three large firms, usually canners or processers, which effectively control the output of the individual farmer, and may themselves be the principal producers of the crop. This gives rise to the now-familiar generalization that in California farming is not a 'way-of-life' but a 'business', and that the part of it which deals with speciality crops is, in many ways, organized more like industry than agriculture.

In the development of the whole of California's agriculture, irrigation has played a vital part. Today, with more than 7 million acres under irrigation, California leads all other states in this respect. While this acreage includes a large number of scattered, private enterprises, three areas outrank all others in importance. The first, and largest, is the Central Valley, the second is the Los Angeles area, and the third the Imperial–Coachella Valleys in the extreme south.

The Central Valley Project of the Bureau of Reclamation has been based on a bold but simple concept. The valley is occupied by two main rivers, the Sacramento in the north and the San Joaquin in the south, the two joining to reach the sea at San Francisco Bay. Along their courses, some 9 million acres of the valley floor are irrigable; about two-thirds of this are along the San Joaquin, and one-third along the Sacramento. But to make use of this land, the valley's natural water-supply is badly distributed; some two-thirds are produced in the north, where remaining irrigable land is scarce, and only one-third in the southern half, where it is plentiful.

The project was designed, therefore, to transfer part of the unused flow of the Sacramento into the San Joaquin. By this means, some 650,000 acres of new lands could be irrigated, and, equally important, added security could be given to farmers already depending on the limited water-supplies in the San Joaquin Valley.

The main task of water transfer is achieved by means of the Delta–Mendota Canal, from the lower Sacramento to Mendota on the San Joaquin. North of Mendota, therefore, the canal water can substitute for the waters of the San Joaquin, thus making the entire flow of the latter available for use south of this point. Here a widespread system of new regulating works and canals has brought assured water-supply to both old and new irrigated lands between Fresno and the Kern River at the southern tip of the valley. Altogether, the farming of some 5 million acres has been affected by the project.

On the new farm lands of the Central Valley the Bureau of Reclamation hoped to encourage farmers to adopt a balanced agriculture of crops and livestock. But instead, the valley has continued the modern Californian trend to crop specialization. The particular agricultural phenomenon of these lands has been the remarkable development of cotton growing since 1939.

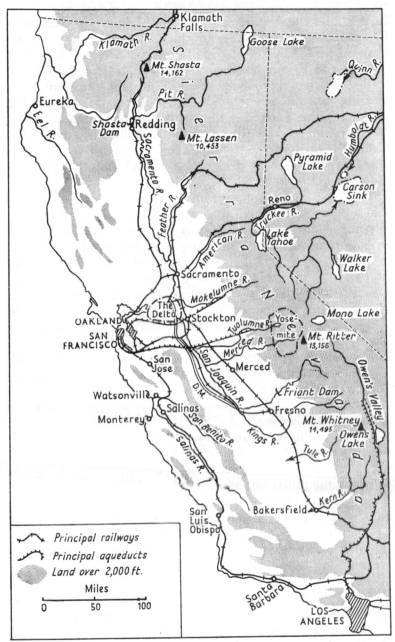

FIG. 70. Central California: Location Map. (DM=Delta–Mendota Canal.)

In that year there were 334,000 acres of cotton in California. By 1961, in spite of quota restrictions, there were 815,000, and California had the second largest output of cotton of any state. Most of this cotton is grown under irrigation in the Central Valley; much of it (70–80 per cent.) is mechanically harvested, and the state law whereby all cotton farmers are required to grow the same variety of the plant has made for maximum efficiency in research, production, and harvesting, so that California's cotton yields—which average about 1,000 lb. per acre—are more than twice the national average, and the highest for any state.

The second important area under irrigation is in the counties that surround the city of Los Angeles. Here, on the dry alluvial fans at the foot of the San Gabriel and Santa Ana Mountains, irrigation has brought into being an agricultural area whose output is truly remarkable. While the area is best known for its orange groves, other forms of production abound. Orange County has the largest concentration of orange trees in the U.S.A.; Ventura County, to the north-west of the metropolis, is noted for its lemons and its vegetables (especially lima beans); and Los Angeles County itself leads the nation both in total value of farm produce and in value of dairy products sold.

The third main irrigated zone of California is in the Imperial and Coachella Valleys. The first of these was brought to agricultural life as a private project as early as 1901, but it was swept out of existence again in 1905, when the Colorado River in flood broke its west bank, flowed into the desert, and created the Salton Sea. A new project replaced it, and this, together with the Coachella Project farther north-west, was given new security and added water resources by the opening in 1935 of the government's Hoover Dam, which controls the Colorado, and by the All-American Canal (see Fig. 72). Today these lands produce citrus fruits, cotton, dates, and vegetables (notably carrots and lettuce), and claim, like corresponding areas of Florida and Texas, the title of Winter Garden.

California's agricultural output is one of the marvels of the American economy. But to put this phenomenon in its true setting we must recall the point made in Chapter IV—that great as this agricultural production may be, it is only one source of income to a state in which urban and residential land uses are spreading so swiftly across former farm land: more important, it is only one competitor among many for the available water supply. As a result, the amount of space that can be devoted to agriculture has shrunk, especially in southern California, and this has given rise to a particular kind of 'urban farming' which requires a minimum of space. It is typified by the 'dry-lot' dairy farming of the Los Angeles suburbs, where cattle are stall-fed on purchased feeds; that is, it is dairy farming without the fields. Unfortunately, however, no one can grow oranges without orange groves, and so the orchard lands are constantly disappearing beneath new housing estates. Too many people want to live in southern California to leave room for the old style of farm.

4. Californian Industry

The number of employees in California's industries increased from 300,000 in 1939 to 1·3 million in 1961. This great industrial growth was both cause and effect of the rise in California's population over the same period. On the one hand, the war in the Pacific from 1941 to 1945 created a demand for manufactured goods on the west coast, and workers moved into the state in large numbers to meet this need. On the other hand, they and their families created an expanded market to satisfy which, after the war, manufacturers set up plants in the west. Then again, the abundant labour supply provided by the immigrants, together with the specific Californian locational advantages such as the climate, set off a new round of industrialization, and so the process has continued.

In 1939 it was the food processing industries that dominated California's manufacturing, giving employment to almost three times as many workers as any other group of industries. Since the war, however, the manufacture of transport equipment has taken first place, thanks in part to war-time developments in shipbuilding, but more particularly to the rise of the Southern Californian aircraft industry. This is an industrial giant which, having grown from small beginnings in the 1920's, now rings Los Angeles with aircraft and missile plants, and provides nearly 30 per cent. of its industrial employment. Other industries which, in conformity with national developments, have contributed to the rapid increase in the state's production are the manufacture of metal goods, machinery, and chemicals. The automobile industry, as has been its practice, has established plants near San Francisco and Los Angeles for local assembly of the motor vehicles which Californians own in such numbers; in the Los Angeles area there is one car to every 2·2 persons.

This has been an industrialization for which the materials usually considered basic—coal and iron ore—are almost entirely lacking. It is true that California has a small steel production—to which the best-known contributor is the Fontana Works, set among the orange groves east of Los Angeles. But the State's coal supplies are meagre, and steel output is based largely on scrap. California's more obvious natural resources are its oilfields, which are scattered widely through the southern part of the state, and its hydro-electricity, which has been made available by the construction of the numerous flood control and irrigation schemes.

In California, at the 1960 census, the population was 85 per cent. urban, a proportion exceeded only by a few states in the metropolitan north-east. This fact calls attention to the drawing power, in the migration to California, of the two great metropolitan areas of the Los Angeles Lowland (including the large separate centre of San Diego) and the San Francisco Bay region. It is here that the new-comers settle; it is here, too, that industry tends to concentrate (at the 1958 census, the two S.M.S.A.'s and San Diego County contained 80 per cent. of the state's production workers), and commercially one dominates northern, as the other dominates southern, California.

San Francisco achieved early prominence as the port of entry for the goldfields after 1848. Devastated by the earthquake of 1906, it lost its lead in population to Los Angeles during the following decade. In 1960 the city had a population of 740,000; its sister city across the Bay, Oakland, had 367,000 inhabitants; and the S.M.S.A. included a further 1,675,000 in other communities along the shores of San Francisco Bay.

The industries of the Bay region are very varied; but, as might be expected of an area that handles almost a third of the water-borne commerce of the United State's Pacific coast, ship-

PLATE XXI

The Columbia River Gorge at Crown Point, Oregon, looking upstream. Road and railway routes follow each bank of the river, utilizing the only low-level route through the western mountains in the 1,200 miles between the Fraser River and Los Angeles

PLATE XXII

The Columbia River: Grand Coulee Dam, Washington. The Grand Coulee, with its reservoir (see Fig. 75), lies off the picture to the right

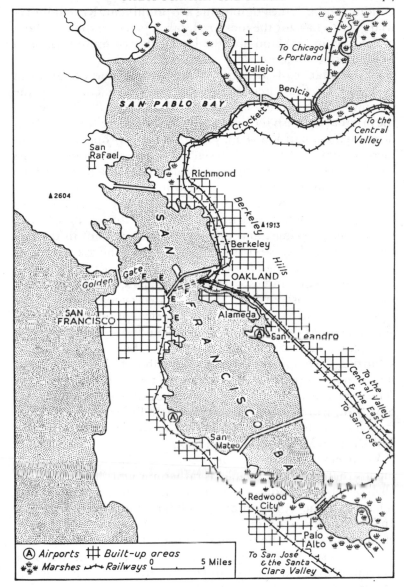

FIG. 71. California: The San Francisco Bay Region. Notice EE, the Embarcadero, where the piers of San Francisco's port are situated. F is the old rail ferry connexion between the city and the railheads in Oakland.

building and marine engineering are prominent. Recent industrial growth has, for the most part, taken place on the east shore of the Bay, in Oakland and the Upper Bay communities, such as Richmond (80,000).

This last fact calls attention to the nature—and the problem —of the San Francisco metropolitan area. Its core is on the narrow, hilly peninsula between the Pacific and the Bay, where the original Spanish settlement stood, and where there remains no room for expansion. Today San Francisco proper is the commercial centre—'the City' to central California—and is a port handling passenger traffic in particular, while Oakland and the outlying communities are industrial and residential, and handle much of the freight traffic of the Bay Harbour. This means that a high proportion of San Francisco's workers live, spend their earnings, and pay their local taxes not in the city but across the Bay, and travel to work over the great bridges (see Fig. 71) that span it.

Between San Francisco and Los Angeles, judged as cities, there is little comparison: San Francisco occupies one of the world's finest urban settings; Los Angeles sprawls disjointedly across 50 miles of plains and foothills, and it is separated from the coast and from its port, near Long Beach, by a belt of suburban development interspersed with oilfields. Yet it is the southern metropolis that has outgrown the northern. The 1960 census gave a population of 6·7 millions for the Los Angeles S.M.S.A., which meant that it had risen by nearly 2½ millions from its 1950 level of 4·3 millions. The 1960 population of the San Diego S.M.S.A. was 1,033,000.

What employment can the newcomers find? The employment structure of Los Angeles is rather unusual. Apart from the 50,000 persons employed in 'entertainment and recreation', it has the highest proportion of its labour force in construction and retail trade to be found in any large American city. This is, of course, a sign of the tremendous growth and great wealth of the city. Los Angeles also has important commercial functions in relation to oil, insurance, and foreign trade, and many federal agencies use it as a regional headquarters. Manufacturing employs a third of the labour force. Apart from consumer goods industries for the huge local market, this 'manufacturing' in the Los Angeles area means aircraft and missiles.

Here, if anywhere, is the point of weakness in the regional economy. The air vehicle industry is one which is very susceptible to fluctuations in demand and cancellation of contracts, simply because progress in it is so rapid that it is hard to know what will be needed next. In 1947, employment in the aircraft industry was 150,000. In 1957, it was 555,000, and in 1958 it was 377,000. While there is no doubt that, over a period, this is a growth industry, it is risky for a region to depend too heavily on it for employment.

This is a lesson which southern California, like the Boston area (p. 222) has had to learn, and one which is most evident if we move on from Los Angeles to San Diego. Such has been the growth of Los Angeles that it is easy to overlook San Diego, 125 miles away to the south. Yet San Diego is a city of more than a million people which, in any other company, would rank as a great urban centre. It grew up as a fishing port and naval base, and as a place to retire to in the sun. But then came an industrial boom based on the air and space vehicle industry, and its fortunes since that time have fluctuated rather seriously.

In the absence of any major relief obstacles the Los Angeles area has developed what seems likely to become the typical urban pattern of this motor-car–electricity–social planning century, much as 'dark, Satanic mills' epitomized the century of the Industrial Revolution. The core of the metropolitan area —central Los Angeles itself—contains public buildings, offices, car parks—and a giant cross-roads (see Fig. 33). The commercial and social life of the community is carried on not so much here as in a series of centres that surround the core at a distance of 5 to 15 miles—Pasadena, Hollywood, Santa Monica, Long Beach—and that offer a full range of services. They function as cities in their own right and, in turn, have their own suburbs and satellites. In such a layout road communications are vital, and the huge volume of daily inter-urban movement carried on in Los Angeles has made necessary the construction of scores of miles of 'freeways' since the Second World War.

Inevitably, the question arises how long California, and especially southern California, can maintain its breakneck rate of population growth and economic development. Employment openings have so far kept up with population increase,

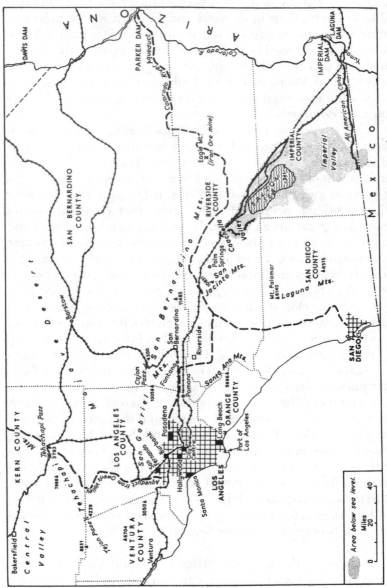

FIG. 72. Southern California: Relief, Routes, and Water-supply.

and although, in the immediate neighbourhood of the cities, space is becoming a problem, yet settlement is continually being carried into new areas on the desert edges. The real limiting factor is water, and the real problem is to decide how best to use it. It seems true to say that, unless a technique can soon be developed for obtaining fresh water from the sea on a large scale, California will be forced to choose between irrigation agriculture and the expansion of population and industry. The state's 7 million acres of irrigated land make astronomical demands on the limited water available; they represent, in fact, an extravagance which, after another decade of population increase at the present rate, the state could hardly support. Already the water table in many of the irrigated areas has fallen dangerously, and in doing so has rendered adjacent areas barren.[1] The use of water for irrigation competes directly with its use in cities and factories; already Californian industries, in order to conserve water, have had to modify their practices in such a way as to use water several times over instead of dis-charging it.

We have seen how, in the Central Valley, the problem is that there is water to spare at the northern end of the valley and a shortage at the southern end. Exactly the same thing is true for the state as a whole: the northern end has the water, and the southern end has the population and the demand. Con-sequently, southern California has had to reach farther and farther afield for its water supplies. Up till now, its two main sources have been the Colorado River to the east, and Owens Valley, 250 miles away to the north. From both of these points aqueducts bring the water to Los Angeles (Fig. 72). But California's share of the Colorado water is limited by the Colorado River Compact, which divides the flow of the 'Nile of America' between the states of the upper and lower basins and Mexico. Although California's allocation is over half the total water available, it has tried repeatedly to have its share increased—and has naturally been opposed by the equally ambitious state of Arizona. In Owens Valley, the frustration is much the same: the Los Angeles catchment area runs to the

---

[1] For details, see such studies as 'Water Problems in the United States', by P. Meigs, or 'The Southern California Water Problem in the Oxnard Area', by H. F. Gregor, *Geog. Review*, vol. xlii, pp. 346–66 and 16–33 respectively.

crest of the Sierras—where it is blocked by the domain of San Francisco, whose water is drawn from the west side of the mountains.

To crowd 8 million people into a plain with an annual rainfall of 12–15 inches, 200 miles from a major river, is to pose a problem of supply and demand that might make even a Californian quail. But two solutions are proposed. One is already under construction—the Feather River Project. This is the Central Valley Project over again, this time carrying the water not merely to the southern part of the valley, but by a series of aqueducts to San Francisco Bay and southern California as well. In all, over 3 million acre-feet will be supplied to the drier parts of the state.

The other, and more radical, solution proposed is to set up a federal 'water grid' for the country as a whole, and transmit water in the same way as electricity is transmitted to the point of demand. California could then draw on the great water resources of the Pacific North-West, which lie outside its control. With such a federal grid, it would hope to be supplied with water enough to do what it certainly proposes to do—go on growing.

FURTHER READING

THE most recent textbooks on this state are *California and the Southwest*, ed. C. M. Zierer, and *California, The New Empire State*, by P. E. Griffin and R. N. Young. Climate is dealt with by R. J. Russell in 'Climates of California', *Univ. of Calif. Pubs. in Geog.*, vol. ii, No. 4, pp. 73–84; specific topics are covered by C. P. Patton in 'Climatology of Summer Fogs in the San Francisco Bay Area', *Univ. of Calif. Pubs. in Geog.*, vol. x, No. 3, pp. 113–200, and by M. K. Bennett in 'Climate and Agriculture in California', *Econ. Geog.*, vol. xv, pp. 153–64.

On settlement in early California, see S. J. Jones, 'Some Regional Aspects of Native California', *S.G.M.*, vol. lxvii, pp. 19–30, and R. Gentilcore, 'Missions and Mission Lands in Alta California', *A.A.A.G.*, vol. li, pp. 46–72. *California Agriculture*, ed. C. B. Hutchison, is the standard work on the state's farming; see also 'The Local Supply Agriculture of California', in *A.A.A.G.*, vol. xlvii, pp. 267–75, which is by H. F. Gregor, who is the most prolific writer on Californian agriculture and land use. Special topics are covered by the following: G. J. Fielding, 'The Los Angeles Milkshed: A Study of the Political Factor in Agriculture', *Geog. Review*, vol. liv, pp. 1–12, P. Meigs, 'Current Trends in California Orchards and Vineyards', *Econ. Geog.*, vol. xvii, pp. 275–86; D. C. Large, 'Cotton in the San Joaquin Valley', *Geog. Review*, vol. xlvii, pp. 365–80, and C. M. Zierer, 'The Citrus Fruit

Industry of the Los Angeles Basin', *Econ. Geog.*, vol. x, pp. 53–73. Studies of smaller regions of the state include those on the Santa Lucia Region by J. W. Coulter, *Geog. Review*, vol. xx, pp. 469–79; the Santa Clara Valley, by E. N. Torbert, ibid., vol. xxvi, pp. 247–63; Owens Valley, by Ruth E. Baugh, *Econ. Geog.*, vol. xiii, pp. 17–34; the Ventura Lowland, by H. F. Gregor, ibid., vol. xxix, pp. 340–61; the Central Valley Project, by Elizabeth Eiselen, ibid., vol. xxiii, pp. 22–31; the Ygnacio Valley, by D. Goodau and T. C. Shatto, ibid., vol. xxiv, pp. 135–48, and the Coachella, by R. M. Glendinning, *Geog. Review*, vol. xxxix, pp. 221–8.

On California's population, see W. S. Thompson, *Growth and Changes in California's Population*, and E. L. Ullman, 'Amenities as a Factor in Regional Growth', *Geog. Review*, vol. xliv, pp. 119–32; also two articles by H. F. Gregor, 'Urban Pressures on California Land', *Land Economics*, vol. xxxiii, pp. 311–25, and 'Spatial Disharmonies in California Population Growth', *Geog. Review*, vol. liii, pp. 100–22. See also 'Geographical Setting of San Francisco', by E. Rostlund, *Journ. Geog.*, vol. liv, pp. 441–8; 'Recent Land-Use Changes in the San Francisco Bay Area', by R. N. Young and P. C. Griffin, *Geog. Review*, vol. xlvii, pp. 396–405, and H. Gilliam's *San Francisco Bay* and M. Scott's *The San Francisco Bay Area; A Metropolis In Perspective*. On southern California, see the symposium, 'Man, Time and Space in Southern California', ed. W. L. Thomas and published as a supplement (120 pp.) to *A.A.A.G.*, vol. xlix. On industry, see J. J. Parsons, 'California Manufacturing', *Geog. Review*, vol. xxxix, pp. 229–41, W. G. Cunningham's *The Aircraft Industry*, and 'The Unorthodox San Francisco Bay Area Electronics Industry', by C. L. White and H. M. Forde, *Journ. Geog.*, vol. lix, pp. 251–8.

On the Los Angeles water supply, see 'The Colorado River; Its Utilization by Southern California', by G. P. Curti, *Geography*, vol. xlii, pp. 230–8.

XVIII

THE PACIFIC NORTH-WEST

1. The Region and its Resources

As they run northward, the two great mountain chains of western North America converge upon each other, confining the narrow tip of the High Plateaux Province between them. Behind this formidable double barricade some 6 million Canadians and Americans live in almost complete physical isolation from the remainder of the continent. Even to the southward the line of the Pacific Coast troughs, which elsewhere provide a lowland route, is interrupted by the wild mass of the Klamath Mountains, blocking the Oregon–California boundary and dominated by the huge double cone of Mt. Shasta (14,162 feet). There is no single line of easy access into this remote corner of the continent, economically vital though it is as the major producer of timber and hydro-electricity.

Most of the population is to be found in the Pacific coast lowlands, and much of it in the line of port-cities whose largest members are Vancouver (790,000), Seattle (1,107,000), Tacoma (321,000), and Portland (822,000). Inland the population is scattered, for the most part, in long streamers up the valley routeways through the mountains. But circumstances of topography and history have drawn into the sphere of the Pacific North-West two larger settled areas which are really parts of the High Plateaux. One is the Columbia Basin of central Washington and southern British Columbia, the 'Inland Empire' whose capital is Spokane (278,000); it is linked with the coastal region largely by grace of the Columbia River Gorge behind Portland. Of this Inland Empire the fertile, south-facing valleys of southern British Columbia form a physical part, since the Columbia and its tributary, the Kootenay, follow zigzag courses that cut across the international boundary and give a geographical unity to the interior lowlands.

The links between the Pacific coast and the second inland area—the Snake River Plains—are even more tenuous. These plains of southern Idaho are physically a part of the Great

Basin of Utah and Nevada, and economically they are in some ways part of the hinterland of Salt Lake City. The Snake River

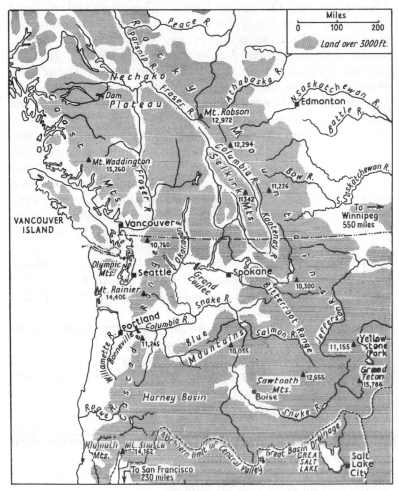

FIG. 73. The Pacific North-West: Physical Features. This is a region bounded and isolated by mountains on the east and by desert to the south.

itself is far from forming a bond between them and the coastal centres, for it cuts through the mountain barrier of eastern Oregon in a 5,500-foot gorge that is all but impassable. But the plains are linked with the Pacific North-West in the historical association of the Oregon Trail, now represented by the railway and the road which climb through the labyrinthine valleys of the Blue Mountains. As we shall shortly see, both the Snake River Plains and the Inland Empire lie on the market side of the Pacific North-West, and their trade tends to follow the same general direction as that of the coast.

Few regions of North America present a greater variety of physical conditions than the Pacific North-West. Though the general structure conforms to the north–south fold-and-fault pattern of the major mountain ranges, the pattern has been disturbed by widespread lava flows; the mountains of northern Oregon run from east to west; and the Columbia and Snake, once clear of the Rockies, conform to no drainage pattern but their own. While most of the terrain of the interior is rugged, the lowlands of the Snake and the central Columbia Basin, levelled by their covering of lava, present favourable surfaces for agriculture at elevations between 500 and 3,000 feet. British Columbia is less favoured by its Fraser River; comparable low-level surfaces are scarce in the southern, populated part of the province, and only appear in the Nechako Plateau round Prince George, so that agriculture in interior British Columbia is largely restricted to the 'trenches' that lie between the ranges of the mountainous south-east.

The variety of climatic conditions within the Pacific North-West has already been suggested in Chapter I. The coastal mountains attract the continent's highest precipitation (most of it falling in winter, when snows are very heavy), while the plateau sections are semi-arid or arid. Thus Wenatchee and Yakima, in the irrigated orchard region of the western Columbia Basin, have 8·7 and 6·8 inches of rain per annum respectively, and the Okanagan Valley 10 to 12 inches. East and south across the basin precipitation increases to 15 and then to 25 inches, making possible the wheat growing for which this moister section of the basin is famous.

The agricultural significance of these abrupt climatic differences may be summarized in a few general statements. (1) Agriculture in the Pacific North-West can be divided into valley agriculture, for which the water must usually be supplied by irrigation, and plateau agriculture, where rainfall may be adequate but the frost-free season is short on account of the altitude. (2) Over much of the North-West the warm-season

rainfall is inadequate for crop growth (between 2 and 4 inches
in the central Columbia Basin), but the heavy snows of winter

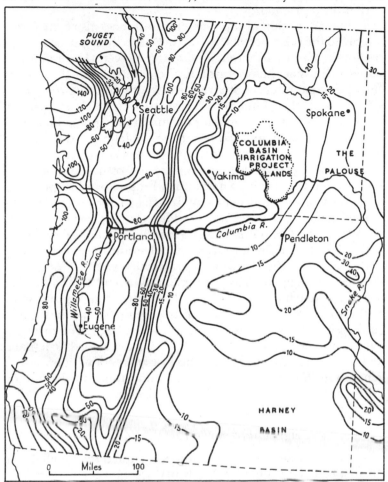

Fig. 74. U.S.A.: Rainfall Map of the North-Western States. The map
emphasizes the marked rain shadow effect of the Olympic Mountains over
Puget Sound, and of the Cascades over the deserts of the Harney and
Columbia Basins.

form a most valuable reservoir. In the interior, if not on the
coast, the melt-water is released into the rivers in a manner well
suited to the irrigation farmer's needs; peak flow on the
Columbia usually occurs in June. (3) Because of the proximity
of areas of high and low rainfall, and because of the seasonal

character of precipitation in the region, some areas require *both* winter drainage *and* summer irrigation to be maintained in agricultural production.

This combination of physical circumstances also contributes largely to the existence of the North-West's three prime natural resources: forests, fisheries, and water power. The mountain slopes, with their heavy rainfall, are clothed with the continent's principal reserves of virgin softwoods, and the region has well earned the name of 'Sawdust Empire'.[1] Its salmon fisheries constitute an important element in regional income— an element of sufficient value for the depletion of the fisheries to cause acute concern and require the Canadian and U.S. governments to take in hand restoration of the salmon runs. Finally, the Columbia, Snake, and Fraser together possess a large part of the continent's hydro-electricity potential. The harnessing of this potential by large-scale projects is quite recent; on the Columbia it dates from the general depression, when the great dams at Grand Coulee and Bonneville were authorized as relief measures under the public works programme of 1933. By 1955 the Columbia and Snake had an installed capacity of 3·5 million kilowatts (roughly the same as the hydro-electric capacity of the Tennessee at that date). In British Columbia, power sites are widely scattered throughout the province, and are gradually being developed as demand increases. The principal river, the Fraser, is not used for power generation, however, because of its importance to the salmon fisheries.

2. *Agriculture in the Pacific North-West*

While fur traders and gold miners occupied the limelight, in the first half of the nineteenth century, the first genuine agricultural settlements on the Pacific coast came quietly into being in the fertile Willamette Valley in the 1830's. The area rapidly gained in popularity, so that the 1840's saw a marked increase in the number of settlers trekking west along the Oregon Trail, and the beginnings of settlement in the central Columbia Basin. In British Columbia, however, there was little agricultural development before the miners arrived in 1858. From these

---

[1] See H. M. Brier, *Sawdust Empire: The Pacific Northwest*, Knopf, 1958.

varied beginnings local specializations have grown, until today we can recognize four main types of farming.

(a) *Dairy farming*, with subsidiary poultry, fruit, and vegetable production. This is the type of farming which occupies the main lowland areas from the Fraser Valley and Puget Sound to the southern Willamette Valley. The great urban centres of the lowlands provide markets for dairy produce, and fodder crops, irrigated and non-irrigated, occupy a large part of the cultivated land. Fruit and vegetable crops account for much of the remainder.

(b) *Fruit and vegetable growing*, with subsidiary dairy farming. This second type is distinguished from the first simply by emphasis; it is a combination of the same elements in different proportions. Away from the principal cities the market for dairy produce is less favourable, so that in these areas the production of fruit and vegetable crops, the North-West's main agricultural speciality, assumes major importance.

It is this type of farming which is found in the valleys that open into the central Columbia Basin. Sheltered but dry, the river and lakeside terraces provide suitable locations for irrigated orchards. The largest orchard areas are those of the Wenatchee, Yakima, and Okanagan Valleys, where apples and pears are the principal fruit crops, but the range of lesser crops is very wide. It includes nuts, hops, holly grown for Christmas decorations, and little-known fruits like youngberries and boysenberries (named for the Northwesterners who developed them), as well as the more familiar soft fruits. From the Rogue River Valley in south-western Oregon with its pear orchards to the apple lands of south central British Columbia, farmers in the sheltered valleys of the North-West have developed temperate fruits as cash crops, in much the same way as the Californians, in more southerly latitudes, have specialized in sub-tropical fruits. The areas form two halves of a Pacific Coast Fruit Belt.

An equally wide range of vegetables is produced, the most important of them being potatoes, onions, beans, and peas. Potatoes are the special cash crop of the Snake River Plains. Idaho has a larger acreage under this crop than any other state although yields are lower than in Maine which is, in consequence, the largest producer.

(c) *Commercial wheat farming.* The eastern end of the central Columbia Basin is an area of natural grassland, the Palouse, and it forms the Wheat Belt of the west coast. On the north, east, and south it is defined by relief, and terminates at the foot of the mountains (roughly on the 3,000-foot contour). On the west, as on the Great Plains, wheat farming is rendered first unwise, and then impossible, by diminishing rainfall towards the dry heart of the basin, with its 6–8 inches of annual precipitation. But the gently rolling surface of the Palouse, with its good grassland soils, encouraged the farmers to plough and plant wheat with dangerous abandon, and erosion has been very serious.

Much of the Palouse wheat is grown by dry-farming methods. For some years past farmers in the moister, eastern edge of the area, on the Washington–Idaho boundary, have used the fallows left by dry-farmed wheat for growing peas, and these have become a local speciality. As on the Great Plains, however, the real, continuing need has been to plant more cover crops on these badly worn wheatlands.

(d) *Ranching.* On those parts of the region which are too dry for wheat and too rugged for irrigation, stockraising replaces cultivation, as it does everywhere in the Mountain West. Between the green patches of irrigated land and the tree-covered mountains, the ranges spread over much of eastern Oregon, the Snake and Columbia lowlands, and the Fraser and Nechako Plateaux of British Columbia. Because of the heavy tree cover in the mountains, however, there is a more definite upper limit to the ranching zone than in other parts of the west; the high grazings are limited in extent, and ranching in the North-West belongs mainly to the middle altitudes.

These, then, are the four types of regional agriculture found in the north-west. When the Columbia Basin Project for a million acres of new irrigated lands was conceived, the question naturally arose as to which of these four types of farming should be practised on it. It was in 1952 that the first irrigation water from the Columbia flowed on to an area whose annual rainfall of 8 to 10 inches had seemed to doom it to permanent uselessness. The scheme makes use of the waters of Lake Roosevelt, impounded behind the largest of all western dams—the Grand Coulee. Close by the dam, a former course of the Columbia

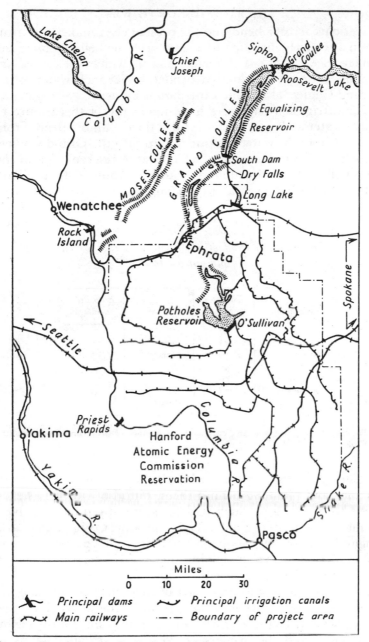

FIG. 75. The Columbia Basin Project. The Coulees are valleys cut into the
lava plateau, and represent former courses of the Columbia or its overflow
channels; they can thus be dammed and used for water storage.

River cuts across a bend that the present river makes as it turns from a westerly direction to a southerly one before joining the Snake (See Fig. 75). This former course, which was carved out by the waters of a Columbia swollen by ice melt-water, is the Grand Coulee, after which the dam is named.

The irrigation engineers have made use of this feature to carry water to the dry western end of the Columbia Bend. From Lake Roosevelt, water is siphoned up into the Grand Coulee, which has been dammed to form a large reservoir. From the reservoir water is distributed, with the gradient, to a million acres of land lying south of the Coulee.

State of Oregon
Percentage of Production of Selected Crops which is sold out-of-state

Commodity	Estimated percentage	Commodity	Estimated percentage
Cattle	30	Pears	97
Sheep	70	Nuts	90
Wool	90	Peas	97
Wheat	50	Beans	97
Apples	78	Dairy products	50

Source: *Oregon Agriculture*. An Analysis by the Faculty of the School of Agriculture of Oregon State College, 1946, p. 9.

The new farmers set out with all the advantages of federal finance and planning behind them, but also with very heavy costs to meet, costs which had to be met by producing high values of output per acre. Dairy products, vegetables, and sugar beet are among the commodities the project farmers market. In doing so, they join other north-western farmers in confronting the problem which dominates the region's life— the need to market a large part of their produce outside the region. In this connexion, the figures in the table above are very relevant. To these figures, and their meaning for the region in general and the farmers of the newly irrigated lands in particular, we must shortly return.

PLATE XXIII

The Canadian Northlands: A scene on the Alaska Highway, which runs from Dawson Creek in British Columbia to Fairbanks, Alaska

PLATE XXIV

Dawson City on the Yukon River. Site of a settlement since the Klondike gold rush of 1896, it once had a population of over 25,000

3. Forests and Industries

Manufacturing in the Pacific North-West is dominated by the forest products industries. Forestry supports thousands of sawmills, from portable one-man plants to giant combinations of mill, furniture factory, and by-products industries, which in one case at least have given rise to a whole town—Longview, Washington—of 20,000 inhabitants. It chokes the smaller harbours on the coast with timber, and makes its presence felt even in the heart of so large a city as Vancouver or Portland, where the rafts of lumber are towed down the Willamette beneath the city's bridges. It provides bulk freight for the railways, and part-time employment for farmers in remote valleys of the Cascades.

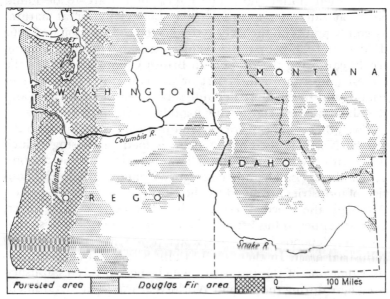

Fig. 76. U.S.A.: Forests of the North-Western States. (British Columbia's forests are included on the map of Canada's forest belts, Fig. 8.)

The Pacific North-West, with its massive firs and pines, is essentially a saw-timber producer, and its leading forest product has up till now been basic lumber, rather than pulp and paper. The last two or three decades have seen a great improvement in the technique of exploiting the forest resource, principally (and most necessarily) in the United States section of the region, where the smallholders of the forest have often left a trail of desolation behind them, after buying, logging off, and abandoning their land. The practice of 'tree farming' by the large firms has placed the industry on a sounder footing; and in British Columbia the provincial government exercises vigilant control. Nevertheless, the situation is serious in the best and most accessible timber areas; whatever the average cut for the region as a whole, these accessible lands continue to be worked at considerably above replacement rate. There are other hazards, too; near Tillamook, on the Oregon coast, an area of prime Douglas fir 300,000 acres in extent was wiped out by three separate fires between 1933 and 1945.

The size of the lumber mills varies fairly directly with the size of their hinterlands. The largest plants are to be found either at tidewater locations (like Longview), or at natural assembly points on the river system (such as Lewiston or Cœur d'Alene in Idaho), or at road centres, to which the huge logging trucks can bring the timber. In British Columbia most of the largest mills are on the coast or the east side of Vancouver Island, and the sheltered channels between the mainland and the islands are used for towing log rafts to the mills.

Two other main categories of industry are to be found in the Pacific North-West. One of these is food processing, which deals with the output of the salmon fisheries and the region's vegetable crops. The other category is more varied, and consists of industries attracted by the North-West's electric power. Although the North-West is rich in minerals such as silver, lead or copper, it has little coal and imports petroleum, so that industry depends heavily on water power, the region's main industrial asset. In these circumstances it is not surprising to find that one of the industries which most firmly established itself here during the Second World War was light metal smelting. Aluminium plants were established at numerous points, such as Troutdale, near Portland, and at Spokane. Although the demand for these metals depended to a rather dangerous degree on defence expenditures, the industry weathered a post-war recession, and with the construction of the giant Kitimat smelter on the coast of British Columbia the region has reaffirmed its faith in it.

Apart from these regional specializations, the coastal cities possess a range of industries roughly appropriate to their size. Vancouver, the third city of Canada, and the only large city on Canada's west coast, has grown impressively in the post-war years. Apart from its importance as a market and as a manufacturing centre (its sawmills and shipyards are of particular importance), it is gradually adding to its significance as Canada's 'back door'; traffic to and from the interior of the country is routed via the west coast rather than the east.

Seattle, on Puget Sound, dominates a coastal lowland that contains a number of smaller cities, and it has outstripped Tacoma, farther up the Sound, which was the original Pacific coast terminal of the first transcontinental railway to the North-West. Seattle's industry is dominated by the Boeing aircraft works; even the lumber industries take second place. Like other Pacific coast cities, it has a small steel output, based on scrap. But it is as a port that Seattle has chiefly come to prominence; thanks to its location and to the strategic importance of the Northlands today, it has thriven on its connexion with Alaska.[1]

The advantages enjoyed by the port of Seattle on the seaward side, however, are balanced by the limitations of its hinterland. In its rivalry with Portland for the industry and commerce of the North-West, it suffers a severe handicap: it possesses no Columbia Gorge. Portland stands at the seaward end of the single water-level route from the interior, while behind Seattle, in winter, the snow may be piled up at roof-top height on the passes. The Columbia Gorge has been of inestimable value to Portland, and even those railways which make for Puget Sound prudently provide themselves with an alternative route down the Columbia. Portland, with the Inland Empire at its back and the fertile Willamette Valley on its flank, has great commercial importance within the region. Its industries, although concentrated on lumber, pulp, and paper, also include shipbuilding, machinery, and textiles.

4. Basic Problems of the Pacific North-West

Such is the geography of this isolated region beyond the

[1] See W. R. Siddall, 'Seattle: Regional Capital of Alaska', *A.A.A.G.*, vol. xlvii, pp. 277–84.

Ff

mountains, a region in which frontiers of settlement are still advancing. But isolation poses economic problems, and without a consideration of those we can have little understanding of how this region fits into the geography of the continent as a whole.

There are two main economic problems. The first is that, at least until the Second World War, the Pacific North-West possessed only 'colonial' status in relation to the east. The marks of this status were (1) that the region was a primary producer, whose resources were largely exploited by outside financial interests, and (2) that the 'balance of trade' of the region showed a large outflow of bulky raw materials, and an inflow of manufactured goods, of higher value but smaller bulk. Further, the value of the region's total 'exports' was greater than that of its material 'imports', the balance being made up by invisibles —services rendered by the East.

Balance of Trade of the Pacific North-West States[1]
Annual Average, 1934–9

Commodity	Quantity balance ('ooo tons)	Value balance ($ 'ooo)
Products of Agriculture . .	+3,600	+143,085
Animals and Products. . .	+ 456	+ 93,366
Products of Mines . . .	−6,771	− 69,630
Products of Forests . . .	+8,285	+178,318
Manufactures and Miscellaneous .	− 262	−221,798
Total	+5,308	+123,341

+indicates an excess of shipments out of the region;
−indicates an excess of receipts.

Source: *The External Trade of the Pacific Northwest*, Pacific Northwest Regional Planning Commission, Portland, Ore., 1942, pp. 23 and 25.

This 'colonial' position, analogous to that of the African colonies of the European powers, is well indicated by the balance of trade drawn up in 1942 by the region's planning commission in the U.S.A.

The figures tell their own story: a huge volume of timber and agricultural produce left the region, while a small quantity of manufactured goods entering it more than balanced, in value,

[1] Includes the states of Washington, Oregon, Idaho, and Montana.

8 million tons of forest products. At the same time, had the pre-war North-West not been deficient in power and fuel (the Products of Mines received were largely petroleum), the 'export surplus' of the region would have been much larger.

The war and the post-war increase in the Pacific North-West's population altered this situation to a certain extent, by stimulating local industries and enlarging the local market. When a region exports its raw materials to have them processed elsewhere, then the increase in value which manufacture brings is lost to that region. It is therefore possible to judge the economic progress of a 'colonial' area, whether in Africa or North America, by the extent to which it is processing its own raw materials. By this criterion, the Pacific North-West has made real progress; its manufacturing is constantly increasing in range and size. Perhaps the best single indication of this is the growth of a north-western pulp and paper industry, alongside the old forest products industry which produced saw timber and plywood, commodities with only a low 'value added by manufacture'. The greater the degree of processing, the larger is the increment of value obtained by the region from its resources.

However, the North-West has not been so favoured in this respect as some other regions. The basic need of any colonial area is capital, and capital is much more forthcoming in an area with a fast-yielding resource to exploit—oil is the obvious case—than with the much slower-yielding North-Western resources of forests and fisheries.

The second problem of the Pacific North-West is simply that of distance from markets. It is a problem that hangs over all the region's agriculture and forestry. We have already noted that a very high proportion of the output of some items must be sold outside the region, because they represent speciality crops produced for a national market. The same is true to a considerable degree, however, of basic production—wheat and dairy produce—because of the limited market afforded by the 6 million people who live in the region. Disposal of the huge timber output is equally dependent on national markets.

Like California, the North-West must sell in distant markets. But, unlike California, the region has additional handicaps.

California's produce at least has the advantage that much of it consists of crops for which the state is the only, or the major, producer in North America, so that it has a certain rarity value. But the Pacific North-West, less favoured climatically, is seeking to market produce—wheat, timber, fruit—in regions which produce, or could produce, these commodities themselves. To market their products, North-Western farmers must carry them past the doors of their competitors to reach the east. As an Oregonian put it to the author, 'It's always bad business to carry wheat through wheat country.'

Two examples may be briefly mentioned: apples and timber. British Columbia produces 40 per cent. of the Canadian apple crop, and Washington some 20 per cent. of that of the U.S.A. Growers have secured markets for these apples, in spite of distance, by attention to appearance, packaging, and flavour. But such advantages are hard to maintain, and are ill-suited to hold off the challenge of growers in Ontario, Michigan, or New York, 2,000 miles nearer their markets. As the Washingtonians have noted, 'Imitation may be the sincerest form of flattery, but in the merchandising of fruits and vegetables it is also one of the surest forms of effective competition.'[1] The result for Washington growers has been declining sales in the east and, to add to their difficulties, per capita consumption of apples in the U.S.A. had dropped by one-third between the 1930's and 1953–6.[2]

In forest products the problem is somewhat more specific; Washington and Oregon must compete in the main United States market with the softwood producers of the south-eastern states. Their difficulty in doing so can best be expressed graphically, as in Fig. 77. This diagram, based on sample railway loadings between states, shows how much of the North-West's rail-borne timber must be marketed at long range. If we consider that some of the most distant markets on the continent are reached not by rail but by water, via Panama, the proportion which has to travel more than 3,000 miles is higher still.

---

[1] W. Calhoun and F. E. Scott, 'Market Prospects for Washington Apples and Certain Other Fruits', State College of Washington, Institute of Agricultural Sciences, Bull. 496, 1947, p. 29.

[2] The north-western states of the U.S.A. market nearly 40 per cent. of their fruit in New England and the Middle Atlantic states. To reach this market they must pay from ½ to 1 cent. per lb. more than their U.S. competitors for transport. (U.S. Dept. of Ag., Marketing Report No. 441, 1960.)

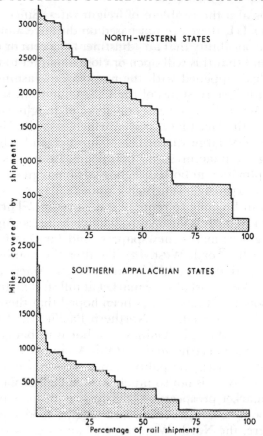

Fig. 77. The North-Western U.S.A.: Lumber Marketing Problems. The diagrams show the distance which forest products shipped by rail from four North-Western states (Washington, Oregon, Idaho, and Montana) have to travel to market, compared with the journey to market of lumber from the Southern Appalachian forest region. While little of the latter is shipped more than 1000 miles outside the region, more than 60 per cent. of the former exceeds this distance. (Detail calculated from *Carload Waybill Analyses, 1948; State to State Distribution of Tonnage by Commodity Groups*, I.C.C. Statement, Washington, D.C., 1949. Distances calculated as to the centres of receiving states.)

In this situation it is not distance alone which tells against the Pacific North-West, and it is certainly not lack of transport facilities, for, besides coastal shipping lines, there are no less than six transcontinental lines serving the area—more, indeed, than the traffic of the region makes strictly necessary.

There is also the problem of freight rates. Since, as we saw
in Chapter III, these are not based on distance alone, there is
always the possibility that an adjustment of a cent or two will be
ordered and that this will open or close a market to the North-
West. (This happened with the market for Washington grain
in the south-eastern states of the U.S.A.; indeed, it happened
several times.) And the general level of freight rates is also
affected by the fact that a region which, like the North-West,
ships out very large quantities of lumber and wheat, while
importing manufactures and petroleum, cannot use the same
trucks or pipelines in both directions. It is a region with a large
number of expensive 'returned empties'.

What can be done to remedy this situation? There are two
courses: (1) To press for favourable freight rates. Agitation for
these by governments, newspapers, and farmers has become
routine in the North-West. (2) To alter the market position.
Considering that, to reach the main North American centres,
the North-West must always market at full stretch, fresh outlets
must be sought. It has always been hoped that these would be
found in Asia; indeed, the Northern Pacific, the first railway
into the area, adopted a Chinese symbol as its badge, as a kind
of declaration of its true goal. But this Asian market has proved
unreliable, so swiftly do political and economic circumstances
change. Today, it is not so much Asia as California that offers
the best market prospects—California, with its soaring population, booming construction, and lagging food supply. Here,
if anywhere, the North-West can find an eastern-style, urban-
industrial market within its reach.

If the North-West's marketing problems have been eased by
demand in California, however, they have also been intensified
by the additional burden of marketing output from the million
acres of new farmland on the Columbia Basin Project, which
was described earlier. In a region already facing serious
marketing problems, to increase by so large an amount the
agricultural output seemed to many observers to be asking for
trouble, when the first irrigation water flowed in 1952. The
production side of the project had been scrupulously planned,
but proposals for marketing the produce were necessarily less
precise, although much was hoped for from California and from
the region's own increasing population. It seems to have been

assumed that, since the farmers on the new lands were encouraged to produce a variety of crops and stock, they would be able to enter whatever market openings existed, on at least equal terms with other North-Western farmers and without swamping any one commodity market.

The project was launched in years of high price supports, and the farmers were cushioned as far as was humanly possible (actually about 85 per cent.) against having to carry the cost of irrigating their land: this cost was borne by other agencies. Such favoured treatment would presumably give them an advantage, in a time of recession, over other farmers in the region who had paid their own way. Yet the project farmers have actually encountered many setbacks. Some of these have been technical problems like drainage, but the main difficulty has been the restricted size of the farms laid out by the Bureau of Reclamation. These have proved too small to be worked economically, and permission has had to be given for enlargement. Today, as many as eight of the original units are farmed as a single block. In this sharp reversal of policy and the abandonment of the ideal for which it stood, is to be seen a measure of the farmers' difficulties on this remote and costly project.

We come, finally, to the special case of British Columbia. We have already referred, in Chapter XVI, to the concept of an economic 'continental divide', from which goods flow to the east and west coasts. In the early days of the West, this divide lay, effectively, close to the west coast, and the railways drew off western produce to the east, while their freight rates encouraged the movement. With the rise of the West, however, in population and economic strength, the divide has been pushed back. In the case of British Columbia, at least, the means by which this has been done are fairly clear. On the one hand, every inducement has been offered to attract commerce from the Prairie Provinces to use the 'back door' of Canada, and to this the agitation about freight rates has contributed. On the other hand, the communications necessary to make this possible have been built. The Prairie oilfields and gas supplies are linked by pipeline not only to the Canadian east but also to the Pacific coast. New roads have been constructed: the Trans-Canada Highway has brought Calgary within a day's drive from Van-

couver, and provincial roads like the Hart Highway to the
Peace River link Vancouver with its provincial hinterland.

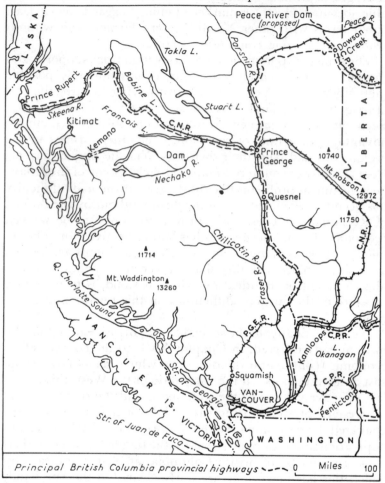

FIG. 78. British Columbia: Communications. The map shows how the
Pacific Great Eastern Railway (P.G.E.R.) has been extended to run from
Vancouver to Dawson Creek and Fort St. John, thus connecting British
Columbia's Peace River frontier with the Pacific. At Kemano a tunnel (T)
carries the waters of the Nechako River, which has been dammed and
reversed, down to the power station supplying the smelter at Kitimat.

Perhaps the most interesting step has been the completion of
the Pacific Great Eastern Railway. This line, long the butt
of local humour, began at Squamish, 40 miles by sea from

Vancouver—there was no road—and ran to Quesnel, 60 miles from Prince George, passing nothing of note on the way. Now, however, the joke is dead; the line is secured at both ends to reality, and links Vancouver firmly to the advancing frontier of settlement and mining on the Peace River, with its agriculture, its gas, and its hydro-electricity, and draws that region into the sphere of influence of the west coast.

FURTHER READING

BASIC information about the region is provided by *The Pacific Northwest*, ed. O. W. Freeman and H. M. Martin, by the *Atlas of the Pacific Northwest*, ed. R. M. Highsmith, the *Atlas of British Columbia Resources* and the *Proceedings* of the annual *British Columbia Natural Resources Conference*. On special aspects of the physical geography, see 'Physiographic Divisions of the Columbia Intermontane Province', by O. W. Freeman and others, *A.A.A.G.*, vol. xxxv, pp. 53–75, and 'British Columbia; A Study in Topographic Control', by G. Taylor, *Geog. Review*, vol. xxxii, pp. 372–402.

On agriculture, useful references are 'The Growth of Agricultural Regions in the Far West, 1850–1910', by D. W. Meinig, *Journ. Geog.*, vol. liv, pp. 221–32; 'The Physical Basis of the Orchard Industry of British Columbia', by R. R. Krueger, *Geog. Bull.*, No. 20 (1963), pp. 5–38; 'The Physical Basis of Agriculture in British Columbia', by D. Kerr, *Econ. Geog.*, vol. xxviii, pp. 229–39; 'The Physical Basis of Ranching in the Interior Plateau of British Columbia', by T. R. Weir, *Geog. Bull.*, No. 3 (1953), pp. 1–22; 'Geography of the Fruit Industry of Yakima Valley', by E. E. Miller and R. M. Highsmith, *Econ. Geog.*, vol. xxv, pp. 285–95, and their 'The Hop Industry of the Pacific Coast', *Journ. Geog.*, vol. xlix, pp. 63–77; 'The Washington Apple Industry', by H. Lemons and R. D. Tousley, *Econ. Geog.*, vol. xxi, pp. 161–82 and 252–68; 'Irrigation in the Willamette Valley', by R. M. Highsmith, *Geog. Review*, vol. xlvi, pp. 98–110, and O. W. Freeman's 'The Pacific Northwest Pea Industry', *Econ. Geog.*, vol. xix, pp. 118–28. On the Palouse, there are numerous articles by W. A. Rockie including 'The Palouse', *Yearbook Assocn. Pacific Coast Geog.*, vol. xv, pp. 3–10 and 'Man's Effects on the Palouse', *Geog. Review*, vol. xxix, pp. 34–45. On Columbia Basin irrigation see 'From Sagebrush to Roses on the Columbia', by L. A. Borah, *Nat. Geog. Mag.*, vol. cii, pp. 571–611, but this must be balanced by G. Machinko's 'The Columbia Basin Project', *Geog. Review*, vol. liii, pp. 185–99.

Forestry is poorly covered, outside official reports and the *Atlases*; for a general study, see *A World Geography of Forest Resources*, ed. S. Haden-Guest and others, and also W. Hardwick's *Forest Industry of Coastal British Columbia*, and 'Economy of Douglas Fir in the Pacific Northwest', by R. F. Keniston, *Sci. Monthly*, vol. lxxvi, pp. 173–81. Fisheries are dealt with by G. W. Hewes in 'The Fisheries of Northwestern North America', *Econ. Geog.*, vol. xxviii, pp. 66–73, and by O. W. Freeman in 'Salmon Industry of the Pacific Coast', ibid., vol. xi, pp. 109–29, but see also 'The Conflict Between Fish and Power

Resources in the Pacific Northwest', by M. E. Marts and W. Sewell, *A.A.A.G.*, vol. l, pp. 42–50.

On rivers and power, see 'Rivers as Regional Bonds: The Columbia–Snake Example', by E. L. Ullman, *Geog. Review*, vol. xli, pp. 210–25; 'Harnessing the Columbia River', by G. R. Barbour, *Geog. Journ.*, vol. xcvi, pp. 233–42; 'Search for Power in the British Columbia Coast Range', by R. C. Farrow, *Geog. Journ.*, vol. cvi, pp. 89–117; *Uncle Sam in the Pacific Northwest*, by C. McKinley. The industrial application of power is covered by 'Kitimat, A Saga of Canada', by P. Clark, *Can. Geog. Journ.*, vol. xlix, pp. 152–73; 'Industrial Trends in the Pacific Northwest', by O. W. Freeman and H. F. Raup, *Journ. Geog.*, vol. xliii, pp. 175–84, and 'Industrial Development in the Vancouver Area', by P. D. McGovern, *Econ. Geog.*, vol. xxxvii, pp. 189–206.

XIX

THE NORTHLANDS

1. *Physical Conditions*

THE Northlands of the continent, considered politically, are made up of Alaska, Yukon, and the Northwest Territories, with a total area of 2·1 million square miles. If, however, we use the term to include all those areas which lie north of the limits of continuous settlement, then the area covered by this last great region of North America is much larger, for it includes Labrador, much of Quebec, and the northern parts of Ontario, the Prairie Provinces, and British Columbia.

Over so large an area, physical conditions are very varied. All types of relief are to be found, while even within this area, of which the layman's impression is simply that it is cold and barren, significant differences in climate and vegetation occur. We can list here only the major physical factors that govern the use of the Northlands.

RELIEF, CLIMATE, AND SOILS

J. L. Robinson has suggested[1] that it is simplest to think of the Northlands as comprising two separate regions: the North-West and the Arctic. The differences between the two are (1) differences of relief. Most of the North-West is made up of the northward extension of the Cordillera and the Pacific Coastlands, and so is mountainous, while the mainland Arctic is underlain by the Laurentian Shield, and is an area of gentle relief.

The differences are also (2) climatic. As we saw in Chapter I, the climatic heart of the American Arctic is offset somewhat to the eastern side of the Northlands. In summer the isotherms run from north-west to south-east, so that, while parts of the North-West have a short, but agriculturally useful, summer season, the Arctic receives much less heat in summer.

The effect of this climatic difference is seen (3) in the vegetation of the two areas. The North-West is a mountainous area in which (as in southern British Columbia and in Washington) lower slopes are forested and upper slopes are barren, but the

[1] In *Canadian Regions*, p. 480.

Arctic is treeless tundra. The northern limit of trees, which runs diagonally across Canada from the mouth of the Mackenzie to north-eastern Manitoba, forms a natural boundary between the two areas.

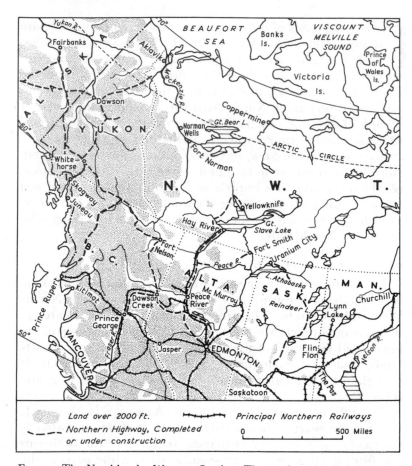

Land over 2000 ft.   ┣━━━━━━┫ Principal Northern Railways

╲╴╴╴╴ Northern Highway, Completed   0   500 Miles
or under construction

Fig. 79. The Northlands: Western Section. The roads and railways shown are not all completed as yet. Some of the roads form part of the 'Roads to Resources' programme of the federal government, referred to in the text, and these are being built by stages, as funds are made available.

The soils of the Northlands are also varied. Besides the podsols and peat which might be expected in these latitudes, there are areas where glaciation has swept away the soil, lowland areas which are lake beds of the glacial epochs, covered by lacustrine clays and sands, and also areas where the drainage

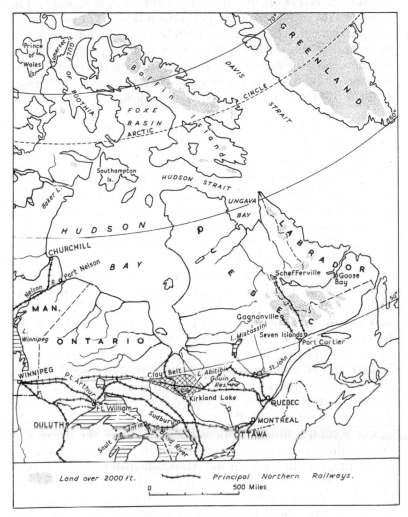

FIG. 80. The Northlands: Eastern Section.

has been interrupted and swamps or muskegs have formed, covered with peat. This peat cover must often be stripped off before land can be brought into use for agriculture.

Soils in these high latitudes have two general characteristics which complicate their use by man. The first of these is that the rate of decomposition and humus formation is slow, so that in the surface layers organic matter is held 'in cold storage'. The second is the existence of the permafrost layer. The presence of this impermeable layer affects both leaching and drainage, by interrupting the water-cycle in the soil. The potentialities of northern soils for agriculture thus depend on the depth of the summer thaw and the quality of soil drainage, which must prevent the thaw from causing waterlogging.

PHYSICAL LIMITATIONS ON AGRICULTURE

What are the prospects for agriculture under such physical conditions? Apart from the limitations imposed by relief and soils, it is widely assumed that the main determinant is the cold of the Northlands. But experience has shown that this is not wholly true. Although the frost-free season is very short and highly unreliable in its occurrence, some crops can nevertheless be raised in the Far North, where summer days are long, even if the summer season is short.

The two main climatic limitations are lack of summer heat and, rather surprisingly, drought. The first of these marks, as we have seen, an important difference between the North-West and the Arctic. There are crops which can be grown on the Lower Mackenzie, beyond the Arctic Circle, which will not ripen in central Quebec, 15° farther south. At Dawson, in Yukon (64° N.), the mean temperature is above 50° F. for almost three months in summer, which is nearly a month longer than at Fort Mackenzie, in Quebec (57° N.), and only a little shorter than at Gaspé (49° N.).

The second limiting factor is drought. Over the interior of the Northlands precipitation is generally between 10 and 20 inches per annum; only on the Alaska–British Columbia coast does it rise to 40, or even 80 inches. This means that the Canadian Arctic, with its cool summers, is sub-humid in climate, while the North-West is definitely semi-arid, and irrigation has as much relevance for its few cultivators as concern over frost danger.

Finally, not merely the amount, but also the seasonal distribution, of precipitation must be borne in mind. Not only does most of the north-east have a short, cool summer, but its 10 to

20 inches of precipitation arrive with a late-summer maximum, too late to be of much help to the would-be cultivator. Thus the Arctic, and in particular northern Ontario and northern Quebec, suffers the triple drawback to land use of lack of soil, lack of sunshine, and lack of growing-season rainfall. Farther west, in the Peace River Country and the Mackenzie Valley, the amount of precipitation is no greater, and evaporation rates are higher, but the rainfall régime is of a Great Plains type and shows a growing-season maximum.

The factors so far considered combine to distinguish five sections of the Northlands according to their physical prospects for agriculture. These are:

(a) *Northern Quebec and Ontario*. The potentialities of this section appear to be very slight. While the eastern Shield has adequate rainfall, it has neither soil nor summer heat; July is usually the only frost-free month. The prospects for local agriculture to support the new iron ore communities (see p. 136) are poor.

(b) *The Northern Clay Belts*. These represent former glacial lake beds, areas of deposition and, consequently, of somewhat less sterility than the ice-swept surface around them. But their cultivation is not easy: before they can be farmed, the clay flats must be de-forested and then sometimes stripped of a layer of peat of varying thickness. The climate is unhelpful; precipitation comes late in the summer, and the frost danger is ever-present. Hay and grain are grown, but there is neither prospect of, nor justification for, much expansion of the farm area on these lands.

(c) *The Peace River Region*. By contrast, this region might be said to represent, in a settlement context, the 'gateway to the north'. The southern edge is fully settled, and forms in fact the northern extremity of the great grain belts of the Agricultural Interior. Beyond this firm base of prosperous farms, where wheat growing is well developed, there is a belt of more scattered farms settled by incomers from the prairies in the drought-and-depression years of the 1930's, while north of this again lie the virgin lands—the fringe of the north. The surface is gently rolling, the soils offer possibilities, and the precipitation is well timed for crops.

(d) *The Mackenzie Basin*. The warm, dry summers make agriculture possible, but there are in fact only a few patches of cultivation within the basin. This is (1) because there is no large market or means of transport to it other than the river itself, and (2) because the small areas of cultivable soils—mostly river terraces—are usually heavily forested.

(e) *The Yukon and Intermontane Areas.* There are some cultivable areas here, along the valleys and on the river terraces, just as there are farther south in British Columbia. But not only are they smaller in extent and remote from any present centres of population; they also have a frost-free season so short as to make any cultivation at best a poor risk.

Because it has no 'prospects for agriculture' at all, our list does not cover the true Arctic. But it is not therefore to be forgotten. It is the home of the Eskimo, a race of hunters and fishers who live without cultivating, and who have built up a distinctive culture which their isolation and their nomadism have enabled them to preserve in its essentials down to the present time.

ECONOMIC LIMITATIONS ON AGRICULTURE

Agricultural settlement in the Northlands is restricted by the physical limitations already considered, and also by economic factors. The first of these is that, in the north, lands suitable for agriculture are widely scattered, mostly on old lake beds and river terraces. To the isolation of the *region* there is added, therefore, the isolation of the *homestead*. This isolation and its counterpart, cost of transport and services, are the great economic handicaps in every northern project. They have been increased by the method of settlement. Where, as in the Peace River country, settlement has been on a homesteading basis, each new-comer has claimed a promising quarter-section, without reference to the location of other settlers, and so the cost of services is increased by the unnecessarily wide scatter of individual homesteads.

The second economic factor is the cost of settlement. In the United States' government's Matanuska Valley Project in Alaska, the cost of clearing the ground before seeding (for much of the potentially cultivable land was under forest) was reckoned as $150 per acre. Thus a problem is created similar to that which we have encountered on irrigation projects in the dry west: that capital is required to make a start. In its pamphlet *Information about Public Lands*, the U.S. Department of the Interior warns would-be settlers in Alaska, 'To develop a farm that will sustain a family in Alaska may require a capital investment of $20,000 to $50,000.' The north suffers the additional handicap that, whereas on irrigated lands higher yields will help to pay for the initial outlay, yields on northern lands will not be appreciably higher—indeed, may be lower— than elsewhere.

If agricultural settlement is to develop, it must clearly be governed by certain principles. (1) Settlement should be made not at the whim of the individual cultivator, but in blocks, as the need for it arises from increasing population pressure or enlarging demand for food. Each of these blocks must be large enough to support the cost of services. (2) Assistance should be available from the federal governments of both countries, to reduce the starting load on settlers' finances. This assistance is needed both for clearance of ground and for the construction of roads and railways, without which the new settlements would be condemned to failure from the start. (3) That such blocks of new lands should be settled only in strict relationship to transport and to market opportunities is, perhaps, the clearest moral to be drawn from northern settlement thus far. In the Peace River country, that laboratory for northern experiments, when the first good lands were opened up, early in the present century, the mistake was made of trying to grow wheat commercially at distances of 50 or 60 miles from a railway. This proved impossible; only as the railway was carried north could this wheat compete with crops grown 10 or 20 miles from a railway in the central Prairies.

On the other hand, the few places where agriculture has proved successful in the north have been places where a market, and in particular a *local* market, has been available. The Matanuska Valley is linked by road and rail with Anchorage, which it supplies, and after initial misjudgements were corrected, results have been excellent. The Peace River country, linked with the Prairies and with British Columbia, is an area of commercial farming. The Ontario Clay Belts supply various mining and forestry communities with food. In short, the only justification for expanding northern agriculture in the future, away from the frontier of continuous settlement at least, will be to supply a specific market within the locality where cultivation is possible.

2. Future Prospects

In 1960, the population of the Canadian northern territories was 37,000, and that of Alaska was 226,000. Of this number, only a small proportion were settled cultivators; the remainder were drawn to the region by employment in mining, transport services, fishing and forestry, or by military duty. Why have so few settlers entered this great region, and under what circumstances might its population increase? The final task in this book is to attempt a brief answer to these questions.

In temperate and long-settled lands, it is normal that agriculture forms the basis of continuous settlement, and that other occupations grow like a pyramid from that base. But it is obvious from what we have already considered that in the Northlands agriculture is likely to play a very small part in future development. Only in one or two places in what has been called the 'Near North' is continuous settlement likely.

Elsewhere, settlement, if it is to take place, will depend on other occupations such as those that predominate in the north today. Because of this, it will almost certainly *not* be continuous, but concentrated—at strategic locations, along routes, or around mineral deposits. These concentrations will become more and more widely spaced, northwards into higher latitudes.

What likelihood of development is there? Several possibilities can be suggested.

(*a*) *Mining.* The Northlands are rich in minerals, and a large part of their sparse population is made up of miners. The Pre-Cambrian rocks of the Shield contain a great variety of metals; the younger formations that underlie the northern end of the Great Plains Province yield coal and petroleum; and in the western mountains lies the gold that blazed the name of Klondike round the world in the 1890's.

Some of these mineral deposits are important on a world scale. Among them are the nickel-copper ores of Sudbury, Ontario, at the southern edge of the Shield, for long the source of some 90 per cent. of the nickel supply of the world, excluding the U.S.S.R. On a continental scale, we have already noted, in Chapter V, the opportune discovery of the central Labrador iron ores, at a time when the Lake Superior supplies were declining.

In the sphere of mining, new developments occur year by year, and with them new communities spring up in the Northlands. The Labrador iron ores prove now to be only a part of a long belt of ore bodies running south-west into Quebec, so that the ore town of Schefferville, which has grown up at the head of the railway from Seven Islands as the principal mining community, has been followed by other similar settlements along the line of the ore workings. The old workings of the radium-uranium beds of Great Bear Lake have now been eclipsed by large-scale operations in the Elliot Lake area on the north shore of Lake Huron, forecast to be the world's richest uranium field. In nickel production the year 1956 brought news of a large-scale operation by the great International Nickel Company, to bring in a new nickel source at Thompson, Manitoba, which is second only to Sudbury as a producing centre.

Development has been particularly swift in petroleum prospecting and production. The 1947 strikes in the Edmonton area (see p. 374) were followed by a move north into the areas round Lesser Slave Lake and the Peace River, where huge reserves of natural gas have been tapped, and these are piped to the west coast. Meanwhile, a fresh attempt is being made to exploit the Athabaska oil sands, which have long baffled commercial producers, while oil has also been struck in the Kenai Peninsula of Alaska.

In an area so huge and so little known as the Northlands, such discoveries are likely to continue. The settlements they create are, however, in many cases ephemeral, so that while agricultural development may be needed to supply the requirements of the miners, it must be based on a clear assessment of the life of the mine. With this reservation, we may assume that the Northlands will continue to be dotted, as at present, with small communities of miners, each associated with pockets of cultivated land, but that the total area of land involved is unlikely to increase much, even if its distribution changes.

GG *

(*b*) *Hydro-electricity*. The Shield and the western mountains of North America possess a huge potential of water power. Schemes are under construction to harness this, and to do for the Peace River what has already been done for the Columbia and Snake in 'putting them to work'. The sort of effect which power development in the north may produce can already be observed in the Kitimat scheme on the coast of British Columbia. Here the flow of one of the Fraser's tributaries has been reversed by damming, the water is diverted down to an underground power station at Kemano, and the power generated there is transmitted to Kitimat, on one of the coastal fiords, where a great aluminium smelter (see p. 433) has been brought into operation. If the triple requirements of capital, access, and markets can be met (and no one is likely to take them for granted in this region), there seems to be no reason why this bold venture should not be followed by others.

Certainly, one outlet for electric power is forestry operations in the region. Sawmills are very widely distributed through the forested zone. As time goes on, these will probably be succeeded, as they are being in British Columbia, by pulp and paper mills, which represent the more stable, long-term element of the forest products industry, and the demand of these mills for electricity is very large.

(*c*) *Strategic considerations*. The Northlands have come into their own in the air age and with the rise of the U.S.S.R. as a military power on the other side of the polar wastes. The knowledge that Alaska was Russian until Seward bought it—in the teeth of fierce criticism—for $7,200,000 in 1867 is a lingering nightmare in the American mind. Of the 1960 population of Alaska, roughly one-quarter were military personnel, while the presence of numerous civilians was also attributable to strategic needs. Of these needs the war-time Alaska Highway, running north-west from Dawson Creek, B.C., is the most obvious geographical expression. Since the war, the U.S.A. and Canada have collaborated in the construction of a DEW (Distant Early Warning) line across the Northlands, as the basis of the continent's radar defences against trans-polar attack.

Such measures tend to open up the north, but involve little permanent settlement outside the few major bases. If, however, we extend the term 'strategic' a little, to cover a wider field, then the general development of northern communications, which will certainly serve strategic purposes, is likely to have the most direct effect on increasing the region's population in the future. At least, the converse is true—that there can be no hope of successful expansion without extension of communications, and that this extension should preferably precede any attempt at further settlement.

(d) *Transport and Tourism*. In the early days of the Northlands, movement was largely by water in summer and pack train in winter. The pack trains are now tractor-hauled, but the same generalization still holds; the Mackenzie, in particular, remains the Main Street of the North-West. To these means of movement have now been added the railways, reaching north from the St. Lawrence and the Prairies to new mining areas and to the ports of Hudson Bay. While railways struggle for survival in other parts of the continent, their mileage is increasing in the Northlands.

In the north-east, the first iron ore railway from the Labrador mines to Seven Islands is now paralleled by another, from mines farther west to Port Cartier. New lines penetrate the Lake Mistassini area of Quebec. Great Slave Lake is linked by rail with the settled lands southward. Elsewhere, roads have been built, under the 'Roads to Resources' programme of the federal government. 4,000 miles of these roads have been planned with the object of opening up the widest possible range of resources in the area they serve. And one purpose which these roads will certainly serve in the future is to carry a growing tourist traffic.

Even more characteristic of the region has been the use of air transport, to carry mining equipment to new projects, or to assist in the export of precious metals, furs, and fish. Most of this northern transport network has, however, to be laid out in acceptance of the fact that, since it is economically 'strategic', its justification is not to be sought in terms of immediate financial returns, but in the long-term development which the coming of transport makes possible within the nation.

That such development is at least feasible is suggested by the following figures:

Population of the Northlands; A Comparison Between North America and the U.S.S.R.

	Arctic	Sub-Arctic	Northlands
North America . .	45,000	1,588,000	1,633,000
U.S.S.R. . . .	250,000	29,475,000	29,725,000

Source: *Geography of the Northlands*, ed. G. H. T. Kimble and D. Good, American Geog. Soc. Special Pubs., No. 32, 1955, p. 274.

ALASKA

The future prospects of Alaska call for special attention, for in addition to the general factors in northern development which we have been considering, there are a number of special elements in the situation confronting the young '49th state' of the U.S.A.

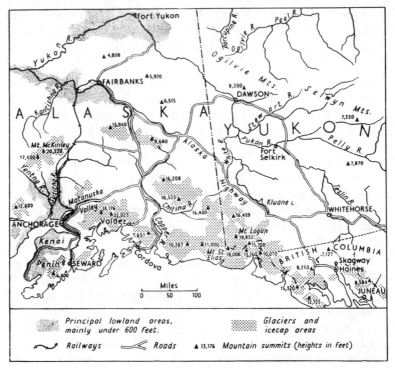

FIG. 81. Alaska: The Mountain Barricades and the Routeways.

On the negative side, the physical character of Alaska is bound to hamper development. While much of the Canadian

Northland is flat and open, and *can* be traversed and even settled if the future so requires, the obstacles to easy movement in Alaska are immense, and the chief of these obstacles are concentrated precisely in the south-eastern corner of the state (that is, nearest to the continental U.S.A.)—mountains, icefields, and deep fiord indentations.

On the positive side, however, there are at least three reasons why we may expect that, over the next decade or two, the rate of development in Alaska will be more rapid than in the Canadian Northlands.

1. Against the lack of obvious resources in the interior of Alaska must be offset the compensation provided by the possession of a coastline, and the wealth it represents. This wealth takes two main forms—exploitable timber reserves, covering 4 million acres of commercial forest land[1] to which access is feasible from the sea, and coastal fisheries, which have an annual value of $30 million or more, mostly for salmon. These forests, in particular, are a source of income which is immediately available for further development. So, too, is the tourist trade.

2. Alaska is a land of 600,000 square miles, being developed with the backing of a nation of 180 million people; the Canadian Northland is an area of about 2½ million square miles, being developed by a nation of 18 million people. It is obvious that the resources which the federal government of the U.S.A. could bring to bear on Alaskan development projects are vastly greater, taxpayer for taxpayer and mile for mile, than those of the Canadian government.

3. This being the case, it is doubly significant that Alaska has attained statehood, while about half of the Canadian Northlands (Yukon and Northwest Territories) remain federal dependencies. In the future it will be possible for Alaska to press, in Washington, for a larger share of federal spending on such projects as hydro-electric construction and defence contracts. For this time-honoured political game, Alaskans have been well prepared by their years of campaigning for statehood.

When Alaska attained its new status, the federal government

---

[1] Land which is (*a*) producing, or physically capable of producing, usable crops of wood, and (*b*) economically available now or prospectively. *Statistical Abstract of the United States, 1957*, p. 692.

gave it as a christening present a large allocation of lands from the public domain, which the state can select, and which it will use to introduce a new 'homestead' system, free from the 160-acre limit and other restrictions inherited from the last century. These lands, together with the very timely payments of oil revenue from the new fields in the Kenai Peninsula, afford the state a valuable nest-egg for further investment and expansion.

CONCLUSIONS

The contrast between the populations of the North American and the Russian 'sub-Arctic' suggests, however, that it is government policy which effectively controls the rate of northern development. In the absence of a powerful stimulus, however contrived, based on official recognition that the nation needs these northern lands whatever the price, people prefer to remain in the less harsh environment of the older settlements.

Yet the lands are there, scattered amidst the wilderness, but available against an uncertain future. They are lands which, given careful organization, government sponsorship, and a willingness to face once more, in the twentieth century, the challenge of a frontier, may yet provide homes for the North Americans of tomorrow.

FURTHER READING

THE basic text on this region is *Geography of the Northlands*, ed. G. H. T. Kimble and D. Good, which treats within one volume the Northlands of both North America and Eurasia, and so affords abundant material for comparisons. A semi-popular account of the area is *North of 55°*, ed. C. Wilson; see also 'Recent Developments in the Canadian North', by H. L. Keenleyside, *Can. Geog. Journ.*, vol. xxxix, pp. 156–76. Land use is covered by 'Land Use in the Arctic', by A. E. Porshild, *Can. Geog. Journ.*, vol. xlviii, pp. 232–43 and vol. xlix, pp. 20–23; 'Agricultural Lands in the Canadian Northwest', by E. S. Archibald, *Can. Geog. Journ.*, vol. xxix, pp. 40–51; 'Land Use Possibilities in Mackenzie District, N.W.T.', by J. L. Robinson, ibid., vol. xxxi, pp. 30–47; 'Agriculture and Forests of Yukon Territory', by J. L. Robinson, ibid., vol. xxxi, pp. 54–72 (see also 'Yukon Territory', by D. Leechman, ibid., vol. xl, pp. 240–67); 'The Settlement of the Peace River Country', by H. M. Leppard, *Geog. Review*, vol. xxv, pp. 62–78 and 'Peace River's Second-Righters', by F. H. Ellis, *Can. Geog. Journ.*, vol. liii, pp. 94–101; 'Trends in the Peace River Country', by B. G. Vanderhill, *The Canadian Geographer*, vol. vii, pp. 33–41; 'Economic Change in the Mackenzie

Valley Area', by W. C. Wonders, *Can. Geog. Journ.*, vol. lxiii, pp. 139–47; 'Agriculture in the Great Clay Belt of Canada', by J. R. Randall, *S.G.M.*, vol. lvi, pp. 12–28, and 'Drought in the Canadian Northwest', by Marie Sanderson, *Geog. Review*, vol. xxxviii, pp. 289–99.

For Alaska see 'Alaska, Land of Opportunity—Limited', by W. J. Eikeman and A. B. Smuts, *Econ. Geog.*, vol. xxvii, pp. 33–42; 'Populating Alaska: The United States Phase', by K. H. Stone, *Geog. Review*, vol. xlii, pp. 384–404; 'A Picture of Matanuska', by W. A. Rockie, ibid., vol. xxxii, pp. 353–71, and 'The Purpose and Source of Seasonal Migration to Alaska', by W. J. Stanton, *Econ. Geog.*, vol. xxxi, pp. 138–48.

On Northern minerals, see E. W. Miller, 'Mineral Regionalism of the Canadian Shield', *The Canadian Geographer*, No. 13 (1959), pp. 17–30; F. K. Hare, 'The Labrador Frontier', *Geog. Review*, vol. xlii, pp. 405–24; G. Humphreys, 'Mining Activity in Labrador–Ungava', *I.B.G. Trans. and Papers, 1961*, pp. 187–99, and 'Schefferville, Que., A New Pioneering Town', *Geog. Review*, vol. xlviii, pp. 151–66. On communications in the Northlands see 'The Development of Transportation in the Canadian North', by C. H. Herbert, *Can. Geog. Journ.*, vol. liii, pp. 188–97, and 'The Mackenzie Waterway: A Northern Supply Route', by T. Lloyd, *Geog. Review*, vol. xxxiii, pp. 415–34; see also his 'Transportation of Ungava Iron Ore' (with D. C. Nutt), *The Canadian Geographer*, No. 15 (1960), pp. 26–36. As a general study of northern problems, there is 'The Northland—Canada's Challenge', in the 1955 *Year Book*, pp. 22–32.

APPENDIX I

Mineral Resources of the U.S.A.

(Extract from *Long-Range Minerals Program*, Hearing Before the Committee on Interior and Insular Affairs, U.S. Senate, 85 Congress, 1st Sess., 4 June 1957, Part I, Appx. I, Commodity Data Summaries.)

Mineral	Chief producing states and their production as % of U.S. total	Ratio between domestic production and quantity imported*	Import sources, and % contribution of each to total imports	Leading world producers
Aluminium .	Pacific North-West 32% Gulf Coast 25%	6·5 : 1	Canada 96%	U.S.A., Canada, Soviet Bloc.
Asbestos .	Vermont	1 : 16·5	Canada 94%	Canada, Africa.
Bauxite .	Arkansas 98%	1 : 3	Jamaica 48%, Surinam 47%	Surinam, Jamaica, British Guiana, Soviet Bloc.
Chromium .	Montana 77%	1 : 12	Philippines 34%, Turkey 23%, S. Africa 21%	Turkey, Philippines, S. Africa, Soviet Bloc.
Cobalt .	Idaho	1 : 7	Belgian Congo 67% Belgium 21%	Belgian Congo, Canada, U.S.A.
Copper .	Arizona 45% Utah 23%	2 : 1	Chile 38%, Canada 18%, N. Rhodesia 12%	U.S.A., Chile, Soviet Bloc, N. Rhodesia.
Gold .	S. Dakota 28% Utah 23%	1 : 1.5	N. America 74%‡	S. Africa, Soviet Bloc, Canada.
Gypsum .	Michigan Texas California	2·5 : 1	Canada 85%	U.S.A., Canada, France.
Iron Ore .	Minnesota 62% Nebraska 24% Missouri 20% Illinois 20%	4·5 : 1	Canada 43%, Venezuela 30%	U.S.A., Soviet Bloc, France.
Lead .		1 : 1·3	Mexico 19%, Canada 13%	U.S.A., Australia, Soviet Bloc.
Magnesium .	Texas 94%‡	33 : 1	Canada 52%, Norway 45%	U.S.A., Soviet Bloc, Canada, Norway.

Mineral	U.S.A. source (%)	Ratio*	Outside supplies (%)	Principal sources
Manganese .	Nevada 35%, Montana 25%	1 : 7	Africa 38%, India 30%	Soviet Bloc, India, S. Africa, Ghana.
Mercury .	California 50%, Nevada 30%	1 : 1	Spain 40%, Italy 30%	Italy, Spain, Mexico.
Molybdenum .	Colorado	—	—	U.S.A.
Nickel .	Oregon 95%	1 : 32	Canada 81%	Canada, New Caledonia.
Platinum Group	New York 37%, New Jersey 21%	1 : 25	Canada 35%, U.K. 28%	S. Africa, Canada.
Silver .	Idaho 37%, Utah 17%	1 : 2	N. America 57%‡	Mexico, U.S.A., Canada.
Sulphur .	Texas 54%, Louisiana 30%	35 : 1	Canada 87%	U.S.A.
Tin .	Texas 100%	1 : 850	Malaya 55%, Bolivia 12%, Belgium 8%, Indonesia 8%, Bolivia 22%, Korea 12%	Malaya, Indonesia, Bolivia.
Tungsten .	Nevada 37%, California 26%	1 : 1·3		Soviet Bloc,** U.S.A., Bolivia.
Zinc .	Pennsylvania 2_%, Montana 21%	1 : 1·3	Canada 42%, Mexico 30%	U.S.A., Soviet Bloc, Canada, Mexico.

* Thus, if the *first* figure is large, the U.S.A. enjoys relative independence from outside supplies; if the *second* figure is large, there is a significant lack of the mineral within the U.S.A.

† From sea water.   ‡ Includes Alaska.   ** Mainly China.

APPENDIX II

Illustrations of North American Geography

A LIST of articles on various sections of North America which have appeared in the *National Geographic Magazine* between 1945 and 1964 is given below. The particular value of these articles lies not so much in the textual material—which is often informal in character— as in the well-known excellence of the photographic coverage they provide. For this reason, the articles have not been included in Further Reading, but are grouped together here, as invaluable aids to visualizing the landscapes described, or to teaching.

Alaska, vol. 109 (1956), vol. 116 (1959). Alberta, vol. 118 (1960). Appalachians, vol. 96 (1949), vol. 102 (1952), vol. 117 (1960), vol. 122 (1962). Arizona, vol. 97 (1950), vol. 123 (1963). Arkansas, vol. 90 (1946). Aroostook, vol. 94 (1948).

British Columbia, vol. 110 (1956), vol. 114 (1958).

California, vol. 95 (1949); California, Central Valley, vol. 90 (1946); California, Coast, vol. 116 (1959); California, Southern, vol. 112 (1957). Canada, vol. 120 (1961). Cape Cod, vol. 122 (1962). Cascade Mountains, vol. 119 (1961). Chesapeake Bay, vol. 126 (1964). Colorado, vol. 106 (1954). Columbia Basin, vol. 102 (1952). Crater Lake, vol. 122 (1962).

Delaware River, vol. 102 (1952). Delmarva Peninsula, vol. 98 (1950). Desert landforms, vol. 88 (1945), vol. 92 (1947), vol. 96 (1949), vol. 101 (1952), vol. 105 (1954), vol. 114 (1958). Desert vegetation, vol. 88 (1945).

Everglades, vol. 93 (1948), vol. 113 (1958).

Florida, Everglades, vol. 93 (1948), vol. 113 (1958); Florida, Coast, vol. 107 (1955); Florida, vol. 124 (1963).

Grand Canyon, vol. 107 (1955). Great Lakes, vol. 115 (1959). Great Smokies, Appalachians, vol. 102 (1952).

Hudson River, vol. 94 (1948), vol. 121 (1962).

Idaho, vol. 118 (1960). Illinois, vol. 104 (1953).

Kansas, vol. 101 (1952). Kitimat, vol. 110 (1956).

Long Island, vol. 99 (1951). Los Angeles, vol. 122 (1962). Louisiana, vol. 113 (1958).

Martha's Vineyard, vol. 119 (1961). Massachusetts, vol. 92 (1947). Merrimack River, vol. 99 (1951). Michigan, vol. 101 (1952). Minnesota, vol. 96 (1949). Mississippi River, vol. 93 (1948). Missouri, vol. 89 (1946). Montana, vol. 97 (1950), vol. 118 (1960). Mount Rainier, vol. 123 (1963).

National Parks, vol. 124 (1963). Nebraska, vol. 87 (1945). Nevada, vol. 89 (1946). New England, vol. 99 (1951), vol. 107 (1955). Newfoundland, vol. 95 (1949). New Jersey, vol. 117 (1960). New Mexico, vol. 96 (1949). New York City, vol. 126 (1964); New York State, vol. 110 (1956). North Carolina, vol. 121 (1962); North Carolina, Coast, vol. 92 (1947). North Dakota, vol. 100 (1951).

Ohio, vol. 107 (1955); Ohio River, vol. 97 (1950). Oklahoma, vol. 111 (1957). Ontario, vol. 104 (1953). Oregon, vol. 90 (1946). Ottawa, vol. 92 (1947), vol. 124 (1963).

Philadelphia, vol. 118 (1960). Pittsburgh, vol. 96 (1949). Potomac River, vol. 88 (1945), vol. 94 (1948).

Quebec Province, vol. 96 (1949).

Rhode Island, vol. 94 (1948). Rockies, Canadian, vol. 91 (1947); Rockies, Central, vol. 109 (1956); Rockies, Colorado, vol. 90 (1946), vol. 100 (1951), vol. 106 (1954).

San Francisco, vol. 110 (1956). Seattle, vol. 117 (1960). Sierra Nevada, vol. 116 (1959). South, The Industrial, vol. 95 (1949). South Carolina, vol. 103 (1953). South Dakota, vol. 91 (1947). Susquehanna River, vol. 98 (1950).

Tennessee River, vol. 93 (1948). Texas, vol. 87 (1945), vol. 119 (1961).

Virginia, Coast, vol. 92 (1947).

Washington, D.C., vol. 91 (1947), vol. 111 (1957). Washington, State, vol. 117 (1960); Washington, Olympic Mountains, vol. 108 (1955). Wisconsin, vol. 111 (1957). Wyoming, vol. 88 (1945).

Yosemite, National Park, vol. 99 (1951). Yukon, vol. 104 (1953).

INDEX

(Note—The Index does not include the names of cities or physical features which are mentioned only once in the text, in the appropriate regional description. It covers topics, together with names which occur more than once, in different sections of the book.)